PENGUIN CLASSICS

THE UPANIṢADS

VALERIE J. ROEBUCK was born in Hertfordshire in 1950. She studied at the University of Cambridge, where she was awarded a BA (Hons.) in Oriental Studies, specializing in Sanskrit and other Indian languages, and a Ph.D. for a thesis on South Indian Bronzes. A freelance scholar and lecturer, she is an Honorary Research Fellow of the University of Manchester. Dr Roebuck has a broad interest in Indian language, culture and religion. She is a Buddhist, practising and teaching meditation in the Samatha tradition, and is involved in interfaith work in Manchester. Her previous publications include *The Circle of Stars: An Introduction to Indian Astrology* (Element Books, 1992).

The Upaniṣads

Translated and edited by
VALERIE J. ROEBUCK

PENGUIN BOOKS

PENGUIN BOOKS

Published by the Penguin Group
Penguin Books Ltd, 80 Strand, London WC2R 0RL, England
Penguin Group (USA) Inc., 375 Hudson Street, New York, New York 10014, USA
Penguin Books Australia Ltd, 250 Camberwell Road, Camberwell, Victoria 3124, Australia
Penguin Books Canada Ltd, 10 Alcorn Avenue, Toronto, Ontario, Canada M4V 3B2
Penguin Books India (P) Ltd, 11 Community Centre, Panchsheel Park, New Delhi – 110 017, India
Penguin Books (NZ) Ltd, Cnr Rosedale and Airborne Roads, Albany, Auckland, New Zealand
Penguin Books (South Africa) (Pty) Ltd, 24 Sturdee Avenue, Rosebank 2196, South Africa

Penguin Books Ltd, Registered Offices: 80 Strand, London WC2R 0RL, England

www.penguin.com

First published by Penguin Books India 2000
This revised edition published 2003
3

Set in 10.25/12.25 pt PostScript Adobe Sabon
Typeset by Rowland Phototypesetting Ltd, Bury St Edmunds, Suffolk
Printed in England by Clays Ltd, St Ives plc

Contents

Acknowledgements

It would be impossible to mention by name all the friends and colleagues who have helped me in their various ways during this project. In the course of it I have been lucky enough to experience the help, encouragement and expertise of many fine scholars in the fields of Indian Studies and Comparative Religion, notably Drs F. R. and B. Allchin, Mr L. S. Cousins, Dr Rupert Gethin, Professor J. R. Hinnells, Dr Jacqueline Suthren Hirst, Mr David Melling, Dr John D. Smith and Dr Karel Werner. Dr Brian Gates of the University College of S. Martin, Lancaster, helped to set the whole process in motion when he arranged a year's teaching fellowship for me to 'do some work on the Bṛhadāraṇyaka Upaniṣad'. Members of Liverpool Hope University College gave encouragement as the project grew, and students there and elsewhere helped me to test the drafts of the translations, giving useful comments on what would and would not work for readers.

The original version of this translation was commissioned by Penguin India, and the patience, understanding and sensitivity of staff there, and particularly of my editor, Kamini Mahadevan, enabled me to bring it to completion. The present version, for Penguin Classics, required a certain amount of rewriting and adaptation, in which I was grateful for the help and encouragement of Hilary Laurie and staff at Penguin UK.

At times the authors of the Upaniṣads seem to expect their readers to be familiar with every imaginable branch of knowledge, like the sage Nārada in the Chāndogya, and my friends must have become used to receiving slightly strange enquiries about their own areas of expertise. Particular thanks are due to Mrs Wendy Hodkinson (archery), Dr Michael Houndsome (natural history) and Dr Francis Beresford (medicine). Thanks, too, to Mr Roberto Raso, Mr Taig McNab and Mr Rob Adkins for help with computer matters, and especially to Miss Erica Adkins, who lent me her computer when mine was stolen. Thanks also to the many scholars who have responded to my enquiries on the Internet. Needless to say, I take full responsibility for the use I have made of knowledge received from all these sources.

Particular thanks to the Wilmslow Vedānta Group, for showing what it means to practise the teachings of the Upaniṣads in daily life: above all to the late and much missed Swami Turiyānanda Saraswati, for her unfailing kindness and encouragement.

Special thanks, of course, to my dear husband, Peter, without whom probably none of this would have happened.

Finally, I wish to dedicate this book to my parents.

Valerie J. Roebuck
Manchester, June 2003

Sanskrit Pronunciation

The following are the closest approximations in Received Standard English to the sounds of the Sanskrit words in this translation. The Roman script has fewer letters than Devanāgarī and other scripts used for writing Sanskrit, so diacritic marks and combinations of letters have to be used to represent some of the sounds.

VOWELS

A as in cup, not as in cap.
Ā as in calm.
I as in pick.
Ī as in peak.
U as in took.
Ū as in tool.
Ṛ is 'vocalic *r*' – *r* as a vowel. It bears the same relation to consonant *r* as *i* does to *y*. At the period of the Upaniṣads it was probably pronounced as a trilled sound, like an *r* continued. Today, however, it is generally pronounced as a short *ri* sound, as in *Kṛṣṇa* ('Krishna'), *Ṛṣi* ('Rishi').
Ḷ, 'vocalic *l*' – *l* as a vowel – in Upaniṣadic times was probably pronounced as in bottle, but today it is generally pronounced like a short 'lri'. It occurs only in the verb *kḷp-*, 'to shape', and its derivatives – see Chāndogya VII.4 and notes.
E as in bake.
Ai as in pike.
O as in boat.

Au as in b<u>ou</u>t.

A, i, u, ṛ, ḷ are short vowels; *ā, ī, ū, e, ai, o, au* are long.

CONSONANTS

K, g, c, j, ṭ, ḍ, t, d, p, b are unaspirated sounds: practically no breath escapes when they are pronounced, so they sound softer than their English equivalents. *Kh, gh, ch, jh, ṭh, ḍh, th, dh, ph, bh* are aspirated: there is a noticeable escape of air, like an *h*, when they are pronounced. *Kh, gh* etc. are written with single characters in the Indian scripts, and count as single sounds in pronunciation. Double consonants, such as *kka, kkha* etc., are fully pronounced (as in Italian).

C as in <u>ch</u>at, not as in <u>c</u>at (which would be spelled with a *k* in this sy<u>s</u>tem).

J as in lo<u>dg</u>e, not as in mira<u>g</u>e.

Kh as in bloc<u>kh</u>ead, not as in lo<u>ch</u>.

Gh as in e<u>gg</u>head.

Ch as in <u>ch</u>at, but with a more marked escape of breath.

Jh as in bri<u>dg</u>ehead.

Ph as in cu<u>ph</u>ook, not as in <u>ph</u>ysics.

Bh as in a<u>bh</u>or.

There are two groups of T and D sounds. *T* and *d* are true dentals, pronounced with the tongue on the teeth, as in French. *Ṭ* and *ḍ* are those distinctively Indian sounds, the retroflex consonants. In pronouncing them, the tongue starts from a position bent back against the roof of the mouth, and is brought slightly forward during speech, much as for *r*.

There is a similar relationship between dental *n* and retroflex *ṇ*, and between dental *s* (like English *s*) and retroflex *ṣ* (a soft *sh* sound). In Vedic Sanskrit there is also a retroflex consonant *ḷ*, which occurs in this book only in the name Iḷā. (Although it is transliterated with the same symbol as the vowel *ḷ*, both are so rare that there is no possibility of confusion.)

To the Indian hearer, the T, D and N sounds of English tend to sound more like retroflexes than dentals, so that in Indian scripts 'London' is spelled *laṇḍan*.

Th, dh, ṭh, ḍh are aspirated versions of the T and D sounds, as in pot̲h̲ook and bloo̲d̲hound, not as in t̲h̲eme or t̲h̲is.

Ś is a palatal *sh* sound, made with the tongue in the same place as for *j*, as in pus̲h̲chair.

Ñ usually comes before *c, ch, j* or *jh*, and sounds as in pi̲n̲ch, a̲n̲gel: on its own it sounds as in Espa̲ñ̲a.

Jñ, as in Yājñavalkya, is pronounced rather like 'dny', or in some parts of India like 'gy'.

Ṅ usually comes before *k, kh, g* or *gh*: it is the sound in pi̲n̲k, a̲n̲gle, ki̲n̲g.

Ṃ nasalizes the preceding vowel, rather like the *n* in French *bon*.

V sounds somewhere between *v* and *w*, on its own sounding more like *v*, but after another consonant more like *w*.

STRESS ON WORDS

The stress on words in Sanskrit is determined by long and short syllables. For this purpose, a syllable containing a long vowel, or any vowel which is followed by more than one consonant, is long. A syllable containing a short vowel followed by a single consonant is short.

In a two-syllable word, the stress is always on the first syllable: Y̲ama, d̲harma, J̲uhū.

In a three-syllable word, if the last syllable but one is long, it is stressed (Mait̲reyī). If not, then the first syllable is stressed, regardless of length: P̲ārvatī, J̲anaka, A̲sura.

In words of four syllables or more, if the second-to-last syllable is long, it is stressed (Yājñav̲alkya). If not, but if the third-to-last syllable is long, that syllable is stressed (Viśv̲āvasu, Bṛh̲aspati, Bṛhadār̲aṇyaka). If that, too, is short, the fourth-to-last syllable is stressed, regardless of its length (A̲numati, Ā̲ṅgirasa). So 'Upaniṣad' should strictly be stressed on the first syllable, though among English speakers it has become conventional for it to be stressed on the second. The stress on words in Sanskrit is not quite as heavy as that in English.

Abbreviations

AA	Aitareya Āraṇyaka
AB	Aitareya Brāhmaṇa
AG	Āśvalāyana Gṛhya-sūtra
AU	Aitareya Upaniṣad
AV	Atharvaveda
BhG	Bhagavadgītā
BU	Bṛhadāraṇyaka Upaniṣad
CU	Chāndogya Upaniṣad
GM	Gāyatrī (Sāvitrī) Mantra
IU	Īśāvāsya Upaniṣad
JAOS	*Journal of the American Oriental Society*
JB	Jaiminīya Brāhmaṇa
JRAS	*Journal of the Royal Asiatic Society*
JU	Jaiminīya Upaniṣad (not in this collection)
KauU	Kauṣītakī Upaniṣad
Kena	Kena Upaniṣad
Kaṭha	Kaṭha Upaniṣad
ManU	Māṇḍūkya Upaniṣad
MaiU	Maitrī Upaniṣad
Mbh	Mahābhārata
MDh	Mānava Dharma-śāstra
MG	Mānava Gṛhyasūtra
MuU	Muṇḍaka Upaniṣad
PG	Pāraskara Gṛhya-sūtra
PU	Praśna Upaniṣad
RV	Ṛgveda
SA	Śāṅkhāyana Āraṇyaka
SBr	Śatapatha Brāhmaṇa
SG	Śāṅkhāyana Gṛhya-sūtra
SM	Southern recension of Maitrī Upaniṣad
SU	Śvetāśvatara Upaniṣad
SV	Sāmaveda
TA	Taittirīya Āraṇyaka
TB	Taittirīya Brāhmaṇa
TS	Taittirīya Saṃhitā (Yajurveda)
TU	Taittirīya Upaniṣad
V	Vulgate recension of Maitrī Upaniṣad
VS	Vājasaneya Saṃhitā (Yajurveda)
WZKS	*Wiener Zeitschrift für die Kunde Sud-asiens*

Introduction

The Upaniṣads are among the world's most influential creative works. Not only did they play a large part in shaping Hinduism as it is today, but the debates that they helped to initiate also influenced, either directly or by reaction, the development of the other South Asian religious traditions, including Buddhism. In the last two centuries they have also begun to influence religious and philosophical thought outside Asian cultural areas. So it is probably no exaggeration to say that at least half the people in the world have been affected in some way by the ideas of the Upaniṣads.

The word 'Upaniṣad', however we derive it,[1] implies an esoteric teaching, concerned not with the outward forms of religion but with the inner meaning. Typically, an Upaniṣad recounts one or more sessions of teaching, often setting each within the story of how it came to be taught. A renowned spiritual teacher is about to leave the household life to live as a renunciant in the forest: one of his wives refuses her share of his wealth, and asks for knowledge instead. A serious young boy, taking his angry father at his word, goes to the house of Death: while there, he takes the opportunity to question the god about the afterlife. A king sends his chamberlain to look for a great teacher of whom he has heard: he finds a rude and uncouth man, sitting scratching himself under a cart. The knowledge that is sought in these encounters is aimed not at material success or even intellectual satisfaction, but at enabling the questioner to become free of worldly suffering and limitations: 'to attain fearlessness', 'to cross beyond sorrow', 'to dig up the supreme treasure'.

There are several hundred works that have the status of

Upaniṣads for at least some groups of Hindus. Many of these are late texts, expounding specialized ways of practice such as Yoga or Tantra, or teaching devotion to one great god or goddess. In fact the most famous Hindu text of all, the Bhagavadgītā, is a devotional Upaniṣad of this kind, embedded within the great epic of the Mahābhārata. It even keeps the traditional format, with the divine charioteer Kṛṣṇa as the teacher and the warrior prince Arjuna as the seeker for knowledge.

It follows that any selection of Upaniṣads like the present one must be to some extent arbitrary. However there are thirteen texts, often called the 'Principal Upaniṣads', which would be recognized by almost all Hindus as forming the foundation of their philosophy, and it is these which are translated in this book. Eleven are those on which the great philosopher Śaṅkara wrote commentaries in the eighth to ninth century CE,[2] confirming their canonical status for later generations. In addition to these, there are several others to which Śaṅkara made reference, though he did not write commentaries on them: one of these is the Kauṣītakī, which is now universally accepted among the 'Principal' group.[3] Its world-view and language seem very close to those of the early Upaniṣads, particularly the Chāndogya and the Bṛhadāraṇyaka.

The Maitrī or Maitrāyaṇī is sometimes included among the 'Principal Upaniṣads', and sometimes not. Patrick Olivelle's recent translation (Olivelle 1996b) omits it. As we have it, it seems to be somewhat later than the other Upaniṣads in this collection. However, it contains a wealth of material of significance for anyone interested in the development of Hinduism or of meditation, and I felt its inclusion here was necessary. Along with the Māṇḍūkya, it helps to show some of the directions in which the Upaniṣadic tradition was taken in later times. While the Māṇḍūkya lays stress on knowledge, the Maitrī is principally concerned with practice. Both give great importance to the symbolism of the syllable OṂ.[4]

THE BACKGROUND

The Upaniṣads form part of the tradition of religious literature[5] that is known as the Veda, literally 'knowledge'. This tradition begins with the four Saṃhitās or 'Collections', themselves more frequently known as 'the Vedas': the Ṛgveda, Yajurveda, Sāmaveda and Atharvaveda. Each Saṃhitā is a collection of metrical prayers and hymns for use in sacred ritual, associated with a particular class of priests who specialized in it and handed it down within their families.[6] Of the four, the Ṛgveda is probably the earliest.[7] It consists of hymns (*ṛc*) for use in the elaborate sacrifice (*yajña*) which was at the heart of Vedic religion. The Yajurveda consists of ritual formulae (*yajus*) to be uttered during the activities of the sacrifice, while the Sāmaveda consists of hymns (*sāman*) arranged for chanting. Both the Yajurveda and the Sāmaveda share a large part of their content with the Ṛgveda, adapted for the different purposes of the priests who used them.

The Ṛgveda is performed in the main as simple syllabic chant, on a narrow range of tones which follow the accents marked in its text. The Yajurveda follows a similar system, though the tones used for each accent are not the same as those for the Ṛgveda. But the Sāmaveda is sung in an elaborately ornamented style, in which one syllable may be extended and sung over a number of notes.[8]

The Atharvaveda stands a little apart from the other three. The early Upaniṣads generally group the Ṛg-, Yajur- and Sāmavedas together,[9] and treat the Atharvaveda as something slightly separate.[10] Subsequently, the Atharvaveda comes to be regarded as a fourth Veda, on a level with the other three. Its verses (called *atharvan*, like the priests who used them) often resemble magical spells, used to cast out misfortunes, gain success in love, and so on. They are generally concerned with the triumphs and problems of the individual, rather than with public sacrifices. But the distinction is by no means always a sharp one. The three earlier Vedas contain personal, as well as public, material, and the Atharvaveda contains many hymns that would not be out of place in the other Saṃhitās.

The basis of Vedic religion was the sacrifice, which no doubt began as a way of nourishing and placating the gods, but expanded to become something of huge symbolic complexity, even to being seen as a means of keeping the cosmos in existence. The sacrificial enclosure and the altar within it, like the temple in later Hinduism, were interpreted as a kind of *maṇḍala* or diagram of the universe. Each part of it, every action performed within it, and all the equipment and offerings took on multiple layers of significance, of which the skilled priest was expected to be aware as he carried out his duties.

In ancient times, at least, the sacrifice involved the ritual slaughter of animals. (Modern revivals, like that documented by Frits Staal, use symbolic replacements.)[11] The supreme examples of the sacrifice were elaborate rituals sponsored by kings, such as the horse sacrifice.[12] It is perhaps debatable how often such costly and time-consuming rituals were carried out in full; however, their structure served as the pattern on which less ambitious kinds of ritual were based.

Once the ritual had taken on this complex symbolic power, a new kind of literature was required to provide instruction in it. This was the role of the Brāhmaṇas,[13] liturgical commentaries on the sacrifice for use by the priests, which formed the second stratum of the Vedic literature. The next stage was that of the Āraṇyakas, which overlap to some extent with the Brāhmaṇas, but are concerned with the inner symbolism of the rituals rather than their external forms. Often they take one of the rituals of the sacrifice and turn it into a form of inner contemplation.

The Vedas, Brāhmaṇas and Āraṇyakas, together with the principal Upaniṣads, are regarded by Hindus as *śruti* – 'that which is heard', revelation – as distinct from *smṛti* – 'that which is remembered', epics, legends, law books, etc. Each Saṃhitā has come down to us in various lineages (*śākhās*, 'branches'), each of which may have its own associated Brāhmaṇas, Āraṇyakas and Upaniṣads. The Yajurveda exists in two recensions, the 'Black' (*kṛṣṇa*) and 'White' (*śukla*) versions, each with its own *śākhās*: in the 'Black' tradition, the verses of the Saṃhitā are interspersed with the Brāhmaṇa material, while in the

'White' they are kept separate. The diagram (overleaf) shows the lineages of the Upaniṣads which are translated in this book.

In some cases, the Upaniṣads have a genuine and early connection with the Vedas to which they are attached. For example the Bṛhadāraṇyaka is closely related to the Śatapatha Brāhmaṇa of the Yajurveda, and is itself, as its name implies, regarded as an Āraṇyaka as well as an Upaniṣad. The first chapter of Book I of this Upaniṣad, internalizing the symbolism of the horse sacrifice, is typical of the Āraṇyakas. The Chāndogya, which is allotted to the Sāmaveda, addresses the concerns of the priests who were responsible for the chanting that accompanied the sacrifice. Book II of the Chāndogya, for example, is devoted to the symbolism of different elements of the chant. But in the case of the later Upaniṣads the attributions to particular Vedas seem to spring mainly from a desire to fit them into the pattern. In general, when there was no clear reason to attach them to another Saṃhitā, they seem to have been allotted to the Atharvaveda.[14]

In certain respects the Upaniṣads mark the changing point between the religion of the Vedas, now generally called 'Brahmanism', and Hinduism as it later developed. Although Hindus regard the whole Vedic literature as the foundation of their tradition, in practice the Brāhmaṇas and Āraṇyakas, and even most of the hymns of the Saṃhitā, are now the province of specialists. But the Upaniṣads are still loved, studied and treated as guides to life by Hindus today, more perhaps than any text apart from the Bhagavadgītā.

In certain respects the Upaniṣads anticipate developments that remain important to the present day. They include what are thought to be the earliest mentions of religious practices, such as Bhakti (devotional worship); philosophical schools, such as Sāṅkhya and Vedānta; and even deities, such as the goddess Umā and a teacher called Kṛṣṇa son of Devakī.[15] In other respects they look back to an older way of life, reflecting a society that is more socially fluid than that described in later texts, such as the law books.

According to the formulations of classical Hinduism,

			Yajurveda			
Saṃhitā:	Ṛgveda		White Yajurveda		Black Yajurveda	
Śākhā (lineage):	Aitareya	Śāṅkhāyana	Vājasaneya		Taittirīya	Kāṭhaka
Brāhamaṇa:	Aitareya	Kauṣītaki/ Śāṅkhāyana		Śatapatha	Taittirīya	Kāṭhaka
Āraṇyaka:	Aitareya	Kauṣītaki/ Śāṅkhāyana		(Bṛhad-āraṇyaka Upaniṣad)	Taittirīya	
Upaniṣad:	Aitareya	Kauṣītakī	Īśā	Bṛhad-āraṇyaka	Taittirīya	Kaṭha

Lineages of the Principal Upaniṣads

knowledge of the Vedic literature was restricted to men of the upper three classes (*varṇas*) who had become 'twice-born' by undergoing initiation with the sacred thread. But in the Upaniṣads we meet women who can debate *śruti* as equals with men. In the Bṛhadāraṇyaka Upaniṣad, Yājñavalkya's wife Maitreyī is called a 'scholar of sacred lore',[16] and her interest is treated as entirely admirable. In the great debate of Bṛhadāraṇyaka Book III, Gārgī Vācaknavī disputes on equal terms with the male scholars. Not only does she regard herself as the equal of anyone there except Yājñavalkya himself (III.8.1, 12), but the other Brāhmaṇas[17] seem to take her at her own estimation. (In view of what subsequently happens to Vidagdha Śākalya,[18] I do not think we can take Yājñavalkya's warning about 'asking too many questions' (BU III.6.1) as being patronizing.)

We also find men of doubtful social background giving or receiving teaching. A good example is the story of Satyakāma Jābāla in Chāndogya IV.4. Later commentators have great difficulty with this story, and sometimes go to considerable lengths to explain away the clear meaning: that Satyakāma's

		Sāmaveda		Atharvaveda		
	Maitrāy-aṇīya	Tāṇḍya	Talavakāra/ Jaiminīya	Paippalāda		
	Maitrāy-aṇīya	Chāndogya	Jaiminīya-upaniṣad Brāhmaṇa	Paippalāda		
Śvetāśvatara	Maitrī	Chāndogya	Kena	Praśna	Muṇḍaka	Māṇḍūkya

parents either were not married or at most had some very informal contract.[19] Yet such explanations seem to take away from the impact of the story, with its clear message about the overriding importance of truthfulness.

One of the most striking developments in the Upaniṣads is in the attitude to family life and the renunciation of it. The Vedas take for granted the overwhelming importance of the desire, even the duty, of a man to marry and leave sons to carry on his family traditions. In the early Upaniṣads, too, this theme is strongly represented: in the Bṛhadāraṇyaka, for example, we find many passages that are concerned with the traditional obligation for a man to leave a son behind him (I.5.16–17) and the sexual rituals thought to ensure that this would happen (VI.4). But there are other passages, particularly those concerned with the teaching of the sage Yājñavalkya, where we find approval of the urge to renounce such worldly needs:

> Desiring it [*brahman*, the supreme reality] as their world, renouncers wander. Knowing it, the ancients did not desire offspring,

> for they thought, 'What is offspring to us, when the self is our world?' Leaving behind desires for sons, desires for wealth and desires for worlds, they lived on alms. For desire for sons is desire for wealth, and desire for wealth is desire for worlds: both are merely desires.[20]

Such teachings are associated with *śramaṇas*,[21] ascetics who wandered from place to place in search of truth, studying with a teacher, or challenging rivals to debate. *Śramaṇas*, like Indian sādhus today, seem to have followed a variety of practices, some wearing distinctive robes or animal skins, others going naked; some with shaven heads, others with long matted locks.[22]

Both Buddhism and Jainism originated in *śramaṇa* circles, as did a number of other movements that have not survived to the present, such as that of the Ājīvikas. These movements all rejected the authority of the Vedas – one of the reasons why they are regarded as religions in their own right, and not as branches of Hinduism – though their influence also fed back into Hinduism as it developed, particularly in such matters as the increasing emphasis on non-violence (*ahiṃsā*) and the rejection of animal sacrifice. But there were others among the *śramaṇas* who continued to accept the authority of the Vedas, while interpreting them in new ways. Their influence can be strongly seen in the Upaniṣads, and in the subsequent development of Hinduism.

Śramaṇas did not have to come from the Brāhmaṇa class, and might bring with them ideas that came from outside the Brahmanical tradition. It has often been noted that both the Buddha and Mahāvīra, the founder of Jainism, were born in the Kṣatriya, not the Brāhmaṇa, *varṇa*, and that their followers came from every level of society. But we see similar tendencies in the Upaniṣads. In Bṛhadāraṇyaka VI.2.8 and Chāndogya V.3.7, a Kṣatriya, Pravāhaṇa Jaivali, claims knowledge about the human destiny after death that has not previously been known to Brāhmaṇas.

The tension between the urge to live in society and carry on one's family and the urge to renounce worldly life in a whole-hearted search for liberation has remained a live and creative one for Hindus to the present day. Often a solution was sought by assigning different priorities to different times of life. It was recommended that a man should first marry and father a family, and that only after fulfilling these duties should be abandon the household life and live as a renunciant.

This solution was eventually formalized into the system of four *āśramas* or stages of life. The *āśramas*, in their fullest form, were offered as the ideal plan for the life of a Brāhmaṇa man, though there were comparable structures for men of the other 'twice-born' classes. According to this system, when he was old enough to go to a teacher's house, a boy was expected to become a celibate student (*brahmacārin*). At the end of his studies he was expected to marry and become a householder (*gṛhastha*). When his children had grown up and had children of their own, he should leave the household life and become a forest-dwelling ascetic (*vanaprastha*). At the end of his life he should give up all worldly things to become a homeless renunciant (*sannyāsin*). Sometimes the four *āśramas* were associated with the four parts of *śruti*: it was said that the *brahmacārin* should study one or more of the Saṃhitās, the *gṛhastha* the Brāhmaṇas, the *vanaprastha* the Āraṇyakas, and the *sannyāsin* the Upaniṣads. In the Upaniṣads themselves, although there are clear references to different stages of life, there is no explicit statement of the *āśrama* system in its classical form.

It is arguable how far the *āśrama* scheme was ever actually practised: certainly there seems no evidence that any of the groups of sacred texts were restricted to one particular *āśrama*. In fact it was early recognized that not all the details of it were practicable in the present age of the world.[23] And there seem always to have been a number of men, and even a few women, who left conventions behind and became ascetics at any time of life.

It should not be forgotten, either, that there were great scholars and teachers who contemplated higher realities while living the household life. They included royal sages such as Janaka and Ajātaśatru, and Brāhmaṇa sages who achieved renown and wealth as sacrificing priests. The triumphs of Yājñavalkya described in the Bṛhadāraṇyaka Upaniṣad all take place while he is living in a family with his two wives, and winning wealth in cattle that would have made him a millionaire in modern terms. He is clearly believed to have achieved liberation while in the household state. In many cases, however, we are told next to nothing about the background of the characters. We simply do not know, for example, whether Gārgī Vācaknavī was a *śramaṇī* or a married woman.

The trend in recent research on the Upaniṣads has been to rediscover their connection with the earlier parts of Vedic literature. This is important, but it should not lead us to minimize their originality. The world they describe is not the pastoral society of the Vedic hymns, but a city-based culture deriving its wealth from industries such as weaving, pottery and mining, as well as from agriculture. The sages may be based in the forest, but they mingle with kings and princes. And although most people still have the perennial human concerns that we find in the Saṃhitās, with creating a prosperous life for themselves and their families, others now question the satisfaction to be found in the whole realm of existence, and renounce the household life entirely. It is clearly the same world that we find in the early texts of the Buddhists and Jains.

DATING THE UPANIṢADS

The date of the Upaniṣads is still a matter of debate. For many traditional Hindus the question is irrelevant, since in essence, at least, the whole of *śruti* literature is considered to be *apauruṣeya*, not of human origin, and of primordial antiquity, containing truths to be rediscovered in every age of the world.[24] But the view among most scholars is that the Saṃhitās of the Veda date back to about 1500–1000 BCE, the Brāhmaṇas and Āraṇyakas to 1000 BCE on, and the Upaniṣads from about 700 BCE on. Attempts to set the whole body of literature further back[25] always come up against the fact that the period of the early Upaniṣads clearly cannot be too far removed from that of the Buddha and of Mahāvīra, both of whom were traditionally placed in the sixth century BCE, but are now thought by most scholars to have been active around 400 BCE.[26]

It seems probable, at least, that the main teachings of the Bṛhadāraṇyaka Upaniṣad, attributed to the sage Yājñavalkya, are immediately pre-Buddhist. (Parts of the rest are if anything older.) Yājñavalkya presents the doctrine of reincarnation as a new and unfamiliar one, whereas in the earliest Buddhist texts that we have it is already fully developed.[27]

There is little internal evidence to link the Upaniṣads to historical events that are known from elsewhere.[28] The most that we can say with confidence is that the material culture described in the earlier Upaniṣads appears entirely compatible with what the archaeological evidence tells us of the city-based culture of the sixth and fifth centuries BCE.

It is possible to place the Upaniṣads in a rough sequence among themselves. The Bṛhadāraṇyaka, Chāndogya, Taittirīya and Aitareya Upaniṣads are generally agreed to be the earliest. All have strong links with the earlier Vedic material, and are mainly in prose with verse passages. The Kauṣītakī Upaniṣad follows a similar format, though its versions of the material that it shares with the Bṛhadāraṇyaka and Chāndogya give the impression of being later reworkings.

The Kena, Kaṭha, Śvetāśvatara and Muṇḍaka seem to belong together. The last three are almost entirely in verse, the Kena in a mixture of verse and prose. All seem to anticipate later developments in Hindu philosophy, including Yoga, Sāṅkhya and Bhakti. The Īśāvāsya is generally thought to belong here, though its clear link with verse passages of the Bṛhadāraṇyaka suggests an earlier date.[29]

The Praśna and Māṇḍūkya revert to the prose format of the early Upaniṣads, but contain ideas that clearly have later origins, particularly in their interpretation of the sacred syllable OṂ. The Maitrī is a different case again. It seems to contain material from different periods, including a core that is related to the Taittirīya, but the main body of it appears much later, and includes references to astronomical ideas that were probably not current until the second century CE.

So we are brought back to the consensus view that the principal Upaniṣads were composed from about 700 BCE, perhaps incorporating some older material. The early prose Upaniṣads could well date from about 700–400 BCE, the verse Upaniṣads two or three centuries later, and the Praśna and Māṇḍūkya from the end of the last millennium BCE. The Maitrī could have been put into its present form as late as the second or third century CE.[30]

Such is my own view about the dating of the Upaniṣads. I hope that those who take a different view will not let it deter them from reading my translation with an open mind. After all, the date of a text is not the most important thing about it, though it may help to provide a context for what we are reading. Surely much that is most important about the Upaniṣads is timeless: perhaps what was originally meant by calling them *apauruṣeya*, and attributing them to a primordial past.

AUTHORSHIP AND TRANSMISSION

The authorship of the Principal Upaniṣads is as enigmatic as their date. According to tradition, they were transmitted by the sages who act as teachers in the texts: Yājñavalkya in the Bṛhadāraṇyaka Upaniṣad, Uddālaka Āruṇi and others in the Chāndogya, Śvetāśvatara in the Upaniṣad that bears his name. The most detailed account is in the 'lineage chapters' of the Bṛhadāraṇyaka,[31] which trace the teaching back from one Pautimāṣya or Pautimāṣī-putra,[32] via some fifty generations of human and divine students and teachers, to its ultimate source, either Āditya, the sun-god,[33] or the supreme reality itself.[34] Yājñavalkya himself appears in one of these lists.[35]

But these lists seems to refer to the content of the texts – the truths believed to be embodied in them – rather than the words in which the texts are expressed. It is clear from the Upaniṣad itself that Yājñavalkya gave his teachings in his own words, to suit the circumstances and the people questioning him, and it seems reasonable to assume that the other teachers in the lineage did the same. So the tradition seems to have nothing to say about the actual form in which these teachings were handed on, or who assembled them into the literary form in which we have them today.

The early Upaniṣads, at least, bear clear signs of having been created and originally transmitted as part of the oral tradition. We do not know at what stage they were put into writing. At the other extreme, the Maitrī, with its remarkable complexity of structure, must surely have been assembled in a written form, albeit one that was strongly influenced by the conventions of the oral form.[36]

We know something of the ways in which ancient Indian texts were memorized and preserved from accidental corruption. In the case of the Vedic hymns themselves, there was an elaborate process of memorization. The students would learn the hymns by heart, both in their normal sequence and in a number of variations (*krama-pāṭha*) in which the syllables were rearranged in different patterns, ranging in complexity from 1–2, 2–3, 3–4, 4–5, etc., to 1–2–2–1–1–2–3–3–2–1–2–3, 2–3–3–2–2–3–4–4–3–2–3–4, . . .[37] The effectiveness of this system can be seen in the fact that the Vedas have survived in an ancient form of Sanskrit (generally known as Vedic) with words and grammatical forms that had dropped out of the spoken language even before the time of the Upaniṣads. The learning system must have helped to ensure that these features were not smoothed over and replaced by more familiar forms.

The method of learning the early Buddhist texts seems to have been a less formal one: monks who knew the texts would meet and chant them together to make sure that mistakes had not crept in. Perhaps some similar process was involved in the transmission of the early Upaniṣads.

The stress on memorization seems to be universal in the South Asian traditions. Even today, when teachings of all kinds are readily available in print, many Hindu, Buddhist and Jain teachers can draw upon extensive internal libraries of memorized texts, and hearing is still viewed as a more effective way of learning about spiritual matters than reading.

KEY CONCEPTS

The Upaniṣads often teach through riddles, images and suggestions, rarely through statements of dogma. However, certain important concepts recur throughout.

Brahman

'*Brahman*' was in origin one of a group of words and names which clustered around the idea of 'priestly power' and its central manifestation, 'sacred speech'.[38] It could mean sacred lore as a whole, or some particular powerful saying. It could be 'priesthood': either the priestly class as a whole or the power embodied in it – counterpart to *kṣatra*, 'royalty', the power of the ruling class. In the Upaniṣads all these meanings are still present, but the word has developed to mean the sacred power not just of some particular person, word or class, but of the whole universe: hence the first cause, absolute or supreme reality. There is an overlap in the different meanings, and sometimes we can only guess which was uppermost in the author's mind. The scholars of *brahman* (*brahmavādin*) of Śvetāśvatara I.1 are certainly expert in the sacred lore, but they also seek the reality or first cause behind it.

'*Brahman*' is a neuter word, and indicates an abstract concept. The masculine form from the same stem is 'Brahmā', referring to a male being who embodies the quality of *brahman* (in its various senses).[39] In later Hinduism, the neuter and masculine forms of the word are clearly differentiated, and attached to two distinct concepts. *Brahman* now refers exclusively to the abstract power, and Brahmā to a creator-god with his own attributes and characteristics. In the Upaniṣads the distinction is much less sharp. In the chapters on creation in Bṛhadāraṇyaka I, the creator-figure seems to shift between the neuter power and the masculine deity. In the Kena, the neuter *brahman* takes an active part in the narrative, appearing before the gods as a mysterious being (*yakṣa*).

Sometimes we cannot be sure which of the two is meant. The

words differ in only a few of their grammatical forms, and in compounds they are indistinguishable. Does *brahmaloka* mean the world of the god Brahmā, or the world or state achieved by a person who realizes *brahman*? In Book I of the Kauṣītakī the two appear to be the same. Where there is real ambiguity I have tried to indicate it.

I have normally left the word '*brahman*' untranslated, and saved any comment on usage for the notes. When a translation seems to be required, I have added the original word in brackets.

Ātman

Another complex term is '*ātman*', a word whose origin is disputed. Some consider that it was originally a term for the breath (which would make it a parallel to *prāṇa*, below). In everyday usage it was the reflexive pronoun – myself, yourself, themselves, etc. In the Upaniṣads it becomes the subject of speculation: What is the self? Who, in reality, am I? It comes to be seen as a real, unchanging part within each changing being, just as *brahman* is within the changing universe. The existence of such an unchanging part was among the main points of contention between early Hinduism and Buddhism. In the translation, *ātman* appears both as 'the self', and as 'myself', 'oneself' etc. Where it seemed appropriate, I have added the Sanskrit word in brackets.

Puruṣa

By the time of the later Upaniṣads included in this book, *brahman* and *ātman* have become the accepted way of discussing the nature of reality. However in the earlier period the sages seem still to be experimenting with different ways of talking about it.

In the early Upaniṣads, the inner part of a human being is often called *puruṣa*, 'man' or 'person', rather than *ātman*. (I generally use 'person', to avoid the implication that it is exclusive to the male: for the authors of the Upaniṣads, every being contained both male and female aspects.)[40] Here the inner reality is pictured in almost physical form as a tiny being moving inside the body, a 'dwarf' (Katha V.3), 'a thumb in length' (e.g. Katha IV.12, 13 and VI.17; SU III.13 and V.8), 'like a rice-grain or a barleycorn' (BU V.6.1; CU III. 14.3), yet mysteriously as large as space (see CU VIII.1.3). Some of the texts (e.g. TU II) envisage a series of *puruṣas* or *ātmans*, of increasingly subtle form, from the physical body to the inmost self.

The concept of *puruṣa* is first found in a famous hymn of the Ṛgveda, in which a giant man with 'a thousand heads, a thousand eyes . . . who is all this, whatever has been and whatever is to be', is sacrificed by the gods, and his dismembered body used to create the world.[41] As so often in the development of the Vedic tradition, what was originally a cosmic concept then became internalized through inner contemplation.

Prāṇa

'*Prāṇa*' means 'breath', that which gives life to every being. Within the body, it is said to divide itself into five separate breaths, each also called *prāṇa*. The five *prāṇas* all have names derived from the verb *an*, 'to breathe', with different prefixes denoting direction of movement. Unfortunately for the translator, ideas about their functions changed over time.

In later Hindu physiology, the functions of the breaths are clearly defined. The first is *prāṇa* itself, literally 'breathing forth', as the process of breathing in and out: it is based in the chest, and has its seat in the heart. *Apāna*, 'breathing away', is the lower breath, based in the intestine, thought to be responsible for the process of digestion and the elimination of waste matter from the body. *Vyāna*, 'breathing apart, breathing in different directions', is the diffused breath, thought to pervade the whole body. *Udāna*, 'breathing up', is the up-breath, based in the throat, and *samāna*, 'breathing together', is the central breath, based in the navel. This system seems to anticipate the later theory of the *cakras*, in which energy flows are thought to be centred on particular points within the body.

In the Praśna Upaniṣad, the *prāṇas* are clearly described in the above terms. In the Aitareya, too, the *prāṇa* and *apāna* seem to have their later roles. But in the earliest references the situation is more complicated. Chāndogya I.3.3–5 makes sense only if we assume that *vyāna* means 'between-breath', the point at which the breath stops in mid-respiration, and *prāṇa* and *apāna* are the out-breath and in-breath or vice versa. In Bṛhadāraṇyaka I, *prāṇa* is the organ that experiences scents, which would connect it to the in-breath, while in III.2.2 of the same Upaniṣad it is *apāna* that has that function. Elsewhere in the Bṛhadāraṇyaka there are traces of yet another system, with references to the 'breath of the mouth' (*ayāsya prāṇa*: I.3.7–8) and the 'middle breath' (*madhyama prāṇa*: I.4.21,22; II.2.1). Because the translations of these words are somewhat speculative, I have generally added the original terms in brackets.

Apart from these technical uses, the word '*prāṇa*' can also be used of the senses, of the bodily functions in general, and even of living beings seen as embodying the *prāṇas*. The central importance of the breath in its various forms is repeatedly stressed, notably in the fable found in several Upaniṣads of the competition for supremacy between the human faculties, in which only the breath proves itself indispensable.[42]

The Cosmos

For the authors of the Upaniṣads, the inner and outer worlds are closely interrelated. Human nature and the nature of the universe are seen as microcosm and macrocosm. Often we encounter a list of correspondences, taken from the earlier Brāhmaṇa literature, in which the sun corresponds to the eye, the moon to the mind, wind to the breath, fire to speech and so on.[43] Typically, both the cosmic powers and the faculties within the human being are called *devas*, or gods.

Therefore accounts of the creation of the universe as we know it (*sarvam idam*, 'all this') are intimately connected with ideas about the nature of the human being. There is generally an attempt to describe the way in which an original pure, undifferentiated state of being came to fall into the diverse and less pure state in which we see ourselves and the universe to be today. This attempt in turn is the key to finding a way to return to the original, purer, state. There are traces of an ancient debate between those who saw the original state as 'being' (*sat*) and those who saw it as 'not-being' (*asat*).[44] These debates use some of the terminology of the speculative passages in the Veda, such as the Puruṣa Hymn and the 'Creation Hymn':[45] however, they unite it with a new preoccupation with finding a way to achieve liberation from a world which is now seen as a cycle of otherwise unending bondage. The force that causes the fall from the original state is identified with desire in some form or another – hunger for food, or desire for a companion.

The Upaniṣads do not in general envisage the creation of something from nothing: the language used is that of emanation, begetting (or giving birth), or the ordering of a chaotic original material. In the early Upaniṣads the being responsible for this is described in a number of ways: as Death or Hunger; as Brahmā/*brahman*; as Hiraṇyagarbha, the Golden Embryo; and as Prajāpati, Lord of Offspring, whose children include gods, demons and human beings.

In the middle Upaniṣads we find the growth of a more developed kind of theism. In the Kaṭha, the supreme deity is variously identified with Agni, the Vedic fire-god, Dhātṛ, the Arranger, and Aditi, the mother of the gods. In the Śvetāśvatara, Rudra, identified with the solar deity Savitṛ, already has many of the titles and attributes of Śiva. Particularly in Book III, the deity becomes the focus of personal worship and devotion, tinged with awe and a touch of fear, rather as Kṛṣṇa does in the great vision of Book XI of the Bhagavadgītā.

THE UPANIṢADS AS LITERATURE

Many of the distinctive features of the Upaniṣads as literature are connected with their origins in an oral tradition. The literary devices that are used seem to be chosen primarily as means of conveying teaching. Perhaps the most striking of these devices is repetition, which takes several forms.

There are a number of passages that are found in different versions in more than one Upaniṣad. Such, for example, are the passages on the triumph of the breath, and on the two ways by which a person can go after death.[46] Since each of the Upaniṣads was in origin a separate work, this is not so much repetition as a case of different authors drawing on the same fund of oral material and interpreting it in their own ways. Sometimes the same kind of repetition occurs within an Upaniṣad, as with the two different versions of the dialogue of Yājñavalkya and Maitreyī in the Bṛhadāraṇyaka.[47] It is possible that both were originally separate versions of the same teaching, each handed down through a slightly different chain of teachers.[48] However, the authors of the Upaniṣad as we have it must have felt that both versions were distinct enough to include, and indeed each contains material that is not in the other, though the second version is slightly fuller and more detailed than the first.

More typically there is a deliberate use of repetition within an Upaniṣad for dramatic or teaching purposes. For example, in Bṛhadāraṇyaka II.1 the sage Gārgya attempts to teach Ajātaśatru, but finds the king more than a match for him in debate. Gārgya puts forward twelve different forms in which he visualizes *brahman*, each time using the same form of words: 'I worship as *brahman* the person who is in the sun', and so on through a series of twelve persons or *puruṣas*. Ajātaśatru rejects each of these visualizations, not as wrong, since each is said to bring great benefits to the one who practises it, but as being inadequate as a way of understanding *brahman*: 'Do not talk to me about him. I worship him as the topmost, the head and king of all beings. Whoever worships him as such becomes the topmost, the head and king of all beings.'

The word translated here as 'worship' is *upās-*, and these visualizations are often called *upāsanā* – an untranslatable word combining the ideas of meditation, worship and contemplation.[49] Often the seeker is advised to contemplate something as a symbol or embodiment of something else, as in the first words of the Chāndogya Upaniṣad: 'One should contemplate the syllable OṂ as the Udgītha.' *Upāsanā* is often used as a way of moving from grosser to subtler concepts of truth. Gārgya is unable to do this, and in the end has to ask Ajātaśatru to teach him instead.

Sometimes the repetition seems designed to act like the

recitation of a mantra, putting the hearer in the right frame of mind for understanding to arise, as in Yājñavalkya's answer to Uddālaka Āruṇi's question about the nature of the 'inner controller':[50]

> That which, resting in the earth, is other than the earth; which the earth does not know; of which the earth is the body; which controls the earth from within: this is your self, the inner controller, the immortal.
>
> That which, resting in the waters, is other than the waters; which the waters do not know; of which the waters are the body; which controls the waters from within: this is your self, the inner controller, the immortal.

– and so on for twenty verses, through the rest of the cosmic powers, through beings as a whole, and through the faculties of the individual being: 'in relation to deities' (*adhidaivatam*), 'in relation to beings' (*adhibhūtam*) and 'in relation to oneself' (*adhyātmam*), as these different levels are called in the Upaniṣads. Finally Yājñavalkya brings it all together:

> It is the unseen seer, the unheard hearer, the unthought-of thinker, the unknown knower. Other than this there is no seer; other than this there is no hearer; other than this there is no thinker; other than this there is no knower. This is your self, the inner controller, the immortal: what is other than this is suffering.

These words are themselves picked up again in his next answer, to Gārgī, so helping to bind the different chapters of Book III together. For their intended effect such passages have to be read in full – preferably aloud.

The favoured means of conveying teaching in the Upaniṣads is dialogue, which takes a variety of forms. Sometimes the situation is the expected one, with a seeker humbly asking a sage for instruction, but at other times there is an element of challenge or competition, as rival sages seek to test themselves against one another. Sometimes, as with Ajātaśatru and Gārgya, a less regarded person may prove more knowledgeable than a teacher who is reputed to be wise.

This way of teaching belongs to a tradition of verbal combat that is first found in the Brāhmaṇas.[51] The sage who wished to excel in it needed not only a profound knowledge of ritual and its meaning, but also powerful debating skills, and the ability to ask and answer questions in new and unexpected ways. Riddle and paradox are essential to this style of teaching, partly as ways of opening the hearer's mind to unfamiliar concepts, and partly for sheer delight, for 'the gods seem to love the mysterious, and hate the obvious.'[52] In the Upaniṣads, the riddle was particularly apt as a way of suggesting ideas about *brahman* and *ātman* which could not readily be conveyed in conventional terms:

> The one for whom priesthood and royalty,
> Both, are the rice
> And death is the sauce:
> Who, truly, knows where he is?[53]

> Two birds, companions and friends,
> Cling to the same tree.
> One of them eats the sweet pippala-berry:
> The other looks on, without eating.[54]

An important part of the sages' debating skills was wordplay, often in the form of puns or punning etymologies. A typical instance is Bṛhadāraṇyaka I.3.25–7, where the ideas of property (*sva*), tone (*svara*) and gold (*suvarṇa*) are linked together through the similarity of their sounds. Such conceits, though playful, have a serious purpose. The authors were almost certainly aware of the true derivations of these words, but regarded verbal resemblances as something more than coincidence. For them, it appears, the sound of a word had a genuine relationship to the thing it named.

Throughout the texts of the Upaniṣads we see the delight of the authors in the resources of the Sanskrit language, with its huge vocabulary, its versatility, and its wide range of consonants which make possible striking effects of assonance and alliteration. Such resources can be used not only for communicating abstract concepts, but also for more earthy purposes, as we see in the wonderfully scornful description of unworthy ascetics in Maitrī VII.8:

> . . . *aṭa-jaṭa-naṭa-bhaṭa-pravrajita-raṅgāvatāriṇo rājakarmaṇi patitādayo* . . .
>
> . . . vagabonds, wearers of matted locks, dancers, mercenaries, who have gone forth yet appear on the stage, renegades who work for kings, and so on . . .

This complexity of detail exists in tension with a powerful simplicity and directness. Stories are told with little scene-setting or explanation, and the characters appear with the minimum of introduction, leaving us to judge them by their own words and actions. The prose is generally clear and unadorned, drawing on universal experiences:

> As a caterpillar, reaching the end of a blade of grass and taking the next step, draws itself together, so the self, dropping the body, letting go of ignorance and taking the next step, draws itself together.
>
> As a weaver, unpicking a pattern from her weaving, fashions another, newer and more beautiful shape, so the self, dropping the body and letting go of ignorance, creates another, newer and more beautiful shape . . .[55]

Verse passages are generally in the simplest of the available metres, the *Anuṣṭubh* ('*śloka*'), helping to make important teachings easy to memorize:

> *yadā sarve pramucyante*
> *kāmā ye 'sya hṛdi śritāḥ*
> *atha martyo 'mṛto bhavaty*
> *atra brahma samaśnute.*
>
> When all the desires that dwell
> In one's heart are let go,
> Mortal becomes immortal:
> One reaches *brahman* here.[56]

In such passages, the Upaniṣads seem to speak directly to the heart of the reader, regardless of distance in time, place or background from the world of their authors.

NOTES

1. The word is derived from *upa-ni-sad-*, 'to sit down close to'. Traditionally this has been taken to refer to a session of teaching, with the student sitting close to the teacher. Within the texts themselves, however, it often refers to another kind of connection, in the hidden correspondences between things (cf. Olivelle 1996b: lii–liii, 303, n. 1.20). These two meanings are not necessarily exclusive. In Taittirīya I.1.2–3 the relationship between teacher and student is given as one of the five 'great connections'.
2. I have preferred the neutral terms BCE and CE to BC and AD.
3. Radhakrishnan 1994: 21.
4. I have written the syllable in this form in the translation because it generally has its own special character in Indian scripts.
5. The words 'literature' and 'text' here should not be taken necessarily to imply something written down: they are just less clumsy terms than the available alternatives.
6. See the Glossary under *Priests*.
7. According to most scholarly opinion, around 1500 BCE, though incorporating earlier material. The question of the dating of ancient Indian texts is a difficult and controversial one: see following section.
8. This is similar to what is called 'melisma' by scholars of early music in the European tradition. Examples of Vedic chanting can be found on the internet at http://www.ahista.com/vedchant/#contents and http://sanskrit.bhaarat.com/Dale/ index.html.
9. E.g. as the threefold knowledge (*trayī vidyā*, BU V.14.2, CU I.1.9, I.4.2–3, KauU II.6; *tretā [vidyā]*, Muṇḍaka I.2.1). The forms Ṛg-, Yajur- and Sāmaveda represent the words *ṛc*, *yajus* and *sāman* in compound, with the appropriate sound changes (sandhi) before initial 'v'.
10. E.g. '[the verses of] the Atharvans and Aṅgirases' (*atharvāṅgirasaḥ*), BU II.4.10 and CU III.4. Cf. CU VII.1.2 and its n. 1.
11. Staal 1983; I, 303, 308–9, 311–12; II, 456–65.
12. See BU I.1 and notes.
13. Bearing the same name as members of the priestly class: see the Glossary.

14. In the case of the Praśna Upaniṣad, the connection is genuine, since it is attributed to the *atharvan* sage Pippalāda. These attributions are discussed further in the headnotes to each individual Upaniṣad.
15. Oberlies's theory (see n. 29) would give precedence to the references to Bhakti, Sāṅkhya and Vedānta in the Bhagavadgītā: the Upaniṣadic references are in the Śvetāśvatara, SU VI.23, VI.13 and VI.22. The Bhagavadgītā has Bhakti as a major theme, but its references to Sāṅkhya and Vedānta are not at all specific. In BhG 2.39 Sāṅkhya seems to refer to 'theory' as distinct from 'practice'. In BhG 15.15, Kṛṣṇa calls himself *vedāntakṛt*, 'maker of the Vedānta', which may refer to the Upaniṣads themselves as 'end of the Veda' rather than to the philosophy derived from them. The Upaniṣadic references to Umā and Kṛṣṇa are distinctly early: for Umā, Kena III.12; for Kṛṣṇa, CU III. 17.6.
16. *Brahmavādinī* (BU IV.5.1): the female equivalent of the *brahmavādins* in SU I.1.
17. In this translation I have used this form of the name for the priestly class in preference to Anglicized forms such as 'brahmin'. It is the same name as that of the liturgical texts: see Glossary.
18. BU III.9.26.
19. See for example Śaṅkara (Gambhīrānanda 1983: 265–6), who thinks that Jabālā was too busy to ask her husband about his *gotra*, and that he left her shortly after their marriage.
20. BU IV.4.22.
21. The word *śramaṇa*, in its Prakrit form *śamaṇa*, spread under Buddhist influence into the languages of Central Asia, from which it entered Chinese (as *sha-men*) and Japanese (as *shamon*). Via Tungus and Russian, it appears also to be the origin of the English 'shaman' (Blacker 1975: 23, 317–18).
22. The Vrātya ascetic of the Atharvaveda was perhaps a forerunner of the *śramaṇas* – AV 15: cf. PU II.11 and the Glossary entry for *Vrātya*.
23. For a comprehensive study of the *āśramas* in theory and practice, see Olivelle 1993.
24. *apauruṣeyaṃ vākyaṃ vedaḥ*, 'The Veda is speech which is not of human origin', according to the Arthasaṃgraha of Laugākṣi Bhāskara (Radhakrishnan 1977: 388). This is a late (*c.* seventeenth-century) text on Mīmāṃsā, the philosophy of ritual, but the idea is derived from the fundamental text of Mīmāṃsā, the Jaiminīya Mīmāṃsā Sūtra (I.27–32).
25. E.g. Frawley 1994.

26. See Bechert 1991, 1992; Cousins 1996.
27. Bronkhorst (1986: 112–13) disputes this. He considers the Bṛhadāraṇyaka to be later than the Buddhist texts, explaining the difference in teachings by the different surroundings in which the two religions grew up: 'The former [Bṛhadāraṇyaka] was part of an esoteric movement confined to Brahmans who dwelt in villages; the latter [early Buddhism] centred in the cities.' This seems to conflict with the view of society portrayed in either group of texts. The Buddha is recorded as having debated with learned Brāhmaṇas, and several of his chief monks were Brāhmaṇas with a traditional Vedic education. It seems impossible to accept any theory about the dating of the Upaniṣads that depends upon such a slow movement of ideas, in either direction.
28. Numerous kings and princes are mentioned, but none whose dates are even approximately known, with the possible exception of Ajātaśatru of Kāśi, mentioned in both the Bṛhadāraṇyaka (II.1) and the Kauṣītakī (IV.1). Most scholars think that this is not the same as the Ajātaśatru (Pāli Ajātasattu) of Magadha, mentioned as a contemporary of the Buddha and Mahāvīra; though the Magadhan king is actually said to have become the ruler of Kāśi in later life, when he conquered the states of the Vajjian confederacy. (For the Buddhist account, see *Dīghanikāya* Suttas II, XVI: Walshe 1987: 91–2, 108–9, 231–2, 568.) The two Ajātaśatrus are portrayed as markedly different in character. Though both are shown debating with religious teachers, the motive of the Ajātaśatru of the Buddhist texts is a search for peace of mind, to allay his mental torment over the dynastic murder of his father. Bronkhorst identifies the two, explaining the discrepancies by dating the texts very late, after the details of the king's life had been forgotten. (This seems improbable, in view of the memory training undergone by those who handed on both Vedic and Buddhist texts.) I think it more likely that Ajātaśatru of Magadha, 'son of the Videhan princess' (*vedehiputta*), was a later king, perhaps named after Ajātaśatru of Kāśi, an illustrious member of his mother's family.
29. Thomas Oberlies (1988, 1995) has recently argued for a date for the Śvetāśvatara Upaniṣad, and by implication for the other middle-period Upaniṣads, later than the conventional one. He argues that the passages shared between this text and the Bhagavadgītā belong more naturally in the latter, making the Śvetāśvatara the later of the two. In his opinion, the differences between the Sāṅkhya philosophy of the Śvetāśvatara and the classical

Sāṅkhya system arose not, as has previously been thought, because the version in the Upaniṣad is earlier and less developed, but because of the impetus to reconcile the Sāṅkhya system with developing theistic ideas. Oberlies would date the Śvetāśvatara to the early centuries of the Common Era. However, this would depend on the date allotted to the Bhagavadgītā, which is also a matter of debate. Current scholarly consensus would place the Bhagavadgītā around the second century BCE, and there is no need to place the Śvetāśvatara much later than this. Even if the shared verses were first found in the Bhagavadgītā, they could quickly have gained popular currency and become widely known.

30. Ranade and Belvalkar (1927: 95–6) date the Māṇḍūkya later than the Maitrī, because it analyses the syllable OṂ into four parts instead of three.
31. BU II.6, IV.6, VI.5.
32. BU VI, n. 55.
33. BU VI.5.3.
34. *Brahman* (see 'Key Concepts', p. xxviii): BU II.6.3, IV.6.3, VI.5.4.
35. BU VI.5.3.
36. Van Buitenen 1962: 23–5.
37. See the Vedic Trust web page on the subject: http://www.ahista.com/dvt/ vedchant.html#noerror.
38. Others include Brahmā, *bṛhat* ('great', as in Bṛhad-āraṇyaka), Brāhmaṇa, Bṛhaspati.
39. In the Upaniṣads, it is also found as the title of one of the sacrificing Priests (BU III.1.6, 9; CU IV.16), and as a term of respect for a (very young) Brāhmaṇa (Kaṭha I.9).
40. BU IV.2.3.
41. RV X.90: O'Flaherty 1981: 29–31.
42. BU VI.1.7–14; CU V.1.7–15; KauU III.3. See also the closely related fable of the breath in the mouth as the supreme chanter-priest (Udgātṛ) who enables the gods to triumph over the demons: BU I.3 and CU I.2.
43. E.g. in SBr VIII.1.2.1–7. In Sanskrit, such correspondences are called *bandhutā*, 'kinship'.
44. Cf. CU VI.2.1–2 and note.
45. 'There was neither non-existence [*asat*] nor existence [*sat*] then . . .' (RV X.129): O'Flaherty 1981: 25–6.
46. See BU VI.2, CU IV.15 and V.3.
47. BU II.4 and IV.5.
48. As given in BU II.6 and IV.6.

49. It is derived from *upa* + *ās*-, 'to sit close to', hence 'attend on' or 'worship': clearly a concept related to that of *upaniṣad* itself.
50. BU III.7.3–23.
51. Melling 1997.
52. BU IV.2.2.
53. Kaṭha II.25.
54. SU IV.6 and MuU III.1.
55. BU IV.4.3–4.
56. BU IV.4.7.

Bibliography

SUGGESTIONS FOR FURTHER READING

Brockington, J. [1981] 1996. *The Sacred Thread: Hinduism in its Continuity and Diversity* (Edinburgh: Edinburgh University Press)

Deussen, P. [1906] 1966. *The Philosophy of the Upanishads*, trans. A. S. Geden (New York: Dover)

Hiriyanna, M. [1949] 1995. *Essentials of Indian Philosophy* (Delhi: Motilal Banarsidass)

King, R. 1999. *Indian Philosophy: An Introduction to Hindu and Buddhist Thought* (Edinburgh: Georgetown University Press)

McEvilley, T. 2002. *The Shape of Ancient Thought: Comparative Studies in Greek and Indian Philosophies* (New York: Allworth Press)

Ranade, R. D., and Belvalkar, S. K. 1927. *History of Indian Philosophy*, Vol. 2: *The Creative Period* (Poona: Bilvakunda Publishing House)

WORKS CONSULTED

Allchin, B., and Allchin, F. R. 1982. *The Rise of Civilization in India and Pakistan*, Cambridge World Archaeology (Cambridge: Cambridge University Press)

Alter, R., trans. 1996. *Genesis: Translation and Commentary* (New York and London: W. W. Norton & Co.)

Anon., ed. 1968. *The Bṛhadāraṇyaka Upaniṣad, containing the original text with word-by-word meanings, running translation, notes and introduction* (Madras: Sri Ramakrishna Math)

Anon., ed. [1938] 1970. *Śvetāśvataropaniṣad Sānuvād Śaṅkarabhāṣyasahit* (Gorakhpur: Gītā Press, Samvat 1995 [= CE 1938], repr. 2027 [= CE 1970])

Anon., ed. [1937] 1971a. *Chāndogyopaniṣad Sānuvād Śaṅkarabhāṣyasahit* (Gorakhpur: Gītā Press, Samvat 1994 [= CE 1937], repr. 2028 [= CE 1971])

Anon., ed. [1935] 1971b. *Kaṭhopaniṣad Sānuvād Śaṅkarabhāṣyasahit* (Gorakhpur: Gītā Press, Samvat 1992 [= CE 1935], repr. 2028 [= CE 1971])

Anon., ed. [1935] 1971c. *Kenopaniṣad Sānuvād Śaṅkarabhāṣyasahit* (Gorakhpur: Gītā Press, Samvat 1992 [= CE 1935], repr. 2028 [= CE 1971])

Anon., ed. [1936] 1972. *Aitareyopaniṣad Sānuvād Śaṅkarabhāṣyasahit* (Gorakhpur: Gītā Press, Samvat 1993 [= CE 1936], repr. 2029 [= CE 1972])

Anon., ed. [1935] 1973a. *Muṇḍakopaniṣad Sānuvād Śaṅkarabhāṣyasahit* (Gorakhpur: Gītā Press, Samvat 1992 [= CE 1935], repr. 2030 [= CE 1973])

Anon., ed. [1934] 1973b. *Praśnopaniṣad Sānuvād Śaṅkarabhāṣyasahit* (Gorakhpur: Gītā Press, Samvat 1992 [= CE 1935], repr. 2030 [= CE 1973])

Basham, A. L. 1951. *History and Doctrines of the Ājīvikas: A Vanished Indian Religion* (London: Luzac)

Bechert, H., 1991, 1992. *The Dating of the Historical Buddha. Die Datierung des Historischen Buddha* (Göttingen: Vandenhoeck & Ruprecht, 2 vols.)

Bell, J. L., and Maule, G. A. 1989. *A Wee Worship Book: Wild Goose Worship Group* (Glasgow: Pearce Institute)

Blacker, Carmen, 1975. *The Catalpa Bow: A Study of Shamanistic Practices in Japan* (London: George Allen & Unwin)

Bloomfield, M. 1906. *A Vedic Concordance*, Harvard Oriental Series, Vol. 10 (Cambridge, Mass.: Harvard University Press)

Brereton, J. 1986, '*Tat Tvam Asi* in Context', *Zeitschrift der Deutschen Morgenländischen Gesellschaft*, 136: 98–109

Bronkhorst, J. 1986. *The Two Traditions of Meditation in Ancient India* (Stuttgart: Franz Steiner)

Brough, J. 1971. 'Soma and *Amanita Muscaria*', *Bulletin of the School of Oriental and African Studies*, 34: 2, 331–62

Brown, G. W. 1919. 'Prāṇa and Apāna', *JAOS*, 19: 39, 104–12

Buitenen, J. A. B. van. 1962. *The Maitrāyaṇīya Upaniṣad: A Critical Essay* (The Hague: Mouton)

Cousins, L. S. 1996. 'The Dating of the Historical Buddha: A Review Article', *JRAS* Series 3, 6:1, 57–63

Craddock, P. T., et al. 1989. 'The Production of Lead, Silver and Zinc in Early India', *Archaometallurgie der Alten Welt, Symposium* (Bochum: Deutschen Bergbau Museums)

Daniélou, A. 1964. *Hindu Polytheism* (London: Routledge & Kegan Paul)

Deussen, P. [1906] 1966. *The Philosophy of the Upanishads*, trans. A. S. Geden (New York: Dover)

Gambhīrānanda, Swāmī, trans. 1957, 1958. *Eight Upaniṣads with the Commentary of Śrī Śaṅkarācārya* (Calcutta: Advaita Ashrama, 2 vols.) (Vol. 1 contains the Īśā, Kena, Kaṭha and Taittirīya; Vol. 2 the Aitareya, Muṇḍaka, Māṇḍūkya with Kārikā, and Praśna)

—— trans. 1983. *Chāndogya Upaniṣad with the Commentary of Śrī Śaṅkarācārya* (Calcutta: Advaita Ashrama)

—— trans. 1986. *Śvetāśvatara Upaniṣad with the Commentary of Śrī Śaṅkarācārya* (Calcutta: Advaita Ashrama)

Gombrich, R. 1984. 'Notes on the Brahminical Background to Buddhist Ethics', in G. Dhammapala, R. Gombrich and K. R. Norman, eds., *Buddhist Studies in Honour of Hammalava Saddhātissa* (Nugegoda: University of Jayawardenepura)

——. 1990a. 'How the Mahāyāna Began', in T. Skorupski, ed., *The Buddhist Forum*, Vol. 1 (London: School of Oriental and African Studies; Delhi: HarperCollins)

——. 1990b. 'Recovering the Buddha's Message', in T. Skorupski, ed., *The Buddhist Forum*, Vol. 1 (London: School of Oriental and African Studies; Delhi: Heritage Publishers)

——. 1996. *How Buddhism Began: The Conditioned Genesis of the Early Teachings* (London and Atlantic Highlands, NJ: Athlone)

Gonda, J. 1981. *The Vedic Morning Litany (Prātaranuvāka)* (Leiden: E. J. Brill)

Griffith, R. T. H. [1895–6] 1985. *Hymns of the Atharvaveda translated with a popular commentary* (Delhi: Munshiram Manoharlal, 2 vols.)

——. [1889] 1987. *Hymns of the Ṛgveda translated with a popular commentary* (Delhi: Munshiram Manoharlal, 2 vols.)

——. [1895] 1986. *Hymns of the Sāmaveda translated with a popular commentary* (Delhi: Munshiram Manoharlal, 2 vols. repr. as one vol.)

Guénon, R. 1981. *Man and his Becoming according to the Vedānta*, trans. R. C. Nicholson (Delhi: Oriental Books Reprint Corporation)

Handelman, D., and Shulman, D. 1997. *God Inside Out: Śiva's Game of Dice* (Oxford and New York: Oxford University Press)

Hinnells, J. R., ed. 1991. *Who's Who of World Religions* (London: Macmillan, and New York: Simon & Schuster)

Hopkins, E. W. 1907. 'The Sniff-Kiss in Ancient India', *JAOS*, 28: 120–34

Hume, R. E. [1887] 1995. *The Thirteen Principal Upanishads translated from the Sanskrit* (Delhi: Oxford University Press, 2nd edn revised)

Johnson, E. H. 1930. 'Some Sāṃkhya and Yoga Conceptions of the Śvetāśvatara Upaniṣad', *JRAS*, 855–78

Killingley, D. H. 1981, 1983. 'Notes on the Kaṭha Upaniṣad' (unpublished)

——. 1983. 'Notes on the Śvetāśvatara Upaniṣad' (unpublished)

——. 1986. 'Oṃ: the Sacred Syllable in the Veda', in J. J. Lipner, ed., *A Net Cast Wide: Investigations into Indian Thought in Memory of David Freedman* (Newcastle upon Tyne: Grevatt & Grevatt)

Larson, G. L. 1979. *Classical Sāṃkhya: An Interpretation of its History and Meaning* (Santa Barbara: Ross/Erikson)

Lienhard, S. 1978. 'On the Meaning and Use of the Word *Indragopa*', in *Indologica Taurinensia*, Vol. 6 (Turin: Edizioni Jollygraphica), 177–88

Mādhavānanda, Swāmī, trans. 1934. *Bṛhadāraṇyaka Upaniṣad with the Commentary of Śrī Śaṅkarācārya* (Calcutta: Advaita Ashrama)

Markel, S. 1990. 'The Imagery and Iconographic Development of the Indian Planetary Deities Rāhu and Ketu', *South Asian Studies*, 6: 9–26

Mascaró, J. 1965. *The Upanishads* (Harmondsworth: Penguin)

Melling, D. 1993. 'Indian Philosophy Before the Greeks', Manchester Metropolitan University, Nehru Lecture: on Internet at http://www.philo.demon.co.uk/preGreek.htm (accessed 10 May 2003)

——. 1997. 'Verbal Combat in the Brāhmaṇas': on Internet at http://www.philo.demon.co.uk/verbal.htm (accessed 10 May 2003)

Mitchiner, J. E. 1982. *Traditions of the Seven Ṛṣis* (Delhi: Motilal Banarsidass)

Müller, F. M. [1879, 1894] 1962. *The Upaniṣads* (New York: Dover, 2 vols.)

Norman, K. R. 1991. 'Theravāda Buddhism and Brahmanical Hinduism: Brahmanical Terms in a Buddhist Guise', in T. Skorupski, ed., *The Buddhist Forum*, Vol. 2: *Seminar Papers 1988–90* (London: School of Oriental and African Studies)

Oberlies, Thomas. 1988. 'Die Śvetāśvatara-Upaniṣad: Eine Studie ihrer Gotteslehre (Studien zu den "mittleren" Upaniṣads I).' *WZKS*, 32: 35–62

——. 1995. 'Die Śvetāśvatara-Upaniṣad: Einleitung – Edition und Übersetzung von Adhyaya I (Studien zu den "mittleren" Upaniṣads II – 1. Teil).' *WZKS*, 39: 61–102.

——. 1996. 'Die Śvetāśvatara-Upaniṣad: Einleitung – Edition und Übersetzung von Adhyaya II-III (Studien zu den "mittleren" Upaniṣads II – 2. Teil).' *WZKS*, 40: 123–160

——. 1998. 'Die Śvetāśvatara-Upaniṣad: Einleitung – Edition und Übersetzung von Adhyaya IV-VI (Studien zu den "mittleren" Upaniṣads II – 3. Teil).' *WZKS*, 42: 77–138

O'Flaherty, W. D. 1981. *The Rig Veda* (Harmondsworth: Penguin)

Olivelle, P. 1993. *The Āśrama System: The History and Her-*

meneutics of a Religious Institution (Oxford and New York: Oxford University Press)

——. 1996a. '*Dharmaskandhāḥ and Brahmasaṃsthaḥ*: A Study of *Chāndogya Upaniṣad* 2.23.1', *JAOS*, 116:2, 204–219

——. 1996b. *Upaniṣads* (Oxford and New York: Oxford University Press)

Panoli, V. 1994–6. *Upanishads in Sankara's Own Words*. 4 Vols. Vol. 1: *Īśā, Kena, Kaṭha and Māṇḍūkya with Kārikā of Gauḍapada* (2nd edn, 1995). Vol. 2: *Praśna, Muṇḍaka, Taittirīya and Aitareya* (2nd edn, 1996). Vol. 3: *Chāndogya* (2nd edn, 1995). Vol. 4: *Bṛhadāraṇyaka* (1994) (Calicut: Mathrabhumi)

Pingree, D. 1981. *Jyotiḥśāstra: Astral and Mathematical Literature*, A History of Indian Literature, Vol. 6, Fasc. 4 (Wiesbaden: Harrassowitz)

Radhakrishnan, S. [1923] 1977. *History of Indian Philosophy*, Vol. 2 (London: George Allen & Unwin, and New York: Humanities Press; repr. Bombay: Motilal Banarsidass)

——. [1953] 1994. *The Principal Upaniṣads* (London: Allen & Unwin; repr. Delhi: Heritage Press)

Rajaram, Navaratna S., and Frawley, David. 1995. *Vedic 'Aryans' and the Origins of Civilization: A Literary and Scientific Perspective* (Saint-Hyacinthe, Quebec: World Heritage Press)

Ranade, R. D., and Belvalkar, S. K. 1927. *History of Indian Philosophy*, Vol. 2: *The Creative Period* (Poona: Bilvakunda Publishing House)

Renou, L. 1953. 'Le Passage des Brāhmaṇa aux Upaniṣad', *JAOS*, 73: 138–44

Roebuck, V. J. 1992. *The Circle of Stars: An Introduction to Indian Astrology* (Shaftesbury, Dorset, and Rockport, Mass: Element)

Sharma, A., and Young, K. K. 1990. 'The Meaning of *ātmahano janāḥ* in Īśā Upaniṣad 3', *JAOS*, 110: 595–602

Shastri, J. L., ed. 1970. *Upaniṣatsaṃgrahaḥ containing 188 Upaniṣads* (Delhi: Motilal Banarsidass)

Staal, F. 1983. *Agni: The Vedic Ritual of the Fire Altar* (Berkeley: Asian Humanities Press, 2 vols.)

Taimni, I. K. 1974. *Gāyatrī: The Daily Religious Practice of the Hindus* (Adyar: Theosophical Publishing House)

Thieme, P., trans. 1965. 'Īśopaniṣad (= Vājasaneyī-Saṃhitā 40) 1–14', *JAOS*, 85: 89–99 (repr. Paul Thieme, *Kleiner Schriften*, ii, 228–38)

Vogel, J. P. 1962. *The Goose in Indian Literature and Art*, Memoirs of the Kern Institute No. 2 (Leiden: E. J. Brill)

Walshe, M., trans. 1987. *Thus Have I Heard: The Long Discourses of the Buddha: Dīgha Nikāya* (London: Wisdom Publications)

Whitney, W. D. [1905] 1984. *Atharva-Veda-Saṁhitā*, rev. and ed. C. R. Lanman (Delhi: Motilal Banarsidass, 2 vols.)

Zaehner, R. C. 1966. *Hindu Scriptures* (London and New York: Everyman, Dutton/Dent)

Zysk, K. G. 1993. 'The Science of Respiration and the Doctrine of the Bodily Winds in Ancient India', *JAOS*, 113: 198–213

About the Translation

When I began the present translation, I had for some years been involved in teaching courses on Indian religious traditions to students of a wide range of ages and backgrounds, and had frequently found myself cautioning them about the translations of the Upaniṣads that were available to them. Some seemed inaccurate or partial, others coloured too strongly by the translators' own religious convictions. Others, though excellent in certain ways, were written in language that the students found difficult to read, leaving them with the feeling that the original texts must themselves have been crabbed and archaic in their expression. So the project began as an attempt to provide students and the general reader with a complete, accurate and readable version of these important texts.

Since I began the work, Patrick Olivelle's translation has appeared, providing one fresh answer to these problems. Olivelle is a great scholar of the Vedic tradition, and I feel a certain temerity in offering another translation so soon after his. While revising my text I have been grateful for his insights into many aspects of the meaning of the Upaniṣads, as the reader will observe from the notes.

However, I feel that there is still room for another approach to a group of texts as full of layers of meaning as the Upaniṣads. I have been particularly concerned to try to retain something of their quality as literature – to convey something of the different ways in which they express their teachings.

The Upaniṣads, as we have seen, were either oral literature or very close to the oral form. Students would have studied them by learning them by heart, and even now scholars of Vedānta will often quote favourite passages in the original Sanskrit. For this reason I have included the invocations that begin and end each Upaniṣad in traditional recitation, usually omitted in Western translations. It is not clear how long these verses have been attached to the Upaniṣads, but in themselves they seem to be ancient, referring to distinctively Vedic gods and concepts.

My basic principle has been to represent accurately what is in the original text, so that readers with no knowledge of Sanskrit may have confidence that anything that they find in the translation corresponds to something in the original. Most readers would probably regard this as the minimum requirement for a translation. However, some of the earlier translators took considerable liberties with the text, importing large amounts of commentarial material into their versions. An extreme example is Juan Mascaró, who renders the sentence which literally means 'Yājñavalkya went to Janaka of Videha: he thought, I will not teach' into 'To Janaka king of Videha came once Yājñavalkya meaning to keep in silence the supreme secret wisdom'.[1]

Other translators, without going to such extremes, have tried to smooth out what is irregular or startling in the original, so depriving the Upaniṣadic authors of one of their most powerful teaching tools. For example:

andhaṃ tamaḥ praviśanti
ye 'vidyām upāsate.
tato bhūya iva te tamo
ya u vidyāyāṃ ratāḥ.

They who worship ignorance
Enter blind darkness:
They who delight in knowledge
Enter darkness, as it were, yet deeper.[2]

Max Müller translates this as 'All who worship what is not real knowledge (good works), enter into blind darkness: those who delight in real knowledge, enter, as it were, into greater darkness.'[3] But clearly the original passage was intended to shock the hearers, as a Zen or Tantric teaching might, in order to wake them up. They had, after all, devoted their lives to Vedic knowledge, and now they would wonder, 'Have I been worshipping ignorance or knowledge? Which is worse?' By inserting the word 'real', Müller has reduced the impact of the verse.

Similarly, one of the effects of Mascaró's additions, quoted above, is to turn Yājñavalkya into a cliché of a guru figure, instead of the complex man that we meet in the Upaniṣad and the Śatapatha Brāhmaṇa.

In translating the early Upaniṣads, I have tried to retain something of the oral style. I have not attempted to retain all the words that denoted the teacher's gesture – *that* sun, *this* fire – or the many particles expressing linkage or emphasis. In English it becomes cumbersome if it is 'yonder sun' at every mention, or if every new sentence begins with a 'therefore' or an 'indeed'. However, I have aimed for a conversational quality in the prose passages, shading into a certain raciness where it seemed appropriate in the dialogues. The verse passages, in Sanskrit metres of various degrees of complexity, have been translated into a form of free verse which I hope will set them slightly apart from the prose. (Sanskrit verse, like that in classical Greek and Latin, depends for its structure on fairly strict patterns of long and short syllables, rather than on rhyme or stress.) I have not attempted to imitate the original forms, except in a very limited way.

I did not want to strew the pages of the translation with additions in square brackets, so where different linguistic or cultural assumptions have required an extra word of explanation I have made a rule of mentioning the fact in the notes. However, I allowed myself the following exceptions. In passages of dialogue where all the speakers are referred to by pronouns I thought it legitimate to add names, or titles such as 'the king', to make it clear who is speaking. As well as pronouns, impersonal verbs are used in Sanskrit far more freely than in English, and the authors of the Upaniṣads are particularly fond of expressions such as 'they say' or 'they call it', referring to people in general. To avoid awkwardness or ambiguity, I have often translated these as 'folk say', 'folk call it'. And where the word 'this' in the feminine gender incontrovertibly means 'this earth', I have translated it as such – partly to avoid confusion with 'this' or 'all this', in the neuter gender, as a term for the whole universe, such a typically Upaniṣadic expression that I wanted to keep it unchanged. (One can almost see the sweep of the teacher's arm.)

While in the latter stages of this work, I came across Robert Alter's new translation of the first book of the Hebrew Bible, and found that much of what he had to say in his introduction expressed for me the special problems and excitements of translating these ancient texts. I was particularly struck by his warning about the perils of 'explaining away':

> The unacknowledged heresy underlying most modern English versions of the Bible is the use of translation as a vehicle for *explaining* the Bible instead of representing it in another language, and in the most egregious instances this amounts to explaining away the Bible . . . Modern translators, in their zeal to uncover the meanings of the biblical text for the instruction of a modern readership, frequently lose sight of how the text intimates its meanings – the distinctive, artfully deployed features of ancient Hebrew prose and poetry that are the instruments for the articulation of all meaning, message, insight, and vision.[4]

When in doubt, I have felt it safest to assume that the original authors of the Upaniṣads knew what they were doing.

NUMBERING

Most of the Upaniṣads consist of several major divisions, which in the case of the longest are divided into subdivisions, themselves divided into individual verses. In different Upaniṣads, both the larger and the smaller divisions tend to have different, and often colourful, names, which are given in the notes to the texts. In the translation itself I have standardized these names, calling the major divisions 'books' and the subdivisions 'chapters'. (I have made an exception in the case of the Praśna Upaniṣad, which is divided into a series of questions (*praśna*): here I have followed the original and called the divisions 'questions'.) In cross-references, the first division in each case is given as a Roman numeral, so that BU 1.2.3 denotes Bṛhadāraṇyaka Upaniṣad Book I, Chapter 2, Verse 3, and SU VI.20 denotes Śvetāśvatara Upaniṣad Book VI, Verse 20. The two shortest Upaniṣads, the Īśā and the Māṇḍūkya, are simply numbered by verses – for example IU 3.

NOTES

1. Mascaró 1965, on BU IV.3.1.
2. IU 9, BU IV.4.10.
3. Müller 1879, I: 312.
4. Alter 1996: xii.

GĀYATRĪ MANTRA

We meditate on the lovely
Glory of the god Savitṛ
That he may stimulate our minds.

Ṛgveda III.57.10

ĪŚĀVĀSYA OR ĪŚĀ UPANIṢAD

'Pervaded by the Lord'

OṂ. *That is full; this is full;*
Fullness comes forth from fullness:
When fullness is taken from fullness,
Fullness remains.[1]

OṂ. *Peace, peace, peace.*

1. All this, everything that moves in this moving world,[2]
Must be pervaded by the lord.[3]
Enjoy what has been abandoned.[4]
Do not covet anyone's wealth.

2. You must seek to live[5] a hundred years
Just doing work (*karman*) here.
There is no other way for you but this:
This way, work does not stick to a man.

3. Those worlds, covered with blind darkness,
Are 'Sunless'[6] by name.
Those people who are self-slayers[7]
Go to them on departing.

4. One, unmoving, swifter than mind,
The gods cannot catch it, as it goes before:
Standing still, it outruns others that are running.
Mātariśvan sets the waters[8] in it.

5. It moves, it does not move;
It is far and near likewise.
It is inside all this:
It is outside all this.

6. Whoever sees
All beings in the self (*ātman*)[9]
And the self in all beings
Does not shrink away from it.[10]

7. For the one who knows,
In whom all beings have become self,
How can there be delusion or grief
When he sees oneness?

8. He has encompassed the bright,[11] the bodiless,
the unwounded,
The sinewless, the pure, the unpierced by evil:
The wise seer, conqueror, self-born,
He has arranged objects according to their nature
Through eternal years.

9. They who worship ignorance
Enter blind darkness:
They who delight in knowledge
Enter darkness, as it were, yet deeper.[12]

10. It is different, they say, from knowledge;
It is different, they say, from ignorance:
So we have heard from those wise ones
Who have revealed it to us.

11. Whoever knows knowledge and ignorance –
Both of them, together –
By ignorance crosses over death.
And by knowledge reaches immortality.

12. They who worship non-becoming
Enter blind darkness:
They who delight in becoming[13]
Enter darkness, as it were, yet deeper.

13. It is different, they say, from becoming;
It is different, they say, from non-becoming:
So we have heard from those wise ones
Who have revealed it to us.

14. Whoever knows becoming and destruction –
Both of them, together –
By destruction crosses over death
And by becoming reaches immortality.

15. The face of truth is concealed
By a vessel made of gold.[14]
Reveal it, Pūṣan, to my sight,
Which has truth as its *dharma*.[15]

16. Pūṣan, Ekarṣi, Yama, Sūrya, son of Prajāpati,
Draw apart your rays and draw them together.
I see the light that is your most beautiful form.
That very person – I am he.[16]

17. My breath (*vāyu*) to immortal air:
This body has ended in ashes.
OṂ! Will, remember! Remember the deed!
Will, remember! Remember the deed![17]

18. Agni, god who knows all ways,
Lead us by a good road to prosperity.
Overcome our crooked faults,[18]
And we will render you the utmost reverence.

OṂ. *That is full; this is full;*
Fullness comes forth from fullness:
When fullness is taken from fullness,
Fullness remains.

OṂ. *Peace, peace, peace.*

BṚHADĀRAṆYAKA UPANIṢAD

The Great Forest Teaching

OṂ. *That is full; this is full;*
Fullness comes forth from fullness:
When fullness is taken from fullness,
Fullness remains.

OṂ. *Peace, peace, peace.*

BOOK I

CHAPTER I

1. OṂ. Dawn is the head of the sacrificial horse.[1] The sun is the eye of the sacrificial horse, the wind his breath, the fire that is in all men[2] his open mouth, the year his body (*ātman*). The sky is his back, middle-air[3] his belly, earth his flanks, the directions[4] his two sides, the intermediate directions his ribs, the seasons his limbs, the months and half-months[5] his joints, the days and nights his feet, the constellations[6] his bones, the clouds his flesh. The food in his stomach is the sands; the rivers are his bowels, liver and lungs; the mountains, plants and trees are his hairs; the rising sun is his front half, the setting sun his rear half; when he yawns, it lightens; when he shakes himself, it thunders; when he urinates, it rains; speech is his voice.[7]

2. Day arose as the sacrificial vessel[8] in front of the horse: its birthplace[9] was in the eastern ocean. Night arose as the sacrificial vessel behind him: its birthplace was in the western ocean. These two came into being as the vessels at either end of the horse.

Becoming Steed, he carried the gods; becoming Charger, he carried the *gandharvas*; becoming Courser, he carried the demons; becoming Horse,[10] he carried human beings. The ocean was his kinsman, the ocean his birthplace.

CHAPTER 2

1. In the beginning there was nothing here: this[11] was covered by Death, by Hunger, for Hunger is Death.[12] Death made up his mind: 'If only I could have a self (*ātman*)!' Shining (*arc-*),[13] he moved about, and, as he shone, the waters[14] were born of him. 'As I shone, water (*ka*)[15] came to me,' he thought: that is why water is called *arka*.[16] Water will come to the one who knows in this way why water is called *arka*.[17]

2. The waters are *arka*. The foam of the waters was compacted together. It became the earth. He toiled on it, and, as he toiled and grew hot, his brightness,[18] his essence, became fire.

3. He divided himself into three, one third being the sun and one third the air.[19] As breath, too, he was divided into three. The eastern direction became his head; that one and *that* one[20] became his forequarters; that one and *that* one[21] became his hindquarters. The southern and northern directions became his two sides, the sky his back, middle-air his belly, this[22] his breast. He stands firm on the waters. Knowing this, one stands firm wherever one goes.

4. He desired that a second self might be born of him. By means of mind, Hunger, that is Death, joined with Speech[23] in sexual union. The seed[24] became the year. Before that there was no year. He carried it for so much time. After so much time, a year, he sent it out.[25] He opened his jaws to eat his offspring. It made the noise 'Bhāṇ!'[26] That became speech.

5. He realized that if he were to kill it he would make less food for himself. With that speech, that self, he sent out all this, whatever there is: the Ṛgveda, Yajurveda and Sāmaveda, the metres,[27] people and animals. Whatever he sent forth he began to eat. Because he eats (*ad-*) everything, space is called Aditi. Whoever knows that this is why space is called Aditi becomes the eater of all this: all this becomes his food.

6. He desired that he might sacrifice again with a greater sacrifice. He toiled, he raised heat;[28] and as he toiled and grew hot his splendour, his vigour, departed. The breaths (*prāṇa*) are

splendour, vigour. Once the breaths had departed, his body began to swell, but mind was still in his body.

7. He desired that that body of his should become fit for sacrifice, and that by it he should become embodied.[29] Then his body became a horse. 'Since it has swollen (*aśvat*),' he thought, 'it has become fit for sacrifice (*medhya*).' That is why the horse sacrifice is the *aśvamedha*. Whoever knows this, knows the horse sacrifice.

Letting it go free, he contemplated it. After a year, he sacrificed it to himself.[30] He offered the animals[31] to the deities. That is why folk offer the horse, which is consecrated to all the deities, as an offering to Prajāpati.

The one who gives heat[32] is the horse sacrifice: the year is his self. Fire is *arka:*[33] the worlds[34] are his bodies. They are two, the shining one and the horse sacrifice. Then again, they are just one deity, Death. He who knows this conquers re-death;[35] Death does not get him; Death becomes his body (*ātman*); he becomes one of the deities.

CHAPTER 3

1. The descendants of Prajāpati are of two kinds: the gods and the demons. The gods are the younger, the demons the elder, and they vied for these worlds. The gods said, 'Come, let us defeat the demons at the sacrifice by means of the Udgītha!'

2. The gods said to speech, 'Chant the Udgītha for us!'

'I will!' said speech, and chanted it for them. Whatever enjoyment there is in speech, it sang into being for the gods: but the fact that it sang well was for itself.[36]

The demons thought, 'By means of this Udgātṛ they will defeat us,' and, attacking it, pierced it with evil. That evil is the evil that anyone does when he says what is not proper.

3. The gods said to breath (*prāṇa*),[37] 'Chant the Udgītha for us!'

'I will!' said breath, and chanted it for them. Whatever

enjoyment there is in breath it sang into being for the gods: but the fact that it smelled well was for itself.

The demons thought, 'By means of this Udgātṛ they will defeat us,' and, attacking it, pierced it with evil. That evil is the evil that anyone does when he smells what is not proper.

4. The gods said to the eye,[38] 'Chant the Udgītha for us!'

'I will!' said the eye, and chanted it for them. Whatever enjoyment there is in the eye it sang into being for the gods: but the fact that it saw well was for itself.

The demons thought, 'By means of this Udgātṛ they will defeat us,' and, attacking it, pierced it with evil. That evil is the evil that anyone does when he sees what is not proper.

5. The gods said to the ear, 'Chant the Udgītha for us!'

'I will!' said the ear, and chanted it for them. Whatever enjoyment there is in the ear it sang into being for the gods: but the fact that it heard well was for itself.

The demons thought, 'By means of this Udgātṛ they will defeat us,' and, attacking it, pierced it with evil. That evil is the evil that anyone does when he hears what is not proper.

6. The gods said to mind, 'Chant the Udgītha for us!'

'I will!' said mind, and chanted it for them. Whatever enjoyment there is in mind it sang into being for the gods: but the fact that it imagined well was for itself.

The demons thought, 'By means of this Udgātṛ they will defeat us,' and, attacking it, pierced it with evil. That evil is the evil that anyone does when he imagines what is not proper.

In the same way they afflicted the other deities with evil, they pierced them with evil.

7. The gods said to the breath in the mouth (*ayāsya prāṇa*), 'Chant the Udgītha for us!'

'I will!' said the breath in the mouth, and chanted it for them.

The demons thought, 'By means of this Udgātṛ they will defeat us,' and, attacking it, desired to pierce it with evil. As a turf would be scattered if it struck a rock, they perished, scattered in all directions. Then the gods prevailed and the demons were overcome. Whoever knows this himself[39] prevails, and the adversary[40] who hates him is overcome.

8. They said, 'Where is the one we had dealings with just now?'

'He is here in the mouth.' He is Ayāsya Āṅgirasa, the essence (*rasa*) of the limbs (*aṅga*).

9. That deity is called Dūr, for death is far (*dūra*) from him. Death is far from the one who knows this.

10. That deity, having driven away evil – that is, death – from these deities, took it to the end of the directions. There he set down their evils. So one should not go to the people there, one should not go to the end of the directions, lest one should meet with evil, with death.

11. That deity, having driven away evil – that is, death – from these deities, then carried them beyond death.

12. First he carried speech across. When speech escaped death, it became fire. Fire, having passed beyond death, blazes.

13. Next he carried breath across. When breath escaped death, it became wind. Wind, having passed beyond death, purifies.

14. Next he carried the eye across. When the eye escaped death, it became the sun. The sun, having passed beyond death, gives heat (*tap-*).

15. Next he carried the ear across. When the ear escaped death, it became the directions. The directions have passed beyond death.

16. Next he carried the mind across. When the mind escaped death, it became the moon. The moon, having passed beyond death, shines.

Whoever knows this, these deities carry him beyond death.

17. Next he sang into being good food[41] for himself. Whatever food is eaten is eaten by him, and he is supported on it.

18. The gods said, 'You have sung all this into being as food for yourself. Give us a share in this food.'

'Then sit round me.'

'We will,' they said, and surrounded him. So whatever food one eats by means of him the gods too enjoy.

Whoever knows this is surrounded by his own people: he becomes the lord, the best, the foremost of his own people, an eater of food, an overlord. If someone knows this, and one among his own people desires to rival him, that rival is not even adequate to support his own dependants. But if someone who helps him desires to support his own dependants, that helper is adequate to support his own dependants.

19. He is called Ayāsya Āṅgirasa, for he is the essence of the limbs. Breath is the essence of the limbs. Breath is the essence of the limbs. So when breath departs from any limb, it dries up, for it is the essence of the limbs.

20. It is also Bṛhaspati. Speech is *bṛhatī* and it is its lord (*pati*), so it is also Bṛhaspati.

21. It is also Brahmaṇaspati. Speech is *brahman* and it is its lord, so it is also Brahmaṇaspati.

22. It is also the *sāman*. Speech is the *sāman*. It is she (*sā*) and he (*ama*).[42] It is equal (*sama*) to a gnat, equal to a fly, equal to an elephant, equal to the three worlds, equal to all this, so it is the *sāman*. Whoever knows the *sāman* in this way attains union with the *sāman*, shares a world with it.[43]

23. It is also the Udgītha. The breath (*prāṇa*) is *ud* (up), for all this is upheld by breath. Speech is song (*gīthā*). *Ud* and *gīthā* make Udgītha.

24. On this, Brahmadatta Caikitāneya, while drinking the King,[44] said, 'May the King make this man's[45] head split apart if Ayāsya Āṅgirasa chanted the Udgītha by anything else but this! He chanted it only by speech and by breath.'

25. Whoever knows the property (*sva*) of the *sāman* obtains property. Its property is tone (*svara*).[46] So one who is about to fulfil the office of a priest should wish for good tone in his speech. With speech possessing good tone he can fulfil the office of a priest. So at a sacrifice people desire to see a priest with good tone, and one who therefore has property. Whoever knows as such the wealth of the *sāman* obtains property.

26. Whoever knows the gold (*suvarṇa*) of the *sāman* obtains gold. Its gold is tone. Whoever knows as such the gold of the *sāman* obtains gold.

27. Whoever knows the support (*pratiṣṭhā*) of the *sāman* stands firm (*prati-sthā-*). Its support is speech. The breath sings when it is supported on speech. Some say, 'supported on food'.

28. Now there is the praying of the prayers of purification. The

Prastoṭr chants the *sāman*. While he chants, one[47] should mutter these prayers:

> 'From the unreal lead me to the real.
> From darkness lead me to light.
> From death lead me to immortality.'

When he says, 'From the unreal lead me to the real': death is the unreal, immortality is the real. He means, 'From death lead me to immortality, make me immortal.'

'From darkness lead me to light': death is darkness, immortality is light. He means, 'From death lead me to immortality, make me immortal.'

'From death lead me to immortality': there is nothing here that seems obscure.

In whatever other hymns of praise there are, one should sing into being good food for oneself. In them one may choose a boon, for whatever desire one may desire. The Udgāṭr who knows this sings into being, either for himself or for the patron of the sacrifice, whatever desire he desires.

So it[48] is called 'World-Conquering': and whoever knows the *sāman* as such has no prospect of ever being without a world.

CHAPTER 4

1. In the beginning this was self (*ātman*), in the likeness of a person (*puruṣa*). Looking round he saw[49] nothing but himself (*ātman*). First he said, 'I am!' So the name 'I'[50] came to be. Even now, when someone is addressed, he first says, 'It is I', and then speaks whatever other name he has. Since, before (*pūrva*) all this, he burnt up (*uṣ-*) all the evils from everything, he is *puruṣa*. Whoever knows this burns up anyone who wants to be before him.

2. He was afraid: so when alone one is afraid. Then he realized, 'There is nothing else but me, so why am I afraid?' Then his fear departed. For why should he be afraid? Fear arises from a second.

3. He had no pleasure either: so when alone one has no

pleasure. He desired a companion.[51] He became as large as a woman and a man embracing. He made that self split (*pat-*) into two: from that husband (*pati*) and wife (*patnī*) came to be. Therefore Yājñavalkya used to say, 'In this respect we two are each like a half portion.'[52] So this space is filled by a wife. He coupled with her, and from that human beings were born.

4. She realized, 'How can he couple with me when he begot me from himself? Ah, I must hide!' She became a cow, the other a bull, and so he coupled with her. From that, cattle were born. She became a mare, the other a stallion; she became a she-donkey, the other a he-donkey: and so he coupled with her. From that, solid-hoofed animals were born. The one became a nanny-goat, the other a billy-goat; the one became a ewe, the other a ram: and so he coupled with her. From that, goats and sheep were born. In that way he created every pair, right down to the ants.

5. He knew, 'I am creation, for I created all this.' So he became creation. Whoever knows this comes to be, in this, his creation.

6. Then he rubbed like *this* and with his hands created Agni from his mouth as from the womb (*yoni*). So both these are hairless on the inside, for the vagina (*yoni*)[53] is hairless on the inside.

When they say, 'Sacrifice to that one!' 'Sacrifice to that one!' – some god or other – that is his varied creation, and he himself is all the gods.

Then he created from seed whatever is moist, and that is Soma. All this is just food and the eater of food. Soma is food, and Agni is the eater of food.

This is the higher creation of Brahmā,[54] since he created gods who are better than he: and also because, being mortal,[55] he created immortals, it is his higher creation. Whoever knows this comes to be, in this, his higher creation.

7. Then this was undifferentiated. It became differentiated by name and form: 'He is so-and-so by name. He has such-and-such a form.' Therefore even now this is differentiated by name and form: 'He is so-and-so by name. He has such-and-such a form.'

He entered in here right to the tips of the nails, as a razor slips into a razor-case, or a scorpion[56] into a scorpion's nest. They do not see him, for he is incomplete. When he breathes, he is called 'breath', when he speaks, 'speech'; when he sees, 'eye'; when he hears, 'ear'; when he thinks, 'mind'. They are just the names of his works. Whoever worships one or other of them does not know, for with just one or other he is incomplete. One should worship him as 'self' (*ātman*), for in that all these become one.

The self is the trace of all this: by it one knows all this, just as one can find someone by a footprint. And so whoever knows this finds glory and renown.

8. The self is dearer than a son, dearer than wealth, dearer than any other thing, and deeper within. If someone were speaking of something other than the self as dear, and one were to say of him, 'He will weep for what is dear to him', one would very likely be right. One should worship only the self as dear: then what is dear to one is not perishable.

9. They say, 'Since human beings think that they will become all through knowledge of *brahman*, what did *brahman* know, that it became all?'

10. In the beginning, *brahman* was this. It knew only itself: 'I am *brahman*.' Through that it became all. Whichever of the gods woke up to it became that; whichever of the Ṛṣis, likewise; whichever of human beings, likewise. Seeing that, the Ṛṣi Vāmadeva began his hymn: 'I have become Manu and Sūrya too.'[57]

Even today, whoever knows 'I am *brahman*' becomes all this. Even the gods are not able to prevent it, for he becomes their self. Whoever worships another god, thinking, 'He is one and I am another', does not know. He is like a domestic animal (*paśu*) for the gods. As many animals are useful to a man, so each man is useful to the gods. When even one animal is taken away, one does not like it, let alone when many are. So the gods do not like it when human beings know this.

11. In the beginning, *brahman*[58] was all this, just one. Being just one, it was not complete. So it created over itself a better form, royalty (*kṣatra*), those who are royalty among the gods: Indra, Varuṇa, Soma, Rudra, Parjanya, Yama, Mṛtyu and Īśāna. Therefore there is nothing higher than royalty: therefore at a king's anointing the Brāhmaṇa sits below the Kṣatriya, and he confers this honour on royalty alone.

Brahman is the source (*yoni*) of royalty. So, even if a king attains the highest state, in the end he takes refuge in the priesthood (*brahman*) as his own source. So whoever harms the priesthood attacks his own source: he becomes more evil, like one who has harmed a superior.

12. He[59] still was not complete. So he created the people (*viś*), those kinds of gods who are named in groups: the Vasus, the Rudras, the Ādityas, the Viśvedevas and the Maruts.

13. He still was not complete. So he created the Śūdra class, Pūṣan. This earth is Pūṣan, for it nourishes (*puṣ-*) all this, whatever there is.

14. He still was not complete. So he created over himself a better form, *dharma*.[60] *Dharma* is the royalty of royalty, so there is nothing higher than *dharma*. Through *dharma* a weaker man overcomes a stronger one, as though through a king. *Dharma* is truth: so they say of one who speaks truth, 'He speaks *dharma*', or of one who speaks *dharma*, 'He speaks truth'. Both are the same.

15. So there were *brahman* (priesthood), *kṣatra* (royalty), *viś* (the people) and *śūdra* (the labourer). *Brahman*[61] came into being among the gods through Agni; as a Brāhmaṇa among human beings; as a Kṣatriya through the Kṣatriya; as a Vaiśya through the Vaiśya; and as a Śūdra through the Śūdra. So folk seek a world among the gods in Agni, and a world among human beings in the Brāhmaṇa, for *brahman* came into being through these two forms.

Whoever leaves this world without knowing his own world, it, unknown, is of no use to him, just like the Veda unrecited, or some other work undone. Even if someone does a great and meritorious work without knowing it, that work of his perishes in the end.

One should worship only the self as one's world. If someone worships only the self as his world, his work does not perish; for he creates from the self whatever he desires.

16. Oneself (*ātman*) is a world for all beings. When one makes offerings, when one sacrifices, one becomes a world for the gods. When one learns by heart,[62] one becomes a world for the Ṛṣis. When one makes offerings to the ancestors, when one

wishes for offspring, one becomes a world for the ancestors. When one gives shelter to human beings, when one gives them food, one becomes a world for human beings. When one finds grass and water for animals, one becomes a world for animals. When wild beasts and birds, and all creatures right down to the ants, find a living in one's house, one becomes a world for them. As one desires safety for one's own world, all beings desire safety for the one who knows this. This is well known and considered.

17. In the beginning, the self was all this, just one. He desired: 'If only I had a wife, so that I might have offspring! If only I had wealth, so that I might do work (*karman*)!' This is all that desire is: even if one wishes, one cannot find more than this. So even now a man alone desires: 'If only I had a wife, so that I might have offspring! If only I had wealth, so that I might do work!' So long as he does not get one or other of these, he thinks he is incomplete.

But his completeness is this:[63] his mind is himself (*ātman*); speech is his wife; breath is his offspring; the eye is his human wealth (*vitta*), because he finds (*vid-*) it with the eye; the ear is his divine wealth, because he hears it with the ear. His body (*ātman*) is his work, because he does work with the body.

The sacrifice is fivefold; the animal is fivefold; the person is fivefold;[64] all this, whatever there is, is fivefold. Whoever knows this obtains all this.

CHAPTER 5

1. When by intelligence and heat (*tapas*)
   The Father produced seven foods,
One of his foods was common to all,
   Two he allotted to the gods,
Three he made for himself,
   One he gave to the animals.
On it everything is supported,
   What breathes and what does not.

Why do they not perish
When they are eaten all the time?
Whoever knows this imperishability
Eats food with his face:
He joins the gods;
He lives on strength.

So say the verses.

2. 'When by intelligence and heat the Father produced seven foods', for the father produced them by intelligence and heat. 'One of his foods was common to all': this is common food (*anna*), that which is eaten (*ad-*). Whoever eats this food does not get rid of evil, for it is mixed.[65]

'Two he allotted to the gods', the *huta* and the *prahuta*:[66] therefore one offers the *huta* and the *prahuta* to the gods. But some say also that it means the new-moon and full-moon sacrifices. Therefore one should not offer a lesser sacrifice.[67]

'One he gave to the animals', that is, milk, for in the beginning both human beings and animals live only on milk. So in the beginning they give the newborn infant ghee to lick, or put it to the breast: and they call a newborn calf 'not grass-fed'. 'On it everything is supported, what breathes and what does not', for all this is supported on milk, what breathes and what does not. So when they say, 'Whoever makes offerings with milk for a year conquers re-death', one should not understand it like that. He conquers re-death on the very day he first makes the offering,[68] if he knows this: for he is offering all his good food to the gods.

'Why do they not perish when they are eaten all the time?' The person is imperishability, for he produces food again and again. 'Whoever knows this imperishability': the person is imperishability, for he produces food by repeated meditations, his works. If he did not do this, it would perish. 'Eats food with his face': 'face' means 'mouth' – he eats food with his mouth. 'He joins the gods; he lives on strength': this is praise.

3. 'Three he made for himself': mind, speech, breath – he made them for himself. Someone may say, 'I had my mind elsewhere: I did not see. I had my mind elsewhere: I did not

hear.' For one sees with the mind, hears with the mind. Desire, imagination,[69] doubt, faith, lack of faith, constancy, inconstancy, shame, meditation, fear – all this is mind. So even when one is touched on the back one knows it through mind.

Whatever sound there is is speech. It may rest on an object, or it may not.[70]

The breath (*praṇa*), the lower breath (*apāna*), the diffused breath (*vyāna*), the upbreath (*udāna*) and the central breath (*samāna*) are all 'breath' (*ana*). All this is breath (*prāṇa*). The self (*ātman*) consists of this: it consists of speech, mind and breath.

4. The three worlds are these. Speech is this world, mind is the world of middle-air, and breath is the world of the sky.

5. The three Vedas are these. Speech is the Ṛgveda, mind is the Yajurveda, and breath is the Sāmaveda.

6. Gods, ancestors and human beings are these. Speech is the gods, mind is the ancestors, and breath is human beings.

7. Father, mother and offspring are these. Mind is the father, speech is the mother, and breath is the offspring.

8. The known, the to-be-known and the unknown are these. Whatever is known is a form of speech, for speech is known. Speech, by becoming the known, protects one.

9. Whatever is to be known is a form of mind, for mind is to be known. Mind, by becoming the to-be-known, protects one.

10. Whatever is unknown is a form of breath, for breath is unknown. Breath, by becoming the unknown, protects one.

11. Earth is the body of speech, fire its form of light. As far as speech goes, earth goes, and fire goes.

12. Sky is the body of mind, the sun its form of light. As far as mind goes, the sky goes, and the sun goes.

They two[71] came together in sexual union. From it, breath was born. He is Indra: he is the unrivalled. A second is a rival. Whoever knows this has no rival.

13. The waters are the body of breath, the moon its form of light. As far as breath goes, the waters go, and the moon goes.[72] All these are the same, all infinite. Whoever worships them as finite wins a finite world: but whoever worships them as infinite wins an infinite world.

14. The year is Prajāpati, of sixteen portions.[73] His nights are fifteen portions. His fixed portion is the sixteenth. Only in his nights does he wax and wane. On the new-moon night[74] he enters into all this that has breath, and in the morning is born from it again. So on that night one should not cut off the breath of anything that has breath, even a lizard, out of reverence for that deity.

15. Any person who knows this is himself the Prajāpati of sixteen portions who is the year. His wealth is the fifteen portions: his self (*ātman*) is the sixteenth portion. Only in his wealth does he wax and wane. The self is the hub of a wheel, wealth the rim. So even if he loses everything, but himself lives, they say, 'He has got off with the loss of a wheel-rim.'[75]

16. There are three worlds: the world of human beings, the world of the ancestors, and the world of the gods. The world of human beings can be won only through a son,[76] not by any other work. The world of the ancestors can be won by work; the world of the gods by knowledge. The world of the gods is the best of the worlds: and so folk praise knowledge.

17. Now the handing on.

When a Brāhmaṇa[77] thinks he is about to depart, he says to his son, 'You are *brahman*. You are sacrifice (*yajña*). You are the world.'

The son replies, 'I am *brahman*. I am sacrifice. I am the world.'

'*Brahman*' means the unity of everything that has been learned. 'Sacrifice' means the unity of all the sacrifices that there are. 'World' means the unity of all the worlds that there are. So much is all this. The father thinks, 'Since he is all this, may he help me from this world!' So a son who has been taught they call 'world-winning': that is why they teach him.

When one who knows this departs from this world, with the breaths (*prāṇa*) he enters his son. And if he has done anything amiss, the son frees him from it all. That is why he is called *putra* (son).[78]

Through his son he is established in this world. Then the divine, immortal breaths enter him.

18. From earth and fire the divine speech enters him. The divine speech is that by which whatever one says comes to be.

19. From sky and the sun the divine mind enters him. The divine mind is that by which one is joyful and never grieves.

20. From the waters and the moon the divine breath enters him. The divine breath is that which, whether moving or not moving, does not suffer, does not come to harm.

The one who knows this becomes the self of all beings. What that deity is he is. Just as all beings favour that deity, all beings favour the one who knows this. Whatever sorrow creatures have remains at home with them. Only good goes to him. No evil goes to the gods.

21. Now an investigation of vows.[79]

Prajāpati created the activities (*karman*). Once created, they vied with each other. Speech resolved, 'I will speak'; the eye, 'I will see'; the ear, 'I will hear'; and so with the other activities, each according to its activity. Death, becoming tiredness, took possession of them and held them. Holding them, he stopped them. So speech grows tired, the eye grows tired, the ear grows tired. But he was not able to hold the one who is the middle breath.[80]

They resolved to know it. 'It is the best of us,' they said, 'for, whether moving or not moving, it does not suffer, does not come to harm. Come, let us all become a form of it!'

They all became a form of it, and therefore they are called 'breaths' after it.[81] Any family in which there is someone who knows this comes to be called after him.

And whoever vies with the one who knows this gradually dries up: he dries up and in the end he dies.

So much regarding oneself.

22. Now regarding deities:

Fire resolved, 'I will burn'; the sun, 'I will give heat'; the moon, 'I will shine'; and so with the other deities, each according to its deity. Like the middle breath among the breaths is Vāyu among the deities. Other deities set, but not Vāyu. Vāyu is the deity who never goes down in the west.

23. There is a verse:

> That from which the sun rises
> And into which it sets . . .

It rises from breath and sets into breath.

> . . . The gods made it *dharma*.
> It is, today, and tomorrow, too.

What they resolved to do then they still do today. So one should undertake just one vow: one should breathe out and breathe in,[82] thinking, 'May not evil, may not death, hold me!' And when one undertakes it, one should desire to bring it to completion. Then one wins union with that deity, shares a world with him.[83]

CHAPTER 6

1. All this is a triplicity: name, form and action. What is called 'speech' is the Uktha of all the names that there are, for all names arise (*ut-thā-*) from it. It is their *sāman*, for it is equal (*sama*) to all names. It is their *brahman*, for it bears (*bhṛ-*) all names.
2. What is called 'the eye' is the Uktha of all the forms that there are, for all forms arise from it. It is their *sāman*, for it is equal to all forms. It is their *brahman*, for it bears all forms.
3. What is called 'the body' (*ātman*) is the Uktha of all the actions that there are, for all actions arise from it. It is their *sāman*, for it is equal to all actions. It is their *brahman*, for it bears all actions.

This triplicity is one, the self: the self, being one, is a triplicity. This is immortality, hidden by truth. Breath is immortality: name and form are truth. The breath is hidden by them.

BOOK II

CHAPTER I

1. OṂ. Bālāki the Proud, the Gārgya, was a learned man. He said to Ajātaśatru of Kāśī, 'I must teach you about *brahman*.'[1]

Ajātaśatru said, 'We will give you a thousand cows[2] for such a teaching. People will run crying, A Janaka, a Janaka!'[3]

2. Gārgya said, 'I worship as *brahman* the person (*puruṣa*) who is in the sun.'

Ajātaśatru said, 'Do not talk to me about him. I worship him as the topmost, the head and king of all beings. Whoever worships him as such becomes the topmost, the head and king of all beings.'

3. Gārgya said, 'I worship as *brahman* the person who is in the moon.'

Ajātaśatru said, 'Do not talk to me about him. I worship him as the great King Soma, dressed in white. Whoever worships him as such, Soma[4] is pressed and re-pressed for him every day, and his food never fails.'

4. Gārgya said, 'I worship as *brahman* the person who is in the lightning.'

Ajātaśatru said, 'Do not talk to me about him. I worship him as the bright (*tejasvin*). Whoever worships him as such becomes bright, and his offspring become bright.'

5. Gārgya said, 'I worship as *brahman* the person who is in space.'

Ajātaśatru said, 'Do not talk to me about him. I worship him as the full, the unmoving. Whoever worships him as such is filled with offspring and animals, and his offspring do not vanish from this world.'

6. Gārgya said, 'I worship as *brahman* the person who is in the wind.'

Ajātaśatru said, 'Do not talk to me about him. I worship him as Indra Vaikuṇṭha, the unvanquished army.[5] Whoever worships him as such becomes victorious, unvanquished, a conqueror of foes.'

7. Gārgya said, 'I worship as *brahman* the person who is in fire.'

Ajātaśatru said, 'Do not talk to me about him. I worship him as the courageous.[6] Whoever worships him as such becomes courageous, and his offspring become courageous.'

8. Gārgya said, 'I worship as *brahman* the person who is in the waters.'

Ajātaśatru said, 'Do not talk to me about him. I worship him as likeness. Whoever worships him as such, what is like him[7] comes to him, not what is unlike, and what is like him is begotten from him.'

9. Gārgya said, 'I worship as *brahman* the person who is in the mirror.'

Ajātaśatru said, 'Do not talk to me about him. I worship him as the shining. Whoever worships him as such becomes shining, and his offspring become shining, and he outshines those he meets.'

10. Gārgya said, 'I worship as *brahman* the sound which follows one as one moves.'

Ajātaśatru said, 'Do not talk to me about him. I worship him as life (*asu*). Whoever worships him as such attains his full span in this world, and his breath does not leave him before his time.'

11. Gārgya said, 'I worship as *brahman* the person who is in the directions.'

Ajātaśatru said, 'Do not talk to me about him. I worship him as the companion who never leaves us. Whoever worships him as such has a companion,[8] and is never deprived of company.'

12. Gārgya said, 'I worship as *brahman* the person made of shadow.'

Ajātaśatru said, 'Do not talk to me about him. I worship him as death. Whoever worships him as such attains his full span in this world, and death does not come to him before his time.'

13. Gārgya said, 'I worship as *brahman* the person who is in the body (*ātman*).'

Ajātaśatru said, 'Do not talk to me about him. I worship him as embodied.[9] Whoever worships him as such comes to be embodied, and his offspring come to be embodied.'

Then Gārgya fell silent.

14. Ajātaśatru said, 'Is that all?'

'That is all.'

'It is not known by this.'

Gārgya said, 'I must come to you as your student.'[10]

15. Ajātaśatru said, 'It is against the natural order[11] that a Brāhmaṇa should come to a Kṣatriya to be taught about *brahman*. However, I shall make it known to you.'

He took him by the hand and stood up. They came to a man who was asleep, and the king called him by these names: 'O great King Soma, dressed in white!' He did not get up. But by patting him with his hand, he woke him, and he got up.

16. Ajātaśatru said, 'When he fell asleep, where was the person made of knowledge, and where has he come back from?'

Gārgya did not know.

17. Ajātaśatru said, 'When he fell asleep, the person made of knowledge, by knowledge taking his knowledge with him, lay down in the space within the heart. When the person takes these to himself, he is said to be asleep: the breath is taken, the eye is taken, the ear is taken, the mind is taken.

18. 'When in dreams he moves about, these are his worlds. He seems to become a great king, or a great Brāhmaṇa, or to move high and low. Just as a great king, taking his subjects with him, moves about at will in his own country, so he, taking his senses (*prāṇa*) with him, moves about at will in his own body.

19. 'When he is deeply asleep, when he knows nothing at all, he moves along the seventy-two thousand channels called *hitā*[12] from the heart to the citadel of the heart.[13] Having moved quietly along them he lies down in the citadel. He lies there as a young

prince or a great king or a great Brāhmaṇa would lie on reaching the utmost ecstasy of bliss.

20. 'As a spider moves up along its thread, as small sparks fly up from a fire, so all breaths, all worlds, all gods, all beings come up out of the self. Its inner meaning (*upaniṣad*) is "the truth of the truth": the breaths are the truth, and it is the truth of them.'

CHAPTER 2

1. Whoever knows the baby with his home, his covering, his post and his rope keeps away seven adversaries who hate him. The baby is the middle breath; this[14] is his home; this[15] is his covering; the breath is his post; food is his rope.[16]

2. Seven unfailing ones wait on him. By the red streaks which are in the eye, Rudra is brought into contact with him; by the waters which are in the eye, Parjanya; by the pupil, Āditya; by the iris, Agni; by the white, Indra; by the lower lid, Pṛthivī is brought into contact with him; by the upper lid, Dyaus. The food of the one who knows this does not fail.

3. There is a verse about it:

> There is a bowl with its rim below and its base above.
> In it is placed the glory which possesses all forms.
> On its edge sit the Seven Ṛṣis,
> And Vāc, as the eighth, communing with *brahman*.[17]

The 'bowl with its rim below and its base above' is the head, for it is a bowl with its rim below and its base above. 'In it is placed the glory which possesses all forms': the breaths are the glory which possesses all forms. 'On its edge sit the Seven Ṛṣis': the breaths are the Ṛṣis; here he speaks of the breaths. He says, 'Vāc, as the eighth, communing with *brahman*', because speech, as the eighth, communes with *brahman*.

4. These two[18] are Gotama and Bharadvāja: this one is Gotama, this one Bharadvāja. These two[19] are Viśvāmitra and Jamadagni: this one is Viśvāmitra, this one Jamadagni. These

two[20] are Vasiṣṭha and Kaśyapa: this one is Vasiṣṭha, this one Kaśyapa. Speech[21] is Atri, for by speech food is eaten. 'To eat' (*ad-*) is the same as Atri. The one who knows this becomes the eater of everything: everything becomes his food.

CHAPTER 3

1. There are two forms of *brahman*: the shaped and the unshaped, the mortal and the immortal, the still and the moving, the present and the beyond.[22]

2. The shaped is what is other than the wind and the middle-air: this is the mortal, the still, the present. The essence of the shaped, the mortal, the still, the present is the one who gives heat,[23] for this is the essence of the present.

3. The unshaped is the wind and the middle-air: this is the immortal, the moving, the beyond. The essence of the unshaped, the immortal, the moving, the beyond is the person (*puruṣa*) in the circle,[24] for this is the essence of the beyond. This in respect of deities.

4. In respect of oneself: the shaped is what is other than the breath and the space which is within the self – this is the mortal, the still, the present. The essence of the shaped, the mortal, the still, the present is the eye, for this is the essence of the present.

5. The unshaped is the breath and the space which is within the self: this is the immortal, the moving, the beyond. The essence of the unshaped, the immortal, the moving, the beyond is the person who is in the right eye, for this is the essence of the beyond.

6. The form of this person is like a saffron garment, a white woollen cloth, a rain-mite,[25] a flame of fire, a white lotus,[26] a sudden flash of lightning. Hence the symbolic statement,[27] 'Not this, not this', for there is nothing – 'not this' – higher than this. Its name is 'the truth of the truth': the breaths are the truth, and it is the truth of them.

CHAPTER 4

1. Yājñavalkya said, 'Maitreyī, I am going forth from this state.[28] I must make a settlement on you and Kātyāyanī.'

2. Maitreyī said, 'Blessed one, if I had this whole earth, filled with riches, would I become immortal by it?'

'No,' said Yājñavalkya. 'Your life would be as the life of the wealthy, but there is no hope of immortality through riches.'

3. Maitreyī said, 'What use to me is something by which I cannot become immortal? Blessed one, teach me what you know.'

4. Yājñavalkya said, 'Ah, you have always been dear to me, and now you speak what is dear too. Come, sit down, I will teach you: but, as I explain, meditate upon it.'

5. He said, 'It is not for the love of a husband that a husband is dear: it is for the love of the self (*ātman*) that a husband is dear. It is not for the love of a wife that a wife is dear: it is for the love of the self that a wife is dear. It is not for the love of children that children are dear: it is for the love of the self that children are dear. It is not for the love of riches that riches are dear: it is for the love of the self that riches are dear. It is not for the love of priesthood (*brahman*) that priesthood is dear: it is for the love of the self that priesthood is dear. It is not for the love of royalty (*kṣatra*) that royalty is dear: it is for the love of the self that royalty is dear. It is not for the love of the worlds that the worlds are dear: it is for the love of the self that the worlds are dear. It is not for the love of the gods that the gods are dear: it is for the love of the self that the gods are dear. It is not for the love of beings that beings are dear: it is for the love of the self that beings are dear. It is not for the love of the all that the all is dear: it is for the love of the self that the all is dear. It is the self that must be seen, heard, thought of and meditated upon: by seeing, hearing, thinking of and understanding the self, Maitreyī, all this is known.

6. 'Whoever understands priesthood as other than the self, priesthood has given him over.[29] Whoever understands royalty as other than the self, royalty has given him over. Whoever

understands the worlds as other than the self, the worlds have given him over. Whoever understands the gods as other than the self, the gods have given him over. Whoever understands beings as other than the self, beings have given him over. Whoever understands the all as other than the self, the all has given him over. This priesthood, this royalty, these worlds, these gods, these beings, this all are what this self is.

7. 'As, when a drum is beaten, one cannot seize the sounds as something outside it, but by seizing the drum or the drummer one has seized the sound;

8. 'As, when a conch is blown, one cannot seize the sounds as something outside it, but by seizing the conch or the conch-blower one has seized the sound;

9. 'As, when a lute[30] is played, one cannot seize the sounds as something outside it, but by seizing the lute or the lute-player one has seized the sound;

10. 'As smoke billows out in all directions from a fire that has been laid with damp fuel, just so is everything breathed out from this great being: the Ṛgveda, the Yajurveda, the Sāmaveda, the hymns of the Atharvans and Aṅgirases, history, legend, science, the Upaniṣads, verses, *sūtras*, explanatory passages and expositions, all these are breathed out from it.

11. 'As the ocean is the one meeting-place of all waters, so the skin is the one meeting-place of all touches, the nostrils are the one meeting-place of all smells, the tongue is the one meeting-place of all tastes, the eye is the one meeting-place of all shapes, the ear is the one meeting-place of all sounds, the mind is the one meeting-place of all decisions, the heart is the one meeting-place of all knowledges, the hands are the one meeting-place of all works, the loins are the one meeting-place of all pleasures, the anus is the one meeting-place of all excretions, the feet are the one meeting-place of all roads, and the voice is the one meeting-place of all the Vedas.

12. 'As a lump of rock-salt thrown into water would dissolve in the water, and there would be none, as it were, to take out again, yet wherever one took water it would be salty, so this great being, endless, boundless, consists entirely of knowledge. Having arisen from these elements, it vanishes along with them,

for after it has departed there is no consciousness:[31] that is what I say,' said Yājñavalkya.

13. Maitreyī said, 'Blessed one, you have confused me by saying that after it has departed there is no consciousness.'

He said, 'I do not speak to confuse you: this is enough for knowledge.

14. 'For where there is duality, one smells another, one sees another, one hears another, one speaks to another, one thinks of another, one knows another. But where everything in one has become self, how can one smell – and whom? How can one see – and whom? How can one hear – and whom? How can one speak – and to whom? How can one think – and of whom? How can one know – and whom? How can one know that by which one knows all this? How can one know the knower?'

CHAPTER 5

1. The earth is the honey[32] of all beings, and all beings are the honey of the earth. The radiant, immortal person[33] who is in the earth, or – in respect of oneself[34] – the radiant, immortal person of the body, is the self (*ātman*). This is the immortal, *brahman*, the all.

2. The waters are the honey of all beings, and all beings are the honey of the waters. The radiant, immortal person who is in the waters, or – in respect of oneself – the radiant, immortal person of the seed, is the self. This is the immortal, *brahman*, the all.

3. Fire is the honey of all beings, and all beings are the honey of fire. The radiant, immortal person who is in fire, or – in respect of oneself – the radiant, immortal person who is made of speech, is the self. This is the immortal, *brahman*, the all.

4. Air is the honey of all beings, and all beings are the honey of air. The radiant, immortal person who is in air, or – in respect of oneself – the radiant, immortal person who is made of breath, is the self. This is the immortal, *brahman*, the all.

5. The sun is the honey of all beings, and all beings are the

honey of the sun. The radiant, immortal person who is in the sun, or – in respect of oneself – the radiant, immortal person of the eye, is the self. This is the immortal, *brahman*, the all.

6. The directions are the honey of all beings, and all beings are the honey of the directions. The radiant, immortal person who is in the directions, or – in respect of oneself – the radiant, immortal person of the ear, of the echo, is the self. This is the immortal, *brahman*, the all.

7. The moon is the honey of all beings, and all beings are the honey of the moon. The radiant, immortal person who is in the moon, or – in respect of oneself – the radiant, immortal person of the mind, is the self. This is the immortal, *brahman*, the all.

8. The lightning is the honey of all beings, and all beings are the honey of the lightning. The radiant, immortal person who is in the lightning, or – in respect of oneself – the radiant, immortal person of brightness, is the self. This is the immortal, *brahman*, the all.

9. The thundercloud is the honey of all beings, and all beings are the honey of the thundercloud. The radiant, immortal person who is in the thundercloud, or – in respect of oneself – the radiant, immortal person of sound, of tone, is the self. This is the immortal, *brahman*, the all.

10. Space is the honey of all beings, and all beings are the honey of space. The radiant, immortal person who is in space, or – in respect of oneself – the radiant, immortal person of the space within the heart, is the self. This is the immortal, *brahman*, the all.

11. *Dharma* is the honey of all beings, and all beings are the honey of *dharma*. The radiant, immortal person who is in *dharma*, or – in respect of oneself – the radiant, immortal person of *dharma*, is the self. This is the immortal, *brahman*, the all.

12. Truth is the honey of all beings, and all beings are the honey of truth. The radiant, immortal person who is in truth, or – in respect of oneself – the radiant, immortal person of truth, is the self. This is the immortal, *brahman*, the all.

13. Humankind is the honey of all beings, and all beings are the honey of humankind. The radiant, immortal person who is in humankind, or – in respect of oneself – the radiant, immortal

person of humanity, is the self. This is the immortal, *brahman*, the all.

14. The self is the honey of all beings, and all beings are the honey of the self. The radiant, immortal person who is in the self, or – in respect of oneself – the radiant, immortal person who is the self, is the self. This is the immortal, *brahman*, the all.

15. The self is the overlord of all beings, the king of all beings. As all the spokes are held together in the hub and rim of a chariot-wheel, so all beings, all gods, all worlds, all breaths, all selves are held together in the self.

16. Dadhyac Ātharvaṇa spoke of this honey to the Aśvins. Seeing it, the Ṛṣi said:

'Twin heroes, I proclaim, as thunder proclaims the rain,
The strange, terrible thing you did for greed,
When Dadhyac Ātharvaṇa, through the head of a horse,
Taught you about the honey.'[35]

17. Dadhyac Ātharvaṇa spoke of this honey to the Aśvins. Seeing it, the Ṛṣi said:

'Aśvins, you placed a horse's head
On Dadhyac Ātharvaṇa.
Keeping truth, he told you, wonderful ones,
Of Tvaṣṭṛ's honey – to be your secret.'[36]

18. Dadhyac Ātharvaṇa spoke of this honey to the Aśvins. Seeing it, the Ṛṣi said:

'He made citadels (*pur*) with two feet;
He made citadels with four feet;
First (*puras*) becoming a bird,
The person entered the citadels.'

This person (*puruṣa*) is lying-in-the-citadel (*puri-śaya*) in all citadels. There is nothing that is not covered by him, nothing that is not surrounded by him.

19. Dadhyac Ātharvaṇa spoke of this honey to the Aśvins. Seeing it, the Ṛṣi said:

'He shifted shape to match every shape,
To manifest his shape.
Indra, by his magical powers,[37] goes in many shapes.
His bay horses, hundreds and ten, are yoked.'

He is the bay horses; he is ten, many thousands, and infinities. He is *brahman*, without a before, without an after, without an inside, without an outside. This self, all-embracing, is *brahman*.

That is the teaching.

CHAPTER 6

1. Now the lineage of the teaching. Pautimāṣya received it[38] from Gaupavana, Gaupavana from Pautimāṣya,[39] Pautimāṣya from Gaupavana, Gaupavana from Kauśika, Kauśika from Kauṇḍinya, Kauṇḍinya from Śāṇḍilya, Śāṇḍilya from Kauśika and Gautama, Gautama

2. from Āgniveśya, Āgniveśya from Śāṇḍilya and Ānabhimlāta, Ānabhimlāta from Ānabhimlāta, Ānabhimlāta from Ānabhimlāta, Ānabhimlāta from Gautama, Gautama from Saitava and Prācīnayogya, Saitava and Prācīnayogya from Pārāśarya, Pārāśarya from Bhāradvāja, Bhāradvāja from Bhāradvāja and Gautama, Gautama from Bhāradvāja, Bhāradvāja from Pārāśarya, Pārāśarya from Baijavāpāyana, Baijavāpāyana from Kauśikāyani, Kauśikāyani

3. from Ghṛtakauśika, Ghṛtakauśika from Pārāśaryāyaṇa, Pārāśaryāyaṇa from Pārāśarya, Pārāśarya from Jātūkarṇya, Jātūkarṇya from Āsurāyaṇa and Yāska, Āsurāyaṇa from Traivaṇi, Traivaṇi from Aupajandhani, Aupajandhani from Āsuri, Āsuri from Bhāradvāja, Bhāradvāja from Ātreya, Ātreya from Māṇṭi, Māṇṭi from Gautama, Gautama from Gautama, Gautama from Vātsya, Vātsya from Śāṇḍilya, Śāṇḍilya from Kaiśorya Kāpya, Kaiśorya Kāpya from Kumārahārita, Kumārahārita from Gālava, Gālava from Vidarbhī-Kauṇḍinya, Vidarbhī-Kauṇḍinya from Vatsanapāt Bābhrava, Vatsanapāt Bābhrava from Pathin Saubhara, Pathin Saubhara from Ayāsya Āṅgirasa,

Ayāsya Āṅgirasa from Ābhūti Tvāṣṭra, Ābhūti Tvāṣṭra from Viśvarūpa Tvāṣṭra, Viśvarūpa Tvāṣṭra from the Aśvins, the Aśvins from Dadhyac Ātharvaṇa, Dadhyac Ātharvaṇa from the Divine Atharvan, the Divine Atharvan from Mṛtyu Prādhvaṃsana,[40] Mṛtyu Prādhvaṃsana from Pradhvaṃsana,[41] Pradhvaṃsana from Ekarṣi,[42] Ekarṣi from Vipracitti,[43] Vipracitti from Vyaṣṭi,[44] Vyaṣṭi from Sanāru, Sanāru from Sanātana, Sanātana from Sanaga,[45] Sanaga from Parameṣṭhin,[46] Parameṣṭhin from *brahman*. *Brahman* is self-born: homage to *brahman*.

BOOK III

CHAPTER I

1. OṂ. Janaka of Videha offered a sacrifice, with munificent gifts for the priests.[1] There the Brāhmaṇas of the Kurus and Pañcālas were gathered together. It occurred to Janaka of Videha to wonder which of the Brāhmaṇas was most learned. So he penned off a thousand cows, and ten gold pieces were attached to the horns of each.

2. He said to them, 'Blessed Brāhmaṇas, whoever is the truest Brāhmaṇa[2] among you, let him drive away these cows.' The Brāhmaṇas dared not.

But Yājñavalkya called[3] to his own student, 'Sāmaśravas, good lad; drive out these cows!' And he drove them out.

The Brāhmaṇas were angry, thinking, 'How can be claim to be the truest Brāhmaṇa among us?'

Aśvala was Hotṛ[4] to Janaka of Videha. He asked him, 'Yājñavalkya, are you the truest Brāhmaṇa among us?'

He said, 'We pay respect to the truest Brāhmaṇa: we just want the cows.'

Then Aśvala the Hotṛ undertook to question him.

3. 'Yājñavalkya,' he said, 'since all this is seized by death, all this is overpowered by death, by what means does the patron of the sacrifice become free from the grip of death?'

'By the Hotṛ priest, by fire, by speech. Speech is the Hotṛ of the sacrifice; what speech is, fire is; that is the Hotṛ. That is freedom; that is utter freedom.'

4. 'Yājñavalkya,' he said, 'since all this is seized by days and nights, all this is overpowered by days and nights, by what

means does the patron of the sacrifice become free from the grip of days and nights?'

'By the Adhvaryu priest, by the eye, by the sun. The eye is the Adhvaryu of the sacrifice; what the eye is, the sun is; that is the Adhvaryu. That is freedom; that is utter freedom.'

5. 'Yājñavalkya,' he said, 'since all this is seized by bright fortnights and dark fornights,[5] all this is overpowered by bright fortnights and dark fortnights, by what means does the patron of the sacrifice become free from the grip of bright fortnights and dark fortnights?'

'By the Udgātṛ priest, by wind, by breath. Breath is the Udgātṛ of the sacrifice; what breath is, wind is; that is the Udgātṛ. That is freedom; that is utter freedom.'

6. 'Yājñavalkya,' he said, 'since the middle-air is, as it were, without a support, by what way does the patron of the sacrifice climb to the heaven-world?'

'By the Brahmā priest, by mind, by the moon. Mind is the Brahmā of the sacrifice; what mind is, the moon is; that is the Brahmā. That is freedom; that is utter freedom.'

That was the passage on utter freedoms: now come the attainments.

7. 'Yājñavalkya,' he said, 'how many kinds of verses will the Hotṛ employ in the sacrifice today?'

'Three.'

'What are the three?'

'The verse of invitation, the verse accompanying the sacrifice, and the verse of blessing as the third.'

'What does one win by them?'

'Whatever has breath.'

8. 'Yājñavalkya,' he said, 'how many kinds of offerings will the Adhvaryu offer in the sacrifice today?'

'Three.'

'What are the three?'

'Those which blaze up when offered, those which overflow when offered, and those which sink down when offered.'

'What does one win by them?'

'By those which blaze up when offered, one wins the world of the gods, for the world of the gods, as it were, shines; by those which overflow when offered, one wins the world of the ancestors, for the world of the ancestors is, as it were, beyond; and by those which sink down when offered, one wins the human world, for the human world is, as it were, below.'

9. 'Yājñavalkya,' he said, 'with how many gods will the Brahmā on the southern side protect the sacrifice today?'

'One.'

'What is the one?'

'The mind.'

Indeed, the mind is infinite; the Viśvedevas are infinite; by knowing it one wins an infinite world.

10. 'Yājñavalkya,' he said, 'how many praises will the Udgātṛ chant in the sacrifice today?'

'Three.'

'What are the three?'

'The chant of invitation, the chant accompanying the sacrifice, and the chant of blessing as the third.'

'What are they in relation to oneself?'

'The chant of invitation is the breath, the chant accompanying the sacrifice the lower breath, and the chant of blessing the diffused breath.'

'What does one win by them?'

'By the chant of invitation, one wins the world of the earth; by the chant accompanying the sacrifice, the world of the middle-air; and by the chant of blessing, the world of the sky.'

Then Aśvala the Hotṛ fell silent.

CHAPTER 2

1. Then Jāratkārava Ārtabhāga questioned him. 'Yājñavalkya,' he said, 'how many graspers are there; how many over-graspers?'[6]

'Eight graspers; eight over-graspers.'

'What are they, the eight graspers, the eight over-graspers?'

2. 'The out-breath (*prāṇa*) is the grasper. It is grasped by the

in-breath (*apāṇa*) as its over-grasper, for by the in-breath one smells smells.

3. 'Speech is the grasper. It is grasped by name as its over-grasper, for by speech one utters names.

4. 'The tongue is the grasper. It is grasped by taste as its over-grasper, for by the tongue one discerns tastes.

5. 'The eye is the grasper. It is grasped by form as its over-grasper, for by the eye one sees forms.

6. 'The ear is the grasper. It is grasped by sound as its over-grasper, for by the ear one hears sounds.

7. 'The mind is the grasper. It is grasped by desire as its over-grasper, for by the mind one desires desires.

8. 'The hands are the grasper. It is grasped by action as its over-grasper, for by the hands one performs actions.

9. 'The skin is the grasper. It is grasped by touch as its over-grasper, for by the skin one feels touches. These are the eight graspers and the eight over-graspers.'

10. 'Yājñavalkya,' he said, 'since all this is the food of death, who is the deity of whom death is the food?'

'Fire is death: he is the food of the waters. He who knows this[7] conquers re-death.'

11. 'Yājñavalkya,' he said, 'when a person dies, do his breaths go up out of him or not?'

'No,' said Yājñavalkya, 'they are gathered together just here, and he swells up, becomes inflated. The dead man lies inflated.'

12. 'Yājñavalkya,' he said, 'when a person dies, what does not leave him?'

'Name.'

Name is infinite; the Viśvedevas are infinite; by it one wins an infinite world.

13. 'Yājñavalkya,' he said, 'when a person dies, and his voice goes into fire, his breath into air, his eye into the sun, his mind into the moon, his ear into the directions, his body into the earth, his self into space, his body-hair into plants, and his head-hair into trees, and his blood and seed are placed in the waters, where is the person then?'

'Ārtabhāga, good man, take my hand. Just we two will know of this: it is not for us to discuss in public.'

They went away and discussed it. What they spoke of was action (*karman*); what they praised was action. One becomes good by good action, evil by evil action.

Then Jāratkārava Ārtabhāga fell silent.

CHAPTER 3

1. Then Bhujyu Lāhyāyani questioned him. 'Yājñavalkya,' he said, 'we were wandering as religious students among the Madras, and we came to the house of Patañcala Kāpya. He had a daughter who was possessed by a *gandharva*. We asked the *gandharva*, "Who are you?" He said, "Sudhanvan Āṅgirasa." When we were questioning him about the ends of the worlds, we said to him, "Where have the Pārikṣitas gone?"

'I ask you, Yājñavalkya, where have the Pārikṣitas gone?'

2. He said, 'He told you, "They have gone where those who perform the horse sacrifice go." You said, "Where do those who perform the horse sacrifice go?" He said, "This world is thirty-two days' journey of the god's[8] chariot wide, and the earth surrounds it completely, twice as wide. The ocean surrounds the earth completely, twice as wide. The space between[9] is just as wide as the edge of a razor or the wing of a fly. Indra, becoming an eagle, handed them over to Vāyu. Vāyu placed them in himself and took them where those who perform the horse sacrifice have gone." In some such words the *gandharva* praised Vāyu. So Vāyu is individuality, Vāyu is totality. Whoever knows this conquers re-death.'

Then Bhujyu Lāhyāyani fell silent.

CHAPTER 4

1. Then Uṣasta Cākrāyaṇa questioned him. 'Yājñavalkya,' he said, 'reveal to me the *brahman* that is manifest, not hidden, that is the self within everything.'

'It is *your* self that is within everything.'

'What is within everything, Yājñavalkya?'

'The one that breathes with your breath is your self that is within everything. The one that breathes down with your lower breath is your self that is within everything. The one that breathes apart with your diffused breath is your self that is within everything. The one that breathes up with your up-breath is your self that is within everything. This is your self that is within everything.'

2. Uṣasta Cākrāyaṇa said, 'You have explained it exactly as one might say, "This is a cow, this is a horse." Reveal to me the *brahman* that is manifest, not hidden, that is the self within everything.'

'It is *your* self that is within everything.'

'What is within everything, Yājñavalkya?'

'You cannot see the seer of seeing; you cannot hear the hearer of hearing; you cannot think of the thinker of thinking; you cannot know the knower of knowing. This is your self that is within everything. What is other than this is suffering.'

Then Uṣasta Cākrāyaṇa fell silent.

CHAPTER 5

1. Then Kahola Kauṣītakeya questioned him. 'Yājñavalkya,' he said, 'reveal to me the *brahman* that is manifest, not hidden, that is the self within everything.'

'It is *your* self that is within everything.'

'What is within everything, Yājñavalkya?'

'What goes beyond hunger and thirst, grief, delusion, old age and death. Seeing the self as such, leaving behind desires for sons, desires for wealth, and desires for worlds, Brāhmaṇas live on alms. For desire for sons is desire for wealth, and desire for wealth is desire for worlds: both are merely desires. Therefore a Brāhmaṇa should turn away from learning, and desire to live like a child. When he has turned away from both childhood and learning, he is a "silent one" (*muni*). When he has turned away from both non-silence and silence, he is a Brāhmaṇa.'

'By what would he become a Brāhmaṇa?'

'By whatever it might be, that is how he is. What is other than this is suffering.'

Then Kahola Kauṣītakeya fell silent.

CHAPTER 6

1. Then Gārgī Vācaknavī questioned him. 'Yājñavalkya,' she said, 'since all this is woven on the waters, as warp and weft, on what are the waters woven, as warp and weft?'[10]

'On air, Gārgī.'

'On what is air woven, as warp and weft?'

'On the worlds of middle-air, Gārgī.'

'On what are the worlds of middle-air woven, as warp and weft?'

'On the worlds of the *gandharvas*, Gārgī.'

'On what are the worlds of the *gandharvas* woven, as warp and weft?'

'On the worlds of the sun, Gārgī.'

'On what are the worlds of the sun woven, as warp and weft?'

'On the worlds of the moon, Gārgī.'

'On what are the worlds of the moon woven, as warp and weft?'

'On the worlds of the constellations, Gārgī.'

'On what are the worlds of the constellations woven, as warp and weft?'

'On the worlds of the gods, Gārgī.'

'On what are the worlds of the gods woven, as warp and weft?'

'On the worlds of Indra, Gārgī.'

'On what are the worlds of Indra woven, as warp and weft?'

'On the worlds of Prajāpati, Gārgī.'

'On what are the worlds of Prajāpati woven, as warp and weft?'

'On the worlds of Brahmā, Gārgī.'

'On what are the worlds of Brahmā woven, as warp and weft?'

He said, 'Gārgī, do not ask too many questions, lest your head should split apart. You are asking too many questions about a deity concerning whom too many questions should not be asked. Gārgī, do not ask too many questions.'

Then Gārgī Vācaknavī fell silent.

CHAPTER 7

1. Then Uddālaka Āruṇi questioned him. 'Yājñavalkya,' he said, 'we were living among the Madras, in the house of Patañcala Kāpya, studying the sacrifice. He had a wife who was possessed by a *gandharva*. We asked the *gandharva*, "Who are you?" He said, "Kabandha Ātharvaṇa." He asked Patañcala Kāpya and us students of the sacrifice, "Do you know, Kāpya, the thread on which this world, the other world, and all beings are strung together?" Patañcala Kāpya said, "I do not know, blessed one." He asked Patañcala Kāpya and us students of the sacrifice, "Do you know, Kāpya, the inner controller (*antaryāmin*) who controls this world, the other world, and all beings from within?" Patañcala Kāpya said, "I do not know, blessed one." He told Patañcala Kāpya and us students of the sacrifice, "Kāpya, whoever knows the thread and the inner controller (as it is called) is a knower of *brahman*, a knower of the worlds, a knower of the gods, a knower of the Vedas, a knower of beings, a knower of the self, a knower of everything."

'He told us, and I know it. If you, Yājñavalkya, take those *brahman*-cows without knowing the thread, without knowing the inner controller, your head will split apart.'

He said, 'Gautama, I know the thread and the inner controller.'

'Anyone could say, "I know, I know." Tell us what you know.'

2. He said, 'Air, Gautama, is the thread. On air as the thread, this world, the other world and all beings are strung together. That is why, Gautama, they say of a person who has died, "His limbs are loosed", for they are strung together on air as the thread.'

'So it is, Yājñavalkya. Tell us of the inner controller.'

3. 'That which, resting in the earth, is other than the earth; which the earth does not know; of which the earth is the body; which controls the earth from within: this is your self, the inner controller, the immortal.

4. 'That which, resting in the waters, is other than the waters; which the waters do not know; of which the waters are the body; which controls the waters from within: this is your self, the inner controller, the immortal.

5. 'That which, resting in fire, is other than fire; which fire does not know; of which fire is the body; which controls fire from within: this is your self, the inner controller, the immortal.

6. 'That which, resting in middle-air, is other than middle-air; which middle-air does not know; of which middle-air is the body; which controls middle-air from within: this is your self, the inner controller, the immortal.

7. 'That which, resting in air, is other than air; which air does not know; of which air is the body; which controls air from within: this is your self, the inner controller, the immortal.

8. 'That which, resting in the sky, is other than the sky; which the sky does not know; of which the sky is the body; which controls the sky from within: this is your self, the inner controller, the immortal.

9. 'That which, resting in the sun, is other than the sun; which the sun does not know; of which the sun is the body; which

controls the sun from within: this is your self, the inner controller, the immortal.

10. 'That which, resting in the directions, is other than the directions; which the directions do not know; of which the directions are the body; which controls the directions from within: this is your self, the inner controller, the immortal.

11. 'That which, resting in the moon and stars, is other than the moon and stars; which the moon and stars do not know; of which the moon and stars are the body; which controls the moon and stars from within: this is your self, the inner controller, the immortal.

12. 'That which, resting in space, is other than space; which space does not know; of which space is the body; which controls space from within: this is your self, the inner controller, the immortal.

13. 'That which, resting in darkness, is other than darkness; which darkness does not know; of which darkness is the body; which controls darkness from within: this is your self, the inner controller, the immortal.

14. 'That which, resting in light, is other than light; which light does not know; of which light is the body; which controls light from within: this is your self, the inner controller, the immortal.

'So much regarding deities: now regarding beings:

15. 'That which, resting in all beings, is other than all beings; which all beings do not know; of which all beings are the body; which controls all beings from within: this is your self, the inner controller, the immortal.

'So much regarding beings: now regarding oneself:

16. 'That which, resting in the breath, is other than the breath; which the breath does not know; of which the breath is the body; which controls the breath from within: this is your self, the inner controller, the immortal.

17. 'That which, resting in speech, is other than speech; which speech does not know; of which speech is the body; which controls speech from within: this is your self, the inner controller, the immortal.

18. 'That which, resting in the eye, is other than the eye; which the eye does not know; of which the eye is the body; which

controls the eye from within: this is your self, the inner controller, the immortal.

19. 'That which, resting in the ear, is other than the ear; which the ear does not know; of which the ear is the body; which controls the ear from within: this is your self, the inner controller, the immortal.

20. 'That which, resting in the mind, is other than the mind; which the mind does not know; of which the mind is the body; which controls the mind from within: this is your self, the inner controller, the immortal.

21. 'That which, resting in the skin, is other than the skin; which the skin does not know; of which the skin is the body; which controls the skin from within: this is your self, the inner controller, the immortal.

22. 'That which, resting in knowledge (*vijñāna*), is other than knowledge; which knowledge does not know; of which knowledge is the body; which controls knowledge from within: this is your self, the inner controller, the immortal.

23. 'That which, resting in the seed, is other than the seed; which the seed does not know; of which the seed is the body; which controls the seed from within: this is your self, the inner controller, the immortal.

'It is the unseen seer, the unheard hearer, the unthought-of thinker, the unknown knower. Other than this there is no seer; other than this there is no hearer; other than this there is no thinker; other than this there is no knower. This is your self, the inner controller, the immortal: what is other than this is suffering.'

Then Uddālaka Āruṇi fell silent.

CHAPTER 8

1. Then Vācaknavī said, 'Blessed Brāhmaṇas, listen, I am going to ask him two questions. If he answers them for me, not one of you will defeat him in debate about *brahman*.'

'Ask, Gārgī.'

2. She said, 'Yājñavalkya, as a warrior son of Kāśī or Videha might string his unstrung bow, take in his hand two enemy-piercing arrows, and advance against you, so I have advanced against you, with two questions. Answer them for me.'

'Ask, Gārgī.'

3. She said, 'Yājñavalkya, that which is above the sky; that which is below the earth; that which is between sky and earth; that which they call past, present and future: on what is that woven, as warp and weft?'

4. He said, 'Gārgī, that which is above the sky; that which is below the earth; that which is between sky and earth; that which they call past, present and future: that is woven on space, as warp and weft.'

5. She said, 'Homage to you, Yājñavalkya, since you have solved this for me. Brace yourself for the other one.'

'Ask, Gārgī.'

6. She said, 'Yājñavalkya, that which is above the sky; that which is below the earth; that which is between sky and earth; that which they call past, present and future: on what is that woven, as warp and weft?'

7. He said, 'Gārgī, that which is above the sky; that which is below the earth; that which is between sky and earth; that which they call past, present and future: that is woven on space, as warp and weft.'

'On what is space woven, as warp and weft?'

8. He said, 'That, Gārgī, is what Brāhmaṇas call the imperishable, not thick, not thin, not short, not long, without blood, without oiliness, without shadow, without darkness, without air, without space, without clinging, without taste, without smell, without eye, without ear, without speech, without mind, without light, without breath, without face, without measure, without inside, without outside. It eats nothing, and nobody eats it.

9. 'Under the rule of the imperishable, Gārgī, the sun and moon abide in their separate places. Under the rule of the imperishable, Gārgī, sky and earth abide in their separate places. Under the rule of the imperishable, Gārgī, moments, hours,[11] days and nights, half-months, months, seasons, and the year

abide in their separate places. Under the rule of the imperishable, Gārgī, some rivers flow east from the snowy mountains and others flow west, each in its own direction. Under the rule of the imperishable, Gārgī, human beings praise those who give, gods are attracted to the patron of the sacrifice, and ancestors to the offering-spoon.

10. 'Gārgī, if someone in this world makes offerings, performs sacrifices, and practises asceticism for many thousands of years without knowing the imperishable, that work of his comes to an end. Gārgī, if someone passes on from this world without knowing the imperishable, he is pitiable. But, Gārgī, if someone passes on from this world knowing the imperishable, he is a Brāhmaṇa.

11. 'The imperishable, Gārgī, is the unseen seer, the unheard hearer, the unthought-of thinker, the unknown knower. Other than this there is no seer; other than this there is no hearer; other than this there is no thinker; other than this there is no knower. On the imperishable, Gārgī, space is woven as warp and weft.'

12. She said, 'Blessed Brāhmaṇas, you should think it a fine thing if you can escape from him by paying him homage: not one of you will defeat him in debate about *brahman*.'

Then Vācaknavī fell silent.

CHAPTER 9

1. Then Vidagdha Śākalya questioned him: 'How many gods are there, Yājñavalkya?'

He answered with this invocation: 'As many as it says in the invocation of the hymn to the Viśvedevas, "three hundred and three and three thousand and three".'

'OṂ,' he said. 'How many gods *are* there, Yājñavalkya?'

'Thirty-three.'

'OṂ,' he said. 'How many gods *are* there, Yājñavalkya?'

'Six.'

'OṂ,' he said. 'How many gods *are* there, Yājñavalkya?'

'Three.'

'OṂ,' he said. 'How many gods *are* there, Yājñavalkya?'

'Two.'

'OṂ,' he said. 'How many gods *are* there, Yājñavalkya?'

'One and a half.'

'OṂ,' he said. 'How many gods *are* there, Yājñavalkya?'

'One.'

'OṂ,' he said. 'Who are the three hundred and three and three thousand and three?'

2. He said, 'They are their powers: there are just thirty-three gods.'

'Who are the thirty-three?'

'The eight Vasus, the eleven Rudras and the twelve Ādityas make thirty-one: Indra and Prajāpati make thirty-three.'

3. 'Who are the Vasus?'

'Fire, the earth, the wind, the middle-air, the sun, the sky, the moon and the constellations. All this is placed in them, so they are called the Vasus.'[12]

4. 'Who are the Rudras?'

'The ten breaths in a person, with the self as eleventh. When they leave this mortal body they make folk weep (*rud-*). Since they make folk weep, they are called the Rudras.'

5. 'Who are the Ādityas?'

'The twelve months of the year are the Ādityas. They go (*yanti*), taking (*ā-dā-*) all this with them. Since they go, taking all this with them, they are called Ādityas.'

6. 'Who is Indra? Who is Prajāpati?'

'Indra is the thunderer. Prajāpati is the sacrifice.'

'What is the thunderer?'

'The thunderbolt.'

'What is the sacrifice?'

'The animals (*paśu*).'

7. 'Who are the six?'

'Fire, the earth, the wind, the middle-air, the sun and the sky are the six: the six are all this.'

8. 'Who are the three gods?'

'They are the three worlds, for all the gods are in them.'

'Who are the two gods?'

'Food and breath.'

'Who is the one and a half?'

'He who purifies.[13]

9. 'Some say about this, "He who purifies seems to be just one, so how is he one and a half?" But since all this has grown (*adhyārdhnot*) in him, he is one and a half (*adhyardha*).'

'Who is the one god?'

'Breath: that is *brahman*. They call it "the beyond".'

10. 'If someone were to know the person (*puruṣa*) whose dwelling is the earth, whose world is fire, and whose light is the mind, the ultimate refuge of every self, he would truly be a knower, Yājñavalkya.'

'I know the person you speak of, the ultimate refuge of every self. He is the person of the body. Tell me, Śākalya, who is his deity?'

'Immortality,' he said.

11. 'If someone were to know the person whose dwelling is desire, whose world is the heart, and whose light is the mind, the ultimate refuge of every self, he would truly be a knower, Yājñavalkya.'

'I know the person you speak of, the ultimate refuge of every self. He is the person made of desire. Tell me, Śākalya, who is his deity?'

'Women,' he said.

12. 'If someone were to know the person whose dwelling is forms, whose world is the eye, and whose light is the mind, the ultimate refuge of every self, he would truly be a knower, Yājñavalkya.'

'I know the person you speak of, the ultimate refuge of every self. He is the person in the sun. Tell me, Śākalya, who is his deity?'

'Truth,' he said.

13. 'If someone were to know the person whose dwelling is space, whose world is the ear, and whose light is the mind, the ultimate refuge of every self, he would truly be a knower, Yājñavalkya.'

'I know the person you speak of, the ultimate refuge of every self. He is the person of hearing and of the echo. Tell me, Śākalya, who is his deity?'

'The directions,' he said.

14. 'If someone were to know the person whose dwelling is darkness, whose world is the heart, and whose light is the mind, the ultimate refuge of every self, he would truly be a knower, Yājñavalkya.'

'I know the person you speak of, the ultimate refuge of every self. He is the person made of shadow. Tell me, Śākalya, who is his deity?'

'Death,' he said.

15. 'If someone were to know the person whose dwelling is forms, whose world is the eye, and whose light is the mind, the ultimate refuge of every self, he would truly be a knower, Yājñavalkya.'

'I know the person you speak of, the ultimate refuge of every self. He is the person in the mirror. Tell me, Śākalya, who is his deity?'

'Life,' he said.

16. 'If someone were to know the person whose dwelling is the waters, whose world is the heart, and whose light is the mind, the ultimate refuge of every self, he would truly be a knower, Yājñavalkya.'

'I know the person you speak of, the ultimate refuge of every self. He is the person in the waters. Tell me, Śākalya, who is his deity?'

'Varuṇa,' he said.

17. 'If someone were to know the person whose dwelling is seed, whose world is the heart, and whose light is the mind, the ultimate refuge of every self, he would truly be a knower, Yājñavalkya.'

'I know the person you speak of, the ultimate refuge of every self. He is the person made of one's children. Tell me, Śākalya, who is his deity?'

'Prajāpati,' he said.

18. 'Śākalya,' cried Yājñavalkya, 'have the Brāhmaṇas made you their tool, to pull coals from the fire for them?'[14]

19. 'Yājñavalkya,' said Śākalya, 'what is the *brahman* that you know, that you have out-debated the Brāhmaṇas of the Kurus and Pañcālas?'

'I know the directions with the gods and their supports.'

'If you know the directions with their gods and their supports,

20. 'What deity have you in the eastern direction?'

'I have Āditya as deity there.'

'On what is Āditya supported?'

'On the eye.'

'On what is the eye supported?'

'On forms: for one sees forms with the eye.'

'On what are forms supported?'

'On the heart,' he said, 'for one knows forms with the heart, so forms are supported on the heart.'

'So it is, Yājñavalkya.

21. 'What deity have you in the southern direction?'

'I have Yama as deity there.'

'On what is Yama supported?'

'On the sacrifice.'

'On what is the sacrifice supported?'

'On the gift to the priests (*dakṣiṇā*).'

'On what is the gift supported?'

'On faith (*śraddhā*), for when one has faith one gives the gift, so the gift is supported on faith.'

'On what is faith supported?'

'On the heart,' he said, 'for one knows faith with the heart, so faith is supported on the heart.'

'So it is, Yājñavalkya.

22. 'What deity have you in the western direction?'

'I have Varuṇa as deity there.'

'On what is Varuṇa supported?'

'On the waters.'

'On what are the waters supported?'

'On seed.'

'On what is seed supported?'

'On the heart,' he said. 'That is why, when a baby is born who looks like his father, they say, "He seems to have crept out of his father's heart;[15] he seems to have been fashioned out of his heart."'

'So it is, Yājñavalkya.

23. 'What deity have you in the northern direction?'

'I have Soma as deity there.'

'On what is Soma supported?'

'On initiation (*dīkṣā*).'

'On what is initiation supported?'

'On truth. That is why, when someone is initiated, they tell him, "Speak truth", for initiation is supported on truth.'

'On what is truth supported?'

'On the heart,' he said, 'for one knows truth with the heart, so truth is supported on the heart.'

'So it is, Yājñavalkya.

24. 'What deity have you in the centre?'[16]

'I have Agni as deity there.'

'On what is Agni supported?'

'On speech.'

'On what is speech supported?'

'On the heart.'

'On what is the heart supported?'

25. 'You fool,' said Yājñavalkya, 'for thinking it might be anywhere else but in us! If it were anywhere else but in us, dogs might eat it or birds tear it apart.'

26. 'On what are both you and your self supported?'

'On the breath (*prāṇa*).'

'On what is the breath supported?'

'On the lower breath (*apāna*).'

'On what is the lower breath supported?'

'On the diffused breath (*vyāna*).'

'On what is the diffused breath supported?'

'On the up-breath (*udāna*).'

'On what is the up-breath supported?'

'On the central breath (*samāna*). The self is "not this, not this". Unseizable, it is not seized; indestructible, it is not destroyed; without clinging, it is not clung to; unbound, it does not suffer, does not come to harm.

'There are eight dwellings, eight worlds, eight gods, eight persons. I ask you about the person of the secret teaching,[17] who takes apart and puts together those persons and goes beyond them. If you do not explain him to me, your head will split apart.'

Śākalya did not know about him, and his head split apart. Indeed, robbers stole his bones, thinking they were something else.

27. Then Yājñavalkya said, 'Blessed Brāhmaṇas, let whoever of you wishes to, question me; or let all of you question me; or I will question whoever of you wishes me to; or I will question all of you.' But the Brāhmaṇas dared not.

28. He questioned them with these verses:

'Just like a tree, a lord of the forest,
  Truly, is a man (*puruṣa*).
The hairs of his body are the leaves,
  His skin the outer bark.

'Blood flows out from his skin
  Like sap from the skin of the tree:
When he is wounded, it flows out of him
  Like sap from a tree that has been struck.

'His flesh is the outer wood;
  The fibres, so strong, his sinews;
His bones the hard wood within;
  His marrow made in the likeness of the pith.

'Since a tree, cut down, grows up again,
  In a newer form, from its root,
From what root does a mortal man,
  Cut down by death, grow up again?

'Do not say, "From the seed",
  For that comes from the living.
A tree, too, springing up from seed,
  Is reborn directly, without having died.[18]

'When a tree has been pulled up
  With its root, it cannot grow again.
From what root does a mortal man,
  Cut down by death, grow up again?

'Though born, he is not born again,
For who could beget him again?
Brahman – knowledge, joy, and grace –
Is the final refuge of the giver,

'The one who abides in it, the one who
knows it.'

BOOK IV

CHAPTER I

1. OṂ. Janaka of Videha sat to give audience.[1] Yājñavalkya approached him. Janaka said to him, 'Yājñavalkya, why have you come? Are you wanting cattle, or subtle arguments?'

'Both, your majesty,' he said.

2. 'Let us hear what someone has told you.'

'Jitvan Śailini told me that speech is *brahman*.'

'Śailini says what anyone would say who had a mother, a father and a teacher to teach him,[2] when he says that speech is *brahman*: for what would anyone have who could not speak? But did he tell you its dwelling and support?'

'He did not.'

'Then that is a one-footed *brahman*,[3] your majesty.'

'So *you* tell us, Yājñavalkya.'

'Speech itself is its dwelling, space is its support. One should worship it as knowledge (*prajñā*).'

'What is the nature of this knowledge?'

'Speech itself, your majesty,' he said. 'By speech, your majesty, a friend is known (*pra-jñā-*). The Ṛgveda, the Yajurveda, the Sāmaveda, the hymns of the Atharvans and Aṅgirases, history, legend, science, the Upaniṣads, verses, *sūtras*, explanatory passages, expositions, sacrifice, offering, food, drink, this world, the other world, and all beings are known by speech, your majesty: speech, your majesty, is indeed the supreme *brahman*. The one who knows this, and worships it as such, speech does not desert him; all beings flock to him; and becoming a god he goes to the gods.'

'I give you a thousand cows, with a bull like an elephant,'[4] said Janaka of Videha.

Yājñavalkya said, 'My father used to say that one should not accept gifts without having taught.

3. 'Let us hear what someone has told you.'

'Udaṅka Śaulbāyana told me that the breath is *brahman*.'

'Śaulbāyana says what anyone would say who had a mother, a father and a teacher to teach him, when he says that the breath is *brahman*: for what would anyone have who could not breathe? But did he tell you its dwelling and support?'

'He did not.'

'Then that is a one-footed *brahman*, your majesty.'

'So *you* tell us, Yājñavalkya.'

'The breath itself is its dwelling, space is its support. One should worship it as the dear.'

'What is its dearness?'

'The breath itself, your majesty,' he said. 'For love of the breath, your majesty, one offers sacrifice for someone for whom one should not offer sacrifice, one accepts gifts from someone from whom one should not accept gifts. For love of the breath, your majesty, in whatever direction one goes, there exists the fear of being killed.[5] The breath, your majesty, is indeed the supreme *brahman*. The one who knows this, and worships it as such, the breath does not desert him; all beings flock to him; and becoming a god he goes to the gods.'

'I give you a thousand cows, with a bull like an elephant,' said Janaka of Videha.

Yājñavalkya said, 'My father used to say that one should not accept gifts without having taught.

4. 'Let us hear what someone has told you.'

'Bārku Vārṣṇa told me that the eye is *brahman*.'

'Vārṣṇa says what anyone would say who had a mother, a father and a teacher to teach him, when he says that the eye is *brahman*: for what would anyone have who could not see? But did he tell you its dwelling and support?'

'He did not.'

'Then that is a one-footed *brahman*, your majesty.'

'So *you* tell us, Yājñavalkya.'

'The eye itself is its dwelling, space is its support. One should worship it as truth.'

'What is its trueness?'

'The eye itself, your majesty,' he said. 'For when someone sees with the eye, your majesty, and they ask him, "Have you seen it?", and he says, "I have seen it", that is the truth. The eye, your majesty, is indeed the supreme *brahman*. The one who knows this, and worships it as such, the eye does not desert him; all beings flock to him; and becoming a god he goes to the gods.'

'I give you a thousand cows, with a bull like an elephant,' said Janaka of Videha.

Yājñavalkya said, 'My father used to say that one should not accept gifts without having taught.

5. 'Let us hear what someone has told you.'

'Gardhabhīvipīta Bhāradvāja told me that the ear is *brahman*.'

'Bhāradvāja says what anyone would say who had a mother, a father and a teacher to teach him, when he says that the ear is *brahman*: for what would anyone have who could not hear? But did he tell you its dwelling and support?'

'He did not.'

'Then that is a one-footed *brahman*, your majesty.'

'So *you* tell us, Yājñavalkya.'

'The ear itself is its dwelling, space is its support. One should worship it as the endless.'

'What is its endlessness?'

'The ear itself, your majesty,' he said. 'That is why, your majesty, whatever direction one goes in, one never reaches the end of it. The directions are endless, and the directions, your majesty, are the ear. The ear, your majesty, is indeed the supreme *brahman*. The one who knows this, and worships it as such, the ear does not desert him; all beings flock to him; and becoming a god he goes to the gods.'

'I give you a thousand cows, with a bull like an elephant,' said Janaka of Videha.

Yājñavalkya said, 'My father used to say that one should not accept gifts without having taught.

6. 'Let us hear what someone has told you.'

'Satyakāma Jābāla told me that the mind is *brahman*.'

'Jābāla says what anyone would say who had a mother, a father and a teacher to teach him, when he says that speech is *brahman*: for what would anyone have who had no mind? But did he tell you its dwelling and support?'

'He did not.'

'Then that is a one-footed *brahman*, your majesty.'

'So *you* tell us, Yājñavalkya.'

'The mind itself is its dwelling, space is its support. One should worship it as joy.'

'What is its joyfulness?'

'The mind itself, your majesty,' he said. 'Through the mind, your majesty, one is attracted to a woman, and of her a son is born who looks like oneself. That is joy. The mind, your majesty, is indeed the supreme *brahman*. The one who knows this, and worships it as such, the mind does not desert him; all beings flock to him; and becoming a god he goes to the gods.'

'I give you a thousand cows, with a bull like an elephant,' said Janaka of Videha.

Yājñavalkya said, 'My father used to say that one should not accept gifts without having taught.

7. 'Let us hear what someone has told you.'

'Vidagdha Śākalya told me that the heart is *brahman*.'

'Śākalya says what anyone would say who had a mother, a father and a teacher to teach him, when he says that the heart is *brahman*: for what would anyone have who had no heart? But did he tell you its dwelling and support?'

'He did not.'

'Then that is a one-footed *brahman*, your majesty.'

'So *you* tell us, Yājñavalkya.'

'The heart itself is its dwelling, space is its support. One should worship it as steadfastness.'

'What is the nature of this steadfastness?'

'The heart itself, your majesty,' he said. 'For the heart, your majesty, is the dwelling of all beings; the heart, your majesty, is the support of all beings. The heart, your majesty, is indeed the supreme *brahman*. The one who knows this, and worships it as such, the heart does not desert him; all beings flock to him; and becoming a god he goes to the gods.'

'I give you a thousand cows, with a bull like an elephant,' said Janaka of Videha.

Yājñavalkya said, 'My father used to say that one should not accept gifts without having taught.'

CHAPTER 2

1. Janaka of Videha came quietly down from his throne and said, 'Homage to you, Yājñavalkya: teach me!'

He said, 'Your majesty, as one about to go on a great voyage would get hold of a chariot or a ship, so you have a self well prepared by these inner teachings (*upaniṣad*). You are a leader of men, wealthy: you have studied the Vedas and heard the inner teachings. When you are released from here, where will you go?'

'Blessed one, I do not know where I shall go.'

'Then I will tell you where you will go.'

'Tell me, blessed one.'

2. 'The person in the right eye is called Indha.[6] Though he is Indha, folk call him Indra, mysteriously, because the gods seem to love the mysterious, and hate the obvious.

3. 'The form of a person in the left eye is his wife, Virāj.[7] The place where they meet in praise together is the space within the heart, and their food is the lump of blood within the heart. The path they travel together is the channel that goes upward from the heart. Its channels called *hitā*, like a hair divided into a thousand parts, are established within the heart: through them flows whatever flows. So that self is an eater of choicer food than the bodily self.

4. 'The eastern direction is its eastward breaths; the southern direction its southward breaths; the western direction its westward breaths; the northern direction its northward breaths; the direction above its upward breaths; the direction below its downward breaths; all directions all its breaths. The self is "not

this, not this". Unseizable, it is not seized; indestructible, it is not destroyed; without clinging, it is not clung to; unbound, it does not suffer, does not come to harm. You have attained fearlessness, Janaka,' said Yājñavalkya.

Janaka of Videha said, 'May fearlessness come to you, Yājñavalkya, since you, blessed one, make us see fearlessness. Homage to you! Here are the Videhas, and here am I, at your service.'[8]

CHAPTER 3

1. Yājñavalkya went to Janaka of Videha, intending not to teach. But once, when Janaka of Videha and Yājñavalkya spoke together about the Agnihotra, Yājñavalkya had granted him a boon.[9] The king chose to ask any question he desired, and Yājñavalkya granted it to him. So the first question he asked him was:

2. 'Yājñavalkya, what light has a man (*puruṣa*)?'

'He has the sun as his light. With the sun as his light he sits, goes about, does his work, and returns.'

'So it is, Yājñavalkya.

3. 'When the sun has set, Yājñavalkya, what light has a man?'

'He has the moon as his light. With the moon as his light he sits, goes about, does his work, and returns.'

'So it is, Yājñavalkya.

4. 'When the sun has set, Yājñavalkya, and the moon has set, what light has a man?'

'Fire is his light. With fire as his light he sits, goes about, does his work, and returns.'

'So it is, Yājñavalkya.

5. 'When the sun has set, Yājñavalkya, and the moon has set, and fire has gone out, what light has a man?'

'Speech is his light. With speech as his light he sits, goes about, does his work, and returns. That is why, your majesty, even when one cannot see one's own hand, when speech is uttered, one goes towards it.'

'So it is, Yājñavalkya.

6. 'When the sun has set, Yājñavalkya, and the moon has set, and fire has gone out, and speech has fallen silent, what light has a man?'

'The self (*ātman*) is his light. With the self as his light he sits, goes about, does his work, and returns.'

7. 'What is the self?'

'The person (*puruṣa*) among the breaths who consists of knowledge, the inner light in the heart. Remaining the same, he travels the two worlds, seems to think, seems to move about. Falling asleep, he goes beyond this world, the forms of death.

8. 'When the person is born and gets a body he is joined with evils. Leaving it, when he dies, he leaves evils behind.

9. 'The person has two states: this one and the state of the other world. The third, intermediate, state is that of dreaming sleep.[10] When he rests in the intermediate state, he sees both states: this one and the state of the other world. When he has gone by whatever way it is that one gains the state of the other world, he sees both evils and joys. When he falls asleep, he takes with him the material of this all-containing world, himself breaks it up, himself re-makes it. He sleeps by his own radiance, his own light. Here the person becomes lit by his own light.

10. 'There are no chariots, nor chariot-horses, nor roads there, but he creates[11] chariots, chariot-horses and roads. There are no pleasures, nor enjoyments, nor delights there, but he creates pleasures, enjoyments and delights. There are no ponds, nor lotus-pools, nor rivers there, but he creates ponds, lotus-pools and rivers. For he is a maker.

11. 'There are these verses about it:

Overcoming with sleep the bodily part,
Unsleeping he looks down upon the sleeping.[12]
Taking his light, he returns to his place,
The golden person, the goose who flies alone.[13]

12. Guarding with the breath his nest below,
Immortal he roves outside his nest.
Immortal he goes wherever he desires,
The golden person, the goose who flies alone.

13. In the dream state, going high and low,
A god, he creates many forms.
Enjoying himself with women, laughing,
Or even seeing dreadful sights.

14. They see his pleasure,
But him nobody sees.

'That is why they say, "You should not wake him suddenly", for a cure is hard to find for someone if it[14] does not get back to him. Some say that this is just the same as his waking state, since he sees when asleep the same objects that he sees when awake: but they are wrong,[15] for in this state he is lit by his own light.'

'Blessed one, I give you a thousand cows: speak on, for my liberation.'[16]

15. 'When he has taken pleasure in deep sleep,[17] when he has travelled about in it and seen both good and evil, he runs back again, back where he began, to dream. Whatever he sees there, he is not followed by it, for the person is without attachment.'

'So it is, Yājñavalkya. Blessed one, I give you a thousand cows: speak on, for my liberation.'

16. 'When he has taken pleasure in dream, when he has travelled about in it and seen both good and evil, he runs back again, back where he began, to the waking state. Whatever he sees there, he is not followed by it, for the person is without attachment.'

'So it is, Yājñavalkya. Blessed one, I give you a thousand cows: speak on, for my liberation.'

17. 'When he has taken pleasure in the waking state, when he has travelled about in it and seen both good and evil, he runs back again, back where he began, to the dream state.

18. 'As a great fish travels along both banks, the nearer and the farther, even so the person travels along both states, the dream state and the waking state.

19. 'As a hawk or eagle, tired after flying around in the sky, folds its wings and is carried to its roosting-place, even so the

person runs to the state where he desires no desire and dreams no dream.

20. 'There are in him channels called *hitā*, in minuteness like a hair divided into a thousand parts, filled with white, blue, yellow, green and red. When[18] it seems that folk kill him or overcome him, or an elephant tramples him, or he falls down a hole, he is imagining through ignorance whatever danger he has seen while waking: but when, like a god or a king, he thinks, "I am this! I am all!", that is his highest world.

21. 'That is the form of him which is beyond craving, freed from evil, without fear. As a man closely embraced by a beloved wife knows nothing outside, nothing inside, so the person, closely embraced by the self of wisdom, knows nothing outside, nothing inside. That is the form of him in which his desires are fulfilled, with the self as his desire, free from desire, beyond sorrow.

22. 'Here a father is not a father, a mother is not a mother, the worlds are not the worlds, the Vedas are not the Vedas. Here a thief is not a thief, a murderer not a murderer,[19] a Caṇḍāla not a Caṇḍāla, a Paulkasa not a Paulkasa, a monk (*śramaṇa*) not a monk, an ascetic not an ascetic. There is no following by good, no following by evil, for then he has passed beyond all sorrows of the heart.

23. 'Though then he does not see, yet seeing he does not see. There is no cutting off of the seeing of the seer, because it is imperishable.[20] But there is no second, no other, separate from himself, that he might see.

24. 'Though then he does not smell, yet smelling he does not smell. There is no cutting off of the smelling of the smeller, because it is imperishable. But there is no second, no other, separate from himself, that he might smell.

25. 'Though then he does not taste, yet tasting he does not taste. There is no cutting off of the tasting of the taster, because it is imperishable. But there is no second, no other, separate from himself, that he might taste.

26. 'Though then he does not speak, yet speaking he does not speak. There is no cutting off of the speaking of the speaker,

because it is imperishable. But there is no second, no other, separate from himself, to which he might speak.

27. 'Though then he does not hear, yet hearing he does not hear. There is no cutting off of the hearing of the hearer, because it is imperishable. But there is no second, no other, separate from himself, that he might hear.

28. 'Though then he does not think, yet thinking he does not think. There is no cutting off of the thinking of the thinker, because it is imperishable. But there is no second, no other, separate from himself, of which he might think.

29. 'Though then he does not touch, yet touching he does not touch. There is no cutting off of the touching of the toucher, because it is imperishable. But there is no second, no other, separate from himself, that he might touch.

30. 'Though then he does not know, yet knowing he does not know. There is no cutting off of the knowing of the knower, because it is imperishable. But there is no second, no other, separate from himself, that he might know.

31. 'When there seems to be another, one can see another, smell another, taste another, speak to another, hear another, think of another, touch another, know another.

32. 'He becomes one, water, a seer without duality. This is the world of Brahmā,[21] your majesty.' Yājñavalkya taught him:

'This is his highest way;
This is his highest fulfilment;
This is his highest world;
This is his highest joy.

'All other beings live on a tiny portion of this joy.

33. 'If someone among human beings is healthy, prosperous, a lord over others, fully endowed with all human enjoyments, that is the highest joy of human beings. A hundred joys of human beings make one joy of the ancestors who have won their world. A hundred joys of the ancestors who have won their world make one joy in the world of the *gandharvas*. A hundred joys in the world of the *gandharvas* make one joy of the gods by action, who have achieved their godhead by their actions. A hundred joys of the gods by action make one joy of

the gods by birth, and of one who is learned, straightforward, and not afflicted by desire. A hundred joys of the gods by birth make one joy in the world of Prajāpati, and of one who is learned, straightforward, and not afflicted by desire. A hundred joys in the world of Prajāpati make one joy in the world of Brahmā, and of one who is learned, straightforward, and not afflicted by desire. This is the highest joy: this is the world of Brahmā, your majesty,' said Yājñavalkya.

'Blessed one, I give you a thousand cows: speak on, for my liberation.'

Then Yājñavalkya was afraid, thinking, 'This king is clever: he has driven me out of all my territories!'

34. 'When he has taken pleasure in dream, when he has travelled about in it and seen both good and evil, he runs back again, back where he began, to the waking state.

35. 'As a heavily loaded cart goes along creaking, so this bodily self, ridden by the self which is wisdom, goes along creaking when it is breathing its last.

36. 'When it grows weak – whether it becomes weak through old age or through illness – then, just as a mango or fig or pipal-berry[22] is loosed from its stalk, the person is released from these limbs and runs back again, back where he began, to the breath.

37. 'Just as, when a king approaches, officers, magistrates, charioteers and village headmen await him with food, drink and lodgings, crying, 'He approaches! He is coming!', in the same way all beings await this *brahman*, crying, 'It approaches! It is coming!'

38. 'Just as, when a king wishes to go back, officers, magistrates, charioteers and village headmen accompany him, so at the end all the breaths come together with the self when it is breathing its last.

CHAPTER 4

1. 'When this self (*ātman*) becomes weak and, as it were, confused, the breaths come together with it. Taking with it particles of light (*tejas*), it goes down into the heart. When the person of the eye turns away from it, it ceases to know forms.

2. 'They say,[23] "He is becoming one: he does not see." They say, "He is becoming one: he does not smell." They say, "He is becoming one: he does not taste." They say, "He is becoming one: he does not speak." They say, "He is becoming one: he does not hear." They say, "He is becoming one: he does not think." They say, "He is becoming one: he does not touch." They say, "He is becoming one: he does not know." The top of his heart lights up, and by its light the self departs, either through the eye, or through the head, or through other parts of the body. As he goes, the breath follows; as the breath goes, the senses (*prāṇa*) follow. He becomes a being of consciousness; he follows consciousness. His knowledge and action take hold of him, as does his former experience.[24]

3. 'As a caterpillar, reaching the end of a blade of grass and taking the next step, draws itself together, so the self, dropping the body, letting go of ignorance and taking the next step, draws itself together.

4. 'As a weaver,[25] unpicking a pattern from her weaving, fashions another, newer and more beautiful shape, so the self, dropping the body and letting go of ignorance, creates another, newer and more beautiful shape, either of the ancestors, or of the *gandharvas*, or of the gods, or of Prajāpati, or of Brahmā,[26] or of some other beings.

5. 'The self, made of knowledge, made of mind, made of breath, made of sight, made of hearing, made of earth, made of water, made of air, made of space, made of light (*tejas*), made of darkness (*atejas*), made of desire, made of non-desire, made of anger, made of non-anger, made of right (*dharma*), made of wrong (*adharma*), made of everything, is *brahman*. It is "made

of this, made of that". As one acts, as one behaves, so does one become. The doer of good becomes good, the doer of evil becomes evil. By virtuous action one becomes virtuous, by evil action evil. They say, "As one desires, so does one become, for the person is made of desire." As he desires, so does his will become; as his will is, so is the action he does; as is the action he does, so is what he gets back.[27]

6. 'There is a verse about it:

He, with his action, is attached
To that same mark to which his
mind is bound.

When he reaches the end
Of the action he did here,
He comes back from that world
To this one, to act again.

'That is about the one who desires. The one who does not desire, who is without desire, free from desire, whose desires are fulfilled, with the self as his desire, the breaths do not leave him. Being *brahman* he goes to *brahman*.

7. 'There is a verse about it:

When all the desires that dwell
In one's heart are let go,
Mortal becomes immortal:
One reaches *brahman* here.

'As the slough of a snake lies dead, abandoned, on an ant-hill, so the body lies. But the bodiless immortal breath is *brahman*, light (*tejas*).'

'Blessed one, I give you a thousand cows,' said Janaka of Videha.

8. 'There are these verses about it:

I have touched, I have found
The narrow, long and ancient way.
By it the wise, the knowers of *brahman*,
Go up to a heavenly world, freed from this.

9. On it, they say, are white and blue,
   Yellow, green and red.
The way was found by *brahman*:[28] by it goes
   The knower of *brahman*, the doer of
      good, the radiant.

10. They who worship ignorance
   Enter blind darkness:
They who delight in knowledge
   Enter darkness, as it were, yet deeper.[29]

11. Those worlds, covered with blind darkness,
   Are 'Joyless' by name.
People who are unknowing, unaware,
   Go to them on departing.[30]

12. But if a person knows the self –
   'I am this!'–
Wanting what, for desire of what,
   Would he burn up his body?

13. Whoever has found and woken up to the self
   That has entered this dangerous, inaccessible place,[31]
He is the 'All-Creator', for he is the maker of
      everything:
   His is the world – indeed, he is the world.

14. While we are here, we know this –
   If not, ignorance, great destruction!
Those who know it become immortal:
   The rest go to sorrow again.

15. When one sees it straight,
   The self, the god,
Lord of past and future,
   One does not shrink from it.

16. The one before whom
   The year revolves with its days
The gods worship
   As the light of lights, immortal life.

17. The one in whom the five times five peoples[32]
And space too are established
I honour as the self.
Knowing *brahman*, the immortal, I
am immortal.

18. Those who know the breath of the breath,
The eye of the eye, the ear of the ear,
The mind of the mind have discovered
The ancient supreme *brahman*.

19. It is to be seen only by mind:
There are no differences in it.
Whoever sees differences in it
Gets death after death.

20. It is to be seen as one,
Immeasurable, steadfast.
The self is dustless, beyond space,
Unborn, great, steadfast.

21. Knowing it, a wise Brāhmaṇa
Should cultivate wisdom.
He should not think on many words,
For that is mere weariness of speech.

22. 'It is the great, unborn self among the breaths that consists of knowledge. It lies in the space that is within the heart, controller of all, ruler of all, overlord of all. It does not become bigger by good actions, or smaller by bad ones. It is the lord of all, the overlord of beings, the protector of beings. It is the dam separating these worlds so that they do not run together.[33] Brāhmaṇas try to find it through study of the Vedas, through sacrifice, through giving, through asceticism, through fasting: knowing it one becomes a 'silent one' (*muni*). Desiring it as their world, renouncers wander. Knowing it, the ancients did not desire offspring, for they thought, "What is offspring to us, when the self is our world?" Leaving behind desires for sons, desires for wealth and desires for worlds, they lived on alms. For desire for sons is desire for wealth, and desire for wealth is

desire for worlds: both are merely desires. The self is "not this, not this". Unseizable, it is not seized; indestructible, it is not destroyed; without clinging, it is not clung to; unbound, it does not suffer, does not come to harm. It is not overcome by the thoughts "Here I did wrong, here I did right": it overcomes both, and what has been done or not done does not burn it.

23. 'About this, the hymn[34] says:

> This eternal greatness of the Brāhmaṇa
> By works neither increases nor grows less.
> One should know its place: knowing it,
> One is not smeared by evil works.

'So knowing this, and becoming calm, self-controlled, quiet, patient and concentrated, he sees the self in himself, sees the self as all. Evil does not overcome him: he overcomes all evil. Evil does not burn him: he burns all evil. Without evil, without dust, free from doubt, he becomes a Brāhmaṇa.[35] This is the world of Brahmā,[36] your majesty: you have attained it,' said Yājñavalkya.

'Blessed one, I give you the Videhas, and myself to be your slave.'

24. This is the great unborn self, eater of food, giver of wealth. The one who knows this finds wealth.

25. This is the great unborn self, unageing, undying, immortal, fearless, *brahman*. *Brahman* is fearless: the one who knows this becomes fearless *brahman*.

CHAPTER 5

1. Yājñavalkya had two wives: Maitreyī and Kātyāyanī. Of the two, Maitreyī was a scholar of sacred lore (*brahman*), while Kātyāyanī had just a woman's knowledge in it.[37] Now, as Yājña-valkya was about to undertake another course of life –

2. 'Maitreyī,' said Yājñavalkya, 'I am about to go forth from this state. I must make a settlement on you and Kātyāyanī.'

3. Maitreyī said, 'Blessed one, if I had this whole earth, filled with riches, would I become immortal by it?'

'Oh, no, no,' said Yājñavalkya. 'Your life would be as the life of the wealthy, but there is no hope of immortality through riches.'

4. Maitreyī said, 'What use to me is something by which I cannot become immortal? Blessed one, teach me what you know.'

5. Yājñavalkya said, 'Ah, dear as you are to me, you have grown yet dearer. Come, sit down, I will teach you: but, as I explain, meditate upon it.'

6. He said, 'It is not for the love of a husband that a husband is dear: it is for the love of the self that a husband is dear. It is not for the love of a wife that a wife is dear: it is for the love of the self that a wife is dear. It is not for the love of children that children are dear: it is for the love of the self that children are dear. It is not for the love of riches that riches are dear: it is for the love of the self that riches are dear. It is not for the love of cattle that cattle are dear: it is for the love of the self that cattle are dear. It is not for the love of priesthood (*brahman*) that priesthood is dear: it is for the love of the self that priesthood is dear. It is not for the love of royalty that royalty is dear: it is for the love of the self that royalty is dear. It is not for the love of the worlds that the worlds are dear: it is for the love of the self that the worlds are dear. It is not for the love of the gods that the gods are dear: it is for the love of the self that the gods are dear. It is not for the love of the Vedas that the Vedas are dear: it is for the love of the self that the Vedas are dear. It is not for the love of beings that beings are dear: it is for the love of the self that beings are dear. It is not for the love of the all that the all is dear: it is for the love of the self that the all is dear. It is the self that must be seen, heard, thought of and meditated upon, Maitreyī: when the self has been seen, heard, thought of and meditated upon, all this is known.

7. 'Whoever understands priesthood as other than the self, priesthood has given him over. Whoever understands royalty as other than the self, royalty has given him over. Whoever

understands the worlds as other than the self, the worlds have given him over. Whoever understands the gods as other than the self, the gods have given him over. Whoever understands the Vedas as other than the self, the Vedas have given him over. Whoever understands beings as other than the self, beings have given him over. Whoever understands the all as other than the self, the all has given him over. This priesthood, this royalty, these worlds, these gods, these Vedas, these beings, this all are what this self is.

8. 'As, when a drum is beaten, one cannot seize the sounds as something outside it, but by seizing the drum or the drummer one has seized the sound;

9. 'As, when a conch is blown, one cannot seize the sounds as something outside it, but by seizing the conch or the conch-blower one has seized the sound;

10. 'As, when a lute is played, one cannot seize the sounds as something outside it, but by seizing the lute or the lute-player one has seized the sound;

11. 'As smoke billows out in all directions from a fire that has been laid with damp fuel, just so is everything breathed out from this great being: the Ṛgveda, the Yajurveda, the Sāmaveda, the hymns of the Atharvans and Aṅgirases, history, legend, science, the Upaniṣads, verses, *sūtras*, explanatory passages, expositions, sacrifice, offering, food, drink, this world, the other world, and all beings, all these are breathed out from it.

12. 'As the ocean is the one meeting-place of all waters, so the skin is the one meeting-place of all touches, the nostrils are the one meeting-place of all smells, the tongue is the one meeting-place of all tastes, the eye is the one meeting-place of all shapes, the ear is the one meeting-place of all sounds, the mind is the one meeting-place of all decisions, the heart is the one meeting-place of all knowledges, the hands are the one meeting-place of all works, the loins are the one meeting-place of all pleasures, the anus is the one meeting-place of all excretions, the feet are the one meeting-place of all roads, and the voice is the one meeting-place of all the Vedas.

13. 'As a lump of rock-salt is without an inside, without an

outside, and consists entirely of taste, so this self is without an inside, without an outside, and consists entirely of wisdom. Having arisen from these elements, it vanishes along with them, for after it has departed there is no consciousness:[38] that is what I say,' said Yājñavalkya.

14. Maitreyī said, 'Blessed one, you have brought me to extreme confusion: I do not understand this.'[39]

He said, 'I do not speak to confuse you: this self is imperishable, of a nature (*dharma*) that cannot be destroyed.

15. 'For where there is duality, one sees another, one smells another, one tastes another, one speaks to another, one hears another, one thinks of another, one touches another, one knows another. But where everything in one has become self, how can one see – and whom? How can one smell – and whom? How can one taste – and whom? How can one speak – and to whom? How can one hear – and whom? How can one think – and of whom? How can one touch – and whom? How can one know – and whom? The self is "not this, not this". Unseizable, it is not seized; indestructible, it is not destroyed; without clinging, it is not clung to; unbound, it does not suffer, does not come to harm. How can one know the knower? So now, Maitreyī, you have the teaching. This is immortality.' And, so saying, Yājñavalkya departed.

CHAPTER 6

1. Now the lineage of the teaching, from Pautimāṣya.[40] Pautimāṣya received it from Gaupavana, Gaupavana from Pautimāṣya, Pautimāṣya from Gaupavana, Gaupavana from Kauśika, Kauśika from Kauṇḍinya, Kauṇḍinya from Śāṇḍilya, Śāṇḍilya from Kauśika and Gautama, Gautama

2. from Āgniveśya, Āgniveśya from Gārgya, Gārgya from Gārgya, Gārgya from Gautama, Gautama from Saitava, Saitava from Pārāśaryāyaṇa, Pārāśaryāyaṇa from Gārgyāyana, Gārgyāyana from Uddālakāyana, Uddālakāyana from Jābālāyana,

Jābālāyana from Mādhyandināyana, Mādhyandināyana from Saukarāyaṇa, Saukarāyaṇa from Kāṣāyaṇa, Kāṣāyaṇa from Sāyakāyana, Sāyakāyana from Kauśikāyani, Kauśikāyani
3. from Ghṛtakauśika, Ghṛtakauśika from Pārāśaryāyaṇa, Pārāśaryāyaṇa from Pārāśarya, Pārāśarya from Jātūkarṇya, Jātūkarṇya from Āsurāyaṇa and Yāska, Āsurāyaṇa from Traivaṇi, Traivaṇi from Aupajandhani, Aupajandhani from Āsuri, Āsuri from Bhāradvāja, Bhāradvāja from Ātreya, Ātreya from Māṇṭi, Māṇṭi from Gautama, Gautama from Gautama, Gautama from Vātsya, Vātsya from Śāṇḍilya, Śāṇḍilya from Kaiśorya Kāpya, Kaiśorya Kāpya from Kumārahārita, Kumārahārita from Gālava, Gālava from Vidarbhī-Kauṇḍinya, Vidarbhī-Kauṇḍinya from Vatsanapāt Bābhrava, Vatsanapāt Bābhrava from Pathin Saubhara, Pathin Saubhara from Ayāsya Āṅgirasa, Ayāsya Āṅgirasa from Ābhūti Tvāṣṭra, Ābhūti Tvāṣṭra from Viśvarūpa Tvāṣṭra, Viśvarūpa Tvāṣṭra from the Aśvins, the Aśvins from Dadhyac Ātharvaṇa, Dadhyac Ātharvaṇa from the Divine Atharvan, the Divine Atharvan from Mṛtyu Prādhvaṃsana, Mṛtyu Prādhvaṃsana from Pradhvaṃsana, Pradhvaṃsana from Ekarṣi, Ekarṣi from Vipracitti, Vipracitti from Vyaṣṭi, Vyaṣṭi from Sanāru, Sanāru from Sanātana, Sanātana from Sanaga, Sanaga from Parameṣṭhin, Parameṣṭhin from *brahman*. *Brahman* is self-born: homage to *brahman*.

BOOK V

CHAPTER 1

1. OṂ That is full; this is full;
Fullness comes forth from fullness:
When fullness is taken from fullness,
Fullness remains.

OṂ. '*Brahman* is space (*kha*), ancient space, airy space': so the son of Kauravyāyaṇī used to say. This is the Veda that the Brāhmaṇas know. By it one knows what is to be known.

CHAPTER 2

1. The descendants of Prajāpati, of three kinds, gods, human beings and demons, lived as *brahmacārins* with their father Prajāpati. When they had completed their studentship, the gods said, 'Teach us, father.'[1]

He spoke to them the syllable DA. 'Did you understand?'

'We understood,' they said. 'You told us, "Be self-controlled (*dāmyata*)."'

'OṂ,' he said. 'You understood.'

2. Then the human beings said to him, 'Teach us, father.'

He spoke to them the same syllable DA. 'Did you understand?'

'We understood,' they said. 'You told us, "Give (*datta*)."'

'OṂ,' he said. 'You understood.'

3. Then the demons said to him, 'Teach us, father.'

He spoke to them the syllable DA. 'Did you understand?'

'We understood,' they said. 'You told us, "Be compassionate (*dayadhvam*)."'

'OṂ,' he said. 'You understood.'

This is what the divine voice that is thunder repeats: 'DA DA DA', 'Be self-controlled! Give! Be compassionate!' One should practise this set of three: self-control (*dama*), giving (*dāna*) and compassion (*dayā*).

CHAPTER 3

1. The heart (*hṛdaya*) is Prajāpati: it is *brahman*: it is all. It has three syllables: *hṛ-da-yam*.[3] *Hṛ* is one syllable: his own and other people bring (*abhi-hṛ-*) gifts to the one who knows this. *Da* is one syllable: his own and other people give (*dā-*) to the one who knows this. *Yam* is one syllable: the one who knows this goes (*i-*)[4] to a heavenly world.

CHAPTER 4

1. That is *that*.[5] This was that – truth. The one who knows the great, first-born wonder[6] – that truth is *brahman* – wins the worlds. Could he ever be conquered, the one who knows the great, first-born wonder – that truth is *brahman*? For truth is *brahman*.

CHAPTER 5

1. In the beginning the waters were all this. The waters created truth; truth *brahman*; *brahman* Prajāpati; and Prajāpati the gods. The gods worship truth (*satya*). It has three syllables:

sa-ti-yam.[7] *Sa* is one syllable. *Ti* is one syllable. *Yam* is one syllable. Truth is in the first and the last syllable, falsehood in the middle:[8] so falsehood is surrounded on both sides by truth, and becomes truth. Falsehood does not harm the one who knows this.

2. What truth is, the sun is. The person who is in its circle and the person who is in the right eye are supported on one another. That one rests on this one through its rays, and this one rests on that one through its breaths.

When one is about to depart,[9] one sees that circle pure. The rays do not come to one again.

3. The head of the person in that circle is BHŪḤ:[10] the head is one, and that is one syllable. His arms are BHUVAḤ: the arms are two, and that is two syllables. SVAḤ is his support: the supports (*pratiṣṭhā*)[11] are two, and that is two syllables (*su-aḥ*). His inner name (*upaniṣad*) is 'day (*ahar*)'. The one who knows this destroys and gets rid of evil.

4. The head of the person in the right eye is BHŪḤ: the head is one, and that is one syllable. His arms are BHUVAḤ: the arms are two, and that is two syllables. SVAḤ is his support: the supports are two, and that is two syllables. His inner name is 'I (*aham*)'. The one who knows this destroys and gets rid of evil.

CHAPTER 6

1. The person made of mind, the light, the true, is inside the heart, like a rice-grain or a barleycorn. He is the ruler of everything, the overlord of everything: he controls all this, whatever there is.

CHAPTER 7

1. They say, 'Lightning is *brahman*.' It is called lightning (*vidyut*) because it cuts free (*vi-do-*). It cuts free from evil the one who knows in this way that lightning is *brahman*: for lightning *is brahman*.

CHAPTER 8

1. One should worship speech as a milch-cow. She has four udders: the sound SVĀHĀ, the sound VAṢAṬ, the sound HANTA and the sound SVADHĀ.[12] The gods live on two of her udders, the sound SVĀHĀ and the sound VAṢAṬ; human beings on the sound HANTA; and the ancestors on the sound SVADHĀ. Breath is her bull, mind her calf.

CHAPTER 9

1. The fire which is within a person is that which is in all men,[13] by which the food that is eaten is digested.[14] It is *its* sound that one hears when one covers one's ears like *this*. When one is about to depart, one does not hear this sound.

CHAPTER 10

1. When a person goes forth from this world, he comes to the air. It parts there for him like the hole in a chariot-wheel, and he goes up through it. He comes to the sun. It parts there for him like the hole in a tabor,[15] and he goes up through it. He comes to the moon. It parts there for him like the hole in a drum,

and he goes up through it. He comes to a world without sorrow, without snow, and he lives there for eternal years.

CHAPTER 11

1. When one suffers (*tap-*) with illness, that is the highest asceticism (*tapas*).[16] Whoever knows this wins the highest world. When they take the dead out to the forest, that is the highest asceticism. Whoever knows this wins the highest world. When they lay the dead on the fire, that is the highest asceticism. Whoever knows this wins the highest world.

CHAPTER 12

1. Some say that food is *brahman*, but it is not so, for without breath food decays. Some say that breath is *brahman*, but it is not so, for without food breath dries up. But when these two deities become united they reach the highest state.

So Prātṛda said to his father, 'What good could I do to one who knows this? What harm could I do to him?'

His father said, with a gesture of his hand, 'No, Prātṛda. Who reaches the highest state by becoming united with these two?' He said to him also, '*Vi*. Food is *vi*, for all these beings have entered (*viś-*) into food. *Ram*. Breath is *ram*, for all these beings take pleasure (*ram-*) in breath. All beings enter into, all beings take pleasure in, the one who knows this.'[17]

CHAPTER 13

1. Uktha. Breath is the Uktha, for breath makes all this arise (*ut-thā-*). Whoever knows this, a hero[18] who knows the Uktha arises from him: he wins union with the Uktha, shares a world with it.
2. *Yajus*. Breath is the *yajus*, for all beings are joined together (*yuj-*) in breath. Whoever knows this, all beings are joined with him for his betterment: he wins union with the *yajus*, shares a world with it.
3. *Sāman*. Breath is the *sāman*, for all beings are together (*samyac*) in breath. Whoever knows this, all beings come together with him for his betterment: he wins union with the *sāman*, shares a world with it.
4. Royalty (*kṣatra*). Breath is royalty, breath indeed is royalty, for breath protects (*trai-*) one from being injured (*kṣan-*). Whoever knows this attains royalty that needs no protection (*a-tra*): he wins union with royalty, shares a world with it.

CHAPTER 14

1. *Bhūmiḥ, antarikṣam, dyauḥ* (earth, middle-air, sky) – eight syllables.[19] One foot of the Gāyatrī has eight syllables, and this is that foot of it. Whoever knows that foot of it as such wins as much as there is in the three worlds.
2. *Ṛcaḥ, yajūṃṣi, sāmāni* (Ṛgveda, Yajurveda, Sāmaveda) – eight syllables. One foot of the Gāyatrī has eight syllables, and this is that foot of it. Whoever knows that foot of it as such wins as much as there is of this threefold knowledge.
3. *Prāṇa, apāna, vyāna*[20] (breath, lower breath, diffused breath) – eight syllables. One foot of the Gāyatrī has eight syllables, and this is that foot of it. Whoever knows that foot of it as such wins as much as there is that has breath.

Its visible foot, the *turīya*,[21] is the one who gives heat (*tap-*)[22] beyond the darkness. The fourth is the *turīya*. It is called 'the visible foot' because it has become visible. It is 'beyond the darkness'[23] because it gives heat far, far above the darkness. The one who knows that foot of it as such blazes (*tap-*) with splendour, with fame.

4. The Gāyatrī is supported on the fourth (*turīya*), visible, foot, which is beyond the darkness.

That is supported on truth. The eye is truth: the eye, indeed, is truth. So if now two people were to come arguing, one saying, 'I have seen', the other saying 'I have heard', we would believe the one saying, 'I have seen.'

Truth is supported on strength. Breath is strength: it is supported on breath. So they say, 'Strength is more powerful than truth.'

That is how the Gāyatrī is supported in relation to oneself. It has protected the *gayas*. The breaths are the *gayas*.[24] It has protected the breaths. Because it has protected (*trai-*) the *gayas*, it is called Gāyatrī. This is the same Sāvitrī that one teaches. It protects the breaths of the one to whom one teaches it.

5. Some teach the Sāvitrī as an *Anuṣṭubh*,[25] saying, 'Speech is the *anuṣṭubh*, so we teach it as speech.' One should not do so. One should teach the Sāvitrī as a *Gāyatrī*. Even if one who knows this receives much wealth, it is not equal to one foot of the Gāyatrī.

6. If one were to receive the three worlds, full, one would be getting the first foot of the Gāyatrī. If one were to receive as much as there is of this threefold knowledge, one would be getting the second foot of it. If one were to receive as much as there is that has breath, one would be getting the third foot of it. But no one can get its fourth (*turīya*), visible, foot, the one who gives heat beyond the darkness: how could one receive something like this?

7. The way to worship it: 'Gāyatrī, you are one-footed, two-footed, three-footed, four-footed: you are no-footed, for you do not walk. Homage to your fourth, visible, foot beyond the darkness.' One may pray,[26] 'May <name> not attain this!' or 'May his desire not be fulfilled!' If one offers worship in this way about someone, his desire is not fulfilled. Or one may pray, 'May I attain this!'

8. On this matter, Janaka of Videha said to Buḍila Āśvatarāśvi, 'Ha! You have called yourself a knower of the Gāyatrī. How is it that you have become an elephant, carrying?'[27]

'Because I did not know its mouth, your majesty,' he said.

Its mouth is fire. Even if one lays, as it were, much fuel on a fire, it burns it all up. In the same way, even if one who knows this does, as it were, much evil,[28] he swallows it all and becomes pure, cleansed, unageing, immortal.

CHAPTER 15

1. The face of truth is concealed
By a vessel made of gold.[29]
Reveal it, Pūṣan, to my sight,
Which has truth as its *dharma*.

2. Pūṣan, Ekarṣi, Yama, Sūrya, son of Prajāpati,
Draw apart your rays and draw them together.
I see the light that is your most beautiful form.
That very person – I am he.

3. My breath to immortal air:
This body has ended in ashes.
OṂ! Will, remember! Remember the deed!
Will, remember! Remember the deed!

4. Agni, god who knows all ways,
Lead us by a good road to prosperity.
Overcome our crooked faults,
And we will render you the utmost reverence.

BOOK VI

CHAPTER I

1. OṂ. The one who knows the eldest and best becomes the eldest and best of his own people. Breath is the eldest and best. The one who knows this becomes the eldest and best of his own people, and of those of whom he wishes to become so.

2. The one who knows the finest[1] becomes the finest of his own people. Speech is the finest. The one who knows this becomes the finest of his own people, and of those of whom he wishes to become so.

3. The one who knows the support (*pratiṣṭhā*) stands firm (*prati-sthā-*) on even ground, stands firm on rough ground. The eye is the support, for the eye stands firm on even ground, stands firm on rough ground.[2] The one who knows this stands firm on even ground, stands firm on rough ground.

4. The one who knows prosperity attains whatever desire he desires. The ear is prosperity, for all the Vedas are attained in it.[3] The one who knows this attains whatever desire he desires.

5. The one who knows the dwelling-place becomes a dwelling-place for his own folk, a dwelling-place for the people. Mind is the dwelling-place. The one who knows this becomes a dwelling-place for his own folk, a dwelling-place for the people.

6. The one who knows procreation increases in offspring and in animals.[4] The seed is procreation. The one who knows this increases in offspring and in animals.

7. The bodily functions (*prāṇa*) were arguing about who was the best. They went to *brahman* and asked it, 'Who is the finest of us?'

It said, 'The finest of you is the one after whose departure the body is thought to be worst off.'

8. Speech departed and stayed away for a year. When it came back it asked, 'How were you able to live without me?'

They said, 'We lived like the dumb, not speaking with speech, but breathing with the breath, seeing with the eye, hearing with the ear, knowing with the mind, procreating with the seed.'

Then speech went back in.

9. The eye departed and stayed away for a year. When it came back it asked, 'How were you able to live without me?'

They said, 'We lived like the blind, speaking with speech, breathing with the breath, not seeing with the eye, but hearing with the ear, knowing with the mind, procreating with the seed.'

The eye went back in.

10. The ear departed and stayed away for a year. When it came back it asked, 'How were you able to live without me?'

They said, 'We lived like the deaf, speaking with speech, breathing with the breath, seeing with the eye, not hearing with the ear, but knowing with the mind, procreating with the seed.'

Then the ear went back in.

11. The mind departed and stayed away for a year. When it came back it asked, 'How were you able to live without me?'

They said, 'We lived like the simpletons, speaking with speech, breathing with the breath, seeing with the eye, hearing with the ear, not knowing with the mind, but procreating with the seed.'

12. The seed departed and stayed away for a year. When it came back it asked, 'How were you able to live without me?'

They said, 'We lived like the eunuchs, speaking with speech, breathing with the breath, seeing with the eye, hearing with the ear, knowing with the mind, but not procreating with the seed.'

Then the seed went back in.

13. The breath (*prāṇa*), about to depart, dragged those bodily functions (*prāṇa*) together as a fine big stallion of Sindhu might drag its tethering-pegs.

They said, 'Blessed one, do not leave. We will not be able to live without you.'

'Then make me an offering.'

'We will.'

14. Speech said, 'In that I am the finest, you are the finest.'

The eye said, 'In that I am the support, you are the support.'

The ear said, 'In that I am prosperity, you are prosperity.'

The mind said, 'In that I am the dwelling-place, you are the dwelling-place.'

The seed said, 'In that I am procreation, you are procreation.'

'Then what is my food, what is my clothing?'

'Whatever there is, down to dogs, worms, insects and flying things,[5] is your food: water is your clothing.'

Whoever knows in this way the food of the breath will not come to eat anything that is not food, will not come to receive anything that is not food. Knowing this, the learned sip water when they are about to eat, and sip water after they have eaten. They think that they are making the breath (*ana*) not-naked (*anagna*).

CHAPTER 2

1. Śvetaketu Āruṇeya came to an assembly of the Pañcālas. He approached Jaivali Pravāhaṇa, who was being waited on by his entourage.[6] Seeing him, the prince called, 'Young man!'[7]

'Sir?' he called back.

'Have you been educated by your father?'

'OṂ,' he said.

2. 'Do you know,' cried the prince, 'how people, when they depart, go in different directions?'

'No,' he said.

'And do you know how they come back to this world again?'

'No,' he said.

'And do you know how that world does not become full with the many people who depart to it again and again?'

'No' was all he said.

'And do you know how many offerings have to be offered before the waters take on a human voice, rise up, and speak?'

'No' was all he said.

'And do you know how to reach the path that leads to the gods or the one that leads to the ancestors – what they do to reach the path that leads to the gods or the one that leads to the ancestors? For we have heard the saying of the Ṛṣi:

> I have heard of two ways for mortals,
> To the ancestors and to the gods:
> By them goes everything that moves
> Between the father and the mother.'[8]

'I do not know a single one of these things,' he said.

3. The prince invited him to stay with him, but the young man, not honouring his hospitality, ran away. He came to his father and said, 'Now, father, you said before that we had been educated!'

'What of it, clever one?'

'A princeling[9] asked me five questions, and I do not know a single one of them.'

'What are they?'

'These' – and he told him the subjects.

4. He said, 'You should know me, son: whatever I know, I have taught you. But come, we two will go to him and live with him as his students.'

'*You* go, father.'

Gautama went to Pravāhaṇa Jaivali's house. The prince offered him a seat, had water brought for him, and welcomed him as an honoured guest. He said, 'We grant a boon to the blessed Gautama.'

5. He said, 'I accept the boon. Tell me the words you spoke in the presence of the young man.'

6. He said, 'Gautama, that falls among boons for the gods. Name something that belongs to human beings.'

7. He said, 'It is well known that I have plenty of gold, cows

and horses, slave-women, coverings and clothing. Sir, do not stint me of what is great, endless, unlimited.'

'Then, Gautama, you should ask for it in the proper way.'

The ancients used to go to their teachers by saying, 'I come to you, sir': and so Gautama became his student by announcing[10] that he was going to him.

8. He said, 'Gautama, may you not be displeased with us, nor your grandfathers either, but this knowledge has never before lived in any Brāhmaṇa. But I will teach it to you: for who could refuse you when you ask in this way?

9. '*That* world[11] is a fire, Gautama. The sun is its fuel; the rays its smoke; the day its flame; the directions its embers; the intermediate directions its sparks. In that fire the gods offer faith (*śraddhā*). From that offering King Soma arises.

10. 'Parjanya is a fire, Gautama. The year is his fuel; the clouds his smoke; the lightning his flame; the thunderbolt his embers; the hailstones his sparks. In that fire the gods offer King Soma. From that offering rain arises.

11. '*This* world is a fire, Gautama. The earth is its fuel; fire its smoke; the night its flame; the moon its embers; the constellations its sparks. In that fire the gods offer rain. From that offering food arises.

12. 'A man (*puruṣa*) is a fire, Gautama. The open mouth is his fuel; breath his smoke; speech his flame; the eye his embers; the ear his sparks. In that fire the gods offer food. From that offering the seed arises.

13. 'A young woman is a fire, Gautama. The loins are her fuel; the body-hairs her smoke; the vagina her flame; what one does inside, her embers; the pleasures her sparks. In that fire the gods offer the seed. From that offering a person arises.[12] He lives as long as he lives, and when he dies –

14. 'They carry him to the fire. Then his fire becomes the fire; his fuel the fuel; his smoke the smoke; his flame the flame; his embers the embers; his sparks the sparks. In that fire the gods offer the person. From that offering a person of the colour of light arises.

15. 'Those who know this, and those who in the forest worship faith as truth,[13] go into the flame, from the flame into the

day, from the day into the waxing fortnight, from the waxing fortnight into the six months in which the sun goes northward,[14] from the months into the world of the gods, from the world of the gods into the sun, from the sun into that which is made of lightning. The person of mind goes to those beings of lightning and leads them to the world of Brahmā.[15] Exalted, far above, they dwell in the worlds of Brahmā. For them there is no returning.

16. 'But those who win worlds by sacrifice, giving and asceticism go into the smoke, from the smoke into the night, from the night into the waning fortnight, from the waning fortnight into the six months in which the sun goes southward,[16] from the months into the world of the ancestors, from the world of the ancestors into the moon.

'Reaching the moon, they become food. There the gods partake of them, as they do of King Soma,[17] saying, "Grow full!" "Wane!"

'When that passes away for them, they enter into space, from space into the air, from the air into the rain, from the rain into the earth.

'Reaching the earth, they become food. They are offered again in the fire of a man, and from that are born in the fire of a young woman, rising again to the worlds. So they circle around. But those who do not know the two paths become worms, flying things, and everything that bites.'

CHAPTER 3

1. If someone desires to achieve greatness, then in the northward passage of the sun, on a lucky day of the waxing fortnight, he takes an *upasad* vow lasting twelve days. Then he puts together all the herbs called 'fruits' in a cup or dish made of pipal-wood. He sweeps up and smears around,[18] builds a fire, and covers it with grass. He prepares the clarified butter in the usual way. Then, under a masculine constellation, he prepares the stirred mixture[19] and makes an offering:

'As many gods as there are in you, Jātavedas,
Who, crossing them, thwart a person's desires,
I offer them all a share.
May they be pleased, and please me with
all desires.
SVĀHĀ!

'And you who cross our desires,[20]
Saying, "I am the Separator",
With a stream of ghee
I sacrifice to you as the Reconciler.
SVĀHĀ!'

2. Saying, 'To the eldest, SVĀHĀ! To the best, SVĀHĀ!', he makes an offering into the fire and pours the remainder into the stirred mixture.

Saying, 'To breath, SVĀHĀ! To the finest,[21] SVĀHĀ!', he makes an offering into the fire and pours the remainder into the stirred mixture.

Saying, 'To speech, SVĀHĀ! To the support, SVĀHĀ!', he makes an offering into the fire and pours the remainder into the stirred mixture.

Saying, 'To the eye, SVĀHĀ! To prosperity, SVĀHĀ!', he makes an offering into the fire and pours the remainder into the stirred mixture.

Saying, 'To the ear, SVĀHĀ! To the dwelling-place, SVĀHĀ!', he makes an offering into the fire and pours the remainder into the stirred mixture.

Saying, 'To the mind, SVĀHĀ! To procreation, SVĀHĀ!', he makes an offering into the fire and pours the remainder into the stirred mixture.

Saying, 'To the seed, SVĀHĀ!', he makes an offering into the fire and pours the remainder into the stirred mixture.

3. Saying, 'To Agni, SVĀHĀ!', he makes an offering into the fire and pours the remainder into the stirred mixture.

Saying, 'To Soma, SVĀHĀ!', he makes an offering into the fire and pours the remainder into the stirred mixture.

Saying, 'BHŪḤ, SVĀHĀ!', he makes an offering into the fire and pours the remainder into the stirred mixture.

Saying, 'BHUVAḤ, SVĀHĀ!', he makes an offering into the fire and pours the remainder into the stirred mixture.

Saying, 'SVAḤ, SVĀHĀ!', he makes an offering into the fire and pours the remainder into the stirred mixture.

Saying, 'BHŪḤ, BHUVAḤ, SVAḤ, SVĀHĀ!', he makes an offering into the fire and pours the remainder into the stirred mixture.

Saying, 'To priesthood (*brahman*), SVĀHĀ!', he makes an offering into the fire and pours the remainder into the stirred mixture.

Saying, 'To royalty (*kṣatra*), SVĀHĀ!', he makes an offering into the fire and pours the remainder into the stirred mixture.

Saying, 'To the past, SVĀHĀ!', he makes an offering into the fire and pours the remainder into the stirred mixture.

Saying, 'To the future, SVĀHĀ!', he makes an offering into the fire and pours the remainder into the stirred mixture.

Saying, 'To the universe, SVĀHĀ!', he makes an offering into the fire and pours the remainder into the stirred mixture.

Saying, 'To all, SVĀHĀ!', he makes an offering into the fire and pours the remainder into the stirred mixture.

Saying, 'To Prajāpati, SVĀHĀ!', he makes an offering into the fire and pours the remainder into the stirred mixture.

4. Then he touches it, saying, 'You are the wandering, you are the blazing, you are the full, you are the rigid, you are the one meeting-place, you are the sound *hiṅ*,[22] you are the sounding of *hiṅ*, you are the Udgītha, you are the chanting of the Udgītha, you are what is recited,[23] you are what is recited back,[24] you are what burns in what is wet,[25] you are the all-pervading, you are the powerful, you are food, you are light, you are the ending, you are the drawing together.'

5. Then he lifts it up, saying, '*Āmaṃsy āmaṃhi te mahi.*[26] He is the ruler of kings, the overlord: may the ruler of kings make me the overlord!'

6. Then he sips it and says:

'*We meditate on the lovely* –[27]
Sweetly[28] the winds blow for the good,
Sweetly the rivers flow.
Sweet be the herbs for us.
BHŪḤ SVĀHĀ!

'*Glory of the god Savitṛ* –
Sweet be the night and the dawns too,
Sweet-filled be the dust of the earth,
Sweet be the sky our father.
BHUVAḤ SVĀHĀ!

'*That he may stimulate our minds* –
Sweet-filled be the lord of the wood,[29]
Sweet-filled be the sun,
Sweet be the cows to us.
SVAḤ SVĀHĀ!'

He recites the whole of the Sāvitrī and all the 'Sweet-filled' verses. Then: 'May I become all this! BHŪḤ, BHUVAḤ, SVAḤ, SVĀHĀ!' Finally, when he has sipped it, he washes his hands and lies down behind the fire-altar with his head towards the east.

In the morning he worships the sun, saying 'You are the one white lotus of the directions: may I become the one white lotus of humankind!' He goes back by the way he came, sits down behind the fire-altar, and recites the lineage.[30]

7. Uddālaka Āruṇi taught this to his student Vājasaneya Yājñavalkya, and said, 'If one were to sprinkle this even on a dried-up stump, branches would grow, and leaves would sprout.'

8. And Vājasaneya Yājñavalkya taught this to his student Madhuka Paiṅgya, and said: 'If one were to sprinkle this even on a dried-up stump, branches would grow, and leaves would sprout.'

9. And Madhuka Paiṅgya taught this to his student Cūla Bhāgavitti, and said, 'If one were to sprinkle this even on a dried-up stump, branches would grow, and leaves would sprout.'

10. And Cūla Bhāgavitti taught this to his student Jānaki Āyasthūna, and said, 'If one were to sprinkle this even on a dried-up stump, branches would grow, and leaves would sprout.'
11. And Jānaki Āyasthūna taught this to his student Satyakāma Jābāla, and said, 'If one were to sprinkle this even on a dried-up stump, branches would grow, and leaves would sprout.'
12. And Satyakāma Jābāla taught this to his students, and said, 'If one were to sprinkle this even on a dried-up stump, branches would grow, and leaves would sprout.' One should not teach this to anybody who is not a son or a student.
13. Four things[31] are made of pipal-wood. The spoon is of pipal-wood; the bowl is of pipal-wood; the fuel is of pipal-wood; the two churning-sticks are of pipal-wood.

There are ten cultivated grains: rice, barley, sesamum, beans, millet, panic seed, wheat, lentils, peas and vetch.[32] He sprinkles them, ground, on yoghurt, honey and ghee, and makes an offering of melted butter.

CHAPTER 4

1. The earth is the essence of all beings, the waters the essence of earth, plants of the waters, flowers of plants, fruits of flowers, a man (*puruṣa*) of fruits, and the seed of a man.
2. Prajāpati thought, 'Come, I must make a support for him!' He created a woman. When he had created her, he worshipped her below: so one should worship a woman below. He stretched forward his pressing-stone[33] in front of him, and with it he poured[34] into her.
3. Her loins are the altar; her body-hairs the strewing-grass; her skin the Soma-press; her labia the fire in the middle. The one who practises sexual intercourse knowing this gains as great a world as the one who offers the Vājapeya sacrifice,[35] and takes the merit of the women to himself. But the one who practises sexual intercourse without knowing this, the women take his merit[36] to themselves.
4. Knowing this, Uddālaka Āruṇi used to say –

Knowing this, Nāka Maudgalya used to say –

Knowing this, Kumārahārita used to say, 'Many mortals, descendants of Brāhmaṇas,[37] depart from this world impotent, without merit: the ones who practise sexual intercourse without knowing this.'

If, when a man is asleep or awake, *this* much of his seed is spilled,

5. He should touch it, or recite over it:

> 'Whatever seed of mine is spilled on the earth,
> Or has flowed into plants, or into the waters,
> I take back that seed. May my potency,
> My energy, my luck, come back to me!

'May the fire-altar and the side-altars be set again in their proper places!' Then he should take it between ring-finger and thumb and rub it between his breasts or his eyebrows.

6. If it is in water, he should look at himself in the water and recite over it,[38] 'In me be light, potency, goods, merit!'

This is the beauty (*śrī*) of women, when she has taken off her dirty clothes.[39] So when she is glorious, having taken off her dirty clothes, the man should approach and invite her.

7. If she does not give him his desire, he should bribe her. If she still does not give him his desire, he should strike[40] her with a stick or with his hand, saying, 'With my potency, my glory, I take away your glory!': and she becomes inglorious.

8. If she gives him his desire, he should say, 'With my potency, my glory, I place glory in you!': and they both become glorious.

9. If a man desires a woman, wishing, 'May she desire me!', then he should place his sex-organ in her, join mouth with mouth, stroke her loins, and mutter:

> 'You[41] come from every limb,
> You are born in the heart;
> You are the essence of the limbs:
> Make <name> mad for me,
> As though pierced by a poisoned arrow!'

10. If he desires a woman, wishing, 'May she not become pregnant!', then he should place his sex-organ in her, join mouth

with mouth, breathe out into her, and breathe in,[42] saying, 'With my potency, my seed, I take the seed from you!': and she becomes without seed.

11. If he desires a woman, wishing, 'May she become pregnant!', then he should place his sex-organ in her, join mouth with mouth, breathe in, and breathe out into her, saying, 'With my potency, my seed, I place seed in you!': and she becomes pregnant.

12. If a man's wife has a lover, and he hates that lover, he should set a fire in an unfired pot, lay out a strewing of reeds in the opposite order to normal,[43] and offer in the fire those reed arrows in the opposite order to normal, saying:

'You have made an offering in my fire. I take away your out-breath (*prāṇa*) and in-breath (*apāna*), <name>!'

'You have made an offering in my fire. I take away your sons and animals, <name>!'

'You have made an offering in my fire. I take away your sacrifice and merit, <name>!'

'You have made an offering in my fire. I take away your hope and expectation, <name>!'

The one who is cursed by a Brāhmaṇa who knows this departs from this world impotent, without merit. So, knowing this, one should not wish for sexual intercourse with the wife of one who is learned in the Veda, for one who knows this becomes superior.

13. When one's wife has her period, for three days she should not drink from a metal cup nor change her clothes. No low-born man or woman should touch her. At the end of three nights she should bathe and have rice ground.

14. If someone wishes, 'May a white son be born to me! May he learn a Veda! May he live a full span!', the couple should have rice-and-milk cooked and eat it with ghee: and they will be able to have one.

15. If someone wishes, 'May a tawny, yellow son be born to me! May he learn two Vedas! May he live a full span!', the couple should have rice-and-yoghurt cooked and eat it with ghee: and they will be able to have one.

16. If someone wishes, 'May a dark, red-eyed son be born to me! May he learn three Vedas! May he live a full span!', the couple should have rice-and-water cooked and eat it with ghee: and they will be able to have one.

17. If someone wishes, 'May a learned daughter[44] be born to me! May she live a full span!', the couple should have rice-and-sesame cooked and eat it with ghee: and they will be able to have one.

18. If someone wishes, 'May a learned, famous son be born to me, one who goes to assemblies, a speaker of well-received words! May he learn all the Vedas! May he live a full span!', the couple should have rice-and-meat cooked and eat it with ghee: and they will be able to have one – with meat from a bull-calf or a bull.[45]

19. Towards morning, the man should stir ghee in the manner of the *sthālīpāka*,[46] and make a touch-offering,[47] saying, 'To Agni, SVĀHĀ! To Anumati, SVĀHĀ! To the god Savitṛ, of true conception, SVĀHĀ!' After offering it, he takes it up and eats: after eating, he offers it to the other. He washes his hands, fills a water-bowl, and sprinkles her three times, saying:

'Get up from here, Viśvāvasu.
  Look for another young woman.
Leave this wife with her husband.'[48]

20. Then he approaches her, saying:

'I am he, you are she;[49]
You are she, I am he;
I am the *sāman* verse, you the *ṛc* verse;
I am sky, you are earth:
Let us two join together,
Mix our seed together,
To get a male child.'

21. Then he spreads apart her thighs, saying, 'Spread apart, sky and earth.' He places his sex-organ in her, joins mouth with mouth, and strokes her three times in the direction of the hair,[50] saying:

'May Viṣṇu prepare the womb;
May Tvaṣṭṛ fashion the shapes;
May Prajāpati pour in;
May Dhātṛ place the embryo in you.

'Place the embryo, Sinīvalī;
Place the embryo, you with the broad fringe;
May the Aśvins, garlanded with lotuses,
Place the embryo in you.

22. 'Just as the Aśvins
Twirl with their golden fire-sticks,
We invoke for you an embryo
To be born in the tenth month.

'As the earth is pregnant with fire
And the sky is pregnant with Indra,
As air is the embryo of the directions,
I place an embryo in you, <name>.'

23. When she is about to give birth, he sprinkles her with water, saying:

'As the wind ruffles a lotus-pond
On every side,
May your embryo stir
And come down with its afterbirth.

'Indra's enclosure has been made
With its bolt and its fence.
Indra, send out from it
The afterbirth with the embryo.'

24. When a son has been born, he takes him in his lap and puts mixed[51] ghee in a metal cup. He makes a touch-offering of the mixed ghee, saying:

'May I nurture a thousand in this one,
Increasing in my own house.
May his lineage not be cut off
In offspring or in animals.
SVĀHĀ!

'The breaths in me
By mind I offer into you.
SVĀHĀ!

'Whatever in my work I have overdone,
Or whatever I have underdone,
May Agni, the maker-good of sacrifices, knowing it,
Make it a good sacrifice, a good offering, for us.
SVĀHĀ!'

25. Then, close to the child's right ear, he whispers three times, 'Speech, speech.' Then putting together yoghurt, honey and ghee he feeds him with a golden spoon, which he does not put inside his mouth, whispering, 'I place BHŪḤ in you; I place BHUVAḤ in you; I place SVAḤ in you: I place BHŪḤ, BHUVAḤ, SVAḤ, everything in you.'

26. Then, saying, 'You are Veda,' he gives him a name: and that becomes his secret name.

27. Then he gives him to his mother and offers him her breast, saying:

'That breast of yours, ever-flowing, refreshing,
Wealth-bestowing, rich, generous,
With which you nourish all that are fit to be chosen,
Sarasvatī, give it to my baby here to suck.'[52]

28. Then he addresses the mother, saying:

'You are Ilā, daughter of Mitra and Varuṇa.
Heroine,[53] you have borne a hero.
May you always possess heroes,[54]
Since you have given us a hero.'

They say to such a one, 'Ah, you have become greater than your father! Ah, you have become greater than your grandfather!' Ah, he has attained the highest point in splendour, fame and the glory of *brahman* – the son who is born to a Brāhmaṇa who knows this!

CHAPTER 5

1. Now the lineage of the teaching. The son of Pautimāṣī[55] received it from the son of Kātyāyanī, the son of Kātyāyanī from the son of Gautamī, the son of Gautamī from the son of Bhāradvājī, the son of Bhāradvājī from the son of Pārāśarī, the son of Pārāśarī from the son of Aupasvastī, the son of Aupasvastī from the son of Pārāśarī, the son of Pārāśarī from the son of Kātyāyanī, the son of Kātyāyanī from the son of Kauśikī, the son of Kauśikī from the son of Ālambī and the son of Vaiyāghrapadī, the son of Vaiyāghrapadī from the son of Kāṇvī and the son of Kāpī, the son of Kāpī

2. from the son of Ātreyī, the son of Ātreyī from the son of Gautamī, the son of Gautamī from the son of Bhāradvājī, the son of Bhāradvājī from the son of Pārāśarī, the son of Pārāśarī from the son of Vātsī, the son of Vātsī from the son of Pārāśarī, the son of Pārāśarī from the son of Vārkāruṇī, the son of Vārkāruṇī from the son of Vārkāruṇī, the son of Vārkāruṇī from the son of Ārtabhāgī, the son of Ārtabhāgī from the son of Śauṅgī, the son of Śauṅgī from the son of Sāṅkṛtī, the son of Sāṅkṛtī from the son of Ālambāyanī, the son of Ālambāyanī from the son of Ālambī, the son of Ālambī from the son of Jāyantī, the son of Jāyantī from the son of Māṇḍūkāyanī, the son of Māṇḍūkāyanī from the son of Māṇḍūkī, the son of Māṇḍūkī from the son of Śāṇḍilī, the son of Śāṇḍilī from the son of Rāthītarī, the son of Rāthītarī from the son of Bhālukī, the son of Bhālukī from the two sons of Krauñcikī, the two sons of Krauñcikī from the son of Vaidabhṛtī, the son of Vaidabhṛtī from the son of Kārśakeyī, the son of Kārśakeyī from the son of Prācīnayogī, the son of Prācīnayogī from the son of Sāñjīvī, the

son of Sāñjīvī from the son of Prāśnī who lived in Āsuri's house,[56] the son of Prāśnī from Āsurāyaṇa, Āsurāyaṇa from Āsuri, Āsuri
3. from Yājñavalkya, Yājñavalkya from Uddālaka, Uddālaka from Aruṇa, Aruṇa from Upaveśi, Upaveśi from Kuśri, Kuśri from Vājaśravas, Vājaśravas from Jihvāvat Bādhyoga, Jihvāvat Bādhyoga from Asita Vārṣagaṇa, Asita Vārṣagaṇa from Harita Kaśyapa, Harita Kaśyapa from Śilpa Kaśyapa, Śilpa Kaśyapa from Kaśyapa Naidhruvi, Kaśyapa Naidhruvi from Vāc, Vāc from Ambhiṇī, Ambhiṇī from Āditya. These White Yajus verses of Āditya were taught by Vājasaneya Yājñavalkya.

4. The same as far as 'the son of Sāñjīvī'.[57] The son of Sāñjīvī received the teaching from Māṇḍūkāyani, Māṇḍūkāyani from Māṇḍavya, Māṇḍavya from Kautsa, Kautsa from Māhitthi, Māhitthi from Vāmakakṣāyaṇa, Vāmakakṣāyaṇa from Śāṇḍilya, Śāṇḍilya from Vātsya, Vātsya from Kuśri, Kuśri from Yajñavacas Rājastambāyana, Yajñavacas Rājastambāyana from Tura Kāvaṣeya, Tura Kāvaṣeya from Prajāpati, Prajāpati from *brahman*. *Brahman* is self-born: homage to *brahman*.

OṂ. *Together may it protect us two:*[58]
Together may it profit us two:
Together may we do a hero's work.[59]
May we learn intelligently:
May we never hate one another.

OṂ. Peace, peace, peace.

CHĀNDOGYA UPANIṢAD

The Chanters' Teaching

OṂ. *May my limbs, speech, breath, eye, ear, strength and all senses grow strong. Everything is the* brahman *of the Upaniṣads. May I not reject* brahman. *May* brahman *not reject me. May there be no rejecting. May there be no rejecting of me.*[1] *May all the* dharmas *which are in the Upaniṣads be in me, who delight in the self. May they be in me.*

OṂ. *Peace, peace, peace.*

BOOK I

CHAPTER 1

1. OṂ. One should contemplate the syllable OṂ as the Udgītha,[1] for one sings aloud (*ud-gai-*) OṂ. To explain further:
2. The earth is the essence of all beings, the waters the essence of earth, plants the essence of the waters, a man (*puruṣa*) the essence of plants, speech the essence of a man, the *ṛc* the essence of speech, the *sāman* the essence of the *ṛc*, the Udgītha the essence of the *sāman*.
3. This, the Udgītha, is the final essence[2] of essences, the supreme, the ultimate, the eighth.
4. It has been debated, 'Which, which is the *ṛc*? Which, which is the *sāman*? Which, which is the Udgītha?'
5. Speech is the *ṛc*. Breath is the *sāman*. The syllable OṂ is the Udgītha. This is a couple – speech and breath, and *ṛc* and *sāman*.
6. This couple come together in the syllable OṂ. When two come together as a couple, they fulfil one another's desire.
7. The one who, knowing this, contemplates the syllable as the Udgītha becomes a fulfiller of desires.
8. It is the syllable of assent, for when one assents to something one says, 'OṂ.' Assent is accomplishment, and the one who, knowing this, contemplates the syllable as the Udgītha becomes an accomplisher of desires.
9. By it the threefold knowledge[3] exists: one sounds OṂ, one praises OṂ, one chants aloud OṂ,[4] for reverence of the syllable with its greatness and essence.

10. So both do it, the one who knows this and the one who does not know. But knowledge and ignorance are different. What one does with knowledge, faith, the inner meaning (*upaniṣad*), is more powerful.

This is the explanation of the syllable.

CHAPTER 2

1. When the gods and the demons, both descendants of Prajāpati, strove together, the gods took up the Udgītha, thinking, 'With this we will overcome them.'[5]
2. They contemplated the breath in the nose as the Udgītha. The demons pierced it with evil. That is why one smells with it both the sweet-scented and the foul-smelling, because it was pierced with evil.
3. Then they contemplated speech as the Udgītha. The demons pierced it with evil. That is why one speaks with it both truth and falsehood, because it was pierced with evil.
4. Then they contemplated the eye as the Udgītha. The demons pierced it with evil. That is why one sees with it both what should be seen and what should not be seen,[6] because it was pierced with evil.
5. Then they contemplated the ear as the Udgītha. The demons pierced it with evil. That is why one hears with it both what should be heard and what should not be heard, because it was pierced with evil.
6. Then they contemplated the mind as the Udgītha. The demons pierced it with evil. That is why one imagines with it both what should be imagined and what should not be imagined, because it was pierced with evil.
7. Then they contemplated the breath which is in the mouth as the Udgītha. The demons, attacking it, perished, as one attacking a solid rock would perish.
8. The one who wishes ill for and is hostile to the one who knows this perishes as one attacking a solid rock perishes, for he is a solid rock.

9. With it[7] one does not discern the sweet-scented or the foul-smelling, for it is free from evil: what one eats and drinks with it protects the other breaths. At the end, when one does not find it, one departs: for at the end, they say, one has one's mouth open.

10. Aṅgiras contemplated it as the Udgītha: indeed, folk consider it to *be* Aṅgiras, because it is the essence (*rasa*) of the limbs (*aṅga*).

11. So Bṛhaspati contemplated it as the Udgītha: indeed, folk consider it to *be* Bṛhaspati, because speech is *bṛhatī* and it is its lord (*pati*).

12. So Ayāsya contemplated it as the Udgītha: indeed, folk consider it to *be* Ayāsya, because it goes (*ayate*) from the mouth (*āsya*).

13. So Baka Dālbhya knew it. He became the Udgātṛ of the people of the Naimiṣa forest, and used to sing into being all their desires.

14. The one who, knowing this, contemplates the syllable as the Udgītha becomes a singer-into-being of all desires.

So much regarding oneself.

CHAPTER 3

1. Now regarding deities:

One should contemplate the one who gives heat[8] as the Udgītha. Rising, it sings aloud (*ud-gai-*) to creatures. Rising, it destroys darkness and fear. The one who knows this becomes a destroyer of darkness and fear.

2. This one and that one[9] are the same. That one is hot and this one is hot (*uṣṇa*). Folk call this one '*svara*', and that one '*svara*', '*pratyāsvara*'.[10] So one should contemplate this one and that one as the Udgītha.

3. One should contemplate the between-breath (*vyāna*) as the Udgītha. When one breathes out, that is the out-breath (*prāṇa*): when one breathes in, that is the in-breath (*apāna*). The meeting-point of the out-breath and the in-breath is the between-breath.

What the between-breath is, speech is. So one utters speech while neither breathing out nor breathing in.[11]

4. What speech is, the *ṛc* is. So one utters the *ṛc* while neither breathing out nor breathing in. What the *ṛc* is, the *sāman* is. So one sings the *sāman* while neither breathing out nor breathing in. What the *sāman* is, the Udgītha is. So one sings the Udgītha while neither breathing out nor breathing in.[12]

5. Whatever other works there are that require effort, such as rubbing to light a fire, running a race, or drawing a strong bow, one does while neither breathing out nor breathing in. For this reason one should contemplate the between-breath as the Udgītha.

6. One should contemplate the syllables of Udgītha, '*ud, gī, tha*'. The breath is *ud*, since one rises up (*ut-thā-*) by means of the breath. Speech is *gī*, since folk call speech 'voice' (*gir*). Food is *tha*, since all this rests (*sthā-*) on food.

7. Sky is *ud*, middle-air is *gī*, earth is *tha*. The sun is *ud*, air is *gī*, fire is *tha*. The Sāmaveda is *ud*, the Yajurveda is *gī*, the Ṛgveda is *tha*.

Speech gives milk, the milk of speech, for him, and he becomes a possessor of food, an eater of food – the one who, knowing these things, contemplates the syllables of Udgītha, '*ud, gī, tha*'.

8. Now the fulfilment of hopes:

One should contemplate the refuges, as they are called. One should go for refuge to the *sāman* verse which one is about to chant.

9. One should go for refuge to the *ṛc* verse on which it is based, to the Ṛṣi to whom it belongs, and to the deity to whom one is about to chant.

10. One should go for refuge to the metre in which one is about to chant, to the hymn-sequence[13] from which one is about to chant.

11. One should go for refuge to the direction towards which one is about to chant.

12. Finally, taking refuge in oneself (*ātman*), one should chant without carelessness, reflecting on one's desire. So whatever

desire one may have while chanting is quickly fulfilled: whatever desire one may have while chanting.[14]

CHAPTER 4

1. One should contemplate the syllable OṂ as the Udgītha, for one sings aloud OṂ. To explain further:

2. The gods, fearing Death, entered into the threefold knowledge. They covered themselves with the metres. It is because they covered (*chad-*) themselves with them that the metres are called metres (*chandas*).

3. Death saw them there, in the *ṛc*, *sāman* and *yajus*, as one might see a fish in water. Realizing this, they went up out of the *ṛc*, *sāman* and *yajus*, and entered into the sound (*svara*).

4. When one receives a *ṛc* verse, one sounds OṂ: so with a *sāman*, and so with a *yajus*. This sound is what the syllable is: it is immortal, fearless. By entering it the gods became immortal, fearless.

5. The one who, knowing this, reverberates the syllable enters into the syllable, the sound, the immortal, the fearless. By entering it, he becomes immortal as the gods are immortal.

CHAPTER 5

1. What the Udgītha is, the reverberation (*praṇava*) is: what the reverberation is, the Udgītha is. So the sun is the Udgītha: it is the reverberation, since it moves with the sound OṂ.

2. 'I sang only of the one: that is why I have just you,' said Kauṣītaki to his son. 'You must reflect on its rays, then you will have many.'[15]

So much regarding deities.

3. Now regarding oneself:

One should contemplate the breath in the mouth as the Udgītha, since it moves with the sound OṂ.

4. 'I sang only of the one: that is why I have just you,' said Kauṣītaki to his son. 'You must sing of the breaths as abundance, thinking, "I will have many."'

5. What the Udgītha is, the reverberation is: what the reverberation is, the Udgītha is. Knowing this, even if the Udgītha is badly sung, one puts it right again from the Hotṛ's seat. One puts it right again.

CHAPTER 6

1. This[16] is the *ṛc*: fire is the *sāman*. So the *sāman* is carried on the *ṛc*. When the *sāman* is sung it is carried on the *ṛc*. This is *sā*: fire is *ama*.[17] Hence '*sāman*'.

2. Middle-air is the *ṛc*: air is the *sāman*. So the *sāman* is carried on the *ṛc*. When the *sāman* is sung it is carried on the *ṛc*. Middle-air is *sā*: air is *ama*. Hence '*sāman*'.

3. Sky is the *ṛc*: the sun is the *sāman*. So the *sāman* is carried on the *ṛc*. When the *sāman* is sung it is carried on the *ṛc*. Sky is *sā*: the sun is *ama*. Hence '*sāman*'.

4. The constellations are the *ṛc*: the moon is the *sāman*. So the *sāman* is carried on the *ṛc*. When the *sāman* is sung it is carried on the *ṛc*. The constellations are *sā*: the moon is *ama*. Hence '*sāman*'.

5. The white light of the sun is the *ṛc*: the blue light, deeper than black, is the *sāman*. So the *sāman* is carried on the *ṛc*. When the *sāman* is sung it is carried on the *ṛc*.

6. The white light of the sun is *sā*: the blue light, deeper than black, is *ama*. Hence '*sāman*'. The person made of gold who is seen within the sun, with golden beard, golden hair, all golden to the nail-tips,

7. Has eyes like the monkey-face lotus.[18] His name is Ud.[19] He has risen (*udita*) above all evils. The one who knows this rises above all evils.

8. The *ṛc* and the *sāman* are his minstrels.[20] Hence 'Udgītha';

hence, indeed, 'Udgātṛ', since he is Ud's singer (*gātṛ*). 'He rules over the worlds which are beyond that, and over the desires of the gods.'[21]

So much regarding deities.

CHAPTER 7

1. Now regarding oneself:

Speech is the *ṛc*: breath is the *sāman*. So the *sāman* is carried on the *ṛc*. When the *sāman* is sung it is carried on the *ṛc*. Speech is *sā*: breath is *ama*. Hence '*sāman*'.

2. The eye is the *ṛc*: the self is the *sāman*. So the *sāman* is carried on the *ṛc*. When the *sāman* is sung it is carried on the *ṛc*. The eye is *sā*: the self is *ama*. Hence '*sāman*'.

3. The ear is the *ṛc*: the mind is the *sāman*. So the *sāman* is carried on the *ṛc*. When the *sāman* is sung it is carried on the *ṛc*. The ear is *sā*: the mind is *ama*. Hence '*sāman*'.

4. The white light of the eye is the *ṛc*: the blue light, deeper than black, is the *sāman*. So the *sāman* is carried on the *ṛc*. When the *sāman* is sung it is carried on the *ṛc*. The white light of the eye is *sā*: the blue light, deeper than black, is *ama*. Hence '*sāman*'.

5. The person who is seen within the eye – that is the *ṛc*; that is the *sāman*; that is the Uktha; that is the *yajus*; that is *brahman*. This one's form is that one's form;[22] this one's minstrels are that one's minstrels; this one's name is that one's name.

6. 'He rules over the worlds which are below this, and over the desires of human beings.' Those who sing to the lute sing of him, and so are rewarded with wealth.

7. The one who, knowing this, sings the *sāman* sings of both. Through that one he gains the worlds which are beyond that, and the desires of the gods.

8. Through this one he gains the worlds which are below this, and the desires of human beings. Therefore the Udgātṛ who knows this should say,

9. 'What desire of yours should I sing into being?': for the one

who, knowing this, sings the *sāman* has the power of singing desires into being: the one who sings the *sāman*.

CHAPTER 8

1. There were three who were expert in the Udgītha: Śilaka Śālāvatya, Caikitāyana Dālbhya and Pravāhaṇa Jaivali. They said, 'We are expert in the Udgītha: come, let us have a debate about the Udgītha.'

2. 'Agreed,' they said, and sat down together.

Pravāhaṇa Jaivali said, 'Blessed ones, speak first, and I will listen to you two Brāhmaṇas as you speak.'

3. Śilaka Śālāvatya said to Caikitāyana Dālbhya, 'Come, let me ask you a question.'

'Ask,' he said.

4. 'What does the *sāman* go back to?'[23]

'Sound (*svara*),' he said.

'What does sound go back to?'

'The breath,' he said.

'What does the breath go back to?'

'Food,' he said.

'What does food go back to?'

'The waters,' he said.

5. 'What do the waters go back to?'

'That world,' he said.

'What does that world go back to?'

'One should not carry it on beyond the heavenly world,' he said. 'We establish the *sāman* on the heavenly world, for the *sāman* is praised as heaven.'

6. Śilaka Śālāvatya said to Caikitāyana Dālbhya, 'Dālbhya, your *sāman* is unsupported. If someone were to say now, "Your head will split apart", your head *would* split apart.'

7. 'Come then, I must know it from *you*, blessed one.'

'You shall know it,' he said.

'What does that world go back to?'

'This world,' he said.

'What does this world go back to?'

'One should not carry it on beyond this world, the support,' he said. 'We establish the *sāman* on the world, the support, for the *sāman* is praised as the support.'

8. Pravāhaṇa Jaivali said to him, 'Śālāvatya, your *sāman* is finite. If someone were to say now, "Your head will split apart", your head *would* split apart.'

'Come then, I must know it from *you*, blessed one.'

'You shall know it,' he said.

CHAPTER 9

1. 'What does this world go back to?'

'Space,' he said, 'for all beings arise from space and sink back into space. Space is older than they: space is the final end.'

2. The Udgītha is higher than the highest; it is infinite. The one who, knowing this, contemplates the Udgītha as higher than the highest gets what is higher than the highest, conquers worlds which are higher than the highest.

3. Atidhanvan Śaunaka, having taught this to Udaraśāṇḍilya, said, 'As long as those in your progeny know the Udgītha as such, their life in this world will be higher than the highest.

4. 'They will have a world in *that* world, too.'

Likewise, for the one who, knowing this, contemplates it as such, his life in this world is higher than the highest. He will have a world in *that* world, too: a world in that world, too.

CHAPTER 10

1. When the Kuru-country had been battered by hailstones,[24] Uṣasti Cākrāyaṇa, being destitute, lived with his wife Āṭikī in an elephant-keeper's village.[25]

2. He begged alms from the elephant-keeper, who was eating black beans.

The elephant-keeper said, 'There are none but these which have been served to me.'

3. Uṣasti said, 'Give me some of them.'

He gave them to him, and said, 'Come, here is water to go with it.'

Uṣasti said, 'But then I would be drinking leftovers.'

4. 'So weren't *these* leftovers, too?'

'If I had not eaten them, I would not have lived,' he said, 'but drinking the water is up to me.'[26]

5. When he had eaten, he took those that were left, for his wife. She had got good alms earlier, so she took them and put them in store.

6. When he got up in the morning, he said, 'Ah! If only we could get some food! Then we could get a little bit of wealth. The king is going to offer a sacrifice. He would have chosen me for all the priestly offices.'

7. His wife said, 'Well, husband, here are the black beans!' He ate them, and went to the sacrifice which had been prepared.

8. He sat down near the Udgātṛ priests, who were about to sing praises at the praising-place.[27] He said to the Prastotṛ,

9. 'Prastotṛ, if you sing the Prastāva without knowing the deity that is associated with the Prastāva, your head will split apart.'[28]

10. Likewise, he said to the Udgātṛ, 'Udgātṛ, if you sing the Udgītha without knowing the deity that is associated with the Udgītha, your head will split apart.'

11. Likewise, he said to the Pratihartṛ, 'Pratihartṛ, if you sing the Pratihāra without knowing the deity that is associated with the Pratihāra, your head will split apart.'

They ceased and sat in silence.

CHAPTER 11

1. The patron of the sacrifice[29] said, 'Blessed one, I would very much like to know who you are.'

'Uṣasti Cākrāyaṇa,' he said.

2. The patron said, 'Blessed one, I searched for you for all the priestly offices. Because I could not find you, blessed one, I chose the others.

3. 'Blessed one, please act for me in all the priestly offices.'[30]

'I will. But let these still offer praise, under my direction. But you should give me as much wealth as you give them.'

'I will,' said the patron of the sacrifice.

4. Then the Prastotṛ approached him, saying, 'Blessed one, you said to me, "Prastotṛ, if you sing the Prastāva without knowing the deity that is associated with the Prastāva, your head will split apart." Which is that deity?'

5. 'The breath,' he said. 'All beings enter into the breath, rise up with the breath. That is the deity that is associated with the Prastāva. If you had sung the Prastāva without knowing it, your head would have split apart when I told you this.'

6. Then the Udgātṛ approached him, saying, 'Blessed one, you said to me, "Udgātṛ, if you sing the Udgītha without knowing the deity that is associated with the Udgītha, your head will split apart." Which is that deity?'

7. 'The sun,' he said. 'All beings sing (*gai-*) to the sun when it is on high (*uccaiḥ*). That is the deity that is associated with the Udgītha. If you had sung the Udgītha without knowing it, your head would have split apart when I told you this.'

8. Then the Pratihartṛ approached him, saying, 'Blessed one, you said to me, "Pratihartṛ, if you sing the Pratihāra without knowing the deity that is associated with the Pratihāra, your head will split apart." Which is that deity?'

9. 'Food,' he said. 'All beings live by collecting (*prati-hṛ-*) food. That is the deity that is associated with the Pratihāra. If you had sung the Pratihāra without knowing it, your head would have split apart when I told you this – when I told you this.'

CHAPTER 12

1. Now the Udgītha of the dogs:[31]

Once Baka Dālbhya, or Glāva Maitreya, went forth to study.

2. A white dog appeared to him. Other dogs approached that one and said, 'Blessed one, sing into being food for us, for we are hungry.'

3. He told them, 'Meet me just here in the morning.' Baka Dālbhya, or Glāva Maitreya, waited.

4. Just as those who are about to chant the Bahiṣpavamāna glide around holding on to one another,[32] *they* glided around. Then, sitting down together, they uttered the sound *hiṃ*.

5. 'OṂ . . . Let us eat . . . ! OṂ . . . Let us drink . . . ! OṂ . . . May the god Varuṇa, may Prajāpati, may Savitṛ . . . bring food here . . . ! O lord of food . . . bring here . . . bring food here . . . ! OṂ . . . !'[33]

CHAPTER 13

1. This world is the sound *hāu*. Air is the sound *hāi*. The moon is the sound *atha*. The self is the sound *iha*. Fire is the sound *ī*.[34]

2. The sun is the sound *ū*. Invocation is the sound *e*. The Viśvedevas are the sound *auhoyi*. Prajāpati is the sound *hiṃ*. Breath is *svara*. Food is *yā*. Speech is *virāj*.

3. The thirteenth ritual cry, *huṃ*, which is variable, is undefined.

4. Speech gives milk, the milk of speech, for him, and he becomes a possessor of food, an eater of food – the one who knows the inner meaning (*upaniṣad*) of the *sāman*: the one who knows the inner meaning.

BOOK II

CHAPTER 1

1. OṂ. Contemplation of the *sāman* as a whole is good (*sādhu*). What is good, folk call 'prosperity (*sāman*)'; what is not good, 'not prosperity'.
2. They say, too, 'He approached him tactfully (*sāmnā*)',[1] meaning 'He approached him well'; and they say, 'He approached him tactlessly (*asāmnā*)', meaning 'He approached him badly'.
3. And they say, too, 'Oh! Lucky (*sāman*) for us!' meaning 'Oh! Good for us!' when something good happens; and they say, 'Oh! Unlucky (*asāman*) for us!' meaning 'Oh! Bad for us!' when something bad happens.
4. Good *dharmas* will come quickly and do homage to him – the one who, knowing this, contemplates the good as *sāman*.

CHAPTER 2

1. One should contemplate the fivefold *sāman* in the worlds. Earth is the Hiṅkāra; fire is the Prastāva; middle-air is the Udgītha; the sun is the Pratihāra; sky is the Nidhana. That is going upward.
2. But coming downward, sky is the Hiṅkāra; the sun is the Prastāva; middle-air is the Udgītha; fire is the Pratihāra; earth is the Nidhana.
3. Worlds upward and downward are made fit for the one

who, knowing this, contemplates the fivefold *sāman* in the worlds.

CHAPTER 3

1. One should contemplate the fivefold *sāman* in rain. The wind beforehand is the Hiṅkāra; when the rain-cloud forms, that is the Prastāva; when it rains, that is the Udgītha; when it lightens and thunders, that is the Pratihāra; when it ceases, that is the Nidhana.
2. It rains for him, and he makes it rain – the one who, knowing this, contemplates the fivefold *sāman* in the rain.

CHAPTER 4

1. One should contemplate the fivefold *sāman* in all water. When the rain-cloud gathers, that is the Hiṅkāra; when it rains, that is the Prastāva; that which flows east is the Udgītha; that which flows west is the Pratihāra; the ocean is the Nidhana.
2. He does not die in water, but becomes rich in water – the one who, knowing this, contemplates the fivefold *sāman* in all water.

CHAPTER 5

1. One should contemplate the fivefold *sāman* in the seasons. Spring is the Hiṅkāra; summer is the Prastāva; the rainy season is the Udgītha; autumn is the Pratihāra; winter is the Nidhana.
2. The seasons are tempered to him, and he becomes rich in seasons[2] – the one who, knowing this, contemplates the fivefold *sāman* in the seasons.

CHAPTER 6

1. One should contemplate the fivefold *sāman* in the animals (*paśu*). Goats are the Hiṅkāra; sheep are the Prastāva; cows are the Udgītha; horses are the Pratihāra; man (*puruṣa*) is the Nidhana.
2. Animals come to him, and he becomes rich in animals – the one who, knowing this, contemplates the fivefold *sāman* in the animals.

CHAPTER 7

1. One should contemplate the fivefold *sāman*, the higher than the highest, in the breaths. Breath is the Hiṅkāra; speech is the Prastāva; the eye is the Udgītha; the ear is the Pratihāra; the mind is the Nidhana.
2. He gets what is higher than the highest, wins worlds that are higher than the highest – the one who, knowing this, contemplates the fivefold *sāman*, the higher than the highest, in the breaths.

So much about the fivefold.

CHAPTER 8

1. Now about the sevenfold:

One should contemplate the sevenfold *sāman* in speech.[3] Whatever in speech is *huṃ* is the Hiṅkāra; whatever is *pra* is the Prastāva; whatever is *ā* is the Ādi;
2. Whatever is *ud* is the Udgītha; whatever is *prati* is the Pratihāra; whatever is *upa* is the Upadrava; whatever is *ni* is the Nidhana.[4]
3. Speech gives milk, the milk of speech, for him, and he

becomes a possessor of food, an eater of food – the one who, knowing this, contemplates the sevenfold *sāman* in speech.

CHAPTER 9

1. One should contemplate the sevenfold *sāman* as the sun. It is always the same (*sama*), hence it is *sāman*. Everyone thinks,[5] 'It faces me, it faces me.' It is the same for everyone, hence it is *sāman*.

2. One should know that all beings are connected with it. Its form[6] before rising is the Hiṅkāra. The domestic animals (*paśu*) are connected with that: because they share in the Hiṅkāra of the *sāman* they go '*hiṃ*'.[7]

3. Its form when it has first risen is the Prastāva. Human beings are connected with that: because they share in the Prastāva of the *sāman* they are lovers of praise (*prastuti*), lovers of fame.

4. Its form at the time when cattle meet is the Ādi. The birds are connected with that: because they share in the Ādi of the *sāman* they fly around in middle-air relying on just themselves (*ātmānam ādāya*), without a support.

5. Its form just at midday is the Udgītha. The gods are connected with that: because they share in the Udgītha of the *sāman* they are the best of the children of Prajāpati.

6. Its form after midday but before evening falls[8] is the Pratihāra. Embryos are connected with that: because they share in the Pratihāra of the *sāman* they are held together (*pratihṛta*) and do not fall down.

7. Its form after evening falls but before setting is the Upadrava. The forest animals are connected with that: because they share in the Upadrava of the *sāman*, when they see a human being they run away (*upa-dru-*) to a thicket or cave.

8. Its form when it has first set is the Nidhana. The ancestors are connected with that: because they share in the Nidhana of the *sāman*, folk give them a place (*ni-dhā-*).

This is how one contemplates the sevenfold *sāman* as the sun.

CHAPTER 10

1. Then one should contemplate the sevenfold *sāman* as equal to the self, and as beyond death. 'Hiṅkāra' is three syllables: 'Prastāva' is three syllables, so it is equal.
2. 'Ādi' is two syllables: 'Pratihāra' has four syllables. Take one from that to this, then it is equal.
3. 'Udgītha' is three syllables: 'Upadrava' is four syllables. With three each it becomes equal, but a syllable (*akṣara*) is left over. *That* [*a-kṣa-ra*] is three syllables, so it is equal.
4. 'Nidhana' is three syllables, so *that* becomes equal. There are twenty-two syllables here.
5. By twenty-one one reaches the sun: the sun is the twenty-first from here. By the twenty-second one conquers what is beyond the sun, heaven, free from sorrow.
6. He gains victory over the sun – has victory greater than victory over the sun[9] – the one who, knowing this, contemplates the sevenfold *sāman* here as equal to the self, and as beyond death: who contemplates the *sāman*.

CHAPTER 11

1. The mind is the Hiṅkāra: speech is the Prastāva; the eye is the Udgītha; the ear is the Pratihāra; the breath is the Nidhana. This is the *Gāyatra*, woven on the breaths (*prāṇa*).
2. The one who knows the *Gāyatra*, woven on the breaths, becomes alive (*prāṇin*): he attains his full lifespan, lives long, becomes great in offspring and animals, great in fame. One should be of great mind: that should be the vow.

CHAPTER 12

1. When one rubs the sticks together,[10] that is the Hiṅkāra; when smoke is produced, that is the Prastāva; when it bursts into flame, that is the Udgītha; when there are embers, that is the Pratihāra; when it dies down, that is the Nidhana – when it goes out, that is the Nidhana. This is the *Rathantara*, woven on fire.

2. The one who knows the *Rathantara*, woven on fire, becomes radiant with *brahman*, an eater of food: he attains his full lifespan, lives long, becomes great in offspring and animals, great in fame. One should not sip water or spit facing a fire: that should be the vow.

CHAPTER 13

1. When one invites a woman,[11] that is the Hiṅkāra; when one makes known one's desire, that is the Prastāva; when one lies close to the woman, that is the Udgītha; when one lies with her, that is the Pratihāra; when one reaches the climax, that is the Nidhana – when one reaches the end, that is the Nidhana. This is the *Vāmadevya*, woven on the sexual act.

2. The one who knows the *Vāmadevya*, woven on the sexual act, achieves the sexual act, procreates from every sexual act: he attains his full lifespan, lives long, becomes great in offspring and animals, great in fame. One should not reject any woman: that should be the vow.

CHAPTER 14

1. Rising, it is the Hiṅkāra; risen, it is the Prastāva; at midday, it is the Udgītha; in the afternoon, it is the Pratihāra; setting, it is the Nidhana. This is the *Bṛhat*, woven on the sun.

2. The one who knows the *Bṛhat*, woven on the sun, becomes radiant, an eater of food: he attains his full lifespan, lives long, becomes great in offspring and animals, great in fame. One should not speak ill of the one who gives heat: that should be the vow.

CHAPTER 15

1. When clouds gather, that is the Hiṅkāra; when a rain-cloud forms, that is the Prastāva; when it rains, that is the Udgītha; when it lightens and thunders, that is the Pratihāra; when it ceases, that is the Nidhana. This is the *Vairūpa*, woven on Parjanya.
2. The one who knows the *Vairūpa*, woven on Parjanya, pens in all kinds of (*virūpa*) fine-looking (*surūpa*) animals: he attains his full lifespan, lives long, becomes great in offspring and animals, great in fame. One should not speak ill of the one who rains: that should be the vow.

CHAPTER 16

1. Spring is the Hiṅkāra; summer is the Prastāva; the rainy season is the Udgītha; autumn is the Pratihāra; winter is the Nidhana. This is the *Vairāja*, woven on the seasons.
2. The one who knows the *Vairāja*, woven on the seasons, excels (*virāj-*) in offspring and animals and in the radiance of *brahman*: he attains his full lifespan, lives long, becomes great in offspring and animals, great in fame. One should not speak ill of the seasons: that should be the vow.

CHAPTER 17

1. Earth is the Hiṅkāra; middle-air is the Prastāva; sky is the Udgītha; the directions are the Pratihāra; the ocean is the Nidhana. These are the *Śakvarīs*, woven on the worlds.
2. The one who knows the *Śakvarīs*, woven on the worlds, becomes a possessor of worlds: he attains his full lifespan, lives long, becomes great in offspring and animals, great in fame. One should not speak ill of the worlds: that should be the vow.

CHAPTER 18

1. Goats are the Hiṅkāra; sheep are the Prastāva; cows are the Udgītha; horses are the Pratihāra; man is the Nidhana. These are the *Revatīs*, woven on the animals.
2. The one who knows the *Revatīs*, woven on the animals, becomes rich in animals: he attains his full lifespan, lives long, becomes great in offspring and animals, great in fame. One should not speak ill of the animals: that should be the vow.

CHAPTER 19

1. Hair[12] is the Hiṅkāra; skin is the Prastāva; flesh is the Udgītha; bone is the Pratihāra; marrow is the Nidhana. This is the *Yajñāyajñīya*, woven on the parts of the body.
2. The one who knows the *Yajñāyajñīya*, woven on the parts of the body, possesses the parts of the body, and is not maimed in any part: he attains his full lifespan, lives long, becomes great in offspring and animals, great in fame. One should not eat meat for a year: that should be the vow. Or one should not eat meat: that should be the vow.

CHAPTER 20

1. Fire is the Hiṅkāra; air is the Prastāva; the sun is the Udgītha; the constellations are the Pratihāra; the moon is the Nidhana. This is the *Rājana*, woven on the deities.
2. The one who knows the *Rājana*, woven on the deities, shares a world with, shares power with, attains union with the deities:[13] he attains his full lifespan, lives long, becomes great in offspring and animals, great in fame. One should not speak ill of Brāhmaṇas: that should be the vow.

CHAPTER 21

1. The threefold knowledge is the Hiṅkāra; the three worlds are the Prastāva; fire, air and sun are the Udgītha; constellations, birds and light-rays are the Pratihāra; snakes, *gandharvas* and ancestors are the Nidhana. This is the *sāman*, woven on everything.
2. The one who knows the *sāman*, woven on everything, becomes everything.
3. There is a verse about it:

> There is nothing else beyond them, older
> Than the threes, the fivefold threes.

4. The one who knows this knows everything. All the directions bring him tribute. One should contemplate, 'I am everything': that should be the vow. That should be the vow.

CHAPTER 22

1. I recommend the roaring style of *sāman*, called 'animal-like': it is the Udgītha of Agni. The 'indistinct' belongs to Prajāpati, the 'distinct' to Soma, the 'soft and smooth' to Vāyu, the

'smooth and powerful' to Indra, the 'crane-like' to Bṛhaspati, the 'ill-sounding' to Varuṇa. One should practise all of them, but avoid the one that belongs to Varuṇa.

2. Thinking, 'Let me sing into being immortality for the gods!', one should sing it into being. 'Let me sing into being the offering (*svadhā*) for the ancestors, hope for human beings, grass and water for the animals, a heavenly world for the patron of the sacrifice, food for myself!': meditating on these things in the mind, one should chant undistracted.

3. All vowels are the selves of Indra; all sibilants are the selves of Prajāpati; all stops are the selves of Death,[14] If someone finds fault with one regarding one's vowels, one should say, 'I have gone for refuge to Indra: he will answer you.'

4. If someone finds fault with one regarding one's sibilants, one should say, 'I have gone for refuge to Prajāpati: he will crush you.' If someone finds fault with one regarding one's stops, one should say, 'I have gone for refuge to Death: he will burn you up.'

5. One should pronounce all vowels with resonance, with strength, thinking, 'Let me bestow strength on Indra!' One should pronounce all sibilants without swallowing, without dropping, distinctly, thinking, 'Let me give myself up to Prajāpati!' One should pronounce all stops crisply, without slurring, thinking, 'Let me keep myself from Death!'

CHAPTER 23

1. There are three who have *dharma* as their trunk. The first believes in sacrifice, study and giving, the second in asceticism (*tapas*); the third is the *brahmacārin*, living in his teacher's family, completely dedicating himself to his teacher's family. All these win worlds of merit. The one who rests in *brahman* attains immortality.[15]

2. Prajāpati heated up (*abhi-tap-*) the worlds. When they were heated up, the threefold knowledge issued from them. He

heated *that* up. When it was heated up, the sounds[16] BHŪḤ, BHUVAḤ, SVAḤ issued from it.

3. He heated *them* up. When they were heated up, the OṂ issued from them. Just as all leaves are penetrated and joined together by their main vein, all speech is penetrated and joined together by the OṂ. The OṂ is all this. The OṂ is all this.

CHAPTER 24

1. Scholars of *brahman* say, 'Since the morning pressing[17] belongs to the Vasus, the midday pressing to the Rudras, and the third pressing to the Ādityas and the Viśvedevas,

2. 'Where, then, is the world of the patron of the sacrifice?' How could one perform a sacrifice without knowing this? One should perform it knowing this:

3. Before the start of the morning recitation,[18] the patron sits down behind the Gārhapatya fire, facing north, and sings the *sāman* of the Vasus:

4. 'Open . . . up . . . the door of the world . . . that
we may see you . . .
For the sake of king . . . *huṃ* . . . *ā* . . .
ship . . . *o* . . . *ā* . . . !'[19]

5. Then he makes an offering, saying, 'Homage to Agni, dwelling on earth, dwelling in a world. Find a world for me, the patron of the sacrifice. This is the patron's world: here shall I go,

6. 'As patron, after my lifespan. SVĀHĀ!' Then, saying, 'Draw back the bolt!', he stands up. The Vasus offer him the morning pressing.

7. Before the start of the midday pressing, the patron sits down behind the Agnīdhrīya fire, facing north, and sings the *sāman* of the Rudras:

8. 'Open . . . up . . . the door of the world . . . that we
may see you . . .
For the sake of glo . . . *huṃ* . . . *ā* . . .
ry . . . *o* . . . *ā* . . . !'

9. Then he makes an offering, saying, 'Homage to Vāyu, dwelling in middle-air, dwelling in a world. Find a world for me, the patron of the sacrifice. This is the patron's world: here shall I go,

10. 'As patron, after my lifespan. SVĀHĀ!' Then, saying, 'Draw back the bolt!', he stands up. The Rudras offer him the midday pressing.

11. Before the start of the third pressing, the patron sits down behind the Āhavanīya fire, facing north, and sings the *sāman* of the Ādityas and the Viśvedevas:

12. 'Open . . . up . . . the door of the world . . . that we
may see you . . .
For the sake of sovereign . . . *huṃ* . . . *ā* . . .
ty . . . *o* . . . *ā* . . . !'

13. – the Ādityas' *sāman*. Then the Viśvedevas' *sāman*:

'Open . . . up . . . the door of the world . . . that we
may see you . . .
For the sake of em . . . *huṃ* . . . *ā* . . .
pire . . . *o* . . . *ā* . . . !'

14. Then he makes an offering, saying, 'Homage to the Ādityas and the Viśvedevas, dwelling in the sky, dwelling in a world. Find a world for me, the patron of the sacrifice.

15. 'This is the patron's world: here shall I go, as patron, after my lifespan. SVĀHĀ!' Then, saying, 'Draw back the bolt!', he stands up.

16. The Ādityas and the Viśvedevas offer him the third pressing. The one who knows this knows the element[20] of the sacrifice: the one who knows this.

BOOK III

CHAPTER 1

1. OṂ. The sun is the honey of the gods. The sky is its horizontal cane,[1] middle-air its honeycomb, the rays its larvae.[2]
2. Its eastward rays are the eastward honey-veins.[3] The *ṛc* verses are the bees, the Ṛgveda the flower, the nectar of immortality the nectar.[4] The *ṛc* verses
3. heated up the Ṛgveda. When it was heated up, its essence was produced from it, as fame, brightness, strength, energy and good food.[5]
4. It flowed out and settled beside the sun. This is what is now[6] the red form of the sun.

CHAPTER 2

1. Its southward rays are the southward honey-veins. The *yajus* verses are the bees, the Yajurveda the flower, the nectar of immortality the nectar.
2. The *yajus* verses heated up the Yajurveda. When it was heated up, its essence was produced from it, as fame, brightness, strength, energy and good food.
3. It flowed out and settled beside the sun. This is what is now the white form of the sun.

CHAPTER 3

1. Its westward rays are the westward honey-veins. The *sāman* verses are the bees, the Sāmaveda the flower, the nectar of immortality the nectar.
2. The *sāman* verses heated up the Sāmaveda. When it was heated up, its essence was produced from it, as fame, brightness, strength, energy and good food.
3. It flowed out and settled beside the sun. This is what is now the black form of the sun.

CHAPTER 4

1. Its northward rays are the northward honey-veins. The verses of the Atharvans and Aṅgirases are the bees, the histories and legends the flower, the nectar of immortality the nectar.
2. The verses of the Atharvans and Aṅgirases heated up the histories and legends. When they were heated up, their essence was produced from them, as fame, brightness, strength, energy and good food.
3. It flowed out and settled beside the sun. This is what is now the deeper-than-black form of the sun.

CHAPTER 5

1. Its upward rays are the upward honey-veins. The secret symbolic statements[7] are the bees, *brahman* the flower, the nectar of immortality the nectar.
2. The secret symbolic statements heated up *brahman*. When it was heated up, its essence was produced from it, as fame, brightness, strength, energy and good food.
3. It flowed out and settled beside the sun. This is what now seems to tremble in the midst of the sun.

4. These are the essences of essences, for the Vedas are the essences and these are the essences of them. These are the nectars of nectars, for the Vedas are the nectars and these are the essences of them.

CHAPTER 6

1. The Vasus, with Agni as their chief, live on the first of these nectars.[8] Gods do not eat or drink: they are satisfied just by seeing the nectar.
2. They enter into this form,[9] and out of this form they arise.
3. The one who knows the nectar in this way becomes one of the Vasus, with Agni as his chief, and is satisfied just by seeing the nectar. He enters into this form, and out of this form he arises.
4. As long as the sun rises in the east and sets in the west he will encompass the overlordship and kingship of the Vasus.

CHAPTER 7

1. The Rudras, with Indra as their chief, live on the second of these nectars. Gods do not eat or drink: they are satisfied just by seeing the nectar.
2. They enter into this form, and out of this form they arise.
3. The one who knows the nectar in this way becomes one of the Rudras, with Indra as his chief, and is satisfied just by seeing the nectar. He enters into this form, and out of this form he arises.
4. Twice as long as the sun rises in the east and sets in the west, it will rise in the south and set in the north. For so long he will encompass the overlordship and kingship of the Rudras.

CHAPTER 8

1. The Ādityas, with Varuṇa as their chief, live on the third of these nectars. Gods do not eat or drink: they are satisfied just by seeing the nectar.
2. They enter into this form, and out of this form they arise.
3. The one who knows the nectar in this way becomes one of the Ādityas, with Varuṇa as his chief, and is satisfied just by seeing the nectar. He enters into this form, and out of this form he arises.
4. Twice as long as the sun rises in the south and sets in the north, it will rise in the west and set in the east. For so long he will encompass the overlordship and kingship of the Ādityas.

CHAPTER 9

1. The Maruts, with Soma as their chief, live on the fourth of these nectars. Gods do not eat or drink: they are satisfied just by seeing the nectar.
2. They enter into this form, and out of this form they arise.
3. The one who knows the nectar in this way becomes one of the Maruts, with Soma as his chief, and is satisfied just by seeing the nectar. He enters into this form, and out of this form he arises.
4. Twice as long as the sun rises in the west and sets in the east, it will rise in the north and set in the south. For so long he will encompass the overlordship and kingship of the Maruts.

CHAPTER 10

1. The Sādhyas, with Brahmā as their chief, live on the fifth of these nectars. Gods do not eat or drink: they are satisfied just by seeing the nectar.

2. They enter into this form, and out of this form they arise.
3. The one who knows the nectar in this way becomes one of the Sādhyas, with Brahmā as his chief, and is satisfied just by seeing the nectar. He enters into this form, and out of this form he arises.
4. Twice as long as the sun rises in the north and sets in the south, it will rise above and set below.[10] For so long he will encompass the overlordship and kingship of the Sādhyas.

CHAPTER 11

1. Then, when it has risen above, it will not rise and will not set, but will rest, solitary, in the middle. There is a verse about it:

2. It is not there: it has not set
 Nor ever risen.
Gods, by that truth
 May I not be parted from *brahman*!

3. It does not rise or set for him: it is always daytime for the one who knows the inner teaching of *brahman*.[11]
4. In this way Brahmā taught it to Prajāpati; Prajāpati to Manu; Manu to his offspring.[12] In this way his father taught *brahman* to Uddālaka Āruṇi, his eldest son.
5. In this way a father should teach *brahman* to his eldest son or to a trustworthy student,
6. not to anyone else at all, even if someone should give him this whole earth,[13] surrounded by the waters, filled with riches: for this is greater than that.[14] This is greater than that.

CHAPTER 12

1. The Gāyatrī is all this, whatever has come to be.[15] Speech is the Gāyatrī: speech sings (*gai-*) and protects (*trai-*) all this that has come to be.
2. What the Gāyatrī is, this earth is. Whatever has come to be is established on the earth and does not go beyond it.
3. What the earth is, the body is in a person. The breaths are established in it and do not go beyond it.
4. What the body is in a person, the heart is within the person. The breaths are established in it and do not go beyond it.
5. The Gāyatrī is four-footed and sixfold. It is described in a *ṛc* verse:

6. So far goes his greatness,
And the person is greater than that.
A foot of him is all beings:
Three-footed, he has immortality in the sky.[16]

7. What is called *brahman* is the space that is outside a person. The space that is outside a person
8. is the space that is within a person. The space that is within a person
9. is the space that is within the heart. It is the full, the unmoving. The one who knows this wins glory which is full and unmoving.

CHAPTER 13

1. The heart has five divine channels.[17] Its eastern channel is the breath (*prāṇa*); it is the eye; it is the sun. One should contemplate it as brightness (*tejas*), as good food. The one who knows this becomes bright (*tejasvin*), an eater of food.
2. Its southern channel is the diffused breath (*vyāna*); it is the ear; it is the moon. One should contemplate it as glory, as fame. The one who knows this becomes glorious, famous.

3. Its western channel is the lower breath (*apāna*); it is speech; it is fire. One should contemplate it as the radiance of *brahman*, as good food. The one who knows this becomes radiant with *brahman*, an eater of food.

4. Its northern channel is the central breath (*samāna*); it is the mind; it is Parjanya. One should contemplate it as renown, as beauty. The one who knows this becomes renowned, beautiful.

5. Its upward channel is the up-breath (*udāna*); it is air; it is space. One should contemplate it as power, as might. The one who knows this becomes powerful, mighty.

6. These five *brahman*-persons are the door-guardians of the heavenly world. A hero is born in the family of the one who knows these five *brahman*-persons as the door-guardians of the heavenly world. He attains the heavenly world – the one who knows these five *brahman*-persons as the door-guardians of the heavenly world.

7. The light which shines beyond the sky, behind all, behind everything, in the unsurpassed, highest worlds, is the same that is the light within the person.

8. This is what one is seeing when one experiences by touch the heat in the body. This is what one is hearing when one closes one's ears and hears a kind of noise, a roaring like that of a blazing fire. One should contemplate it as the seen and the heard. The one who knows this becomes someone worth seeing, someone heard-of – the one who knows this.

CHAPTER 14

1. 'All this is *brahman*. Calming oneself, one should contemplate it as Tajjalān.[18] The person is made of intention:[19] as is his intention in this world, so does the person become on departing from here. He should form his intention.

2. 'Made of mind, with breath as body, with light as form, of true resolve,[20] with space as self, doing all, desiring all, smelling of all, tasting of all, encompassing all this, unspoken, untroubled.

3. 'This self of mine within the heart is smaller than a rice-grain or a barleycorn or a mustard-seed or a millet-grain or the kernel of a millet-grain. This self of mine within the heart is greater than the earth, greater than middle-air, greater than the sky, greater than these worlds.

4. 'Doing all, desiring all, smelling of all, tasting of all, encompassing all this, unspoken, untroubled, this self of mine within the heart is *brahman*. "Having gone forth from here, I shall be changed into[21] this." Truly he will, the one who has no doubt of this.' So said Śāṇḍilya, Śāṇḍilya.

CHAPTER 15

1. Middle-air its interior, earth its base,
The treasury is not exhausted.
The directions are its corners,
Sky the opening above.

This treasury is the holder of wealth. All this rests in it.

2. Its eastern direction is called Juhū, its southern direction Sahamānā, its western direction Rājñī, its northern direction Subhūtā. Air is their darling child. Whoever knows air as the darling child of the directions never makes mourning for a son. I know air as the darling child of the directions: may I never make mourning for a son!

3. I take refuge in the undamaged treasury with <name>, with <name>, with <name>.[22] I take refuge in the breath with <name>, with <name>, with <name>. I take refuge in BHŪḤ with <name>, with <name>, with <name>. I take refuge in BHUVAḤ with <name>, with <name>, with <name>. I take refuge in SVAḤ with <name>, with <name>, with <name>.

4. When I said, 'I take refuge in the breath', I was saying, 'Breath is all this, whatever there is. I have taken refuge in it.'

5. And when I said, 'I take refuge in BHŪḤ', I was saying, 'I

take refuge in earth; I take refuge in middle-air; I take refuge in sky.'

6. And when I said, 'I take refuge in BHUVAḤ', I was saying, 'I take refuge in fire; I take refuge in air; I take refuge in the sun.'

7. And when I said, 'I take refuge in SVAḤ', I was saying, 'I take refuge in the Ṛgveda; I take refuge in the Yajurveda; I take refuge in the Sāmaveda.'

CHAPTER 16

1. A person is a sacrifice. Twenty-four of his years are the morning pressing.[23] The *Gāyatrī* has twenty-four syllables: the morning pressing is in *Gāyatrī* metre. The Vasus are associated with it. The breaths are the Vasus, for they cause all this to stay (*vas-*).[24]

2. If some illness afflicts him during this period, he should say, 'Breaths, Vasus, extend my morning pressing to the midday pressing. May I, the sacrifice, not be cut off in the middle of the breaths, the Vasus.' Then he gets over it and is cured.

3. Forty-four of his years are the midday pressing. The *Triṣṭubh* has forty-four syllables: the midday pressing is in *Triṣṭubh* metre. The Rudras are associated with it. The breaths are the Rudras, for they cause all this to weep (*rud-*).

4. If some illness afflicts him during this period, he should say, 'Breaths, Rudras, extend my midday pressing to the third pressing. May I, the sacrifice, not be cut off in the middle of the breaths, the Rudras.' Then he gets over it and is cured.

5. Forty-eight of his years are the third pressing. The *Jagatī* has forty-eight syllables: the third pressing is in *Jagatī* metre. The Ādityas are associated with it. The breaths are the Ādityas, for they take (*ā-dā-*) all this.

6. If some illness afflicts him during this period, he should say, 'Breaths, Ādityas, extend my third pressing to a lifespan. May I, the sacrifice, not be cut off in the middle of the breaths, the Ādityas.' Then he gets over it and is cured.

7. Knowing this, Mahidāsa Aitareya once said 'Why do you[25]

afflict me like this? For I will not die from this.' He lived a hundred and sixteen years. The one who knows this lives a hundred and sixteen years.

CHAPTER 17

1. When one is hungry, when one is thirsty, when one takes no pleasure, that is one's initiation.[26]

2. When one eats, when one drinks, when one takes pleasure, one takes part in the *upasads*.[27]

3. When one laughs, when one feasts, when one makes love, one takes part in the hymns and recitations.[28]

4. One's asceticism, giving, honesty, non-violence and truth-speaking (as they are called) are one's gifts to the priests.[29]

5. So they say, 'She will give birth!' 'She has given birth!' This is one's resumption of the sacrifice.[30] Death is one's bath at the end.[31]

6. Ghora Āṅgirasa, having taught this to Kṛṣṇa son of Devakī,[32] said – for he had become free from thirst – 'At the time of death one should take refuge in these three recollections: "You are the unperishing. You are the unfallen. You are the subtlest part of the breath." '[33]

There are two *ṛc* verses about it:

7. Yes, they see the day-like light
   Of the primal seed
   Which is kindled beyond in the sky.[34]

8. Seeing above darkness the highest light,
   Seeing, each for himself, the highest,
   We have reached the sun,
   The god among gods,
   The highest light –
   The highest light.[35]

CHAPTER 18

1. One should contemplate mind as *brahman*. That is regarding oneself. Now, regarding deities: space is *brahman*. Both are taught, regarding oneself and regarding deities.
2. *Brahman* has four feet. Speech is a foot, breath is a foot, eye is a foot, ear is a foot. That is regarding oneself. Now, regarding deities: fire is a foot, air is a foot, the sun is a foot, the directions are a foot.
3. Speech is a quarter, a foot of *brahman*. With fire as its light it shines and gives heat. The one who knows this shines and gives heat with fame, glory, the radiance of *brahman*.
4. Breath is a quarter, a foot of *brahman*. With air as its light it shines and gives heat. The one who knows this shines and gives heat with fame, glory, the radiance of *brahman*.
5. The eye is a quarter, a foot of *brahman*. With the sun as its light it shines and gives heat. The one who knows this shines and gives heat with fame, glory, the radiance of *brahman*.
6. The ear is a quarter, a foot of *brahman*. With the directions as its light it shines and gives heat. He shines and gives heat with fame, glory, the radiance of *brahman*, the one who knows this: the one who knows this.

CHAPTER 19

1. The sun is *brahman*: this is the symbolic statement. To explain further: in the beginning this was not-being. That was being;[36] it came into existence; it turned into an egg. It lay for the space of a year, then cracked open. The two halves of the eggshell became gold and silver.
2. What was the silver half is the earth, and what was the gold half is the sky. What was the chorion is the mountains, and what was the amnion[37] is the mist with the clouds. What were the blood-vessels are the rivers, and what was the amniotic fluid[38] is the sea.

3. What was born is the sun. When it was being born, sounds of ululation went up towards it, and all beings and all desires. So, at its rising and at its setting, sounds of ululation go up towards it, and all beings and all desires.

4. Good sounds will come quickly to him – the one who, knowing this, contemplates the sun as *brahman* – and will fill him with joy: will fill him with joy.

BOOK IV

CHAPTER I

1. OṂ. Jānaśruti the great-grandson[1] was full of faith, very generous, having much food cooked. He had lodging-houses built everywhere, with the idea that everywhere folk would be eating his food.

2. One night, some geese[2] flew over. One goose said to another, 'Hey, hey there, Clearsight, Clearsight! The light of Jānaśruti the great-grandson is spread out like day. Do not get caught in it, or you will burn up!'

3. The other replied, 'So! Who is this that you speak about as though he were Raikva the Yoke-man?'[3]

'What is he like, this Raikva the Yoke-man?'[4]

4. 'Just as the lower throws of the dice go into the winning *kṛta* throw,[5] whatever good deed people do goes to him. I say the same about anyone who knows what he knows.'

5. Jānaśruti the great-grandson overheard that. As soon he got up, he said to his chamberlain,[6] 'So! You speak about me as though I were Raikva the Yoke-man!'

'Who is this Raikva the Yoke-man?'

6. '"Just as the lower throws of the dice go into the winning *kṛta* throw, whatever good deed people do goes to him. I say the same about anyone who knows what he knows."'

7. The chamberlain searched for him and returned, saying, 'I have not found him.'

Jānaśruti said to him, 'Oh! Search for him where you *would* look for a Brāhmaṇa!'[7]

8. He came upon him under a cart, scratching a rash. He said to him, 'Blessed one, are you Raikva the Yoke-man?'

He called back, 'I am. So what?'[8]

The chamberlain returned, saying, 'I have found him.'

CHAPTER 2

1. Then Jānaśruti the great-grandson went to him, taking six hundred cows, a golden jewel, and a chariot drawn by she-mules, and said to him:
2. 'Raikva, here are six hundred cows; here is a golden jewel; and here is a chariot drawn by she-mules. Blessed one, teach me about the deity, the one that you worship.'[9]
3. The other replied, 'Śūdra, you can keep the necklace and the wagon, and the cows too!'

So Jānaśruti the great-grandson went to him again, taking a thousand cows, a golden jewel, a chariot drawn by she-mules, and his daughter.

4. He said to him, 'Raikva, here are a thousand cows; here is a golden jewel; here is a chariot drawn by she-mules; here is a wife; and here is the village in which you live. Blessed one, teach me now.'
5. Raikva turned up her face to him and said, 'Śūdra, you have brought all these, but with this face alone you would have made me talk!'

There are villages in Mahāvṛṣa called the Raikvaparṇas, where he lived at the king's behest.[10] He taught him:

CHAPTER 3

1. 'Air is the drawer-together.[11] When fire goes out, it enters air. When the sun sets, it enters air. When the moon sets, it enters air.

2. 'When water dries up, it enters air. Air draws all these together. So much regarding deities.

3. 'Regarding oneself: the breath is the drawer-together. When one sleeps, speech enters the breath; the eye enters the breath; the ear enters the breath; the mind enters the breath. The breath draws all these together.

4. 'These two are the drawers-together: air among the gods, the breath among the breaths.

5. 'A *brahmacārin* once begged alms of Śaunaka Kāpeya and Abhipratārin Kākṣaseni as they were being served with food, but they did not give him any.

6. 'He said, "One god, Ka,[12] the protector of the world, has swallowed up four of great self. Kāpeya, Abhipratārin, mortals do not see him, for he dwells in many forms – the one to whom this food has not been given."

7. 'Then Śaunaka Kāpeya, in reply, went over to him, saying:

' "Self of the gods, begetter of creatures,
With golden tusks, devourer, no fool is he!
They say his might is great.
Uneaten, he eats what is not food.

' "*Brahmacārin*, it is he that we are not worshipping. – Give him alms!"

8. 'And they gave him some.

'There are five in the one group and five in the other group, ten in all. That is the *kṛta* throw. Therefore the ten in all the directions – the *kṛta* – are food. It is also Virāj,[13] the eater of food – she who sees all this. All that is seen is his, and he becomes an eater of food – the one who knows this: the one who knows this.'

CHAPTER 4

1. Satyakāma Jābāla asked his mother, Jabālā, 'Mother, I want to live the life of a *brahmacārin*. What lineage[14] do I belong to?'
2. She said to him, 'Darling, I do not know what lineage you belong to. I got you in my youth, when I travelled about a great deal as a servant, so I do not know what lineage you belong to. But I am called Jabālā and you are called Satyakāma. You can say you are Satyakāma Jābāla.'[15]
3. He went to Hāridrumata Gautama and said, 'Blessed one, I will live the life of a *brahmacārin* with you. Blessed one, I would come to you as my teacher.'[16]
4. He said, 'Good lad, what lineage do you belong to?'

He said, 'Sir, I do not know what lineage I belong to. I asked my mother, and she answered me, "I got you in my youth, when I travelled about a great deal as a servant, so I do not know what lineage you belong to. But I am called Jabālā and you are called Satyakāma. You can say you are Satyakāma Jābāla." Sir, I am Satyakāma Jābāla.'
5. Hāridrumata said to him, 'No one who was not a Brāhmaṇa could have explained it so. Good lad, bring firewood: I shall initiate you. You have not departed from the truth.' After he had initiated him, he separated out four hundred of his thin and feeble cows and said, 'Good lad, follow these!'

As he drove them off, Satyakāma said, 'I will not come back without a thousand.' He lived away for a number of years. When they had become a thousand –

CHAPTER 5

1. the bull called[17] him: 'Satyakāma!'

'Blessed one?' he replied.

'Good lad, we have reached a thousand. Drive us to the teacher's house –

2. 'and I must tell you about a foot of *brahman*.'

'Tell me, blessed one.'

He told him, 'The eastern direction is a fraction;[18] the western direction is a fraction; the southern direction is a fraction; the northern direction is a fraction. This, good lad, is a foot of *brahman*, in four fractions, called "Shining".[19]

3. 'The one who, knowing this, contemplates a foot of *brahman*, in four fractions, as "Shining" becomes shining in this world and wins shining worlds – the one who, knowing this, contemplates a foot of *brahman*, in four fractions, as "Shining".

CHAPTER 6

1. 'Fire will tell you about a foot.'

The next morning he drove the cows onward. At the place they reached in the evening he lit a fire, penned up the cows, brought firewood, and sat down behind the fire, facing east.

2. Fire called him: 'Satyakāma!'

'Blessed one?' he replied.

3. 'Good lad, I must tell you about a foot of *brahman*.'

'Tell me, blessed one.'

He told him, 'Earth is a fraction; middle-air is a fraction; sky is a fraction; ocean is a fraction. This, good lad, is a foot of *brahman*, in four fractions, called "Unending".

4. 'The one who, knowing this, contemplates a foot of *brahman*, in four fractions, as "Unending" becomes unending in this world and wins unending worlds – the one who, knowing this, contemplates a foot of *brahman*, in four fractions, as "Unending".

CHAPTER 7

1. 'A goose will tell you about a foot.'

The next morning he drove the cows onward. At the place they reached in the evening he lit a fire, penned up the cows, brought firewood, and sat down behind the fire, facing east.

2. A goose alighted and called him: 'Satyakāma!'

'Blessed one?' he replied.

3. 'Good lad, I must tell you about a foot of *brahman*.'

'Tell me, blessed one.'

He told him, 'Fire is a fraction; the sun is a fraction; the moon is a fraction; lightning is a fraction. This, good lad, is a foot of *brahman*, in four fractions, called "Radiant".

4. 'The one who, knowing this, contemplates a foot of *brahman*, in four fractions, as "Radiant" becomes radiant in this world and wins radiant worlds – the one who, knowing this, contemplates a foot of *brahman*, in four fractions, as "Radiant".

CHAPTER 8

1. 'A cormorant[20] will tell you about a foot.'

The next morning he drove the cows onward. At the place they reached in the evening he lit a fire, penned up the cows, brought firewood, and sat down behind the fire, facing east.

2. A cormorant alighted and called him: 'Satyakāma!'

'Blessed one?' he replied.

3. 'Good lad, I must tell you about a foot of *brahman*.'

'Tell me, blessed one.'

He told him, 'Breath is a fraction; the eye is a fraction; the ear is a fraction; the mind is a fraction. This, good lad, is a foot of *brahman*, in four fractions, called "Abiding".[21]

4. 'The one who, knowing this, contemplates a foot of *brahman*, in four fractions, as "Abiding" becomes abiding in this world and wins abiding worlds – the one who, knowing

this, contemplates a foot of *brahman*, in four fractions, as "Abiding".'

CHAPTER 9

1. He reached the teacher's house. The teacher called him: 'Satyakāma!'

2. 'Blessed one?' he replied.

'Good lad, you shine like a knower of *brahman*. Who taught you?'

He replied, 'Ones who were other than human. But, blessed one, *you* tell me, please.

3. 'For I have heard from those like yourself, blessed one, that knowledge learned from one's teacher has the best results.'[22]

He taught it to him. In it, nothing was different. Nothing was different.

CHAPTER 10

1. Upakosala Kāmalāyana lived as a *brahmacārin* with Satyakāma Jābāla. For twelve years he tended his fires. Satyakāma let his other students return home,[23] but he did not let Upakosala return home.

2. Satyakāma's wife said to him, 'The ascetic *brahmacārin* has tended the fires well. Do not let the fires speak to him first. You should teach him.' But he went on a journey without having spoken to him.

3. Then, from grief, Upakosala resolved not to eat. His teacher's wife said, 'Eat, *brahmacārin*. Why do you not eat?'

He said, 'In this person are many desires, sufferings of all kinds. I am full of grief. I shall not eat.'

4. Then the fires spoke together: 'The ascetic *brahmacārin* has tended us well. Come, let us teach him.' They said to him:

5. 'Breath is *brahman*; Ka is *brahman*; Kha[24] is *brahman*.'

He said, 'I know that breath is *brahman*, but I do not know Ka or Kha.'

They said, 'What Ka is, Kha is, and what Kha is, Ka is.' They told him about breath, and then about space.

CHAPTER 11

1. Then the Gārhapatya fire taught him: '"Earth, fire, food, the sun."' The person who is seen in the sun am I. *I* am he.[25]
2. 'The one who knows and contemplates him in this way wards off evil actions, becomes a possessor of worlds, attains his full span, and lives long, and his descendants do not perish. We protect, both in this world and in that, the one who knows and contemplates him in this way.'

CHAPTER 12

1. Then the Anvāhāryapacana fire taught him: '"The waters, the directions, the constellations, the moon."' The person who is seen in the moon am I. *I* am he.
2. 'The one who knows and contemplates him in this way wards off evil actions, becomes a possessor of worlds, attains his full span, and lives long, and his descendants do not perish. We protect, both in this world and in that, the one who knows and contemplates him in this way.'

CHAPTER 13

1. Then the Āhavanīya fire taught him: '"Breath, space, fire, lightning." The person who is seen in the lightning am I. *I* am he.
2. 'The one who knows and contemplates him in this way

wards off evil actions, becomes a possessor of worlds, attains his full span, and lives long, and his descendants do not perish. We protect, both in this world and in that, the one who knows and contemplates him in this way.'

CHAPTER 14

1. They said, 'Upakosala, good lad, you have knowledge of us and knowledge of the self. But your teacher will tell you where they go back to.'[26]

His teacher came back. His teacher called him: 'Upakosala!'

2. 'Blessed one?' he replied.

'Good lad, your face shines like that of a knower of *brahman*. Who taught you?'

'Who could have taught me, sir?' he said, seeming to deny it. He paid respect to the fires, saying, 'Now they look like this, but then they looked different.'[27]

'So what did they tell you, good lad?'

3. 'This . . .,' he replied.

'But did they tell you only about the worlds, good lad? But I will tell you about *that*. When one knows *that*, evil action does not stick to one, just as water does not stick to a lotus petal.'

'Tell me, blessed one.'

And he told him:

CHAPTER 15

1. 'The person who is seen in the eye is the self,' he said. 'It is the immortal, the fearless. It is *brahman*. Even if one sprinkles ghee or water on it, it goes only as far as the eyelids.[28]

2. 'They call him "Unifying the Beautiful", for all beautiful things come together to him. All beautiful things come together to the one who knows this.

3. 'He is also "Bringer of the Beautiful", for he brings all

beautiful things. The one who knows this brings all beautiful things.

4. 'He is also "Light-Bringer"', for he shines in all worlds. The one who knows this shines in all worlds.

5. 'And whether they perform funerary rites for him or not, they[29] go into the light; from light into the day; from the day into the waxing fortnight; from the waxing fortnight into the six months in which the sun goes northward; from the months into the year; from the year into the sun; from the sun into the moon; from the moon into the lightning: then a person who is not human[30] leads them to *brahman*. This is the path of the gods, the path of *brahman*. Those who travel by it do not whirl again in the whirlpool of Manu.[31] They do not whirl again.'

CHAPTER 16

1. The one who purifies[32] is a sacrifice, for as it goes it purifies all this. Since as it goes it purifies all this it is a sacrifice. Mind and speech are ways to it.

2. Of the two, the Brahmā consecrates one with his mind; the Hotṛ, the Adhvaryu and the Udgātṛ the other with speech. When the Brahmā breaks the silence, once the morning recitation[33] has begun, before the closing verse,[34]

3. he consecrates one of the ways, but the other is lacking. As a person walking on one foot, or a chariot running on one wheel, comes to harm, his sacrifice comes to harm. When the sacrifice comes to harm, the patron of the sacrifice comes to harm with it. By sacrificing, he becomes more evil.

4. But when the Brahmā does not break the silence once the morning recitation has begun, before the closing verse, they consecrate both the ways, and neither of them is lacking. As a person travelling on both feet, or a chariot running on both wheels, remains steady (*prati-sthā-*), his sacrifice remains steady. When the sacrifice remains steady, the patron of the sacrifice remains steady with it. By sacrificing, he becomes better.

CHAPTER 17

1. Prajāpati heated up the worlds. As they were heated up, he extracted[35] the essences from them: fire from earth, air from middle-air, the sun from sky.
2. He heated up these three deities. As they were heated up, he extracted the essences from them: *ṛc* verses from fire, *yajus* verses from air, *sāman* verses from the sun.
3. He heated up this threefold knowledge. As it was heated up, he extracted the essences from it: BHŪḤ from the *ṛc* verses, BHUVAḤ from the *yajus* verses, SVAḤ from the *sāman* verses.
4. If it should come to harm from the *ṛc* verses, one should make an offering into the Gārhapatya fire, saying, 'BHŪḤ SVĀHĀ!' Then one repairs the harm to the sacrifice from the *ṛc* verses with the essence of the *ṛc* verses, with the power of the *ṛc* verses.
5. And if it should come to harm from the *yajus* verses, one should make an offering into the Dakṣiṇāgni fire, saying, 'BHUVAḤ SVĀHĀ!' Then one repairs the harm to the sacrifice from the *yajus* verses with the essence of the *yajus* verses, with the power of the *yajus* verses.
6. And if it should come to harm from the *sāman* verses, one should make an offering into the Āhavanīya fire, saying, 'SVAḤ SVĀHĀ!' Then one repairs the harm to the sacrifice from the *sāman* verses with the essence of the *sāman* verses, with the power of the *sāman* verses.
7. Just as one would repair gold with salt,[36] silver with gold, tin with silver, lead with tin, iron with lead, timber with iron, or timber with leather,
8. one repairs the harm to the sacrifice with the power of the three worlds, the three deities, the threefold knowledge. The sacrifice is healed, where one who knows this is the Brahmā.
9. The sacrifice slopes to the north,[37] where one who knows this is the Brahmā. There is a song about the Brahmā who knows this:

Wherever it turns back,
There goes
Manu's son.
10. The Brahmā priest alone
Is the mare who protects the Kurus.[38]

The Brahmā who knows this protects the sacrifice, the patron of the sacrifice, and all the priests. So one should choose as Brahmā one who knows this, not one who does not know this: not one who does not know this.

BOOK V

CHAPTER I

1. OṂ. The one who knows the eldest and best becomes the eldest and best. Breath is the eldest and best.[1]
2. The one who knows the finest becomes the finest of his own folk. Speech is the finest.[2]
3. The one who knows the support stands firm both in this world and in that world. The eye is the support.
4. The one who knows prosperity attains his desires, both divine and human.[3] The ear is prosperity.
5. The one who knows the dwelling-place becomes the dwelling-place of his own folk. Mind is the dwelling-place.
6. Now the bodily functions (*prāṇa*) argued about who was the best.[4] 'I am the best!' 'I am the best!'
7. The bodily functions said to father Prajāpati, 'Blessed one, who is the best of us?'

He said to them, 'The best of you is the one after whose departure the body seems to be in worst case.'

8. Speech departed. It stayed away for a year, and when it returned it asked, 'How were you able to live without me?'

'Like the dumb, not speaking, but breathing with the breath, seeing with the eye, hearing with the ear, thinking with the mind. That is how we lived.'

Then speech went back in.

9. The eye departed and stayed away for a year. When it came back it asked, 'How were you able to live without me?'

'Like the blind, not seeing, but breathing with the breath,

speaking with speech, hearing with the ear, thinking with the mind. That is how we lived.'

Then the eye went back in.

10. The ear departed and stayed away for a year. When it came back it asked, 'How were you able to live without me?'

'Like the deaf, not hearing, but breathing with the breath, speaking with speech, seeing with the eye, thinking with the mind. That is how we lived.'

Then the ear went back in.

11. The mind departed and stayed away for a year. When it came back it asked, 'How were you able to live without me?'

'Like the foolish, without mind, but breathing with the breath, speaking with speech, seeing with the eye, hearing with the ear, not thinking with the mind. That is how we lived.'

Then the mind went back in.

12. The breath (*prāṇa*), intending to depart, dragged together the other bodily functions (*prāṇa*) as a fine stallion might drag its tethering-pegs.

They said, 'Blessed one, do not go. You are the best of us. Do not leave.'

13. Speech said to it, 'In that I am the finest, you are the finest.'

The eye said to it, 'In that I am the support, you are the support.'

14. The ear said to it, 'In that I am prosperity, you are prosperity.'

The mind said to it, 'In that I am the dwelling, you are the dwelling.'

15. Folk do not call them 'speeches', 'eyes', 'ears' or 'minds'. They call them 'breaths'. The breath becomes all these.

CHAPTER 2

1. It said, 'What will be my food?'

They said, 'Whatever there is, down to dogs and birds.'

This is the food (*anna*) of the breath (*ana*). *Ana* is its simple name. For the one who knows this, there is nothing that is not food.

2. It said, 'What will be my clothing?'

They said, 'Water.'

Therefore when folk are about to eat, both before and after, they clothe it with water. It becomes a recipient of garments: it becomes not-naked (*anagna*).

3. Satyakāma Jābāla taught this to Gośruti Vaiyāghrapadya, and said, 'If one were to say this even to a dried-up stump, branches would grow on it, and leaves would sprout.'[5]

4. If one should aspire to greatness, one should undergo initiation on the new-moon day; then on the full-moon night one should prepare a stirred mixture of all herbs with yoghurt and honey. Saying, 'To the eldest, to the best, SVĀHĀ!', one should make an offering of ghee into the fire and pour the remainder into the stirred mixture.

5. Saying, 'To the finest, SVĀHĀ!', one should make an offering of ghee into the fire and pour the remainder into the stirred mixture.

Saying, 'To the support, SVĀHĀ!', one should make an offering of ghee into the fire and pour the remainder into the stirred mixture.

Saying, 'To prosperity, SVĀHĀ!', one should make an offering of ghee into the fire and pour the remainder into the stirred mixture.

Saying, 'To the dwelling-place, SVĀHĀ!', one should make an offering of ghee into the fire and pour the remainder into the stirred mixture.

6. Then, moving quietly away, holding the stirred mixture between one's two hands, one mutters '*Amo nāmāsy amā hi te sarvam idam*;[6] this is the eldest, the best, the king, the overlord; may he make me the eldest, the best, the king, the overlord! May I become all this!'

7. Then he sips with a *ṛc* verse, foot by foot.

> 'We ask for the food' – he sips –
> 'Of the god Savitṛ' – he sips –
> 'Best and most sustaining for all'[7] – he sips –
> 'Swiftly we meditate on Bhaga's might'[8] – he drinks it all.

After washing the bowl or ladle, he lies down behind the fire-altar, either on a hide or on the bare ground, restraining his speech and not careless. If he sees a woman,[9] he knows that his work is successful.

8. There is a verse about it:

> When, in works concerned with desire,
> One sees a woman in dreams,
> One should know success there,
> In the seeing of that dream,
> In the seeing of that dream.

CHAPTER 3

1. Śvetaketu Āruṇeya went to a meeting of the Pañcālas. Jaivali Pravāhaṇa said to him, 'Young man, has your father educated you?'[10]

'He has, blessed one.'

2. 'Do you know where people go on to from here?'

'No, blessed one.'

'Do you know how they come back again?' he cried.[11]

'No, blessed one.'

'Do you know the parting of the ways between the path of the gods and the path of the ancestors?'

'No, blessed one.'

3. 'Do you know how that world does not become full?'

'No, blessed one.'

'Do you know how, in the fifth offering, the waters take on human speech?'

'No indeed, blessed one.'

4. 'So why did you call yourself educated? How can someone who does not know these things call himself educated?'

Distressed, Śvetaketu went to his father's home. He said to him, 'Blessed one, you said you had educated me when you had *not* educated me.

5. 'A princeling asked me five questions, and I could not answer a single one of them . . .'[12]

His father said, 'As you told them to me then, I do not know a single one of them. If I had known them, how would I not have told you?'

6. Gautama went to the king's home. When he got there, the king treated him as an honoured guest. In the morning he went to the assembly and approached him. The king said, 'Blessed Gautama, choose a boon from my human wealth.'

He said, 'O king, human wealth belongs to you. Tell me the words you spoke in the presence of the young man.'

The king was troubled.

7. He invited him to stay for a long time. He said, 'Gautama, since you have said that, you should know that[13] before you the knowledge has not previously gone to Brāhmaṇas. So in all worlds, rulership has belonged to Kṣatriyas.' He told him:

CHAPTER 4

1. '*That* world is a fire, Gautama. The sun is its fuel; the rays its smoke; the day its flame; the moon its embers; the constellations its sparks.

2. 'In that fire the gods offer faith. From that offering King Soma arises.

CHAPTER 5

1. 'Parjanya is a fire, Gautama. Air is his fuel; cloud his smoke; the lightning his flame; the thunderbolt his embers; the hailstones his sparks.

2. 'In that fire the gods offer King Soma. From that offering rain arises.

CHAPTER 6

1. 'The earth is a fire, Gautama. The year is its fuel; space its smoke; the night its flame; the directions its embers; the intermediate directions its sparks.
2. 'In that fire the gods offer rain. From that offering food arises.

CHAPTER 7

1. 'A man (*puruṣa*) is a fire, Gautama. Speech is his fuel; the breath his smoke; the tongue his flame; the eye his embers; the ear his sparks.
2. 'In that fire the gods offer food. From that offering the seed arises.

CHAPTER 8

1. 'A young woman is a fire, Gautama. The loins are her fuel; when one invites her, her smoke; the vagina her flame; what one does within, her embers; the pleasures her sparks.
2. 'In that fire the gods offer the seed. From that offering a foetus arises.

CHAPTER 9

1. 'And so, in the fifth offering, the waters take on human speech. The foetus, covered by the amnion,[14] sleeps inside for ten months or nine or however long it is, and then is born.
2. 'When he is born, he lives out his span of life, and, when

he has passed away at the appointed time, they take him from here to the fire from which he came, from which he came to be.

CHAPTER 10

1. 'Those who know this, and those who in the forest contemplate faith, asceticism,[15] go into the flame, from the flame into the day, from the day into the waxing fortnight, from the waxing fortnight into the six months in which the sun goes northward,

2. 'from the months into the year, from the year into the sun, from the sun into the moon, from the moon into the lightning. Then a person who is not human takes them to *brahman*. This is called the way of the gods.

3. 'But those who in the village contemplate the gift in stored-up merit[16] go into the smoke, from the smoke into the night, from the night into the waning fortnight, from the waning fortnight into the six months in which the sun goes southward: they do not reach the year.

4. 'From the months into the world of the ancestors, from the world of the ancestors into space, from space into the moon. This is King Soma: this is the food of the gods. The gods partake of him.

5. 'They live in it until their fall. Then they return by the same road that they came, into space; from space into the air: having become air it becomes smoke; having become smoke, it becomes cloud.

6. 'Having become cloud it becomes rain-cloud; having become rain-cloud it rains. Here they are born as rice and barley, herbs and trees, sesame and black beans.[17] It is very hard indeed to escape from this. But whenever someone eats the food and emits seed, one again comes into being.

7. 'Those who here are of delightful conduct will quickly attain a delightful womb – a Brāhmaṇa womb, a Kṣatriya womb

or a Vaiśya womb. But those who here are of foul conduct will quickly attain a foul womb – a dog's womb, a pig's womb, or a Caṇḍāla womb.

8. 'But the little beings that travel round many times go by neither of these paths, but to a third state: 'Be born! Die!' So that world is not filled up. Therefore one should be on one's guard. There is a verse about it:

9. A gold-thief, a wine-drinker,
One who enters his guru's bed,[18]
a Brāhmaṇa-slayer –
These four fall, and fifth
The one who associates with these.

10. 'But the one who knows the five fires does not become smeared even if he associates with these. He becomes pure, cleansed, possessor of a meritorious world – the one who knows this: the one who knows this.'

CHAPTER 11

1. Prācīnaśāla Aupamanyava, Satyayajña Pauluṣi, Indradyumna Bhāllaveya, Jana Śārkarākṣya and Buḍila Āśvatarāsvi, great householders and great scholars, came together and held a discussion: 'What is the self? What is *brahman*?'

2. They decided, 'Blessed ones, Uddālaka Āruṇi has direct knowledge of the self of all men.[19] Come, let us approach him!' And they approached him.

3. He decided, 'These great householders and great scholars will question me, and I will not be able to answer everything. Come, let me recommend someone else.'

4. He said to them, 'Blessed ones, Aśvapati Kaikeya has direct knowledge of the self of all men. Come, let us approach him!' And they approached him.

5. When they arrived, he had each one individually welcomed as an honoured guest. In the morning he got up and said:

'There is in my country no thief,
No miser, no drinker of wine,
None who has not lit a fire, none ignorant,
No unchaste man, how then an unchaste woman?

'Blessed ones, I am about to offer a sacrifice. I will give you, blessed ones, as much wealth as I will give to every single priest. Blessed ones, please stay.'

6. They said, 'A man should state the business on which he comes. You have direct knowledge of the self of all men. Teach us about that!'

7. He said to them, 'I will answer in the morning.' Early next day they approached him with fuel in their hands. Without initiating them, he said to them:

CHAPTER 12

1. 'Aupamanyava, what do you worship[20] as the self?'

'Sky, blessed king,' he said.

'Indeed, this is the self of all men as 'Radiant'. Since you worship the self as such, in your family it is seen that Soma is pressed, re-pressed, and pressed again.[21]

2. 'You eat food and see what is pleasant. The one who worships the self of all men as such eats food and sees what is pleasant, and in his family is the radiance of *brahman*. This is the head of the self,' he said. 'Your head would have split apart if you had not come to me.'

CHAPTER 13

1. Then he said to Satyayajña Pauluṣi, 'Prācīnayogya, what do you worship as the self?'

'The sun, blessed king,' he said.

'Indeed, this is the self of all men as "Having All Shapes".

Since you worship the self as such, in your family is plenty, of all shapes.

2. 'You have at hand a chariot drawn by she-mules, slave-women, a gold chain. You eat food and see what is pleasant. The one who worships the self of all men as such eats food and sees what is pleasant, and in his family is the radiance of *brahman*. This is the eye of the self,' he said. 'You would have gone blind if you had not come to me.'

CHAPTER 14

1. Then he said to Indradyumna Bhāllaveya, 'Vaiyāghrapadya, what do you worship as the self?'

'Air, blessed king,' he said.

'Indeed, this is the self of all men as "Travelling Far and Wide". Since you worship the self as such, tribute comes to you from far and wide, and ranks of chariots follow you far and wide.

2. 'You eat food and see what is pleasant. The one who worships the self of all men as such eats food and sees what is pleasant, and in his family is the radiance of *brahman*. This is the breath of the self,' he said. 'Your breath would have gone up out of you if you had not come to me.'

CHAPTER 15

1. Then he said to Jana, 'Śārkarākṣya, what do you worship as the self?'

'Space, blessed king,' he said.

'Indeed, this is the self of all men as "Abundant". Since you worship the self as such, you abound in offspring and in wealth.

2. 'You eat food and see what is pleasant. The one who worships the self of all men as such eats food and sees what is

pleasant, and in his family is the radiance of *brahman*. This is the body of the self,' he said. 'Your body would have wasted away if you had not come to me.'

CHAPTER 16

1. Then he said to Buḍila Āśvatarāśvi, 'Vaiyāghrapadya, what do you worship as the self?'

'The waters, blessed king,' he said.

'Indeed, this is the self of all men as "Wealth". Since you worship the self as such, you are wealthy and prosperous.

2. 'You eat food and see what is pleasant. The one who worships the self of all men as such eats food and sees what is pleasant, and in his family is the radiance of *brahman*. This is the bladder of the self,' he said. 'Your bladder would have burst if you had not come to me.'

CHAPTER 17

1. Then he said to Uddālaka Āruṇi, 'Gautama, what do you worship as the self?'

'Earth, blessed king,' he said.

'Indeed, this is the self of all men as "Support" (*pratiṣṭhā*). Since you worship the self as such, you are supported with offspring and with animals.

2. 'You eat food and see what is pleasant. The one who worships the self of all men as such eats food and sees what is pleasant, and in his family is the radiance of *brahman*. This is the feet of the self,' he said. 'Your feet would have withered away if you had not come to me.'

CHAPTER 18

1. He said to them, 'You seem to know the self of all men in different ways, and you eat food. But the one who worships the self of all men limb by limb, as identified with himself,[22] eats food in all worlds, in all beings, in all selves.
2. 'The head of the self of all men is "Radiant"; his eye is "Having All Shapes"; his breath is the self as "Travelling Far and Wide"; his body is "Abundant"; his bladder is "Wealth"; the earth is his feet;[23] his chest is the altar; his body-hair is the grass-strewing; his heart is the Gārhapatya fire; his mind is the Anvāhāryapacana fire; his mouth is the Āhavanīya fire.

CHAPTER 19

1. 'The food which comes first should be given in offering. The first offering one makes one should offer with the words "To the breath, SVĀHĀ!" Then the breath is content.
2. 'When the breath is content, the eye is content; when the eye is content, the sun is content; when the sun is content, the sky is content; when the sky is content, whatever the sun and the sky rule over is content; with the contentment of that, one is content, with offspring, animals, good food, brightness, and the radiance of *brahman*.

CHAPTER 20

1. 'And the second offering one makes one should offer with the words "To the diffused breath, SVĀHĀ!" Then the diffused breath is content.
2. 'When the diffused breath is content, the ear is content; when the ear is content, the moon is content; when the moon is content, the directions are content; when the directions are

content, whatever the directions and the moon rule over is content; with the contentment of that, one is content, with offspring, animals, good food, brightness, and the radiance of *brahman*.

CHAPTER 21

1. 'And the third offering one makes one should offer with the words "To the lower breath, SVĀHĀ!" Then the lower breath is content.

2. 'When the lower breath is content, speech is content; when speech is content, fire is content; when fire is content, earth is content; when earth is content, whatever earth and fire rule over is content; with the contentment of that, one is content, with offspring, animals, good food, brightness, and the radiance of *brahman*.

CHAPTER 22

1. 'And the fourth offering one makes one should offer with the words "To the central breath, SVĀHĀ!" Then the central breath is content.

2. 'When the central breath is content, the mind is content; when the mind is content, Parjanya is content; when Parjanya is content, the lightning is content; when the lightning is content, whatever the lightning and Parjanya rule over is content; with the contentment of that, one is content, with offspring, animals, good food, brightness, and the radiance of *brahman*.

CHAPTER 23

1. 'And the fifth offering one makes one should offer with the words "To the up-breath, SVĀHĀ!" Then the up-breath is content.
2. 'When the up-breath is content, the skin is content; when the skin is content, air is content; when air is content, space is content; when space is content, whatever air and space rule over is content; with the contentment of that, one is content, with offspring, animals, good food, brightness, and the radiance of *brahman*.

CHAPTER 24

1. 'If one performs the Agnihotra without knowing this, it will be just the same as if one performed it by casting embers on to ashes.
2. 'But if one performs the Agnihotra knowing this, it will have been offered in all worlds, in all beings, in all selves.
3. 'Just as the tip of a reed, when poked in a fire, is burnt up, all one's evils are burnt up if one performs the Agnihotra knowing this.
4. 'So, knowing this, even if one offers leftovers to a Caṇḍāla, it will have been offered to the self of all men in him. There is a verse about it:

5. Just as here hungry children
   Wait around[24] their mother,
So all beings attend
   Upon the Agnihotra:
   Upon the Agnihotra.'

BOOK VI

CHAPTER 1

1. OṂ. There once was a boy called Śvetaketu Āruṇeya.[1] His father said to him, 'Śvetaketu, go and live as a *brahmacārin*. Good lad, there is no one in our family who is just a Brāhmaṇa by birth, without learning.'

2. So at twelve years old he went, and at twenty-four years old he returned, having learned all the Vedas, haughty, proud of his learning, and opinionated. His father said to him, 'Śvetaketu, good lad, since you are haughty, proud of your learning, and opinionated, did you ask for the symbolic statement

3. 'by which the unheard becomes heard, the unthought thought, and the unknown known?'

'Blessed one, what sort of symbolic statement is that?'

4. 'Good lad, just as through one lump of clay everything made of clay is known, so difference of shape is just name, dependent on speech: "clay" is the reality.[2]

5. 'Good lad, just as through one copper ornament everything made of copper is known, so difference of shape is just name, dependent on speech: "copper" is the reality.

6. 'Good lad, just as through one nail-clipper everything made of iron is known, so difference of shape is just name, dependent on speech: "iron" is the reality. Such, good lad, is the symbolic statement.'

7. 'The blessed ones certainly did not know this, for, if they had known it, how would they not have told me? Blessed one, *you* tell me about it.'

'I will, good lad,' he said.

CHAPTER 2

1. 'In the beginning, good lad, this was being, one alone without a second. Some say, "In the beginning this was not-being, one alone without a second. From that not-being, being was produced."[3]
2. 'But, good lad, how could that be?' he said. 'How could being be produced from not-being? In the beginning, good lad, surely this was being, one alone without a second.
3. 'It thought, "Let me become many; let me be born." It created heat.[4] Heat thought, "Let me become many; let me be born." It created the waters. So when and wherever a person grieves or sweats, the waters are born from heat.
4. 'The waters thought, "Let us become many; let us be born." They created food. So when and wherever it rains, food becomes more abundant. So good food is born from the waters.

CHAPTER 3

1. 'Beings have three seeds: the egg-born, the live-born, the shoot-born.
2. 'The deity thought, "Come, I must enter these three deities with life, with the self", and created differences of name and form.[5]
3. 'Thinking, "I must make each one of them threefold – each one threefold",[6] the deity entered the three deities with the life, with the self, and created differences of name and form.
4. 'He made each one of them threefold – each one threefold. Good lad, learn from me how those three deities each became threefold – each one threefold.

CHAPTER 4

1. 'The red form of fire is the form of heat; the white is that of water; the black is that of food. The "fire-ness" of fire has disappeared. Difference of shape is just name, dependent on speech: the three forms are the reality.
2. 'The red form of the sun is the form of heat; the white is that of water; the black is that of food. The "sun-ness" of the sun has disappeared. Difference of shape is just name, dependent on speech: the three forms are the reality.
3. 'The red form of the moon is the form of heat; the white is that of water; the black is that of food. The "moon-ness" of the moon has disappeared. Difference of shape is just name, dependent on speech: the three forms are the reality.
4. 'The red form of lightning is the form of heat; the white is that of water; the black is that of food. The "lightning-ness" of lightning has disappeared. Difference of shape is just name, dependent on speech: the three forms are the reality.
5. 'Knowing this, of old, great householders and great scholars said, "No one of ours will speak of 'the unheard, the unthought, the unknown'", for they knew it through these –
6. 'What seemed red they knew as the form of heat; what seemed white they knew as the form of water; and what seemed black they knew as the form of food.
7. 'What seemed unknown they knew as the combination of these deities. Good lad, learn from me how those three deities become threefold – each one threefold – when they come into contact with the person.

CHAPTER 5

1. 'Food, once eaten, is divided into three. The grossest element becomes faeces; the middling, flesh; the subtlest, mind.
2. 'Water, once drunk, is divided into three. The grossest element becomes urine; the middling blood; the subtlest, breath.

3. 'Heat, once consumed,[7] is divided into three. The grossest element becomes bone; the middling, marrow; the subtlest, speech.
4. 'Good lad, the mind is made of food, the breath is made of water, the speech is made of heat.'

'Blessed one, explain it to me further.'

'I will, good lad,' he said.

CHAPTER 6

1. 'Good lad, when soured milk is churned, the subtle part of it rises to the top. That becomes butter.
2. 'In the same way, good lad, when food is eaten, the subtle part of it rises to the top. That becomes mind.
3. 'Good lad, when water is drunk, the subtle part of it rises to the top. That becomes breath.
4. 'Good lad, when heat is consumed, the subtle part of it rises to the top. That becomes speech.
5. 'Good lad, the mind is made of food, the breath is made of water, the speech is made of heat.'

'Blessed one, explain it to me further.'

'I will, good lad,' he said.

CHAPTER 7

1. 'Good lad, the person has sixteen fractions.[8] Do not eat for fifteen days, but drink water as you wish. The breath is made of water. If you do not drink, your breath will be cut off.'
2. For fifteen days he did not eat. Then he approached him, saying, 'Father, what shall I say?'

'Ṛc verses, *yajus* verses and *sāman* verses, good lad,' he said.

'They do not come clear to me, father.'

3. He said to him, 'Good lad, just as when only one ember,

the size of a firefly, is left of a great fire it cannot burn anything big, now that you, good lad, have only one fraction left of your sixteen fractions you have not the strength for the Vedas. Eat, and you will understand me.'

4. He ate, then approached him. Then he understood whatever he asked him.

5. He said to him, 'Good lad, just as when only one ember, the size of a firefly, is left of a great fire one can make it blaze up by feeding it with grass, and then it can burn something big,

6. 'so, good lad, one fraction was left of your sixteen fractions: when fed with food it blazed up, and so you have the strength for the Vedas. Good lad, the mind is made of food, the breath is made of water, the speech is made of heat.'

Then he understood his teaching: he understood.

CHAPTER 8

1. Uddālaka Āruṇi once said to his son, Śvetaketu, 'Good lad, learn from me about the state of sleep. When a person "sleeps", as it is called, then, good lad, he has entered into being; he is merged with his own. That is why they say of him, "He sleeps" (*svapiti*), for he is merged with his own (*svam apīta*).

2. 'Just as a bird, tied by a thread, flies in every direction but, failing to reach a home elsewhere, returns to its bondage, so, good lad, the mind flies in every direction but, failing to reach a home elsewhere, returns to the breath. For, good lad, the mind is bound to breath.

3. 'Good lad, learn from me about hunger and thirst. When a person here "is hungry", as it is called, then water leads the food (*aśitaṃ nayante*). So they call water "the leader of food" (*aśanāyā* = hunger),[9] just like a leader of cows (*gonāya*), a leader of horses (*aśvanāya*), a leader of men (*puruṣanāya*). Good lad, learn from me where this shoot has sprung from: it cannot be rootless.

4. 'Where else could its root be, but in food? Good lad, through food as the shoot seek for water as the root. Good lad,

through water as the shoot seek for heat as the root. Good lad, through heat as the shoot seek for being as the root. Good lad, all creatures have being as their root, being as their home, being as their base.

5. 'When a person "is thirsty", as it is called, then heat leads the drink. So they call heat "leader of water" (*udanyā* = thirst),[10] just like a leader of cows, a leader of horses, a leader of men. Good lad, learn from me where this shoot has sprung from: it cannot be rootless.

6. 'Where else could its root be, but in water? Good lad, through water as the shoot seek for heat as the root. Good lad, through heat as the shoot seek for being as the root. Good lad, all creatures have being as their root, being as their home, being as their base.

'Good lad, I have said before how those three deities each become threefold – each one threefold – when they come into contact with the person. Good lad, when the person departs, his speech enters into mind, his mind into breath, his breath into heat, his heat into the highest deity.

7. 'This subtle part is what all this has as self.[11] It is truth: it is the self. *You* are that,[12] Śvetaketu.'

'Blessed one, explain it to me further.'

'I will, good lad,' he said.

CHAPTER 9

1. 'Good lad, just as bees secrete honey by collecting the nectars from different kinds of trees, and combine the nectar into oneness,

2. 'and just as there they do not keep any distinction, so as to be able to say, "I am the nectar of that tree", "I am the nectar of *that* tree", so, good lad, all creatures, once they have entered into being, do not know that they have entered into being.

3. 'Whatever they are here – a tiger, a lion, a wolf, a boar, a

worm, a flying thing, a gnat or a mosquito – they become *that*.
4. 'This subtle part is what all this has as self. It is truth: it is the self. *You* are that, Śvetaketu.'

'Blessed one, explain it to me further.'

'I will, good lad,' he said.

CHAPTER 10

1. 'Good lad, the eastern rivers flow east and the western rivers flow west, and from the sea merge into the sea. That is just sea. Just as there they do not know "I am that river", "I am *that* river",
2. 'so, good lad, all creatures, once they have come forth from being, do not know that they have come forth from being. Whatever they are here – a tiger, a lion, a wolf, a boar, a worm, a flying thing, a gnat or a mosquito – they become *that*.
3. 'This subtle part is what all this has as self. It is truth: it is the self. *You* are that, Śvetaketu.'

'Blessed one, explain it to me further.'

'I will, good lad,' he said.

CHAPTER 11

1. 'Good lad, if someone were to strike at the root of this great tree, it would ooze sap but live. If someone were to strike at the middle, it would ooze sap but live. If someone were to strike at the top, it would ooze sap but live. Pervaded by the life, by the self, it stands, happy, ever drinking.
2. 'If the life leaves one branch of it, that branch dries up. If it leaves a second, that dries up. If it leaves a third, that dries up. If it leaves the whole tree, the whole dries up. Good lad, know that this is the same,' he said.
3. 'When separated from the life, *it* dies, but the life does not

die. This subtle part is what all this has as self. It is truth: it is the self. *You* are that, Śvetaketu.'

'Blessed one, explain it to me further.'

'I will, good lad,' he said.

CHAPTER 12

1. 'Bring a banyan-fruit from this tree.'

'Here it is, blessed one.'

'Break it.'

'I have broken it, blessed one.'

'What do you see there?'

'Tiny seeds, blessed one.'

'Now break one of them.'

'I have broken it, blessed one.'

'What do you see there?'

'Nothing, blessed one.'

2. He said to him, 'Good lad, on this subtle part – the subtle part which you do not see – rests the great banyan-tree. Good lad, have faith.

3. 'This subtle part is what all this has as self. It is truth: it is the self. *You* are that, Śvetaketu.'

'Blessed one, explain it to me further.'

'I will, good lad,' he said.

CHAPTER 13

1. 'Put this salt in water, and come to me in the morning.'

He did so. His father said to him, 'Now, bring me the salt that you put in water last night.'

He felt for it, but did not find it.

2. 'Quite,' said his father, 'for it has dissolved. But sip from the side of it. What is it like?'

'Salt.'

'Sip from the middle of it. What is it like?'

'Salt.'

'Sip from the other side of it. What is it like?'

'Salt.'

'Throw it away, then come to me.'

He did so, and said, 'It is there all the time.'

His father said to him, 'You do not see *being* here, but it *is* here.

3. 'This subtle part is what all this has as self. It is truth: it is the self. *You* are that, Śvetaketu.'

'Blessed one, explain it to me further.'

'I will, good lad,' he said.

CHAPTER 14

1. 'Suppose, good lad, that someone were to lead a man blindfold from Gandhāra and then release him in a deserted place; and suppose that he were to be blown to east, north, south or west, crying, "I have been led blindfold and released blindfold!"

2. 'And suppose that someone were to undo the blindfold and tell him, "Gandhāra is in this direction. Walk in this direction." And he, being wise and intelligent, by asking from village to village would reach Gandhāra. In the same way a person who has a teacher knows, "It is only so long until I am released. Then I will reach my goal."[13]

3. 'This subtle part is what all this has as self. It is truth: it is the self. *You* are that, Śvetaketu.'

'Blessed one, explain it to me further.'

'I will, good lad,' he said.

CHAPTER 15

1. 'Good lad, if a man is ill, his relatives wait around him saying, "Do you know me? Do you know me?" So long as his speech has not entered into mind, his mind into breath, his breath into heat, his heat into the highest deity, he knows them.
2. 'But when his speech *has* entered into mind, his mind into breath, his breath into heat, his heat into the highest deity, he does not know them.
3. 'This subtle part is what all this has as self. It is truth: it is the self. *You* are that, Śvetaketu.'

'Blessed one, explain it to me further.'

'I will, good lad,' he said.

CHAPTER 16

1. 'Good lad, suppose they bring a man with his hands bound, saying, "He has stolen! He has committed a theft! Heat up an axe for him." If he is the culprit he makes himself false.[14] Joined with falsehood, hiding himself behind falsehood, when he seizes the heated axe he is burnt, and then he is executed.
2. 'But if he is not the culprit he makes himself true. Joined with truth, hiding himself behind truth, when he seizes the heated axe he is not burnt, and then he is set free.
3. 'As he would not then be burnt . . .[15] It is what all this has as self. It is truth: it is the self. *You* are that, Śvetaketu.'

Then he understood his teaching: he understood.

BOOK VII

CHAPTER I

1. OṂ. Nārada came to Sanatkumāra saying, 'Teach me, blessed one.'

Sanatkumāra said to him, 'Come to me with what you know, and I will tell you of something higher than that.'

He said,

2. 'Blessed one, I know the Ṛgveda, the Yajurveda, the Sāmaveda, the Atharvan which is the fourth,[1] and history and legend the fifth; I know the Veda of Vedas,[2] the ancestral rites,[3] arithmetic,[4] portents,[5] treasure-finding,[6] disputation,[7] the single way,[8] the knowledge of the gods,[9] the knowledge of priesthood,[10] the knowledge of ghosts,[11] the knowledge of royalty,[12] the knowledge of the constellations,[13] and the knowledge of the divine people who are serpents.[14]

3. 'But I am a knower of the mantras, not a knower of the self. I have heard from folk like yourself, blessed one, that "the knower of self crosses beyond sorrow". I am sorrowful, blessed one. Blessed one, take *me* across to the other shore of sorrow.'

Sanatkumāra said to him, 'All this that you have learned is name.

4. 'The Ṛgveda, the Yajurveda, the Sāmaveda, the Atharvan which is the fourth, and history and legend the fifth; the Veda of Vedas, the ancestral rites, arithmetic, portents, treasure-finding, disputation, the single way, the knowledge of the gods, the knowledge of priesthood, the knowledge of ghosts, the knowledge of royalty, the knowledge of the constellations, and the

knowledge of the divine people who are serpents, are name. All this is name. Worship[15] name.

5. 'The one who worships name as *brahman* wins freedom to move as far as name can go – the one who worships name as *brahman*.'

'Blessed one, is there anything greater than name?'

'There *is* something greater than name.'

'Tell me about it, blessed one.'

CHAPTER 2

1. 'Speech is greater than name. Speech makes known the Ṛgveda, the Yajurveda, the Sāmaveda, the Atharvan which is the fourth, and history and legend the fifth; the Veda of Vedas, the ancestral rites, arithmetic, portents, treasure-finding, disputation, the single way, the knowledge of the gods, the knowledge of priesthood, the knowledge of ghosts, the knowledge of royalty, the knowledge of the constellations, the knowledge of the divine people who are serpents; sky, earth, air, space, water, heat;[16] gods, human beings, domestic animals, birds, grass and trees, and wild animals, all the way down to worms, flying things and ants; right (*dharma*) and wrong (*adharma*), truth and falsehood, good and bad, attractive and unattractive. If there had been no speech, then right and wrong, truth and falsehood, good and bad, attractive and unattractive would not have been made known. Speech makes known all this. Worship speech.

2. 'The one who worships speech as *brahman* wins freedom to move as far as speech can go – the one who worships speech as *brahman*.'

'Blessed one, is there anything greater than speech?'

'There *is* something greater than speech.'

'Tell me about it, blessed one.'

CHAPTER 3

1. 'Mind is greater than speech. Just as a fist encloses two myrobalans or two jujubes or two terminalia seeds, mind encloses both speech and name. When one thinks with the mind, "Let me recite mantras", one chants; when one thinks, "Let me perform actions (*karman*)", one performs actions; when one thinks, "Let me wish for sons and animals", one wishes for sons and animals; when one thinks, "Let me wish for this world and that one", one wishes for this world and that one. Mind is the self; mind is the world; mind is *brahman*. Worship mind.
2. 'The one who worships mind as *brahman* wins freedom to move as far as mind can go – the one who worships mind as *brahman*.'

'Blessed one, is there anything greater than mind?'

'There *is* something greater than mind.'

'Tell me about it, blessed one.'

CHAPTER 4

1. 'Will (*saṃkalpa*)[17] is greater than mind. When one wills (*saṃkalpayate*), one thinks; then one utters speech – one utters it as names. In name the mantras become one, and in the mantras actions become one.
2. 'These have will as their sole end, will as their self, and are established on will. Sky and earth have been formed (*sam-kḷp-*), air and space have been formed, the waters and heat have been formed, and rain is formed according to their will (*saṃkḷpti*). Food is formed according to the will of rain. The breaths are formed according to the will of food. The mantras are formed according to the will of the breaths. Actions are formed according to the will of the mantras. The world is formed according to the will of the actions. Everything is formed according to the will of the world. This is will. Worship will.
3. 'The one who worships will as *brahman* wins worlds that

are fitting (*kḷpta*): being constant, he wins constant worlds; being established, established worlds; being sorrowless, sorrowless worlds. He wins freedom to move as far as will can go – the one who worships will as *brahman*.'

'Blessed one, is there anything greater than will?'

'There *is* something greater than will.'

'Tell me about it, blessed one.'

CHAPTER 5

1. 'Intelligence (*citta*)[18] is greater than will. When one reflects (*cetayati*), one wills; then one thinks; then one utters speech – one utters it as names. In name the mantras become one, and in the mantras actions become one.

2. 'These have intelligence as their sole end, intelligence as their self, and are established on intelligence. So even if someone knows much, but is without intelligence, folk say of him, "He is nobody.[19] If he had learned, or knew, he would not be without intelligence like this." But if someone knows little, but has intelligence, folk wish to hear him. Intelligence is the sole end of these; intelligence is their self; intelligence is their basis. Worship intelligence.

3. 'The one who worships intelligence as *brahman* wins worlds that are longed for (*citta*): being constant, he wins constant worlds; being established, established worlds; being sorrowless, sorrowless worlds. He wins freedom to move as far as intelligence can go – the one who worships intelligence as *brahman*.'

'Blessed one, is there anything greater than intelligence?'

'There *is* something greater than intelligence.'

'Tell me about it, blessed one.'

CHAPTER 6

1. 'Meditation[20] is greater than intelligence. Earth seems to meditate. Sky seems to meditate. The waters seem to meditate. The mountains seem to meditate. Gods and human beings seem to meditate. So those among human beings who achieve greatness here seem to share in the reward of meditation. Those who are small are quarrelsome, spiteful, slanderous: those who are powerful seem to share in the reward of meditation. Worship meditation.

2. 'The one who worships meditation as *brahman* wins freedom to move as far as meditation can go – the one who worships meditation as *brahman*.'

'Blessed one, is there anything greater than meditation?'

'There *is* something greater than meditation.'

'Tell me about it, blessed one.'

CHAPTER 7

1. 'Understanding[21] is greater than meditation. By understanding one knows the Ṛgveda, the Yajurveda, the Sāmaveda, the Atharvan which is the fourth, and history and legend the fifth; the Veda of Vedas, the ancestral rites, arithmetic, portents, treasure-finding, disputation, the single way, the knowledge of the gods, the knowledge of priesthood, the knowledge of ghosts, the knowledge of royalty, the knowledge of the constellations, the knowledge of the divine people who are serpents; sky, earth, air, space, water, heat; gods, human beings, domestic animals, birds, grass and trees, and wild animals, all the way down to worms, flying things and ants; right and wrong, truth and falsehood, good and bad, attractive and unattractive, food, flavour, this world, and that world. One knows them through understanding. Worship understanding.

2. 'The one who worships understanding as *brahman* attains worlds full of understanding, full of knowledge. He wins

freedom to move as far as understanding can go – the one who worships understanding as *brahman*.'

'Blessed one, is there anything greater than understanding?'

'There *is* something greater than understanding.'

'Tell me about it, blessed one.'

CHAPTER 8

1. 'Strength is greater than understanding. One man with strength causes a hundred with understanding to tremble. When one becomes strong one can stand up; standing up, one can go about; going about, one can pay attention;[22] paying attention, one can see, can hear, can think, can be aware, can do, can understand. Through strength, the earth stands; through strength, middle-air stands; through strength, the sky stands; through strength, the mountains stand; through strength, gods and human beings stand; through strength, domestic animals, birds, grass and trees, and wild animals, all the way down to worms, flying things and ants stand; through strength, the worlds stand. Worship strength.

2. 'The one who worships strength as *brahman* wins freedom to move as far as strength can go – the one who worships strength as *brahman*.'

'Blessed one, is there anything greater than strength?'

'There *is* something greater than strength.'

'Tell me about it, blessed one.'

CHAPTER 9

1. 'Food is greater than strength. So if one does not eat for ten nights,[23] even if one lives one cannot see, cannot hear, cannot think, cannot be aware, cannot do, cannot understand. But with the coming of food one can see, can hear, can think, can be aware, can do, can understand. Worship food.

2. 'The one who worships food as *brahman* achieves worlds full of food and full of drink. He wins freedom to move as far as food can go – the one who worships food as *brahman*.'

'Blessed one, is there anything greater than food?'

'There *is* something greater than food.'

'Tell me about it, blessed one.'

CHAPTER 10

1. 'The waters are greater than food. So when there is not a good rainfall, living things[24] suffer, thinking, "Food will be short." When there *is* a good rainfall, living things are happy, thinking, "Food will be plentiful." All these are the waters, shaped: earth, middle-air, sky, mountains, gods and human beings, domestic animals, birds, grass and trees, and wild animals, all the way down to worms, flying things and ants. All these are the waters, shaped. Worship the waters.

2. 'The one who worships the waters (*āpaḥ*) as *brahman* obtains (*āp-*) all desires and becomes contented. He wins freedom to move as far as the waters can go – the one who worships the waters as *brahman*.'

'Blessed one, is there anything greater than the waters?'

'There *is* something greater than the waters.'

'Tell me about it, blessed one.'

CHAPTER 11

1. 'Heat (*tejas*) is greater than the waters. By seizing hold of the air, it heats up middle-air. Then folk say, "It is burning! It is boiling! It is going to rain!" It first foreshows and then creates the waters. It travels along as claps of thunder, with flashes of lightning going upward and across. Then folk say, "It lightens! It thunders! It is going to rain!" It first foreshows and then creates the waters. Worship heat.

2. 'The one who worships heat as *brahman*, bright (*tejasvin*), achieves bright worlds, blazing (*tejasvat*), free from darkness. He wins freedom to move as far as heat can go – the one who worships heat as *brahman*.'

'Blessed one, is there anything greater than heat?'

'There *is* something greater than heat.'

'Tell me about it, blessed one.'

CHAPTER 12

1. 'Space is greater than heat. In it are both the sun and the moon, lightning, the constellations, and fire. Through space one calls, through space one hears, through space one replies; in space one takes pleasure, in space one does not take pleasure, in space one is born, into space one grows. Worship space.

2. 'The one who worships space as *brahman* achieves spacious worlds, clear, unobstructed, with plenty of room to move. He wins freedom to move as far as space can go – the one who worships space as *brahman*.'

'Blessed one, is there anything greater than space?'

'There *is* something greater than space.'

'Tell me about it, blessed one.'

CHAPTER 13

1. 'Memory is greater[25] than space. So even if many people were to sit together who did not remember, they would not hear anyone, think of anyone, or know anyone. When they remembered, then they *would* hear, *would* think, *would* know. By memory one knows one's sons; by memory one knows one's animals. Worship memory.

2. 'The one who worships memory as *brahman* wins freedom to move as far as memory can go – the one who worships memory as *brahman*.'

'Blessed one, is there anything greater than memory?'

'There *is* something greater than memory.'

'Tell me about it, blessed one.'

CHAPTER 14

1. 'Hope is greater than memory. Kindled by hope the memory recites mantras, performs actions, wishes for offspring and animals, wishes for this world and that one. Worship hope.

2. 'For the one who worships hope as *brahman*, all his desires are prospered by hope, and his prayers are never in vain. He wins freedom to move as far as hope can go – the one who worships hope as *brahman*.'

'Blessed one, is there anything greater than hope?'

'There *is* something greater than hope.'

'Tell me about it, blessed one.'

CHAPTER 15

1. 'Breath is greater than hope. Just as spokes are held together in a wheel-hub, everything is held together in the breath. Breath moves by breath. Breath gives breath, gives it to breath. Breath is father, breath is mother, breath is brother, breath is sister, breath is teacher, breath is Brāhmaṇa.

2. 'If one says something slightly harsh to father, mother, brother, sister, teacher or Brāhmaṇa, folk say to one, "Shame on you! You are killing your father! You are killing your mother! You are killing your brother! You are killing your sister! You are killing your teacher! You are killing a Brāhmaṇa!"[26]

3. 'But once breath has left them, even if one burns them in a heap, turning them with a spear, folk do not then say to one, "You are killing your father! You are killing your mother! You are killing your brother! You are killing your sister! You are killing your teacher! You are killing a Brāhmaṇa!"

4. 'For the breath becomes all these. The one who sees this, thinks this, knows this, speaks boldly.[27] If folk should say to him, "You speak boldly", he would say, "I *do* speak boldly." He would not deny it.

CHAPTER 16

1. 'He who speaks boldly through truth speaks boldly indeed.'
'Blessed one, let me speak boldly through truth!'
'Then you must seek to know truth.'
'Blessed one, I seek to know truth.'

CHAPTER 17

1. 'When one understands, one speaks truth. If one does not understand, one does not speak truth. If one understands, one *does* speak truth. You must seek to know understanding.'
'Blessed one, I seek to know understanding.'

CHAPTER 18

1. 'When one thinks, one understands. If one has not thought, one does not understand. If one has thought, one *does* understand. You must seek to know thought.'
'Blessed one, I seek to know thought.'

CHAPTER 19

1. 'When one has faith, one thinks. If one has no faith, one does not think. If one has faith, one *does* think. You must seek to know faith.'

'Blessed one, I seek to know faith.'

CHAPTER 20

1. 'When one serves, one has faith. If one does not serve, one has no faith. If one serves, one *has* faith. You must seek to know service.'

'Blessed one, I seek to know service.'

CHAPTER 21

1. 'When one acts, one serves. If one has not acted, one does not serve. If one has acted, one *does* serve. You must seek to know action.'[28]

'Blessed one, I seek to know action.'

CHAPTER 22

1. 'When one attains happiness, one acts. If one has not attained happiness, one does not act. If one has attained happiness, one *does* act. You must seek to know happiness.'

'Blessed one, I seek to know happiness.'

CHAPTER 23

1. 'Abundance is happiness. There is no happiness in smallness. Abundance is happiness. You must seek to know abundance.'

'Blessed one, I seek to know abundance.'

CHAPTER 24

1. 'Where one does not see another, does not hear another, does not know another, that is abundance. Where one sees another, hears another, knows another, that is smallness. Abundance is immortal: smallness is mortal.'

'Blessed one, on what does it rest (*prati-sthā-*)?'

'On its own greatness – or perhaps not on greatness.

2. 'What folk here call greatness is cows and horses, elephants and gold, slaves and wives, fields and houses. That is not what I am saying. I say', he said, 'that it is other, and rests on something other.

CHAPTER 25

1. 'It is below, it is above, it is in the west, it is in the east, it is in the south, it is in the north. It is all this. Hence the symbolic statement on "I": "I am above, I am in the west, I am in the east, I am in the south, I am in the north. I am all this."

2. 'Hence the symbolic statement on "self": "The self is below, the self is above, the self is in the west, the self is in the east, the self is in the south, the self is in the north. The self is all this." Seeing this, thinking this, knowing this – taking pleasure in the self, playing in the self, making love with the self, delighting in the self – one becomes one's own ruler, and wins freedom to

move in all worlds. But those who know it in other ways are ruled by others, live in perishable worlds, and win no freedom to move in all worlds.

CHAPTER 26

1. 'When one sees this, thinks this, knows this, one's breath is of the self; one's hope is of the self; one's memory is of the self; one's space is of the self; one's heat is of the self; one's waters are of the self; one's appearance and disappearance are of the self; one's food is of the self; one's strength is of the self; one's understanding is of the self; one's meditation is of the self; one's intelligence is of the self; one's will is of the self; one's mind is of the self; one's speech is of the self; one's name is of the self; one's mantras are of the self; one's actions are of the self; all this is of the self.

2. 'There is a verse about it:

> The seer[29] does not see death,
> Nor disease, nor suffering:
> The seer sees everything,
> Wins everything, everywhere.

'It is onefold, threefold, fivefold, sevenfold, ninefold; again, it is traditionally called "eleven", "a hundred and ten and one", and "twenty thousand". In purity of food is purity of being; in purity of being is constant memory; in the finding of memory is the undoing of all knots.'

To the one whose impurities have been wiped away,[30] the blessed Sanatkumāra reveals the farther shore of darkness. They call him Skanda: they call him Skanda.[31]

BOOK VIII

CHAPTER I

1. OṂ. Within the tiny lotus-house[1] which is in the city of *brahman* there is a tiny space. That which is in it one must seek for, one must want to know.

2. If folk were to ask him, 'Within the tiny lotus-house which is in the city of *brahman* there is a tiny space. What is found there that one must seek for, one must want to know?', the sage would say:[2]

3. 'The space within the heart is as big as *this* space. Both sky and earth are concentrated within it: both fire and air, both sun and moon, both lightning and constellations, what one has here and what one does not have here – everything is concentrated within it.'

4. If they were to ask him, 'If all this, and all beings, and all desires, are concentrated within the city of *brahman*, when old age seizes it or it perishes, what is left of it?'

5. He would say, 'It does not grow old with the ageing of *this*, nor is it slain with the slaying of *this*. It is the true city of *brahman*. Desires are concentrated within it. The self is free from evil, ageless, deathless, sorrowless, without hunger, without thirst, of true desire,[3] of true resolve.[4] Just as here people follow at command, and live in whatever place, whatever country, whatever share of land they wish for . . .

6. 'Just as here worlds won through action perish, there worlds won through merit perish.[5] While those here who pass on without having known the self and the true desires do not gain freedom to move in all worlds, those here who pass on

having known the self and the true desires *do* gain freedom to move in all worlds.

CHAPTER 2

1. 'If one desires a world of fathers,[6] at one's will fathers appear and one triumphs, blessed with a world of fathers.
2. 'If one desires a world of mothers, at one's will mothers appear and one triumphs, blessed with a world of mothers.
3. 'If one desires a world of brothers, at one's will brothers appear and one triumphs, blessed with a world of brothers.
4. 'If one desires a world of sisters, at one's will sisters appear and one triumphs, blessed with a world of sisters.
5. 'If one desires a world of friends, at one's will friends appear and one triumphs, blessed with a world of friends.
6. 'If one desires a world of perfumes and garlands, at one's will perfumes and garlands appear and one triumphs, blessed with a world of perfumes and garlands.
7. 'If one desires a world of food and drink, at one's will food and drink appear and one triumphs, blessed with a world of food and drink.
8. 'If one desires a world of singing and music, at one's will singing and music appear and one triumphs, blessed with a world of singing and music.
9. 'If one desires a world of women,[7] at one's will women appear and one triumphs, blessed with a world of women.
10. 'Whatever place one longs for, whatever desire one desires, at one's will it appears and one triumphs, blessed with it.

CHAPTER 3

1. 'These true desires are hidden by falsehood. Falsehood is what hides desires that are true, for when any of one's folk passes on from here one is no longer able to see him.

2. 'By going there[8] one finds everything, both those of one's folk who are alive here and those who have passed away, and whatever else one cannot get by desiring: for here one's true desires are hidden by falsehood. Just as those who do not know the land would not find a golden treasure, though they might walk over it again and again, so all these creatures do not find the world of *brahman*, though they go to it every day;[9] for they are kept away by falsehood.

3. 'This self is in the heart. This is the derivation of it: "this in the heart" (*hṛdy ayam*), hence "heart" (*hṛdayam*). The one who knows this goes every day to a heavenly world.

4. 'The blissful one[10] that, leaving this body and entering the light beyond, appears in its own form is the self,' he said. 'This is the immortal, the fearless: this is *brahman*. The name of this *brahman* is "truth" (*satya*).'

5. 'There are three syllables: *sa-tī-yam*.[11] What is *sat* (being) is immortal. What is *ti* is mortal. By that which is *yam* one controls (*yam-*) them both. Since one controls both by it, it is *yam*. The one who knows this goes every day to a heavenly world.'

CHAPTER 4

1. The self is a dam, a separation between worlds so that they do not run together.[12] Day and night do not cross it, nor old age nor death nor grief, nor good action nor bad action. All evils turn back from it, for the world of *brahman* is freed from evil.

2. On crossing this dam, one who was blind is blind no longer; one who was wounded is wounded no longer; one who was suffering suffers no longer. On crossing this dam, night turns into day, for the world of *brahman* is always bright.

3. The world of *brahman* belongs to those who through studentship[13] find the world of *brahman*. They win freedom to move in all worlds.

CHAPTER 5

1. What folk call 'sacrifice' is studentship, for only through studentship does the knower find it. What they call 'offering' (*iṣṭi*) is studentship, for only by seeking (*iṣṭvā*)[14] through studentship does one find the self.
2. What they call 'a sequence of sacrifices' (*sattrāyaṇa*)[15] is studentship, for only through studentship does one find protection (*trāṇa*) of the self which is being (*sat*). What they call 'silent practice' (*mauna*)[16] is studentship, for only by finding the self through studentship does one think (*man-*).
3. What they call 'a period of fasting' (*anāśakāyana*) is studentship, for the self that one finds through studentship does not perish (*na naśyati*).[17] What they call 'going to the forest' (*araṇyāyana*) is studentship, for there are two oceans, Ara and Ṇya, in the world of *brahman*, in the sky, the third from here.[18] There is a lake called Airaṃmadīya;[19] there is a fig-tree called Somasavana;[20] there is a citadel of *brahman* called Aparājitā;[21] there is a golden palace, Prabhu.[22]
4. The world of *brahman* belongs to those who through studentship find the two oceans, Ara and Ṇya. They win freedom to move in all worlds.

CHAPTER 6

1. There exist channels of the heart, of a subtle essence, tawny, white, blue, yellow, red.[23] The sun, too, is tawny, white, blue, yellow, red.
2. Just as a highway reaches both villages, this one and that one, so the rays of the sun go to both worlds, this one and that one. They spread out from the sun, slipping into these channels: they spread out from these channels, slipping into the sun.
3. So when, asleep, withdrawn and perfectly calm, one knows no dream, one has slipped into these channels. No evil touches one, for one is endowed with light (*tejas*).

4. Now when someone is brought to weakness, folk sit around him and say, 'Do you know me? Do you know me?' As long as he has not left the body, he knows them.

5. When he leaves the body, he goes upward by these rays. Chanting OṂ, he passes upward: otherwise not. In the time that it would take to throw the mind there, he goes to the sun. For those who know, this is the door of the world, a way onward, but for those who do not know, it is an obstruction.[24]

6. There is a verse about it:

> A hundred and one are the channels of the heart.
> Of them, one flows out through the head.
> Going up by it, one reaches immortality.
> Others, on departing, go in all directions –
> On departing.[25]

CHAPTER 7

1. 'One must seek for and want to know the self, which is free from evil, ageless, deathless, sorrowless, without hunger, without thirst, of true desire, of true resolve. The one who has found and knows the self attains all worlds and all desires.' So said Prajāpati.

2. Both gods and demons came to know of this. They said, 'Come, we will seek for the self, since by knowing the self one attains all worlds and all desires.' Of the gods, Indra set forth, and of the demons, Virocana, and unbeknown to one another they came into Prajāpati's presence with firewood in their hands.

3. For thirty-two years they lived as *brahmacārins*. Then Prajāpati asked them, 'What did you want, that you came to stay here?'

They said, 'Folk report your saying, blessed one, "One must seek for and want to know the self, which is free from evil, ageless, deathless, sorrowless, without hunger, without thirst, of true desire, of true resolve. The one who has found and knows the self attains all worlds and all desires." That is what we wanted, that we came to stay here.'

4. Prajāpati said to them, 'The person who is seen in the eye is the self.' He said, 'This is the immortal, the fearless: this is *brahman*.'

'Then, blessed one, which is it, the one that is discerned in water, or the one that is discerned in a mirror?'

'It is discerned in all places,' he said.

CHAPTER 8

1. 'Look at yourselves (*ātman*) in a dish of water, then tell me what you do not understand about the self.' They looked in a dish of water. Prajāpati asked them, 'What do you see?'

They said, 'Blessed one, we see ourselves in reflection, from hair to nails.'

2. Prajāpati said to them, 'Make yourselves smart,[26] well-dressed and elegant, and look in a dish of water.' They made themselves smart, well-dressed and elegant, and looked in a dish of water. Prajāpati asked them, 'What do you see?'

3. They said, 'Blessed one, just as we are smart, well-dressed and elegant, so these, blessed one, are smart, well-dressed and elegant.'

'This is the self,' he said. 'This is the immortal, the fearless: this is *brahman*.' And they left, their hearts at peace.

4. Seeing them, Prajāpati said, 'They are leaving without attaining or knowing the self. Those who have this as their inner teaching,[27] whether gods or demons, will be defeated.'

Virocana went to the demons, his heart at peace, and taught them this inner teaching:

'The self must be glorified, the self must be served here.[28] Glorifying and serving the self here, one attains both worlds, this one and that one.'

5. So even here, today, they say of one who does not give, does not have faith, does not sacrifice, 'Alas! He is demonic!', for this inner teaching belongs to the demons. Folk make

ready the body of the departed with alms,[29] clothing and adornments, and think that they will win that world by means of this one.

CHAPTER 9

1. But, before he had reached the gods, Indra saw the danger: 'When the body is smart, it is smart. When the body is well-dressed, it is well-dressed. When the body is elegant, it is elegant. But, in the same way, when the body is blind, it is blind. When the body is lame, it is lame. When the body is mutilated, it is mutilated. On the destruction of the body, it is destroyed. I see no satisfaction here.'

2. He went back with firewood in his hands. Prajāpati said to him, 'Maghavan, you went away with Virocana, your heart at peace. So what did you want, that you came back?'

He said, 'Blessed one, when the body is smart, it is smart. When the body is well-dressed, it is well-dressed. When the body is elegant, it is elegant. But, in the same way, when the body is blind, it is blind. When the body is lame, it is lame. When the body is mutilated, it is mutilated. On the destruction of the body, it is destroyed. I see no satisfaction here.'

3. 'Just so, Maghavan,' he said. 'I will explain it to you further. Stay another thirty-two years.' He stayed another thirty-two years. Then he said to him:

CHAPTER 10

1. 'The one that, triumphing, moves about in dream is the self,' he said. 'This is the immortal, the fearless: this is *brahman*.'

He went away, his heart at peace, but, before he had reached the gods, he saw the danger: 'Though the body becomes blind, it is not blind. Though the body is lame, it is not lame. It is not flawed by its flaws.

2. 'It is not slain with its slaying, nor lamed with its laming. But it *seems* to be killed; it *seems* to be stripped.[30] It seems to experience unpleasant things; it seems to weep. I see no satisfaction here.'

3. He went back with firewood in his hands. Prajāpati said to him, 'Maghavan, you went away, your heart at peace. So what did you want, that you came back?'

He said, 'Blessed one, though the body becomes blind, it is not blind. Though the body is lame, it is not lame. It is not flawed by its flaws.

4. 'It is not slain with its slaying, nor lamed with its laming. But it *seems* to be killed; it *seems* to be stripped. It seems to experience unpleasant things; it seems to weep. I see no satisfaction here.'

'Just so, Maghavan,' he said. 'I will explain it to you further. Stay another thirty-two years.' He stayed another thirty-two years. Then he said to him:

CHAPTER 11

1. 'When, asleep, withdrawn and perfectly calm, one knows no dream, this is the self,' he said. 'This is the immortal, the fearless: this is *brahman*.'

He went away, his heart at peace, but, before he had reached the gods, he saw the danger: 'Surely this does not directly know itself (*ātman*) as "I am this", nor does it know beings. It merges and dissolves.[31] I see no satisfaction here.'

2. He went back with firewood in his hands. Prajāpati said to him, 'Maghavan, you went away, your heart at peace. So what did you want, that you came back?'

He said, 'Blessed one, surely this does not directly know itself as "I am this", nor does it know beings. It merges and dissolves. I see no satisfaction here.'

3. 'Just so, Maghavan,' he said. 'I will explain it to you further, this and nothing else. Stay another five years.' He stayed another five years. Altogether it came to a hundred and one years. So

folk say, 'Maghavan lived as a *brahmacārin* with Prajāpati for a hundred and one years.' Then he said to him:

CHAPTER 12

1. 'Maghavan, the body is mortal. It has been taken by death. But it is the support of the self, which is immortal and bodiless. The embodied has been taken by the pleasant and the unpleasant. For the embodied, there is no escaping the pleasant and the unpleasant. But that which is bodiless the pleasant and the unpleasant do not touch.

2. 'Air is bodiless. Cloud, lightning and thunder – these are bodiless. Just as they, rising up from space and reaching the light beyond, appear in their own form,

3. 'so the blissful one, leaving this body and entering the light beyond, appears in its own form. That is the highest person.[32] Here he moves about, feasting, playing, or taking pleasure with women, chariots or kin, not remembering this appendage, the body. Just as a draught animal is yoked to a carriage, the breath is yoked to the body.

4. 'Where the eye is fixed upon space, that is the person of the eye.[33] The eye is for seeing. The one who experiences "Let me smell this" is the self. The nose[34] is for smelling. The one who experiences "Let me say this" is the self. The speech is for talking. The one who experiences "Let me hear this" is the self. The ear is for hearing.

5. 'The one who experiences "Let me think this" is the self. Mind is its divine eye. It takes pleasure, seeing with this divine eyes, the mind, the desires

6. 'which are in the world of *brahman*. The gods worship the self as such, so all worlds and all desires have been taken by them. The one who has found and knows the self attains all worlds and all desires.' So said Prajāpati. So said Prajāpati.

CHAPTER 13

1. From the dark I take refuge in the dappled,
From the dappled I take refuge in the dark.[35]
Shaking off evil, as a horse shakes its mane,
Shaking off the body, as the moon breaks
free from Rāhu's mouth,[36]
With self achieved (*kṛtāman*), I reach,
I reach the unmade (*akṛta*) world of *brahman*.

CHAPTER 14

1. Space, as it is called, is the bringer into being of name and form. That which contains them[37] is *brahman*, the immortal: that is the self.

I reach the house, the court of Prajāpati.
I become glory. I have attained
The glory of the Brāhmaṇas, glory of the
kings, glory of the people.[38]
The glory of glories, may I not go
To the white, toothless,
Toothless, white and slimy[39] –
May I not go to the slimy!

CHAPTER 15

1. Brahmā taught this to Prajāpati, Prajāpati to Manu, and Manu to his offspring. If one studies the Veda, according to the rule, in the time left over from one's guru's work; if, after returning from the teacher's house into the family, one recites it to oneself in a clean place; if one brings up virtuous children;[40] if one establishes all one's faculties in the self; and if one does

no harm to any beings, other than at the due times:[41] if one conducts oneself like this as long as one lives, one attains the world of *brahman*, and does not return – and does not return.

OṂ. *May my limbs, speech, breath, eye, ear, strength and all senses grow strong. Everything is the* brahman *of the Upaniṣads. May I not reject* brahman. *May* brahman *not reject me. May there be no rejecting. May there be no rejecting of me. May all the* dharmas *which are in the Upaniṣads be in me, who delight in the self. May they be in me.*

OṂ. *Peace, peace, peace.*

TAITTIRĪYA UPANIṢAD

The Taittirīyas' Teaching

OṂ. *May Mitra be kind,*[1] *may Varuṇa be kind,*
May Aryaman be kind to us.
May Indra and Bṛhaspati be kind,
May wide-striding Viṣṇu be kind to us.
Homage to brahman,[2] *homage to you, Vāyu:*
You are brahman *manifest:*
I will speak of you as brahman *manifest.*
*I will speak law (*ṛta*): I will speak truth.*[3]
May that protect me: may that protect the speaker.[4]
May it protect me: may it protect the speaker.

OṂ. *Peace, peace, peace.*

BOOK I: PRONUNCIATION[5]

CHAPTER 1

1. OṂ. May Mitra be kind, may Varuṇa be kind,
May Aryaman be kind to us.
May Indra and Bṛhaspati be kind,
May wide-striding Viṣṇu be kind to us.
Homage to *brahman*, homage to you, Vāyu:
You are *brahman* manifest:
I will speak of you as *brahman* manifest.
I will speak law: I will speak truth.
May that protect me: may that protect the speaker.
May it protect me: may it protect the speaker.

OṂ. Peace, peace, peace.

CHAPTER 2

1. We will explain pronunciation. Letter, accent, length, stress, intonation, sequence:[6] so the teaching on pronunciation is told.

CHAPTER 3

1. May glory, may the radiance of *brahman* be with us two.[7]

Now we will explain the inner teaching (*upaniṣad*) on connection, under five headings: regarding worlds, regarding lights, regarding knowledge, regarding offspring, regarding oneself. Folk call these the great connections.

Regarding worlds: earth is the prior form, sky the latter form, space the connection,
2. air the connector.[8] So much regarding worlds.

Regarding lights: fire is the prior form, the sun the latter form, the waters the connection, lightning the connector. So much regarding lights.

Regarding knowledge: the teacher is the prior form,
3. the student the latter form, knowledge the connection, teaching the connector. So much regarding knowledge.

Regarding offspring: the mother is the prior form, the father the latter form, the offspring the connection, begetting the connector. So much regarding offspring.

4. Regarding oneself: the lower jaw is the prior form, the upper jaw the latter form, speech the connection, the tongue the connector. So much regarding oneself.

These are the great connections. The one who knows the great connections, explained in this way, is connected with offspring, animals, the radiance of *brahman*, good food, a heavenly world.

CHAPTER 4

1. May he who is the bull of the metres, of all forms,
   Who has come into being from immortality over the metres,
Indra, save me by intelligence.
   God, may I become a bearer of immortality.

May my body be very active,
My tongue be most honeyed:
May I hear widely with my ears!
You are the sheath of *brahman*,
hidden by intelligence.
Protect what I have heard.

She[9] comes, bringing, increasing,

2. Soon[10] making her own for ever
My clothing and cattle
And food and drink:
So bring prosperity, wool-clad,[11]
With animals, to me.
SVĀHĀ!

May *brahmacārins* come towards me, SVĀHĀ!
May *brahmacārins* come by different ways to
me, SVĀHĀ!
May *brahmacārins* come forth to me, SVĀHĀ!
May *brahmacārins* be self-controlled, SVĀHĀ!
May *brahmacārins* come in peace,[12] SVĀHĀ!

3. May I be glory among the people, SVĀHĀ!
May I be greater than the richest, SVĀHĀ!
May I enter you, Bhaga, SVĀHĀ!
Enter me, Bhaga, SVĀHĀ!
In you, the thousand-branched,
I cleanse myself, Bhaga. SVĀHĀ!
Just as the waters flow downhill,
Just as the months (while days grow old),[13]
May *brahmacārins* come to me,
Dhātṛ, from every side. SVĀHĀ!
You are my neighbour. Appear to me. Take
refuge in me.[14]

4. Increasing, may *brahmacārins* come in peace, SVĀHĀ!

CHAPTER 5

1. BHŪḤ, BHUVAḤ, SUVAḤ: these are the three utterances.[15] Māhācamasya makes known the fourth of them: MAHAḤ.[16] That is *brahman*: that is the self. The other gods are limbs of it. BHŪḤ is this world. BHUVAḤ is middle-air. SUVAḤ is that world.

2. MAHAḤ is the sun. All the worlds grow great through the sun. BHŪḤ is fire. BHUVAḤ is air. SUVAḤ is the sun. MAHAḤ is the moon. All the lights grow great through the moon. BHŪḤ is the *ṛc* verses. BHUVAḤ is the *sāman* verses. SUVAḤ is the *yajus* verses.

3. MAHAḤ is *brahman*. All the Vedas grow great through *brahman*. BHŪḤ is the breath. BHUVAḤ is the lower breath. SUVAḤ is the diffused breath. MAHAḤ is food. All the breaths grow great through food. These are fourfold, in four ways. The four utterances are fourfold. The one who knows them knows *brahman*: all the gods bring tribute to him.

CHAPTER 6

1. There is a space within the heart. In it is the person made of mind, immortal and golden. The nipple-like thing that hangs down between the two halves of the palate[17] is the birthplace[18] of Indra. He exists where the root of the hair is, dividing the two halves of the skull of the head.[19] As BHŪḤ he rests in fire, as BHUVAḤ in air,

2. as SUVAḤ in the sun, as MAHAḤ in *brahman*. He wins independence, he wins the lord of the mind: he is lord of speech, lord of the eye, lord of the ear, lord of knowledge. From that comes this: *brahman*, with space as its body, truth as its self, breath as its dwelling, mind as its joy, pervaded by peace, immortal. Worship it as such, Prācīnayogya.

CHAPTER 7

1. Earth, middle-air, sky, directions, intermediate directions; fire, air, sun, moon, constellations; the waters, plants, trees, space, self: so much regarding beings. Now regarding oneself: breath, diffused breath, lower breath, up-breath, central breath; eye, ear, mind, speech, skin; cuticle,[20] flesh, sinews, bone, marrow. Dividing them up in this way, the Ṛṣi has said, 'All this is fivefold. By the fivefold, one wins the fivefold.'

CHAPTER 8

1. OṂ is *brahman*. OṂ is all this. OṂ: this is compliance. Indeed, with the words[21] 'O, recite!', they recite. With 'OṂ' they chant the *sāman* verses. With 'OṂ ŚOṂ' they recite the recitations.[22] With 'OṂ' the Adhvaryu utters the response.[23] With OṂ the Brahmā sets it going.[24] With OṂ one[25] authorizes the Agnihotra. With OṂ a Brāhmaṇa, about to recite, says, 'May I win *brahman*.' He wins *brahman*.

CHAPTER 9

1. Law (*ṛta*) and study and teaching. Truth and study and teaching. Asceticism (*tapas*) and study and teaching. Self-control and study and teaching. Peace and study and teaching. The fires and study and teaching. The Agnihotra and study and teaching. Guests and study and teaching. Humanity and study and teaching. Offspring and study and teaching. Begetting and study and teaching. Procreation and study and teaching.

'Truth,' said Satyavacas[26] Rāthītara.

'Asceticism,' said Taponitya[27] Pauruśiṣṭi.

'Just study and teaching,' said Nāka Maudgalya. 'That is asceticism. That is asceticism.'

CHAPTER 10

1. I am the mover of the tree,
   Fame, like the top of the mountain.
As the purifier above,
   I am true nectar in the racehorse,[28]
A radiant treasure,
   Truly intelligent, immortal, indestructible.

Such is Triśaṅku's teaching on the Veda.

CHAPTER 11

1. After teaching him the Veda, the teacher tells the student, 'Speak truth. Do not neglect study. Once you have brought your teacher a fee that is pleasing to him, do not cut off the thread of offspring. You must not neglect truth. You must not neglect *dharma*. You must not neglect what is beneficial.[29] You must not neglect prosperity. You must not neglect study and teaching.

2. 'You must not neglect your duty to gods and ancestors. Hold your mother as a god. Hold your father as a god. Hold your teacher as a god. Hold your guest as a god. You must practise whatever other actions are irreproachable – no others. You must honour whatever actions of ours are good –

3. 'no others. Those Brāhmaṇas who are better than us, you must make comfortable with a seat. You should give with faith; you should not give without faith; you should give with largesse;[30] you should give with modesty; you should give with fear; you should give with fellow-feeling. If there should be doubt about actions, or doubt about behaviour,

4. 'you should behave in those circumstances as Brāhmaṇas would behave who were judicious, restrained,[31] dedicated,[32] not stern, lovers of *dharma*. And towards folk who are spoken against, you should behave as Brāhmaṇas would behave who

were judicious, restrained, dedicated, not stern, lovers of *dharma*.

'This is the symbolic statement; this is the teaching; this is the inner meaning of the Veda; this is the instruction. You should contemplate (*upās-*) it in this way; you must contemplate it in this way.'

CHAPTER 12

1. OṂ. May Mitra be kind, may Varuṇa be kind,
May Aryaman be kind to us.
May Indra and Bṛhaspati be kind,
May wide-striding Viṣṇu be kind to us.
Homage to *brahman*, homage to you, Vāyu:
You are *brahman* manifest:
I have spoken law: I have spoken truth.
That has protected me: that has protected the speaker.
It has protected me: it has protected the speaker.

OṂ. Peace, peace, peace.

OṂ. May Mitra be kind, may Varuṇa be kind,
May Aryaman be kind to us.
May Indra and Bṛhaspati be kind,
May wide-striding Viṣṇu be kind to us.
Homage to brahman, *homage to you, Vāyu:*
You are brahman *manifest:*
I will speak of you as brahman *manifest.*
I will speak law: I will speak truth.
May that protect me: may that protect the speaker.
May it protect me: may it protect the speaker.

OṂ. Peace, peace, peace.

BOOK II: *BRAHMAN*

OṂ. Together may it protect us two.[33]
Together may it profit us two:
Together may we do a hero's work.
May we learn intelligently:
May we never hate one another.

OṂ. Peace, peace, peace.

CHAPTER I

1. OṂ. The knower of *brahman* wins the highest. This is said about it:

The one who knows *brahman*
As truth, as knowledge, as the endless,
Hidden in the secret place and in the highest heaven[34]
Wins all desires,
With *brahman*, the wise one.[35]

Space is born from this self, air from space, fire from air, the waters from fire, earth from the waters, plants from earth, food from plants, a person from food. The person is made of the essence of food. This is his head; this is his right wing; this is his left wing; this is his self.[36] This is his tail, his support. There is this verse about it:

CHAPTER 2

1. Whatever creatures depend on earth
   Are born from food.
By food they live,
   And into it go in the end.

Food is the eldest of beings,
   So it is called 'the panacea'.[37]
Those who worship food as *brahman*
   Win all food.

Food is the eldest of beings,
   So it is called 'the panacea'.
Beings are born from food:
   Born, they grow by food.

It is eaten and it eats (*ad-*) beings,
   Hence it is called food (*anna*).

Different from and inside the self that is made of the essence of food is the self that is made of breath. This one is filled by it. It, too, is man-shaped. This, in its man-shape, matches the man-shape of that one.[38] The breath is its head; the diffused breath is its right wing; the lower breath is its left wing; space is its self; earth is its tail, its support. There is this verse about it:

CHAPTER 3

1. Along with breath breathe gods,
   Human beings and animals.
Breath is the life of beings,
   So it is called 'life of all'.

Those who worship breath as *brahman*
   Reach their full lifespan.
Breath is the life of beings,
   So it is called 'life of all'.

It is the bodily self of the previous one.[39]

Different from and inside the self that is made of the breath is the self that is made of mind. This one is filled by it. It, too, is man-shaped. This, in its man-shape, matches the man-shape of that one. The *yajus* verse is its head; the *ṛc* verse is its right wing; the *sāman* verse is its left wing; symbolic statement is its self; the hymns of the Atharvans and Aṅgirases are its tail, its support. There is this verse about it:

CHAPTER 4

1. The one who knows the joy of *brahman*
 From which speech, along with mind,
Turns back without winning it,
 Is never afraid.

It is the bodily self of the previous one.

Different from and inside the self that is made of mind is the self that is made of knowledge.[40] This one is filled by it. It, too, is man-shaped. This, in its man-shape, matches the man-shape of that one. Faith is its head; law is its right wing; truth is its left wing; *yoga* is its self; MAHAḤ is its tail, its support. There is this verse about it:

CHAPTER 5

1. Knowledge spreads out the sacrifice;
 It spreads out actions, too.
All the gods worship knowledge
 As *brahman*, the eldest.

If one knows knowledge as *brahman*
 And is not neglectful of it,
Abandoning evils in the body
 One attains all desires.

It is the bodily self of the previous one.

Different from and inside the self that is made of knowledge is the self that is made of joy. This one is filled by it. It, too, is man-shaped. This, in its man-shape, matches the man-shape of that one. Dearness is its head; happiness is its right wing; delight is its left wing; joy is its self; *brahman* is its tail, its support. There is this verse about it:

CHAPTER 6

1. One becomes not-being
 If one knows *brahman* as not-being.
 If one knows that *brahman* is,
 Folk know one as being.[41]

It is the bodily self of the previous one.

Now for further questions:

If someone departs, not knowing that world, does he go to it?

If someone departs, knowing that world, does he win it?[42]

He desired: 'Let me become many! Let me be born!' He raised heat. When he had raised heat, he created all this, whatever there is. He entered into it. When he had entered into it, he became the present and the beyond:[43] he became the explained and the unexplained, the based and the unbased, the knowing and the unknowing, truth and falsehood. As truth (*satya*), he became whatever there is: folk call it 'reality' (*satya*). There is this verse about it:

CHAPTER 7

1. In the beginning all this was not-being.
   From not-being, being was born.[44]
It made itself a self:
   So it is called, 'Well done'.[45]

What was well done is essence, for by getting an essence one becomes joyful. Who would breathe, who would draw breath,[46] if there were not this joy in space? It makes one joyful. When one finds the fearless, the support, in this invisible, selfless, unexplained, unresting, then one has reached the fearless. When one makes in it a cavity, a gap, one has fear. This is the fear of one who thinks himself a knower.[47] There is this verse about it:

CHAPTER 8

1. From this fear, wind blows.
   From fear, Sūrya rises.
From this fear both Agni and Indra,
   And Death, as fifth, run on.[48]

This is the enquiry into joy:

Let there be a young man, a good young man, one who studies, very swift, very steadfast, very strong. Let the whole earth, filled with riches, be his. That is one human joy.[49] A hundred human joys make one joy of the human *gandharvas*, and of one who is learned and not afflicted by desire. A hundred joys of the human *gandharvas* make one joy of the divine *gandharvas*, and of one who is learned and not afflicted by desire. A hundred joys of the divine *gandharvas* make one joy of the ancestors who long abide in their world, and of one who is learned and not afflicted by desire. A hundred joys of the ancestors who long abide in their world make one joy of the gods who are born there by birth, and of one who is learned and not afflicted by desire. A hundred joys of the gods who are born there by birth make one joy of the gods by action, who reach the gods through action, and of one who is learned and not afflicted by desire. A hundred joys of the gods by action make one joy of the gods, and of one who is learned and not afflicted by desire. A hundred joys of the gods make one joy of Indra, and of one who is learned and not afflicted by desire. A hundred joys of Indra make one joy of Bṛhaspati, and of one who is learned and not afflicted by desire. A hundred joys of Bṛhaspati make one joy of Prajāpati, and of one who is learned and not afflicted by desire. A hundred joys of Prajāpati make one joy of Brahmā, and of one who is learned and not afflicted by desire. This one who is in the person and that one who is in the sun are one: and the one who leaves this world knowing this goes up to the self made of food, goes up to the self made of breath, goes up to the self made of mind, goes up to the self made of knowledge, goes up to the self made of joy. There is this verse about it:

CHAPTER 9

1. The one who knows the joy of *brahman*
From which speech, along with mind,
Turns back without reaching it,
Is afraid of nothing.[50]

The thought 'Have I not done good? Have I done evil?' does not burn him. The one who knows this saves himself (*ātmānam*) from these. The one who knows this saves himself from both. This is the inner teaching.

OṂ. *Together may it protect us two:*
Together may it profit us two:
Together may we do a hero's work.
May we learn intelligently:
May we never hate one another.

OṂ. *Peace, peace, peace.*

BOOK III: BHṚGU

HARI OṂ. *Together may it protect us two:*
Together may it profit us two:
Together may we do a hero's work.
May we learn intelligently:
May we never hate one another.

OṂ. *Peace, peace, peace.*

CHAPTER 1

1. Bhṛgu Vāruṇi approached his father, Varuṇa, saying, 'Blessed one, teach me about *brahman*.'

He taught him this: food, breath, the eye, the ear, mind, speech. He said to him, 'That from which beings are born; by which, being born, they live; into which they enter when they pass on – seek to know that as *brahman*.'

He practised asceticism. After practising asceticism

CHAPTER 2

1. he realized, 'Food is *brahman*. For from food beings are born; by food, being born, they live; into food they enter when they pass on.' On realizing that, he approached his father, Varuṇa, again saying, 'Blessed one, teach me about *brahman*.'

He said to him, 'Seek to know *brahman* by asceticism. Asceticism is *brahman*.'

He practised asceticism. After practising asceticism

CHAPTER 3

1. he realized, 'Breath is *brahman*. For from breath beings are born; by breath, being born, they live; into breath they enter when they pass on.' On realizing that, he approached his father, Varuṇa, again saying, 'Blessed one, teach me about *brahman*.'

He said to him, 'Seek to know *brahman* by asceticism. Asceticism is *brahman*.'

He practised asceticism. After practising asceticism

CHAPTER 4

1. he realized, 'Mind is *brahman*. For from mind beings are born; by mind, being born, they live; into mind they enter when they pass on.' On realizing that, he approached his father, Varuṇa, again saying, 'Blessed one, teach me about *brahman*.'

He said to him, 'Seek to know *brahman* by asceticism. Asceticism is *brahman*.'

He practised asceticism. After practising asceticism

CHAPTER 5

1. he realized, 'Knowledge is *brahman*. For from knowledge beings are born; by knowledge, being born, they live; into knowledge they enter when they pass on.' On realizing that, he approached his father, Varuṇa, again saying, 'Blessed one, teach me about *brahman*.'

He said to him, 'Seek to know *brahman* by asceticism. Asceticism is *brahman*.'

He practised asceticism. After practising asceticism

CHAPTER 6

1. he realized, 'Joy is *brahman*. For from joy beings are born; by joy, being born, they live; into joy they enter when they pass on.' This is the wisdom of Bhṛgu, of Varuṇa, which stands firm in the highest heaven.[52] The one who knows this stands firm: he becomes a possessor of food, an eater of food; becomes great in offspring and animals and the radiance of *brahman*, great in fame.[53]

CHAPTER 7

1. One should not speak ill of food: that should be the vow. Breath is food: the body is the eater of food. The body stands firm on breath: breath stands firm on the body. So food stands firm on food. The one who knows food as standing firm on food stands firm: he becomes a possessor of food, an eater of food; becomes great in offspring and animals and the radiance of *brahman*, great in fame.

CHAPTER 8

1. One should not reject food: that should be the vow. The waters are food: light is the eater of food. Light stands firm on the waters: the waters stand firm on light. So food stands firm on food. The one who knows food as standing firm on food stands firm: he becomes a possessor of food, an eater of food;

becomes great in offspring and animals and the radiance of *brahman*, great in fame.

CHAPTER 9

1. One should make much of food: that should be the vow. The earth is food: space is the eater of food. Space stands firm on the earth: the earth stands firm on space. So food stands firm on food. The one who knows food as standing firm on food stands firm: he becomes a possessor of food, an eater of food; becomes great in offspring and animals and the radiance of *brahman*, great in fame.

CHAPTER 10

1. One should not refuse anyone in one's house: that should be the vow. So one should get food by any means possible.[54] Folk say, 'Food is prepared for him.' This food is prepared for another first, so it is prepared for him first.[55] This food is prepared for another in the middle, so it is prepared for him in the middle. This food is prepared for another last, so it is prepared for him last –

2. the one who knows this.

'Enjoying' in speech; 'getting and enjoying'[56] in the breath and the lower breath; 'action' in the hands; 'movement' in the feet; 'excretion' in the anus: these are its human titles. As for its divine titles: 'contentment' in rain; 'strength' in lightning;

3. 'glory' in animals; 'light' in the constellations; 'procreation, immortality and joy' in the loins; 'all' in space. One should worship it as the support: one becomes supported. One should worship it as MAHAḤ: one becomes great (*mahat*). One should worship it as mind (*manas*): one becomes respected (*mānavat*).

4. One should worship it as homage: desires pay one homage. One should worship it as *brahman*: one becomes endowed with *brahman*. One should worship it as the dying-around[57] of *brahman*: rivals who hate one die around one, and so do those adversaries[58] who are not dear. This one who is in the person, and that one who is in the sun, are one:
5. and the one who leaves this world knowing this goes up to the self made of food, goes up to the self made of breath, goes up to the self made of mind, goes up to the self made of knowledge, goes up to the self made of joy. He moves about the worlds, with food at his desire, with forms at his desire. He continually sings this *sãman*: 'Oh, bliss . . . ! Oh, bliss . . . ! Oh, bliss . . . ![59] I am food, I am food, I am food. I am the eater of food . . . I am the eater of food . . . I am the eater of food . . . I am the maker of verse. I am the maker of verse. I am the maker of verse. I am the first-born of law . . ., before the gods, in the navel . . . of immortality. You protect . . . the one who gives to me. I eat . . . food and the one who eats food. I have overcome . . . the whole universe.[60] I am light like the sun.'[61]

– The one who knows this. This is the inner teaching.

OṂ. *Together may it protect us two:*
Together may it profit us two:
Together may we do a hero's work.
May we learn intelligently:
May we never hate one another.

OṂ. *Peace, peace, peace.*

OṂ. *May Mitra be kind, may Varuṇa be kind,*
May Aryaman be kind to us.
May Indra and Bṛhaspati be kind,
May wide-striding Viṣṇu be kind to us.
Homage to brahman, *homage to you, Vāyu:*
You are brahman *manifest:*
I will speak of you as brahman *manifest.*

I will speak law: I will speak truth.
May that protect me: may that protect the speaker.
May it protect me: may it protect the speaker.

OṂ. *Peace, peace, peace.*

AITAREYA UPANIṢAD

Aitareya's Teaching

OṂ. *My speech stands firm on mind:*
My mind stands firm on speech.
Appear, appear to me.
Be to me a nail for the Veda.[1]
Do not harm my learning.
With this study I hold days and nights together.[2]

*I will speak law (*ṛta*): I will speak truth.*[3]
May that protect me: may that protect the speaker.
May it protect me: may it protect the speaker, may it protect the speaker.

OṂ. *Peace, peace, peace.*

BOOK I

1. OṂ. In the beginning this was the self, just one, nothing else blinking.[4] He thought, 'Let me create worlds.'
2. He created these worlds: the heavenly water,[5] light-rays, death, the waters. That is the heavenly water, beyond the sky. Sky is the base. Middle-air is the light-rays. The earth is death. What is below is the waters.
3. He thought, 'Here are the worlds: let me create protectors of the worlds.' From the waters he drew out and shaped a man.[6]
4. He heated him up.[7] When he was heated up, a mouth broke out of him, like an egg.[8] From the mouth came speech; from speech, fire. Nostrils broke out. From the nostrils came breath; from breath, air. Eyes broke out. From the eyes came sight;[9] from sight, the sun. Ears broke out. From the ears came hearing; from hearing, the directions. A skin broke out. From the skin came the body-hairs; from the body-hairs, the plants and trees. A heart broke out. From the heart came mind; from the mind, the moon. A navel broke out. From the navel came the lower breath; from the lower breath, death. A phallus broke out. From the phallus came seed; from the seed, the waters.

BOOK II

1. Once the deities had been created, they flew down on to this great ocean.[10] The self afflicted the man with hunger and thirst.[11] They said to him, 'Find us a place where we can settle and eat food.'

2. He brought a cow to them. They said, 'This is not enough for us.' He brought a horse to them. They said, 'This is not enough for us.'

3. He brought a man to them. They said, 'Hurrah! Well done!' A man is something well done.[12] He said to them, 'Enter, each to your place.'

4. Fire became speech and entered the mouth. Air became breath and entered the nostrils. The sun became sight and entered the eyes. The directions became hearing and entered the ears. The plants and trees became body-hairs and entered the skin. The moon became mind and entered the heart. Death became the lower breath and entered the navel. The waters became seed and entered the phallus.

5. Hunger and thirst said to him, 'Find a place for us, too.'

He said to them, 'I allot you a share among these deities. I make you sharers with them.' So, whenever an offering is assigned to any deity, hunger and thirst become sharers with that deity.

BOOK III

1. He thought, 'Here are worlds and world-protectors. Let me create food for them.'

2. He heated up the the waters. When they were heated up a shape was produced from them. The shape that was produced was food.

3. As soon as it had been created, it tried to escape behind him.[13] He tried to seize it with speech. He was not able to seize it with speech. If he had seized it with speech, one would now[14] be able to enjoy food just by uttering it.

4. He tried to seize it with the breath (*prāṇa*). He was not able to seize it with the breath. If he had seized it with the breath, one would now be able to enjoy food just by breathing over it.

5. He tried to seize it with sight. He was not able to seize it with sight. If he had seized it with sight, one would now be able to enjoy food just by seeing it.

6. He tried to seize it with hearing. He was not able to seize it with hearing. If he had seized it with hearing, one would now be able to enjoy food just by hearing about it.

7. He tried to seize it with the skin. He was not able to seize it with the skin. If he had seized it with the skin, one would now be able to enjoy food just by touching it.

8. He tried to seize it with the mind. He was not able to seize it with the mind. If he had seized it with the mind, one would now be able to enjoy food just by thinking about it.

9. He tried to seize it with the phallus. He was not able to seize it with the phallus. If he had seized it with the phallus, one would now be able to enjoy food just by ejaculating it.

10. He tried to seize it with the lower breath.[15] He got it. This

is the seizer of food – air. Air (*vāyu*) is the life of food (*annāyu*).

11. He thought, 'How could this be without me?' He thought, 'Which way shall I enter it?' He thought, 'If uttering is done by speech,[16] if breathing is done by the breath, if seeing is done by the sight, if hearing is done by the hearing, if touching is done by the skin, if thinking is done by the mind, if down-breathing[17] is done by the lower breath, if ejaculating is done by the seed, then who am I?'

12. Opening up (*vi-dṛ-*) the parting,[18] he entered by it as a door. This is the door called the fontanelle (*vidṛti*). It is the bringer of joy. It has three states, three kinds of sleep:[19] this state, this state and *this* state.[20]

13. Once he was born, he looked at the beings, thinking, 'What here has desired to converse with another?'[21] He saw the person, very *brahman*. He cried,[22] 'I have seen it (*idam adarśam*)!'

14. So he is called Idandra: Idandra is his name. Though he is Idandra, folk call him Indra, mysteriously, because the gods seem to love the mysterious: the gods seem to love the mysterious.[23]

BOOK IV

1. In a person, he first becomes an embryo. What the seed is is energy (*tejas*), come together from all the limbs. One carries a self in oneself (*ātman*). When one sprinkles it in a woman, one begets it. That is one's first birth.
2. It becomes own self to the woman, just like a limb of her own, so it does not harm her. She nurtures one's self when it has come here.
3. She, the nurturer, becomes one to be nurtured. The woman carries the embryo. He nourishes the boy before and after birth. When he nourishes the boy before and after birth, he nourishes himself (*ātman*), for the continuance of the worlds: for so the worlds continue. That is one's second birth.
4. He, being one's self, is set in one's place for meritorious actions. Then one's other self, having done what was to be done and reached his age, departs.[24] Departing from here, he is born again. That is one's third birth.
5. It was said by the Ṛṣi:

> While in the womb I fully knew
> The births of all the gods.
> A hundred citadels of iron surrounded me.
> A hawk, I flew out with speed.[25]

Vāmadeva said that while lying in the womb.
6. Knowing this, from the break-up of this body he rose upward; he won in that heavenly world all desires; and he became immortal, became immortal.

BOOK V

1. 'Who is he?'

'We worship him as the self.'

'Which one is the self?'

'The one by whom one sees, by whom one hears, by whom one smells smells, by whom one utters speech, by whom one discriminates what is sweet and not sweet –

2. 'Who is the heart, the mind: consciousness, perception, discrimination, knowledge,[26] intelligence,[27] vision, steadfastness, thought,[28] consideration,[29] swiftness,[30] memory,[31] resolve, intention, life, desire, will.[32] All these are names for knowledge.

3. He is Brahmā, he is Indra, he is Prajāpati and all the gods; the five elements,[33] earth, air, space, the waters, light; those which are, as it were, finely mixed;[34] the various other kinds of seeds, the egg-born, the womb-born, the sweat-born,[35] the shoot-born; horses, cattle, human beings (*puruṣa*), elephants. All that has breath, both walking and flying, and all that is still, is led by knowledge,[36] based on knowledge. The world is led by knowledge. Knowledge is the basis. Knowledge is *brahman*.

4. By the wise[37] self he[38] rose upward; he won in that heavenly world all desires; and he became immortal, became immortal. So it is. OṂ.

OṂ. *My speech stands firm on mind:*
My mind stands firm on speech.
Appear, appear to me.
Be to me a nail for the Veda.
Do not harm my learning.
With this study I hold days and nights together.

I will speak law: I will speak truth.
May that protect me: may that protect the speaker.
May it protect me: may it protect the speaker, may it protect the speaker.

OṂ. *Peace, peace, peace.*

KAUṢĪTAKĪ UPANIṢAD

Kauṣītaki's Teaching

OṂ. *My speech stands firm on mind:*
My mind stands firm on speech.[1]
May you appear, appear as a youth.[2]
By knowledge that nail has held the law (ṛta) *in place.*[3]
Do me no harm.
With this study I hold days and nights together.[4]
Homage to Agni with the libation.
With the libation homage to the Ṛṣis,
Makers of the mantras, lords of the mantras.
Homage to you, O gods.
Gracious lady, be most healing to us, compassionate Sarasvatī.
May we not be separated from your sight.[5]
Unerring mind, quick eye is the sun, best of lights.
Initiation, do me no harm.[6]

BOOK I

1. OṂ. Citra Gāṅgyāyani,[1] about to offer a sacrifice, chose Āruṇi as priest. Āruṇi sent his son, Śvetaketu, telling him to perform the sacrifice.

When he had arrived,[2] Gāṅgyāyani asked him, 'Son of Gautama, is there[3] a closed place in the world in which you will set me? Or is there some other path there, by which you will set me in a world?'[4]

He said, 'I do not know this: come, I must ask my teacher.' He approached his father and asked him, 'He asked me such-and-such: how should I reply?'

He said, 'I do not know this either. Let us study at his house and take what others give us. Come, we both will go.' With fuel in hand he went up to Citra Gāṅgyāyani saying, 'I must come to you as a student.'[5]

Gāṅgyāyani said, 'You are worthy of the sacred knowledge (*brahman*), Gautama, for you have not fallen into conceit. Come, I will explain it to you.'

2. He said, 'All those who depart from this world go to the moon. In the former half of the month it waxes by their breaths, and with its latter half it causes them to be born again.[6] This, the moon, is the door to the heaven-world: the one who answers it it sends onward, but the one who does not answer becomes rain here, and it rains him down. He is reborn here in one place after another as a worm, a flying thing, a fish, a bird, a lion, a boar, a snake, a tiger, a person,[7] or something else, according to his actions, according to his knowledge.

'When he gets there, the moon asks him, "Who are you?"

'He should answer it,

'"From the shining, O seasons, the seed was brought,
From the fifteenfold begotten, from the ancestors' realm.[8]
You caused me to arise in a male as agent:
Through a male as agent, sprinkle me in a mother.

'As such I was born, being reborn[9] as the twelfth or thirteenth succeeding month through a twelve- or thirteenfold father.[10] I know that: I know the reverse of that.[11] Seasons, you have brought me to immortality.[12] By that truth, by that asceticism, I am a season: I am of the seasons. Who am I? I am you.' It sends him onward.

3. 'Entering the path that leads to the gods, he comes to Agni's world; to Vāyu's world;[13] to Varuṇa's world; to Indra's world; to Prajāpati's world; to Brahmā's world.[14] This world has the lake, Āra;[15] watchmen, the Muhūrtas;[16] the river, Vijarā;[17] the tree, Ilya;[18] the public square, Sālajya;[19] the dwelling, Aparājita;[20] the two door-guardians, Indra and Prajāpati; the palace, Vibhu;[21] the throne, Vicakṣaṇā;[22] the couch, Amitaujas;[23] the beloved, Mānasī, and her pair, Cākṣuṣī, who take flowers and weave the two worlds;[24] the *apsarases*, the Ambās and the Ambāyavīs;[25] the rivers, Ambayā.[26] The one who knows this arrives there. Brahmā[27] says, "Run to him! By my glory he has reached the river Vijarā, and he will not grow old."

4. 'Five hundred *apsarases* approach him, a hundred with fruit in their hands, a hundred with unguents in their hands, a hundred with garlands in their hands, a hundred with garments in their hands, a hundred with perfumed powders in their hands. They adorn him with the adornment of Brahmā. Once adorned with the adornment of Brahmā, the knower of *brahman* approaches *brahman*. He comes to the lake, Āra, and crosses it by mind. When they get there, those who know only what is in front of them sink. He comes to the watchmen, the Muhūrtas, and they run away from him.[28] He comes to the river, Vijarā, and crosses it, too, by mind.

'Then he shakes off his good deeds and bad deeds. His dear relations get his good deeds, and those who are not dear his bad deeds. Then, just as one driving a chariot looks down on the two chariot-wheels, he looks down on day and night, good deeds and bad deeds, and all dualities. Free from good deeds, free from bad deeds, the knower of *brahman* approaches *brahman*.

5. 'He comes to the tree, Ilya, and the smell of Brahmā enters him. He comes to the public square, Sālajya, and the taste of Brahmā enters him. He comes to the dwelling, Aparājita, and the brightness of Brahmā enters him. He comes to the two door-guardians, Indra and Prajāpati, and they run away from him. He comes to the hall, Vibhu, and the glory of Brahmā enters him.

'He comes to the throne, Vicakṣaṇā. The *Bṛhat* and *Rathantara sāmans* are its front feet; the *Śyaita* and *Naudhasa* its back feet; the *Vairūpa* and *Vairāja* its side-pieces; the *Śākvara* and *Raivata* its cross-pieces. It is awareness, for by awareness one discerns.[29]

'He comes to the couch, Amitaujas. That is the breath. What has been and what is to be are its front feet; splendour (*śrī*) and refreshment (*irā*) its back feet; the *Bhadra* and *Yajñāyajñīya* its head-pieces; the *Bṛhat* and *Rathantara* its side-pieces; the *ṛc* verses and *sāman* verses its lengthwise cords; the *yajus* verses its crosswise ones; the Soma-stems[30] its mattress; the Udgītha its coverlet; and glory its pillow. On it Brahmā sits. The one who knows this at first sets just one foot on it.[31]

'Brahmā asks him, "Who are you?"

'He should reply to him:

6. ' "I am a season: I am of the seasons. From space as womb I came into being as seed for a wife:[32] as the brightness of the year; as the self of being after being. You are the self of being after being. What you are, I am."

'He says to him, "Who am I?"

'He should say, "Truth (*satya*)."

' "What is that truth?"

' "What is other than the gods and the breaths is being (*sat*), and what is the gods and the breaths is yonder (*tyam*), which is why 'truth' is called by this name. So much is all this. You are all this." This is what he tells him. This is taught in a verse:

7. He whose belly is the *yajus*, whose head is the *sāman*,
Whose form is the *ṛc*, unfailing one,
Should be known as Brahmā,
Great Ṛṣi, made of *brahman*.[33]

'He says to him, "By what does one win my masculine names?"

'He should say, "By the breath (*prāṇa*, masc.)."

' "By what my neuter names?"[34]

' "By mind (*manas*, neut.)."

' "By what my feminine names?"

' "By speech (*vāc*, fem.)."

' "By what my smells?"

' "By the breath."[35]

' "By what my forms?"

' "By the eye."

' "By what my sounds?"

' "By the ear."

' "By what my tastes of food?"

' "By the tongue."

' "By what my actions?"

' "By the hands."

' "By what my joy and sorrow?"

' "By the body."

' "By what my delight, pleasure and procreation?"

' "By the loins."

' "By what my movements?"

' "By the feet."

' "By what my thoughts, that which is to be known, and desires?"

'He should say, "By awareness."

'Brahmā says to him, "The waters[36] are my world: that world is yours." He wins as his victory the victory, the attainment, that is Brahmā's – the one who knows this, the one who knows this.'

BOOK II

1. OṂ. 'Breath is *brahman*': so said Kauṣītaki. Mind is the messenger of the breath, of *brahman*: the eye is its watchman, the ear its herald, speech its maid.[1]

The one who knows the mind as the messenger of the breath, of *brahman*, comes to have a messenger.[2] The one who knows the eye as the watchman comes to have a watchman. The one who knows the ear as the herald comes to have a herald. The one who knows speech as the maid comes to have a maid.

All these deities bring tribute to the breath, to *brahman*, without its asking: likewise all beings bring tribute to it, without its asking. The secret teaching (*upaniṣad*) for the one who knows this is that one should not ask, just as one who had begged in a village without getting anything might sit down, saying, 'I would not eat anything from here if it were given.' Those who refused him before now invite him. This is the *dharma* of the one who does not ask:[3] givers of food invite him, saying, 'Let us give to you.'

2. 'Breath is *brahman*': so said Paiṅgya. The eye of the breath, of *brahman*, is shut behind speech; the ear is shut behind the eye; the mind is shut behind the ear; the breath is shut behind the mind. All these deities bring tribute to the breath, to *brahman*, without its asking: likewise all beings bring tribute to it, without its asking. The secret teaching for the one who knows this is that one should not ask, just as one who had begged in a village without getting anything might sit down, saying, 'I would not eat anything from here if it were given.' Those who refused him before now invite him. This is the *dharma* of the one who does not ask: givers of food invite him, saying, 'Let us give to you.'

3. Now the claiming of a special treasure:

If someone longs for a special treasure, then at one of these junctures[4] – the full-moon day, the new-moon day, or an auspicious constellation in the bright fortnight – he builds a fire, sweeps around, strews, and sprinkles;[5] bending the right knee, he makes offerings of melted butter with the spoon,[6] saying: 'The deity named "Speech" is the Claimer. May it claim this for me from <name>. To it, SVĀHĀ!

'The deity named "Breath" is the Claimer. May it claim this for me from <name>. To it, SVĀHĀ!

'The deity named "Eye" is the Claimer. May it claim this for me from <name>. To it, SVĀHĀ!

'The deity named "Ear" is the Claimer. May it claim this for me from <name>. To it, SVĀHĀ!

'The deity named "Mind" is the Claimer. May it claim this for me from <name>. To it, SVĀHĀ!

'The deity named "Awareness" is the Claimer. May it claim this for me from <name>. To it, SVĀHĀ!'

Then he should smell the scent of the smoke, anoint his limbs with an ointment of melted butter, and go forth restraining his speech. He should state his purpose, or send a messenger: and he gets his wish.

4. Now the longing that belongs to the gods:[7]

If someone wishes to become beloved of any man, or woman, or persons, then at one of these same junctures, by the same method, he makes offerings of melted butter,[8] saying: 'I offer up your speech in me, <name>. SVĀHĀ!

'I offer up your breath in me, <name>. SVĀHĀ!

'I offer up your eye in me, <name>. SVĀHĀ!

'I offer up your ear in me, <name>. SVĀHĀ!

'I offer up your mind in me, <name>. SVĀHĀ!

'I offer up your awareness in me, <name>. SVĀHĀ!'

Then he should smell the scent of the smoke, anoint his limbs with an ointment of melted butter, and go forth restraining his speech. He should seek to touch the person or stand to windward, conversing with them. He becomes beloved, and they long for him.

5. Now Pratardana's method of self-restraint – folk call it the 'inner Agnihotra':

So long as a person is speaking, he cannot breathe: at that time he offers up the breath in speech. So long as a person is breathing, he cannot speak: at that time he offers up speech in the breath. Waking or sleeping, one constantly[9] makes these two unending, immortal offerings. Other offerings have an end, for they are made of actions. The ancients, knowing this, used not to offer the Agnihotra.

6. 'The Uktha is *brahman*':[10] so said Śuṣkabhṛṅgāra. One should worship it as *ṛc*: then all beings praise (*ṛc-*) one, to one's betterment. One should worship it as *yajus*: then all beings are yoked (*yuj-*) to one, to one's betterment. One should worship it as *sāman*: all beings then bow (*sam-nam-*) to one, to one's betterment. One should worship it as splendour: one should worship it as fame: one should worship it as brightness. As it is the most splendid, the most famous, the brightest among the recitations,[11] the one who knows this becomes the most splendid, the most famous, the brightest among all beings.

The Adhvaryu makes ready the self of the sacrifice,[12] which is made of actions. On it he weaves that which is made of the *yajus*. On that which is made of the *yajus*, the Hotṛ weaves that which is made of the *ṛc*. On that which is made of the *ṛc*, the Udgātṛ weaves that which is made of the *sāman*. This is the self of the threefold knowledge. The one who knows this becomes the self of Indra.[13]

7. Now there are three contemplations (*upāsana*) of the all-conquering Kauṣītaki.

The all-conquering Kauṣītaki[14] used to worship (*upās-*) the sun at rising, having put on the sacred thread,[15] fetched water[16] and three times sprinkled with the water-pot, saying, 'You are the drawer:[17] draw evil from me.' By the same method he worshipped it in the middle of its course, saying, 'You are the drawer-up: draw up evil from me.' By the same method he worshipped it at setting, saying, 'You are the drawer-together: draw together evil from me.' So it draws together whatever evil he has done by day or by night.[18] In the same way, the one who knows this worships the sun by this method:[19] it draws together whatever evil he does, by day or by night.

8. Now each month, when the new-moon night comes round,[20] when the moon appears in the west, one should worship it by this method, or cast two green grass-blades at it,[21] saying,

> 'Since my well-formed heart
> Rests in the moon in the sky,
> I think myself a knower of it.
> May I not mourn for harm to a son.'[22]

Then his offspring do not pass away before him. That is for one to whom a son has been born. Now for one to whom a son has not yet been born: after muttering the three *ṛc* verses,

'Wax! May well-being come to you! . . .'[23]

'May juices, may strength come to you . . .'[24]

'Stem that the Ādityas cause to wax! . . .'[25]

he says, 'Do not wax by our breath, offspring, animals. Wax by the breath, offspring, animals, of the one who hates us, of the one that we hate. I turn the turn of Indra:[26] I turn with the sun's turn.' And he turns towards the right hand.

9. Now on the full-moon night, when the moon appears in the east, one should worship it by this method, saying, 'You are King Soma, the shining.[27] You are the five-mouthed Prajāpati.

'The Brāhmaṇa is one mouth of you. With that mouth you eat the kings. With that mouth make me an eater of food.

'The king is one mouth of you. With that mouth you eat the people.[28] With that mouth make me an eater of food.

'The hawk is one mouth of you. With that mouth you eat the birds. With that mouth make me an eater of food.

'Fire is one mouth of you. With that mouth you eat this world. With that mouth make me an eater of food.

'There is a fifth mouth in you. With that mouth you eat all beings. With that mouth make me an eater of food.

'Do not wane with our breath, offspring, animals. Wane with the breath, offspring, animals, of the one who hates us, of the one we hate. I turn the turn of the gods: I turn with the sun's turn.' And he turns towards the right hand.

10. Now when one is about to lie with one's wife, one should stroke her heart, saying,

'O well-formed one, by that which rests
  In your heart, in Prajāpati,
Mistress of immortality,
  May you not endure suffering from a son.'

Then her offspring do not pass away before her.[29]

11. On coming back when one has been away, one should sniff one's son's head,[30] saying,

'You arise from every limb:
  You spring from the heart.
Indeed, son, you are my self.
  Live a hundred autumns, <name>.'[31]

He utters his name, saying:

'Be a rock, be an axe,
  Be invincible gold.
Indeed, son, you are brightness.
  Live a hundred autumns, <name>.'

He speaks his name, then embraces him,[32] saying, 'As Prajāpati has embraced his creatures for their safety, I embrace you, <name>.'[33] Then he mutters in his right ear:

'Give to him, Maghavan, who receive the remnant . . .'[34]

and in his left:

'Bestow on him, Indra, the finest goods . . .'[35]

'Do not be cut off. Do not suffer. Live a hundred autumns of life. Son, with your name I sniff your head.' So saying, he sniffs his head three times. 'I low over you with the lowing of cows.' So saying, he lows over his head three times.

12. Now the dying-around (*parimara*) of the gods:

Brahman shines when fire burns, and it dies when it does not burn. Its brightness (*tejas*) goes to the sun, its breath to the air. *Brahman* shines when the sun is seen, and it dies when it is not seen. Its brightness goes to the moon, its breath to the air. *Brahman* shines when the moon is seen, and it dies when it is not seen. Its brightness goes to lightning, its breath to the air.

Brahman shines when lightning lightens, and it dies when it does not lighten. Its brightness goes to the air,[36] its breath to the air. Though all these deities enter the air and die in the air, they do not perish, and so they arise again.

So much regarding deities. Now regarding oneself:

13. *Brahman* shines when one speaks with speech, and it dies when one does not speak. Its brightness goes to the eye, its breath to the breath. *Brahman* shines when one sees with the eye, and it dies when one does not see. Its brightness goes to the ear, its breath to the breath. *Brahman* shines when one hears with the ear, and it dies when one does not hear. Its brightness goes to the mind, its breath to the breath. *Brahman* shines when one thinks with the mind, and it dies when one does not think. Its brightness goes to the breath, its breath to the breath. Though all these deities enter the breath and die in the breath, they do not perish, and so they arise again. So when someone knows this, even if both mountains, the southern and the northern,[37] were to roll towards him intending to crush him, they would not crush him. But those who hate him, and those whom he himself hates, die around (*pari-mṛ-*) him.

14. Now the attaining of supremacy:[38]

The deities, disputing over who was the best, left the body. It lay there, not breathing, dry, become a log.[39] Speech entered it, and it still lay there, speaking with speech. The eye entered it, and it still lay there, speaking with speech, seeing with the eye. The ear entered it, and it still lay there, speaking with speech, seeing with the eye, hearing with the ear. The mind entered it, and it still lay there, speaking with speech, seeing with the eye, hearing with the ear, thinking with the mind. The breath entered it, and it at once stood up.

All the deities, having acknowledged supremacy in the breath, and understood the breath as the self of awareness, left the body, all of them together.[40] Entering the air,[41] with space as self, they went to heaven.

In the same way, the one who knows this, having acknowledged supremacy in the breath, and understood the breath as the self of awareness, leaves the body with all of them together. Entering the air, with space as self, he goes to heaven. He goes where the gods are. Reaching that, he becomes immortal as the gods are immortal: the one who knows this.[42]

15. Now the Father-and-Son Ceremony – folk call it the handing-on.[43]

When the father is about to depart, he calls his son. Having strewn the house with fresh grass, built a fire and placed nearby a water-pot with a dish, and covered himself with a new garment, the father lies there.[44] The son comes and lies down over him.[45]

The father should hand on to him, either by touching faculties with faculties or with the son sitting facing him.[46] Then he hands on to him:

The father says, 'I must place my speech in you.'
The son says, 'I place your speech in me.'
The father says, 'I must place my breath in you.'
The son says, 'I place your breath in me.'
The father says, 'I must place my eye in you.'
The son says, 'I place your eye in me.'
The father says, 'I must place my ear in you.'
The son says, 'I place your ear in me.'
The father says, 'I must place my tastes of food in you.'
The son says, 'I place your tastes of food in me.'
The father says, 'I must place my actions in you.'
The son says, 'I place your actions in me.'
The father says, 'I must place my joy and sorrow in you.'
The son says, 'I place your joy and sorrow in me.'

The father says, 'I must place my delight, pleasure and procreation in you.'

The son says, 'I place your delight, pleasure and procreation in me.'

The father says, 'I must place my movement in you.'
The son says, 'I place your movement in me.'
The father says, 'I must place my mind in you.'
The son says, 'I place your mind in me.'[47]
The father says, 'I must place my awareness in you.'
The son says, 'I place your awareness in me.'[48]

But if he is not able to say much, the father should say in brief, 'I must place my breaths in you.'

The son should say, 'I place your breaths in me.'

Then the son gets up and goes out,[49] turning to the right. The father calls after him, 'May glory, may the radiance of *brahman*,[50] may fame favour you!'

The other looks back over his left shoulder, hiding his face with his hand or covering it with the end of his garment, and says, 'Win heavenly worlds and desires!'

If he gets well, the father should either live under his son's authority or go forth.[51] If he passes away, they should provide him with those funeral rites with which he ought to be provided – with which he ought to be provided.[52]

BOOK III

1. OṂ. Pratardana Daivodāsi reached the beloved home of Indra through battle and manly deeds.[1] Indra said to him, 'Pratardana, choose a boon (*vara*).'

Pratardana said, '*You* choose for me what you think best for a human being.'

Indra said to him, 'A superior (*vara*) does not choose for an inferior (*avara*). You choose.'

Pratardana said, 'That is no favour (*avara*) to me.'

But Indra did not depart from truth, for Indra is truth. Indra said to him, 'Know me: I think this is best for a human being, that he should know me. I slew the three-headed son of Tvaṣṭṛ;[2] I gave the Arunmukha sorcerers up to the wolves;[3] breaking many treaties, I destroyed the Prahlādīyas[4] in the sky, the Paulomas[5] in middle-air, and the Kālakañjas[6] on earth: yet, such though I was, not a hair of mine grows less. If someone knows me, his world does not grow less by any action of his, not by theft, not by murder,[7] not by the killing of his mother, not by the killing of his father. Though he has committed any evil, the dark colour does not leave his face.'[8]

2. He said, 'I am the breath, the self of awareness: so worship me as immortal life.[9] The life is the breath, the breath is the life. As long as the breath dwells in the body, there is life. By the breath one attains immortality in this world:[10] by awareness one attains true resolve.[11] The one who worships me as immortal life attains a full lifespan in this world: he attains immortality, imperishability, in the heavenly world.'

Some say, 'The breaths become a unity, or no one would be able at once to be made aware of[12] a name with speech, a form with the eye, a sound with the ear, a thought with the mind: but, becoming a unity, the breaths make one aware of all these, one by one. When the speech speaks, all the breaths speak with it; when the eye sees, all the breaths see with it; when the ear hears, all the breaths hear with it; when the mind thinks, all the breaths think with it; when the breath breathes, all the breaths breathe with it.'

'So it is,' said Indra, 'but there is a supremacy among the breaths.

3. 'One lives without speech, for we see the dumb. One lives without the eye, for we see the blind. One lives without the ear, for we see the deaf. One lives without the mind, for we see the foolish. One lives with arms cut off, one lives with legs cut off, for we see it is so. But when the breath, the self of awareness, seizes the body, it causes it to stand up (*ut-thā-*): so one should contemplate it as the Uktha. This is all-attainment in the breath.[13] What the breath is, awareness is; and what awareness is, the breath is: they dwell in the body together, and they leave it together.'

This is the seeing of it, this is the knowing of it:

When the person, asleep, sees no dream, he becomes unified in the breath. Speech enters it with all names; the eye enters it with all forms; the ear enters it with all sounds; the mind enters it with all thoughts. When he wakes up, just as sparks from a burning fire might scatter in all directions, the breaths scatter from the self, each to its proper place;[14] the gods from the breaths, the worlds from the gods.

But when the breath, the self of awareness, seizes the body, it makes it stand up, so one should contemplate it as the Uktha. This is all-attainment in the breath. What the breath is, awareness is; and what awareness is, the breath is.[15]

This is the proof of it, this is the understanding of it:

When the person, ailing and about to die, becomes weak and falls into unconsciousness, folk say of him, 'His consciousness[16] has left him: he does not hear, he does not see, he does not speak with speech, he does not think.' He becomes unified in the breath. Speech enters it with all names; the eye enters it with all forms; the ear enters it with all sounds; the mind enters it with all thoughts.[17] When it leaves the body, it leaves with all these together.

4. Speech releases all names into it: by speech it attains all names. The breath releases all smells into it: by the breath it attains all smells. The eye releases all forms into it: by the eye it attains all forms. The ear releases all sounds into it: by the ear it attains all sounds. The mind releases all thoughts into it: by the mind it attains all thoughts. This is all-attainment in the breath. What the breath is, awareness is; and what awareness is, the breath is.[18] These two live in the body together, and they leave it together.

Now we will explain how all beings become one with this awareness.

5. Speech is one part taken out of it, and name is the external element of being which corresponds to it.[19] The breath is one part taken out of it, and smell is the external element of being which corresponds to it. The eye is one part taken out of it, and form is the external element of being which corresponds to it. The ear is one part taken out of it, and sound is the external element of being which corresponds to it. The tongue is one part taken out of it, and the taste of food is the external element of being which corresponds to it. The hands are one part taken out of it, and action is the external element of being which corresponds to them. The body is one part taken out of it, and joy and sorrow are the external element of being which corresponds to it. The loins are one part taken out of it, and delight, pleasure and procreation are the external element of being which corresponds to them. The feet are one part taken out of it, and movements are the external element of being which corresponds to them. The mind is one part taken out of it, and thoughts and desires[20] are the external element of being which corresponds to it.

6. Rising to speech through awareness, by speech one wins all names.[21] Rising to the breath through awareness, by the breath one wins all smells. Rising to the eye through awareness, by the eye one wins all forms. Rising to the ear through awareness, by the ear one wins all sounds. Rising to the tongue through awareness, by the tongue one wins all tastes of food. Rising to

the hands through awareness, by the hands one wins all actions. Rising to the body through awareness, by the body one wins all joy and sorrow. Rising to the loins through awareness, by the loins one wins all delight, pleasure and procreation. Rising to the feet through awareness, by the feet one wins all movements. Rising to the mind through awareness, by the mind one wins all thoughts.[22]

7. Without awareness, speech cannot make one aware of any name. One says, 'My mind was elsewhere: I was not aware of this name.' Without awareness, the breath cannot make one aware of any smell. One says, 'My mind was elsewhere: I was not aware of this smell.' Without awareness, the eye cannot make one aware of any form. One says, 'My mind was elsewhere: I was not aware of this form.' Without awareness, the ear cannot make one aware of any sound. One says, 'My mind was elsewhere: I was not aware of this sound.' Without awareness, the tongue cannot make one aware of any taste of food. One says, 'My mind was elsewhere: I was not aware of this taste of food.' Without awareness, the hands cannot make one aware of any action. One says, 'My mind was elsewhere: I was not aware of this action.'[23] Without awareness, the body cannot make one aware of any joy or sorrow. One says, 'My mind was elsewhere: I was not aware of this joy or sorrow.' Without awareness, the loins cannot make one aware of any delight, pleasure or procreation. One says, 'My mind was elsewhere: I was not aware of this delight, pleasure or procreation.' Without awareness, the feet cannot make one aware of any movement. One says, 'My mind was elsewhere: I was not aware of this movement.' Without awareness, thought cannot be effective, or be aware of that of which it should be aware.

8. One should not seek to know speech: one should know the speaker. One should not seek to know smell: one should know the smeller. One should not seek to know form: one should know the seer.[24] One should not seek to know sound: one should know the hearer. One should not seek to know the taste of food: one should know the knower of the taste of food. One should not seek to know action: one should know the doer. One should not seek to know joy and sorrow: one should know the knower

of joy and sorrow. One should not seek to know delight, pleasure or procreation: one should know the knower of delight, pleasure and procreation. One should not seek to know movement: one should know the mover. One should not seek to know mind: one should know the thinker.

Those are the ten elements of being in relation to awareness. There are ten elements of awareness in relation to being. For if there were no elements of being there would be no elements of awareness, and if there were no elements of awareness there would be no elements of being, since form cannot be realized from either one of them alone.

It is not various. Just as the rim is fixed to the spokes of a chariot-wheel, and the spokes are fixed to the hub, the elements of being are fixed to the elements of awareness, and the elements of awareness are fixed to the elements of being. Breath is the self of awareness, delight, unageing, immortal.

It does not grow greater by right action or less by wrong action. The one that it wishes to lead up out of these worlds it impels to right action, and the one it wishes to lead down it impels to wrong action. It is the guardian of the world, the overlord of the world, the ruler of the world.[25] One should know: it is *my* self. One should know: it is *my* self.

BOOK IV

1. OṂ. Gārgya Bālāki was famed as being learned, since he had lived among the Uśīnaras, among the Matsyas, among the Kurus and Pañcālas, and among the Kāśis and Videhas. He approached Ajātaśatru of Kāśī and said to him, 'I must teach you about *brahman*.'[1]

Ajātaśatru said to him, 'We will give you a thousand cows.' He thought, 'On such a teaching, people will run crying, "A Janaka, a Janaka!"'

2. *In the sun, the great; in the moon, food; in lightning, truth; in thunder, sound; in the air, Indra Vaikuṇṭha; in space, the full; in fire, the courageous; in the waters, brightness: so much regarding deities. Regarding oneself: in the mirror, likeness; in the shadow, the companion; in the echo, life; in sound, death; in sleep, Yama; in the body, Prajāpati; in the right eye, the self of speech; in the left eye, the self of truth.*[2]

3. Bālāki said, 'I worship the person who is in the sun.'

Ajātaśatru said to him, 'Do not make me talk about him. I worship him as the topmost, the great one dressed in white, the head of all beings. Whoever worships him as such becomes the topmost, the head of all beings.'

4. Bālāki said, 'I worship the person who is in the moon.'

Ajātaśatru said to him, 'Do not make me talk about him. I worship him as King Soma,[3] the self of food. Whoever worships him as such becomes the self of food.'

5. Bālāki said, 'I worship the person who is in the lightning.'

Ajātaśatru said to him, 'Do not make me talk about him. I worship him as the self of truth. Whoever worships him as such becomes the self of truth.'[4]

6. Bālāki said, 'I worship the person who is in the thunder.'

Ajātaśatru said to him, 'Do not make me talk about him. I worship him as the self of sound. Whoever worships him as such becomes the self of sound.'

7. Bālāki said, 'I worship the person who is in the air.'[5]

Ajātaśatru said to him, 'Do not make me talk about him. I worship him as Indra Vaikuṇṭha, the unvanquished army. Whoever worships him as such becomes victorious, unvanquished, a conqueror of foes.'

8. Bālāki said, 'I worship the person who is in space.'

Ajātaśatru said to him, 'Do not make me talk about him. I worship him as the full, the unmoving. Whoever worships him as such is filled with offspring, with animals,[6] with fame, with the radiance of *brahman*, with the heavenly world: he attains his full lifespan.'

9. Bālāki said, 'I worship the person who is in fire.'

Ajātaśatru said to him, 'Do not make me talk about him. I worship him as the courageous. Whoever worships him as such becomes courageous among others.'[7]

10. Bālāki said, 'I worship the person who is in the waters.'

Ajātaśatru said to him, 'Do not make me talk about him. I worship him as the self of brightness. Whoever worships him as such becomes the self of brightness.'[8]

So much regarding deities. Now regarding oneself:

11. Bālāki said, 'I worship the person who is in the mirror.'

Ajātaśatru said to him, 'Do not make me talk about him. I worship him as likeness. For, whoever worships him as such, likeness is born in his offspring, not unlikeness.'

12. Bālāki said, 'I worship the person who is in the shadow.'[9]

Ajātaśatru said to him, 'Do not make me talk about him. I worship him as the companion who never leaves us. Whoever worships him as such gets offspring from a companion and has a companion.'[10]

13. Bālāki said, 'I worship the person who is in the echo.'[11]

Ajātaśatru said to him, 'Do not make me talk about him. I worship him as life.[12] Whoever worships him as such does not fall into unconsciousness before his time.'

14. Bālāki said, 'I worship the person who is in sound.'[13]

Ajātaśatru said to him, 'Do not make me talk about him. I worship him as death. Whoever worships him as such does not pass away before his time.'[14]

15. Bālāki said, 'I worship the person who, asleep, moves about in dream.'[15]

Ajātaśatru said to him, 'Do not make me talk about him. I worship him as King Yama. For, whoever worships him as such, all this is controlled (*yam-*) for his betterment.'

16. Bālāki said, 'I worship the person who is in the body.'

Ajātaśatru said to him, 'Do not make me talk about him. I worship him as Prajāpati. Whoever worships him as such becomes fruitful in offspring, in animals, in fame, in the glory of *brahman*, in a heavenly world: he attains his full lifespan.'[16]

17. Bālāki said, 'I worship the person who is in the right eye.'

Ajātaśatru said to him, 'Do not make me talk about him. I worship him as the self of speech,[17] the self of fire, the self of light. Whoever worships him as such becomes the self of all these.'

18. Bālāki said, 'I worship the person who is in the left eye.'

Ajātaśatru said to him, 'Do not make me talk about him. I worship him as the self of truth, the self of lightning, the self of brightness. Whoever worships him as such becomes the self of all these.'

19. Then Bālāki fell silent. Ajātaśatru said to him, 'Is that all, Bālāki?'

Bālāki said, 'That is all.'

Ajātaśatru said to him, 'You make me talk to no purpose. I must teach you about *brahman*. What one needs to know, Bālāki, is who is the maker of these persons, whose work it is.'

Then Bālāki approached him, fuel in hand, and said, 'I must come to you as your student.'[18]

Ajātaśatru said to him, 'I think it contrary to the proper form[19] that a Kṣatriya should initiate a Brāhmaṇa. But come, I shall make it known to you.' He seized him by the hand and set off. They came to a person who was asleep, and Ajātaśatru called him: 'O great King Soma, dressed in white!' He just lay there. But then Ajātaśatru prodded him with a stick, and he got up.

Ajātaśatru said to Bālāki, 'Where did the person lie then, Bālāki? Where was he? Where has he come from?'

Bālāki did not know.

Ajātaśatru said to him, 'As to where the person lay then, Bālāki, where he was, and where he has come from: the channels of a person,[20] called *hitā*, stretch from the heart to the citadel of the heart. As subtle as a hair a thousandfold divided, they exist on a subtle essence of tawny, white, black, yellow and red. When, asleep, he sees no dream, he is in those channels.

20. 'He becomes unified in the breath. Speech enters it with all names; the eye enters it with all forms; the ear enters it with all sounds; the mind enters it with all thoughts. When he wakes up, just as sparks from a burning fire might scatter in all directions, the breaths scatter from the self, each to its proper place; the gods from the breaths, the worlds from the gods. The breath, the self of awareness, enters the self that is the body right to the hairs and the nails.[21] Like a razor hidden in a razor-case, or a scorpion in a scorpion's nest,[22] the breath, the self of awareness, enters the self that is the body right to the hairs and the nails. These selves depend on that self just as his people receive benefit from a chief. Just as a chief receives benefit from his people or his people receive benefit from a chief, these selves receive benefit from that self.'

As long as Indra did not understand the self, the demons used to overcome him. When he understood it, slaying and conquering the demons he encompassed chiefship, sovereignty and overlordship over all gods and all beings. Likewise, knowing this, defeating all evils, one encompasses chiefship, sovereignty and overlordship over all beings – the one who knows this: the one who knows this.

I will speak law (ṛta): *I will speak truth.*

My speech stands firm on mind:
My mind stands firm on speech.
May you appear, appear as a youth.
By knowledge that nail has held the law in place.

Do me no harm.
With this study I hold days and nights together.
Homage to Agni with the libation.
With the libation homage to the Ṛṣis,
Makers of the mantras, lords of the mantras.
Homage to you, O gods.
Gracious lady, be most healing to us,
    compassionate Sarasvatī.
May we not be separated from your sight.
Unerring mind, quick eye is the sun, best of lights.
Initiation, do me no harm.

OṂ. Peace, peace, peace.

KENA UPANIṢAD

'By Whom?'

OṂ. *May my limbs, speech, breath, eye, ear, strength and all senses grow strong. Everything is the* brahman *of the Upaniṣads. May I not reject* brahman. *May* brahman *not reject me. May there be no rejecting. May there be no rejecting of me.*[1] *May all the* dharmas *which are in the Upaniṣads be in me, who delight in the self. May they be in me.*

OṂ. *Peace, peace, peace.*

BOOK I

1. OṂ. *Urged on by whom does the mind fly?*
Harnessed by whom does breath move, the first?
By whom is urged on the speech that folk utter?
And which god harnesses the eye and ear?[2]

2. He is the ear of the ear, the mind of the mind,
The speech of speech, and the breath of the breath,
The eye of the eye. Knowing this,[3] the wise renounce,
And, when they leave this world, become immortal.

3. The eye does not go there,
Speech does not go, nor mind.
We do not know, we do not understand,
How anyone could teach it.

4. It is different from the known;
It is different, too, from the unknown:
So we have heard from those of old
Who have revealed it to us.[4]

5. What is not expressed by speech –
By which speech is expressed –
Know that as *brahman*,
Not what they worship as such.

6. What one does not think of by the mind –
By which, they say, the mind is thought of –
Know that as *brahman*,
Not what they worship as such.

7. What one does not see by the eye –
By which one sees eyes[5] –
Know that as *brahman*,
Not what they worship as such.

8. What one does not hear by the ear –
By which the ear is heard –
Know that as *brahman*,
Not what they worship as such.

9. What one does not breathe by the breath[6] –
By which the breath is breathed –
Know that as *brahman*,
Not what they worship as such.

BOOK II

1. If you think, 'I know it well', you know just a little the form of *brahman* – that part of it which is you[7] and that part of it which is among the gods. I think you should investigate that unknown:[8]

2. I do not think, 'I know it well',
   And I do not know, 'I don't know it.'
Whoever of us knows it knows it,
   And does not know 'I don't know it.'

3. It is thought of by the one to whom it is unthought;
   The one by whom it is thought of – he does
      not know.
It is not understood by the understanders;
   It is understood by those who do not understand.

4. It is thought of when it is realized by
      awakening to it:
   So one finds immortality.
Through oneself (*ātman*) one finds power:
   Through wisdom one finds immortality.

5. If, here, one has known it, it is truth;
   If, here, one has not known it – great destruction![9]
The wise discern it in every being
   And, when they leave this world, become
      immortal.

BOOK III

1. *Brahman* won a victory for the gods, and the gods were triumphing in the victory of *brahman*. They thought 'This victory is ours! This triumph is ours!'

2. It knew their thought and appeared before them, but they did not know what this wonder[10] was.

3. They said to Agni, 'Jātavedas, find out what this wonder is.'

'I will.'

4. He ran up to it, and it spoke to him: 'Who are you?'

'I am Agni,' he said. 'I am Jātavedas.'

5. 'Then what power is in you?'

'I could burn up everything that is on the earth.'

6. It put down a blade of grass before him. 'Burn this!'

He approached it with all his force, but could not burn it. Then he went back, saying, 'I have not been able to find out what this wonder is.'

7. Then they said to Vāyu, 'Vāyu, find out what this wonder is.'

'I will.'

8. He ran up to it, and it spoke to him: 'Who are you?'

'I am Vāyu,' he said. 'I am Mātariśvan.'

9. 'Then what power is in you?'

'I could carry off everything that is on the earth.'

10. It put down a blade of grass before him. 'Carry off this!'

He approached it with all his force, but could not carry it off. Then he went back, saying, 'I have not been able to find out what this wonder is.'

11. Then they said to Indra, 'Maghavan, find out what this wonder is.'

'I will.'

He ran up to it, and it disappeared.

12. In the same space he came upon a most beautiful woman, Umā Haimavatī.[11] He asked her what this wonder was.

BOOK IV

1. '*Brahman*,' she said. 'You were triumphing in the victory of *brahman*.'

Then he knew it as *brahman*.

2. That is why these gods – Agni, Vāyu, Indra – are somewhat above the other gods: they touched it closest.[12]

3. That is why Indra is somewhat above the other gods: he touched it closest; he was the first to know it as *brahman*.

4. There is this symbolic statement about it: 'As when lightning has flashed – Aaah! – and made us blink – Aaah!'

So much regarding deities.

5. Regarding oneself:

'Mind seems to go to it; and by it the imagination[13] at once remembers.'

6. It is called 'the beloved':[14] it should be worshipped as 'the beloved'. All beings greatly love the one who knows this.

7. *Sir, tell me the secret teaching.*

The secret teaching has been told to you. We have told you the secret teaching of *brahman*.[15]

8. Asceticism (*tapas*), self-control and work (*karman*) are its supports (*pratiṣṭhā*); the Vedas are all its limbs; truth is its dwelling.

9. Whoever knows it as such destroys evil and in the end[16] stands firm (*prati-sthā-*), stands firm in the highest[17] heavenly world.

OṂ. *May my limbs, speech, breath, eye, ear, strength and all senses grow strong. Everything is the* brahman *of the Upaniṣads. May I not reject* brahman. *May* brahman *not reject me. May there be no rejecting. May there be no rejecting of me. May all the* dharmas *which are in the Upaniṣads be in me, who delight in the self. May they be in me.*

OṂ. *Peace, peace, peace.*

KAṬHA UPANIṢAD

The Kaṭhas' Teaching

OṂ. *Together may it protect us two:*
Together may it profit us two:
Together may we do a hero's work.
May we learn intelligently:
May we never hate one another.

OṂ. *Peace, peace, peace.*[1]

BOOK I

1. OṂ. Uśan Vājaśravasa once offered a sacrifice entailing the giving away of all his possessions.[2] He had a son called Naciketas.

2. Though he was just a boy, when the gifts of cattle[3] were being led away, faith entered him and he thought:

3. 'They have drunk their water and eaten their grass,
   Have given their milk, senseless ones:
'"Joyless" are the worlds called
   To which goes the one who gives these.'

4. And he said to his father, 'Daddy,[4] to whom will you give *me*?' A second and a third time he said it.
'I give you to Death!'

5. 'First of many I go;[5]
   Midst of many I go.
What work has Yama to do
   That he will be doing with me?

6. 'Looking towards those before me
   And looking back at those who come after –
Like the crops a mortal ripens
   And like the crops springs up again.'

7. *As fire a Brāhmaṇa*
   Guest enters a house,
And so they quench him.
   Bring water, son of Vivasvat!

8. *From that man of little wit*
In whose house he stays, unfed,
A Brāhmaṇa takes hope and expectation,
Friendship, happiness, action and merit, sons and cattle – everything.[6]

9. 'Brahmā,[7] since you, a guest to be honoured,
Have stayed three nights in my house, unfed, –
Homage to you, Brahmā! May it be well with me! –
Choose three boons.'

10. 'May Gautama, his mind at peace, well-disposed,
His anger towards me gone, O Death,
Greet me, content, when I am released by you.
I choose this as the first of the three boons.'

11. 'Auddālaka Āruṇi,[8] released by me,
Shall be content as before.
He shall sleep well nights, his anger gone,
Once he has seen you set free from the mouth of Death.'

12. 'In the heavenly world there is no fear:
You are not there, nor does one fear old age:
Having crossed over both hunger and thirst,
One rejoices in that heavenly world beyond sorrow.

13. '*You* teach me, Death, about the heavenly fire.
Tell it to me, who have faith.
The heavenly worlds share in immortality.
I choose this by way of my second boon.'

14. 'I will tell you, Naciketas, so listen to me
And learn of the heavenly fire.
Know of this, which is kept in a secret place –
How to win an endless world, and remain there.'[9]

15. He taught him of the fire, the beginning of the world,[10]
What bricks to use and how many, and how to build it –
And he repeated it back as it had been told to him.
Then Death, satisfied, spoke again.

16. The great-hearted (*mahātman*) one, pleased, said,
'Today I give you another favour:
This fire will be known by your name.
Grasp this chain[11] with its many forms.

17. 'The one of three Nāciketa-fires, who has attained union with the three,
Who does the three works,[12] crosses over birth and death.
Knowing the god, worthy of offerings, who knows all that is born from *brahman*,
And building the fires,[13] he reaches this surpassing peace.

18. 'The one of three Nāciketa-fires, knowing this threesome,[14]
Who, knowing this, builds up the Nāciketa,
Thrusting Death's snares from before him,
Going beyond sorrow, rejoices in a heavenly world.

19. 'Naciketas, since you chose the heavenly fire
By way of your second boon,
Folk will speak of this fire as yours.
Naciketas, choose your third boon.'

20. 'There is doubt concerning a man who has departed.
Some say, "He is", and others say, "He is not."
Taught by you, I would know this.
This is the third of my boons.'

21. 'This was doubted here too, by the gods before:
It is a subtle *dharma*, not easily understood.
Choose a different boon, Naciketas.
Do not, do not insist: release me from this.'

22. 'So this was doubted here too, by the gods!
Since you, Death, tell me it is not easily understood,
And no one else can be found who can teach this as you can,
There is no boon to equal this.'

23. 'Choose a hundred years, sons and grandsons,
Many cattle, elephants, gold, horses:
Choose a great estate of land,
And yourself live as many autumns as you will.

24. 'If you think fit, choose another boon, equal to this,
Wealth and long life too.
Naciketas, enter a great realm of desires:
I will make you the enjoyer of your desires.

25. 'Whatsoever desires are hard to obtain in the mortal world,
Ask for them all, at your will.
Here are fair ladies, with chariots, with musical instruments,[15]
Their like not to be won by men.
Enjoy yourself with them – I give them to you –
Naciketas, but do not ask me about dying.'

26. 'Ephemeral things, Ender! Since they wear out
The potency of all a mortal's faculties,
And all life is so short,
The chariots are yours, the dance and song yours still.

27. 'A human being cannot be satisfied by wealth.
Shall we get wealth if we have seen you?
We shall live just as long as *you* decree.
That boon of mine is the only one to choose.

28. 'Once he has encountered the agelessness of the immortals,
How could the ageing mortal, dwelling on earth below, understanding this,
Contemplating their beauty, pleasures and delights,
Find pleasure in very long life?

29. 'Tell us, Death, what people are doubtful of
In the great matter of their passing away.[16]
Naciketas chooses no other boon but this one
That is so deeply hidden.'

BOOK II

1. 'The better is one thing, the pleasanter another:
Both bind a man, to different ends.
Of the two, it is well for the one who chooses the better.
The one who chooses the pleasanter fails of his end.

2. 'When both have examined the better and the pleasanter human course,
The wise one discriminates between the two.
The wise one chooses the better over the pleasanter;
The foolish one chooses the pleasanter, for the sake of getting and enjoying.[17]

3. '*You*, Naciketas, contemplating desires
Both pleasant and pleasant-appearing, have let them go.
You have not taken on this chain[18] made of wealth
Into which many human beings have plunged.

4. 'These two are far apart, disparate,
Ignorance and what is called wisdom.
I think Naciketas is a seeker of wisdom:
Many desires have not distracted you.

5. 'Living in the midst of ignorance,
Wise in their own view, thinking themselves learned,
The foolish rush about,
Like blind men led by one who is blind.

6. 'Intoxicated, deluded by the glamour of riches,
The childish one does not see that he must pass away:[19]
Thinking, "This is the world: there is no other",
Again and again he comes into my power.

7. 'What many will not get the chance even to hear of,
What many, though hearing, do not know –
Wonderful is the speaker of it, skilled the winner of it,
Wonderful the knower of it, taught by a skilled one.

8. 'Through the teaching of an inferior man it cannot easily be known,
Though it be thought about in many ways:
There is no way to it without another's teaching,
For it is subtler than the subtle, not to be reasoned out.

9. 'This thought, which cannot be grasped by reasoning,
Yet is easily known when taught by another,
You, my dear, have grasped. How steadfast in truth you are!
May we find another questioner like you!'

[Naciketas:]

10. 'I know that what is called treasure is impermanent,
That what is constant cannot be got through inconstant means,
So I have built the Naciketa-fire:
Through impermanent objects I have won the permanent.'[20]

[Yama:]

11. 'Fulfilment of desire, a firm foundation in the world,
Infinity of power, the further shore of fearlessness,
Greatness of praise, a wide-ranging foundation,
Naciketas, you have seen, and, being wise, have steadfastly let go.

12. 'By the study of the yoga of the self,[21] the wise one
knows as god
That which is hard to see, that is deeply hidden,
That lies in a secret place, that rests in the depths,
ancient,
And abandons joy and sorrow.

13. 'Hearing and grasping this, a mortal,
Drawing out that which belongs to *dharma*,[22]
attains this subtle one.
Then he rejoices, for he has won what is worthy of
rejoicing.
I consider Naciketas a fitting home for this.[23]

14. 'It is different from *dharma*, different from not-*dharma*,
Different from this that is made and unmade,
Different from both past and future.
Tell me what you see!'

[Naciketas cannot, so Yama continues:]

15. 'The word which all the Vedas recollect,
Of which all ascetic practices speak,
Searching for which folk live as students of *brahman*,
I will tell you in brief.
It is OṂ.

16. 'This syllable is *brahman*.
This syllable is supreme.
Knowing this syllable,
Whatever one wishes for one has.

17. 'This support is the best.
This support is supreme.
Knowing this support,
One is honoured in the world of Brahmā.

18. 'The wise one[24] is not born, nor does it die.
It is not from anywhere, nor was it anyone.
Unborn, everlasting, eternal, primeval,
It is not slain when the body is slain.

19. 'If the slayer thinks it slays;
If the one who is slain thinks *it* is slain:
Neither of them understands.
It does not slay, nor is it slain.[25]

20. 'Subtler than the subtle, greater than the great,
The self is hidden in the secret place of a being.
One without will,[26] through the creator's favour,[27]
Sees the greatness of the self, his sorrow at an end.

21. 'Sitting, it travels far.
Lying down, it goes everywhere.
Who else but I (*mad-*) is able to know
The god who is ever delighted (*madāmada*).[28]

22. 'Knowing this great all-pervading self –
Bodiless among bodies,
Stable among the unstable –
The wise one does not grieve.

23. 'The self cannot be won by speaking,
Nor by intelligence or much learning.
It can be won by the one whom it chooses.
To him the self reveals its own form.

24. 'Neither the one who has not ceased from wrongdoing,
Nor the unpeaceful nor the unconcentrated,
Nor the one of unpeaceful mind
Can win it through knowing.

25. 'The one for whom priesthood (*brahman*) and
royalty (*kṣatra*),
Both, are the rice
And death is the sauce:
Who, truly, knows where he is?

BOOK III

1. 'Two drink law (*ṛta*) in the world of the good deed,
Having entered both the secret place and the utmost height:
Knowers of *brahman* call them 'shadow' and 'light':
So do those with the five fires,[29] and those of three Nāciketa-fires.

2. 'May we be capable of the Nāciketa,
Which is the bridge for those who sacrifice,
Which is the supreme imperishable *brahman*,
The other shore, free from fear, for those who long to cross.

3. 'Know the self as a chariot-owner,
The body as a chariot,
The intelligence (*buddhi*) as a charioteer,
The mind (*manas*) as the reins.

4. 'The senses they call the horses,
The objects of sense their courses.
The self, joined with senses and mind,
The wise call "the enjoyer".

5. 'The senses of the one without understanding,
With mind ever undisciplined,[30]
Are out of his control,
Like evil horses of a charioteer.

6. 'The senses of the one with understanding,
With mind ever disciplined,
Are under his control,
Like good horses of a charioteer.

7. 'The one without understanding,
Unmindful, ever impure,
Does not reach that place,
But goes on to *saṃsāra*.

8. 'The one with understanding,
Mindful, ever pure,
Attains that place
From which he is not born again.

9. 'The man who has understanding as his charioteer
And mind as his reins
Attains the journey's end,
Viṣṇu's highest step.

10. 'For the objects are higher than the senses,
The mind higher than the objects,
Intelligence higher than the mind,
The great self higher than intelligence.

11. 'The unmanifest (*avyakta*) is higher than the great one,
The person (*puruṣa*) higher than the unmanifest.[31]
Nothing is higher than the person:
That is the goal, the highest bourn.

12. 'Hidden in all beings,
The self does not shine forth.
But it is seen with supreme, subtle intelligence
By those of subtle sight.

13. 'The wise one should offer up speech and mind:
He should offer it up into the knowing self.
He should offer up the knowing into the great self:
He should offer up that into the peaceful self.

14. 'Stand up! Wake up!
Now you have got your boons, pay attention![32]
This is a difficult path,
A razor's sharp edge, hard to cross –
So the poets say.

15. 'The one who has seen[33] that which is wordless, untouched, formless, unperishing,
Without taste, too, eternal, without scent,
Beginningless, endless, higher than the great, constant,
Is freed from the mouth of Death.'

16. Speaking and hearing the eternal teaching of Naciketas
Spoken by Death,
The intelligent one
Is honoured in the world of Brahmā.

17. The one who, well prepared, recites this supreme secret
In an assembly of the priesthood
Or at the time of the *śrāddha*-offering
Becomes fitted for immortality –
Becomes fitted for immortality.

BOOK IV

1. 'The self-born has bored holes, facing outward:
Hence one sees outward, not within oneself (*antarātman*).
A certain wise one, desiring immortality, turning his gaze around,
Has looked within at the self.

2. 'Childish folk follow outward desires
And go into the noose of Death, who lies in wait:[34]
But the wise, seeing immortality,
Do not search for the constant in inconstant things.

3. 'By that by which one knows form, taste, smell,
Sounds and sexual contacts,[35]
One knows it too.
What is left here?
This is that.

4. 'Knowing that by which one experiences
Both sleep and waking states
As the great, all-pervading self,
The wise one does not grieve.

5. 'The one who knows this honey-eater[36]
As life, the self, close by,
Lord of past and future,
Does not shrink away from it.
This is that.

6. 'He who was formerly the offspring of
heat (*tapas*) –
Who was formerly born of the waters –
He who, having entered and dwelt in the secret
place,
Looks out through beings –
This is that.[37]

7. 'She who arises through the breath –
Aditi, made of deities –
She who, having entered and dwelt in the secret
place,
Was born through beings –
This is that.

8. 'Agni Jātavedas, hidden in the two fire-sticks
Like an embryo safely carried by pregnant
women,
Worthy of daily worship
By vigilant men bearing offerings –
This is that.

9. 'That from which the sun rises
And into which it sets,
In that the gods are fixed.
No one goes beyond it.
This is that.

10. 'What is here is there:
What is there is here too.
The one who sees things here as various
Gets death after death.

11. 'It can be grasped only by mind.
There is nothing various here.
The one who sees things here as various
Goes from death to death.

12. 'A person (*puruṣa*), a thumb in length,
Rests in the midst of the self,
Lord of past and future . . .
One does not shrink away from it.
This is that.

13. 'A person, a thumb in length,
Like a light without smoke,
Lord of past and future,
It is, today, and tomorrow too.
This is that.

14. 'As rainwater, fallen in a rugged place
Among the mountains, runs away,
One who sees *dharmas* as separate
Runs away after them.

15. 'As pure water, dropping into pure,
Becomes just like it,
So, Gautama, does the self
Of the silent one (*muni*) who understands.

BOOK V

1. 'Ruling the eleven-gated city[38]
Of the unborn whose thought is not crooked,
One does not grieve,
And, when freed from it, is freed.
This is that.

2. 'As the goose in the clear sky, as the Vasu in middle-air,
As the Hotṛ at the altar, as the guest in the house,
In a man, in a boon, in law (*ṛta*), in the sky,
Water-born, cow-born, law-born, mountain-born, great law.[39]

3. 'It leads the breath (*prāṇa*) up:
It throws the lower breath (*apāna*) back:
All the gods[40] worship
The dwarf who sits in the middle.

4. 'When the possessor of the body who rests in the body
Is unloosed
And set free from the body,
What is left here?
This is that.

5. 'Not by the breath, not by the lower breath
Does any mortal live.
They live by something else
On which these two depend.

6. 'Look, Gautama, I will tell you
Of the secret eternal *brahman*
And what the self is like
After reaching death.

7. 'Some go into a womb
So that the possessor of the body may find a body.[41]
Others go into the motionless[42]
According to their actions (*karman*) and learning.

8. 'The one who is awake in the sleeping,
The person shaping desire after desire,
Is the bright, is *brahman*.
It is called the immortal.
On it all the worlds depend.
No one goes beyond it.
This is that.

9. 'Just as the one fire, entering the world,
Takes on forms corresponding to every form,
So the one self within all beings
Takes on forms corresponding to every form, and is outside them.

10. 'Just as the one wind, entering the world,
Takes on forms corresponding to every form,
So the one self within all beings
Takes on forms corresponding to every form, and is outside them.

11. 'Just as the one sun, the eye of the whole world,
Is not contaminated by the external flaws of eyes,
So the one self within all beings
Is not contaminated by the sorrow of the world, being outside it.

12. 'Those wise ones who see, in the self,
The one controlling self within all beings
That makes the one form into many
Have everlasting happiness: no others do.

13. 'Those wise ones who see, in the self,
The one that is permanent among the impermanent, thinker among thinkers,
The one among many who disposes desires,
Have everlasting peace: no others do.

14. 'They know that *this* is that –
The indescribable highest happiness.
How could I understand it?
Does it shine, or is it lit by another's light?[43]

15. 'The sun does not shine there, nor the moon and stars.
Lightning does not shine there, let alone fire.
Everything reflects its shining.
Everything is lit by its light.

BOOK VI

1. 'There is an eternal pipal tree
With its roots above, its branches below.[44]
It is the bright; it is *brahman*;
It is called the immortal.
On it all the worlds depend:
No one goes beyond it.
This is that.

2. 'Whatever there is that moves (*jagat*),[45]
The breath impels it as it is sent forth.
It is a great terror, an upraised thunderbolt.
They who know this become immortal.

3. 'From fear of it, Agni burns.
From fear, Sūrya shines.
From fear both Indra and Vāyu,
And Death, as fifth, run on.

4. 'If one has been able to wake up to it here
Before the break-up of the body,
One is fitted to attain a body
In the worlds of creation.[46]

5. 'In oneself, it appears as though in a mirror;
In the world of the ancestors, as though in a dream;
In the world of the *gandharvas*, as though it appeared in water;
In the world of Brahmā, as though in bright light and shadow.[47]

6. 'Knowing the senses to be separate,
Likewise the rising and setting
Of things that arise separately,
The wise one does not grieve.[48]

7. 'The mind is higher than the senses,
Being (*sattva*) higher than the mind:
The great self is above being,
The unmanifest higher than the great.[49]

8. 'Above the unmanifest is the person,
Pervading and without mark,[50]
Knowing which, a being is liberated
And reaches immortality.

9. 'Its form is not present to the sight –
No one sees it with the eye.
The wise one, adept in mind, sees it in his heart.
Those who know it become immortal.

10. 'When the five knowings[51] cease,
Together with the mind,
And the intelligence does not stir,
They call that the highest bourn.

11. 'This steadfast control of the senses
Is known as "yoga" –
Then one becomes undistracted:
For yoga is the origin and the passing away.

12. 'It cannot be won
By speech or mind or eye.
How can it be grasped in any other way
Than by one saying, "It is!"

13. 'It can be grasped so: "It is!" –
Through the real nature of both.[52]
When it has been grasped so: "It is!" –
Its real nature becomes clear.

14. 'When all the desires that dwell
In one's heart are let go,
Mortal becomes immortal:
One reaches *brahman* here.[53]

15. 'When all the knots of
The heart here are broken,
Mortal becomes immortal:
This is the teaching.

16. 'A hundred and one are the channels of the heart.
Of them, one flows out through the head.
Going up by it, one reaches immortality.
Others, on departing, go in all directions.[54]

17. 'The person, a thumb in length, in the midst of
the self,
Ever resting in the hearts of people,
One should by wisdom[55] draw out from one's
own body
Like the cane from a *muñja*-reed.
One should know it as the bright, the immortal.
One should know it as the bright, the immortal.'

18. Naciketas, having received this knowledge,
taught by Death,
And the complete method of yoga,
Attaining *brahman*, became free of impurity,
deathless,
And so will any other who knows it in relation
to the self.

OṂ. *Together may it protect us two:*
Together may it profit us two:
Together may we do a hero's work.
May we learn intelligently:
May we never hate one another.

OṂ. *Peace, peace, peace.*

ŚVETĀŚVATARA UPANIṢAD

Śvetāśvatara's Teaching

OṂ. *That is full; this is full;*[1]
Fullness comes forth from fullness:
When fullness is taken from fullness,
Fullness remains.

OṂ. *Peace, peace, peace.*

BOOK I

1. OṂ. Scholars of *brahman* say:
What is the cause – brahman?[1] *From what were we born?*
By what do we live? And on what are we based?
Ruled by what do we follow our course
In joys and their opposite, you knowers of brahman?

2. *Should we conceive of it as time, own nature, fate, or chance,*
Elements, a womb, a person?[2]
A conjunction of these? No, because of the existence of the self:
And the self is powerless over the cause of joy and sorrow.[3]

3. Those who have followed the method of meditation[4]
Have seen the god's own power, hidden by his own strands[5] –
One, who rules over all those causes
From 'time' to 'self'.

4. As a wheel with one rim,[6] three tyres,[7] and sixteen ends,[8]
Half a hundred spokes,[9] twenty counter-spokes,[10]
Six eights,[11] one rope that takes every shape,[12]
Three different roads,[13] and one illusion with two causes:[14]

5. As a river with five streams[15] we know it, wild and winding, with five sources,[16]
Five breaths (*prāṇa*) as waves, five perceptions[17] as its wellspring,
Five whirlpools[18] whirling with the power of the five sufferings,[19]
Fifty divisions, with five sections each.[20]

6. In this mighty wheel of *brahman*, life-giver to all, rest to all,[21]
Roves a goose.[22]
Once it knows itself (*ātman*) and the impeller to be different,
Then, finding favour with him, it attains immortality.[23]

7. In song it has been called the supreme *brahman*.
In it are the triad, the good support and the imperishable.[24]
Knowing it and merging into *brahman*,
Knowers of *brahman*, intent upon it, are freed from the womb.

8. The powerful one[25] bears the whole, united,
Perishable and imperishable, manifest and unmanifest.
The self, powerless, is bound through its being an enjoyer.
Once it knows the god, it is freed from all bonds.

9. There are two billy-goats, knower and unknowing, powerful and powerless;
One nanny-goat, yoked to the enjoyer and the objects of enjoyment,[26]
And the infinite self, possessing all forms, not an actor.[27]
When one finds the triad, this is *brahman*.

10. Primal matter is perishable; the taker[28] is the immortal
imperishable.[29]
One god has power over both perishable and self.
Through meditation on him, through practice,
Through his being entity (*tattva*) and more,[30] in
the end the whole artifice (*māyā*)[31] ceases.

11. When one knows the god, all bonds are cast off;
When the afflictions have faded away, birth and
death are ended;
Through meditation on him, there arises a third state:
On the break-up of the body, lordship over all;
absolute,[32] one attains one's desires.

12. One must know the eternal which rests in the self:
There is nothing beyond this to be known.
When the enjoyer knows the object of enjoyment and
the impeller,
Everything has been said. This is the threefold
brahman.

13. As when fire is in its source, its form is not seen,
Nor yet is the mark[33] of it destroyed,
And it may be got again from its source, the
kindling-stick,
So both can be got in the body by the OṂ (*praṇava*).

14. Making one's own body the lower fire-stick
And the OṂ the upper fire-stick,
By practising the friction of meditation
One may see the god in hiding.

15. Like oil in sesame-seeds, butter in curds,
Water in river-beds,[34] and fire in fire-sticks,
Self is found in self
For the one who seeks it by truth and asceticism.

16. The self that pervades everything,
As butter is contained in milk –
The root of self-knowledge and asceticism –
Is the supreme inner teaching of *brahman*:
Is the supreme inner teaching of *brahman*.[35]

BOOK II

1. Savitṛ, first yoking mind,
   Yoking thoughts for truth (*tattva*),
Discerning the light of Agni
   Brought it up from earth.[1]

2. We, with mind yoked,
   Under the inspiration[2] of the god Savitṛ,
   By his power, for the heavenly world[3] . . .

3. Having yoked by mind the heaven-going gods
   That go by thought to the sky,
May Savitṛ inspire them
   To make a great light.

4. The poets of the great inspired poet
   Yoke mind and yoke thoughts.
The one knower of ways has assigned the
      Hotṛ's tasks.
   Great is the praise of the god Savitṛ.

5. I yoke your ancient lore (*brahman*) with praises.
   Let my verse go on the hero's path.[4]
May all the sons of the immortal, who have reached
   The divine abodes, hear.

6. Where fire is kindled,
   Where wind arises,
Where Soma overflows,
   Mind appears.[5]

7. With Savitṛ as inspirer
One should take delight in the ancient lore:
There make your source.
Your good deeds have not perished.[6]

8. Keeping the body straight, its three parts[7] upright,
Causing the senses by mind to enter the heart,
By the boat of *brahman* the wise one should cross over
All the terrifying floods.

9. Suppressing the bodily functions (*prāṇa*), movements controlled,
His breath (*prāṇa*) light, he should breathe through the nose:
The wise one, heedful, should control the mind
As a chariot yoked to bad horses.

10. In a level, clean place, free from gravel, fire and sand,
With soundless water, a dwelling and so on,[8]
Pleasing to the mind and not harsh on the eye,
Secret and sheltered from the wind, one should practise yoga.

11. Forms of mist, smoke, sun, wind, fire,
Fireflies, lightning, crystal, or moon,
Are harbingers in yoga
Which bring manifestations in *brahman*.[9]

12. When earth, water, fire, air and space have arisen
And the fivefold strand of yoga has come forth,
One has neither disease nor old age nor death,
Having won a body made of the fire of yoga.[10]

13. Lightness, freedom from disease, steadiness,
Clarity of complexion, sweetness of voice,
A pleasant smell, little urine or excrement
Tell of the first arising of yoga.

14. Just as a mirror smeared with dirt,
Once cleaned, shines, being bright,[11]
The embodied, seeing the entity of self,
Becomes one, his aim fulfilled, freed from sorrow.

15. But when, concentrated, one sees here, by the entity of self,
As by a lamp, the entity of *brahman*,
Knowing the god as unborn, constant, free of all entities,
One is freed from all bonds.[12]

16. The god faces all directions:
He was born of old and yet is in the womb,
Born and to be born, he stands
In front of people, facing every way.[13]

17. To the god who is in fire, in water,
Who has entered the whole world,
Who is in plants, in trees –
To the god be praise, be praise.[14]

BOOK III

1. There is one who bears a net, who rules with his powers,[1]
   Who rules all worlds with his powers,
   Who is one in arising and ceasing.
   Those who know this become immortal.

2. Rudra is the one – they do not give place to a second –
   Who rules the worlds with his powers.
   He stands in front of people. Protector of all worlds,
   At the ending-time he has drawn them in again.[2]

3. Eyes on every side and faces on every side,
   Arms on every side and feet on every side,
   With his arms and his wings he forges them,
   One god begetting sky and earth.[3]

4. May Rudra, overlord of all, great Ṛṣi,
   The source and origin of the gods,
   Who of old begot the golden embryo,[4]
   Yoke us with clear intelligence.

5. Mountain-dweller Rudra,
   With that gracious (*śivā*) form of yours,
   Not terrifying nor evil-appearing, but most healing,[5]
   Gaze on us always.

6. Mountain-dweller, make gracious (*śiva*)
   The arrow that you hold in your hand to shoot:
   Mountain-protector, do not injure
   Man or moving thing.[6]

7. Higher than that[7] is the supreme *brahman*.
Knowing that powerful one, the great,
Hidden in all beings according to their bodies,
One enveloping all, folk become immortal.

8. I know this great person,
Sun-coloured, beyond darkness.
Knowing him, one goes beyond death:
There is no other path by which to go.

9. All this is filled by the person,
The one, who stands in the sky, firm as a tree.
There is nothing higher or lower than he,
No one[8] smaller or larger.

10. That which is far higher than that[9]
Is formless, without disease:
Those who know it become immortal.
The rest go on to suffering.

11. Possessing all faces, heads and necks,
Living in the secret depth of all beings,
The blessed one is all-pervading:
Therefore he is the omnipresent gracious
one (*śiva*).[10]

12. The person is the great lord,
He who makes being (*sattva*) roll onward,[11]
Ruling over this most pure attainment,[12]
Unfailing light.

13. The person within the self, a thumb in length,
Always living in the heart of people,
Is shaped by the heart, the intelligence, the mind.[13]
Those who know this become immortal.

14. The person with a thousand heads,
A thousand eyes, a thousand feet
Has enfolded the earth on every side
And stood out beyond it by ten thumbs' length.[14]

15. The person is all this,
What has been and what is to be:
And lord of immortality, too –
Whatever grows up on food.[15]

16. With hands and feet on every side,
With eyes, heads and faces on every side,
With ears on every side, it stands
Enfolding everything in the world.[16]

17. Seeming to have the strands of all the senses
But apart from all the senses,
Ruler and lord of all,
Great refuge of all![17]

18. Embodied in the nine-gated city,
The goose flits outside,[18]
Controller of the whole world,
Stationary and moving.

19. A swift seizer without hand or foot,
He sees without eyes, he hears without ears:
He knows what is to be known, and there is none who knows him.
They call him the primeval great person.

20. Subtler than the subtle, greater than the great,
The self is hidden in the secret place of the being.
One sees him as without will, through the creator's favour,
Sees the greatness, the lord, one's sorrow at an end.[19]

21. I know the unageing ancient one,
Self of all,[20] omnipresent through pervading all:
Folk say that cessation of birth belongs to him
Whom scholars of *brahman* call the eternal.

BOOK IV

1. May the one god who, his purpose hidden, through
the yoking of his power in many ways,[1]
Colourless, disposes many colours,
And gathers all together at the end and the beginning,
Yoke us with clear intelligence.

2. That is fire, that is the sun,
That is air, that is the moon likewise:
That is the pure, that is *brahman*,
That is water, that is Prajāpati.[2]

3. You are woman, you are man,
You are youth and maiden too.
Aged, you hobble along with a stick:
Newborn, you have faces on every side.[3]

4. You are the dark-blue moth and the green with
red eyes,[4]
The one who is pregnant with lightning,[5] the
seasons, and the seas;
By all-pervasion you go on without beginning,
You from whom all worlds are born.

5. With the nanny-goat, red, white and black,
Who brings forth many offspring like herself,
Lies one billy-goat, taking pleasure.
The other billy-goat abandons her, who has
had her enjoyment.[6]

6. Two birds, companions and friends,
Cling to the same tree.
One of them eats the sweet pippala-berry:
The other looks on, without eating.[7]

7. In the same tree a man (*puruṣa*) is plunged.
Deluded, he grieves from powerlessness (*anīśāyā*).[8]
When he sees the other, powerful one (*īśa*), content,
Sees his greatness, he is freed from sorrow.[9]

8. To one who does not know the supreme syllable
(*akṣara*) of the Ṛgveda (*ṛc*),
In which, in heaven, all the gods have taken
their seats,
What use is the Ṛgveda?
But those who know it are assembled here.[10]

9. From it the artificer (*māyin*) sends forth all this:
Metres, sacrifices, rites and vows,
What has been, what is to be, and what the
Vedas teach.
The other is trapped in it by the artifice.

10. One should know nature (*prakṛti*) as the artifice,
The great lord[11] as the artificer,
And the whole world as pervaded
By beings that are parts of him.

11. By discerning the one who stands over every womb,
In whom all this is gathered together,
The lord, the boon-granter, the worshipful[12] god,
One attains surpassing peace.

12. May Rudra, the overlord, the great Ṛṣi,
Who is the source and origin of the gods,
Who saw the golden embryo being born,
Yoke us with clear intelligence.

13. Overlord of the gods,
On whom the worlds depend,
Who rules over his two-footed and four-footed ones,
To which god shall we make our offering?[13]

14. Knowing him, subtler than the subtle in the midst of the throng,
Many-formed creator of all,
One enfolder of all, Śiva,
One attains surpassing peace.

15. He is the protector of the world in time,
Overlord of all, hidden in all beings,
To whom are yoked the Ṛṣis of Brahmā and the deities.
Knowing him, one cuts the bonds of death.

16. Knowing him, Śiva, hidden in all beings
Like a subtler distillation than clarified butter,[14]
The god, the one enfolder of all,
One is freed from all bonds.

17. The one god, all-maker,[15] magnanimous,[16]
Always dwelling in the heart of beings,
Shaped by the heart, the intelligence, the mind:
Those who know this become immortal.

18. When there is no darkness, there is neither day nor night,
Neither being nor not-being, just Śiva, absolute.
That is the imperishable: that is the lovely glory of Savitṛ.[17]
The ancient wisdom came forth from that.

19. No one has grasped him, above,
Across, or in the middle.
There is no likeness of him
Whose name is 'great glory'.

20. His form is not accessible to the sight:
No one sees him with the eye.
Those who, with heart and mind,
See him dwelling in the heart become immortal.

21. Afraid, someone takes refuge
In you, as 'unborn'.
Rudra, with that propitious[18] face of yours
Protect me always.

21. Do not hurt us in child or grandchild,
In life, in cows or horses:
Rudra, do not in anger slay our heroes.
We invoke you always, bringing offerings.[19]

BOOK V

1. In the imperishable, infinite supreme *brahman*
   Two are kept in a secret place: knowledge and ignorance.
Ignorance is the perishable, knowledge the immortal:
   But the one who rules knowledge and ignorance is different again –

2. The one who stands over every womb,
   All forms and all wombs,
Who carries the Ṛṣi Kapila,[1] first begotten, in his thoughts
   And can see him being born.

3. The god spreads out net after net, in many ways,
   And draws them together in this field.[2]
When the Yatis – and thus the lord – have created again,
   The magnanimous one becomes overlord of all.[3]

4. As the draught-ox[4] shines, lighting all regions,
   Above, below and across,
The one blessed, lovely god
   Rules over those who have the nature of the womb.[5]

5. One who, womb of all,[6] ripens his own nature,
   Stands over all this whole,
To mature all that is to be ripened,
   To assign all strands.

6. Brahmā knows it as the womb of *brahman*,[7]
That which is hidden in the Upaniṣads that are hidden in the Vedas.
The gods and Ṛṣis who knew it of old,
Becoming of a kind with it, became immortal.

7. The one with the strands, doer of actions which bring fruit,
Is the experiencer of that act.
In all forms, with three strands, with three paths,
The overlord of the breaths wanders according to his own actions.[8]

8. With a form like the sun, he is a thumb in length
When possessing intention and the sense of 'I'.
With just the strand of understanding and the strand of self
He seems in size the lesser point of an awl.[9]

9. The life (*jīva*) should be known as a fraction
Of the hundredth part of a hair-tip
A hundredfold divided –
Yet it is fitted for infinity.[10]

10. It is neither female nor male,
Nor is it neuter.
It is guarded by whatever body
It takes on.

11. By intention, touch, sight and passion
And the rain of food and water, the self grows and is born.[11]
Embodied, it takes in succession to different forms
In different places in accordance with its action.

12. Through its own strands, the embodied
Chooses many shapes, gross and subtle.
Because of the strands of actions and the strands of self,
The cause of their joining seems to be another.[12]

13. Knowing the god, beginningless, endless, in the midst of the throng,
Many-formed creator of all,
Enfolder of all,
One is freed from all bonds.

14. Those who know him, to be found through being, 'nestless' by name,[13]
Śiva, maker of being and not-being,
The god, maker of the creation of parts,[14]
Have left the body behind.

BOOK VI

1. Some poets speak of own nature,
   Others, likewise, of time – being deluded.
It is the greatness of the god in the world
   By which the wheel of *brahman* is made to turn.

2. Directed by him the work unfolds
   Which is thought of as earth, water, fire, air and
      space:
Him by whom all this is ever enfolded,
   Who is knower, time-maker, possessor of the
      strands, all-wise.

3. He did the work and ceased from it again,
   Then entered union with the entity (*tattva*) of entity,
By one, by two, by three, by eight,
   By time and by the subtle strands of self.[1]

4. Since he undertook the works which are endowed with
      strands,
   So as to apportion all existences,
In their absence the work which has been done
      disappears:
   When the work perishes, he goes on, being other
      than entity.[2]

5. He is seen as the beginning, the efficient cause[3] of union,
   Beyond the three times, without fractions –
When one first contemplates in one's own heart
   That worshipful god, of all forms, who has
      become whatever is.

6. He is higher and other than the appearances of time and the tree,
He from whom this proliferation[4] evolves –
When one knows him in the self, as bringer of *dharma*,
Averter of evil, lord of happiness, immortal, abode of all.

7. Let us know him as supreme, great lord of lords,
Supreme deity of deities,
Supreme master of masters, beyond,
The god, worshipful lord of the world.

8. For him there exists nothing to be done and no organ of action.
His equal or superior cannot be seen.
His supreme power[5] is revealed to be manifold.
The action of knowledge and strength is his by nature.

9. He has no master in the world,
No ruler nor any mark:[6]
He is the cause, the overlord of overlords of action:
He has no begetter, nor any overlord.

10. May the one god
Who, spider-like, from his own nature
Enfolds himself with threads produced from primal matter
Ordain for us entry into *brahman*:[7]

11. The one god hidden in all beings,
All-pervading, within the self of all,
Overseer of deeds, dwelling in all beings,
Witness, watcher, absolute, without strands.

12. The wise who see him in the self,
The one controlling the many inactive ones,
Who makes the one seed into many,
Have everlasting happiness: no others do.

13. Knowing the god, the cause, approachable through
Sāṅkhya and Yoga,[8]
Permanent among the impermanent,[9] thinker
among thinkers,
One among many, who disposes desires,
One is released from all bonds.

14. The sun does not shine there, nor the moon and stars.
Lightning does not shine there, let alone fire.
Everything reflects his shining.
Everything is lit by his light.[10]

15. He is the one goose in the midst of the world:
He is the fire dwelling in the water.[11]
Knowing him, one goes beyond death:
There is no other path by which to go.

16. All-making, all-knowing, source of the self,
Who is knower, time-maker, possessor of the
strands, all-wise,
Lord of primal matter and of the conscious mind,[12]
ruler of strands,
Cause of *saṃsāra* and *mokṣa*, stability[13] and
bondage.

17. He who rules this world for ever
Is of such a kind, immortal, resting as the lord,
Knower, omnipresent, protector of this world.
No other cause can be found to rule.

18. Longing for freedom, I go for refuge
To the god who shines with his own intelligence,[14]
Who creates Brahmā of old,
And bestows the Vedas on him,

19. Without fractions, without actions, at peace,
Irreproachable, unstained,
Bridge to the far shore of immortality,
Like a fire with its fuel burnt up.

20. When human folk
Roll space up like a hide,
There will be an end to sorrow
Apart from knowing the god.

21. By the power of asceticism and the god's favour
Śvetāśvatara knew *brahman*:
He taught it rightly to those beyond the stages,
The supreme purifier,[15] pleasing to the community of Ṛṣis.

22. The supreme secret in the Vedānta,
Proclaimed in an earlier age,
Should not be given to one who is not at peace,
Nor yet to one who is not a son or a student.[16]

23. The subjects that have been discussed
Shine clear to the great-hearted one[17]
Who has the highest devotion[18] to the god
And to his guru as to the god –

Shine clear to the great-hearted one.

OṂ. *Together may it protect us two:*
Together may it profit us two:
Together may we do a hero's work.
May we learn intelligently:
May we never hate one another.

OṂ. *Peace, peace, peace.*[19]

MUṆḌAKA UPANIṢAD

The Renouncers' Teaching

OṂ. *Gods, may we hear good fortune*[1] *with our ears!*
You worthy of sacrifice, may we see good fortune with our eyes!
Having praised you with bodies strong of limb,
May we attain, lifelong, what is ordained by the gods!
May Indra, of great swiftness,
May Pūṣan, the all-knowing,[2]
May Tārkṣya Ariṣṭanemi,
May Bṛhaspati ordain well-being for us!

OṂ. *Peace, peace, peace.*

BOOK I

CHAPTER I

1. OṂ. First of the gods, Brahmā came into being,
   Maker of all, protector of the earth.
He taught the knowledge of *brahman*, basis of all knowledge,
   To Atharva, his eldest son.

2. The knowledge of *brahman*, such as Brahmā taught to Atharvan,
   Atharvan of old taught to Aṅgir.
He taught it to Bhāradvāja Satyavaha:
   Bhāradvāja to Aṅgiras, the higher and lower knowledge.

3. Śaunaka, a great householder, approached Aṅgiras in the proper way and asked him, 'Blessed one, what must one know for all this to become known?'

4. He said to him, 'Two knowledges must be known – so say the knowers of *brahman* – the higher and the lower.

5. 'In it, the lower is the Ṛgveda, the Yajurveda, the Sāmaveda, the Atharvaveda,

Phonetics,[3] ritual,[4] grammar,
   Etymology, metre and astronomy;[5]

but the higher is that by which the imperishable (*akṣara*) is understood.

6. 'That which is invisible,[6] unseizable, without lineage,
Without colour,[7] without eye or ear, without
hands or feet,
Eternal, pervading, omnipresent, very subtle –
That is the unfailing, that the wise see as the
source (*yoni*) of beings.

7. 'As a spider emits its thread and seizes on to it,[8]
As plants grow on the earth,
As head- and body-hair from a living person,
All here arises from the imperishable.

8. '*Brahman* increases by heat (*tapas*);
From it, food is produced:
From food come breath, mind, truth,
The worlds: in works grows immortality.[9]

9. 'From the one who is all-knowing, all-wise,
Whose asceticism (*tapas*) is formed of knowledge,
Are born *brahman*,
Name and form, and food.

CHAPTER 2

1. 'This is truth:

'The works which the poets have seen in the mantras
Are laid out in the triple knowledge[10] in many forms.
Practise them constantly, lovers of truth.
This is your path to the world of the good deed.[11]

2. 'As the flame flickers
When the oblation-fire is kindled,
Then one should cast the offerings
Between the two portions of melted butter –
An offering made with faith.

3. 'The one whose Agnihotra is followed by no new-moon sacrifice or full-moon sacrifice, no four-month sacrifice or

harvest sacrifice, is barred to guests, not offered, offered without the Viśvedevas' rite, or improperly offered, destroys his worlds even to the seventh.[12]

4. 'Kālī, Karālī, Manojavā,
Sulohitā, Sudhūmravarṇā,
Sphuliṅginī and divine Viśvarūpī
Are the seven flickering tongues, as they are called.[13]

5. 'Whoever acts while they are blazing[14]
And at the right time,
The offerings, as rays of the sun, take and lead him
To the lord of the gods, the one dweller above.[15]

6. 'Saying, "Come! Come!", the radiant offerings
Carry the patron of the sacrifice by the rays of the sun,
Greeting and praising him with kind words:
"This is your pure world of *brahman*, well-won."[16]

7. 'But the eighteen forms of sacrifice[17] are unsteady boats,
In which is what is called "lower action".
The foolish who delight in that as best
Go on to old age and death again.

8. 'Living in the midst of ignorance,
Wise in their own view, thinking themselves learned,
The foolish roam about,
Like blind men led by one who is blind.[18]

9. 'Living in many kinds of ignorance,
Childish, they think they have achieved their end,
Since, through passion, the doers of works[19] do not know,
In distress they fall down when their worlds are exhausted.

10. 'The foolish, believing stored-up merit[20] the highest thing,
Proclaim there is nothing better.
After winning to heaven's back, well-won,
They enter this world or a lower one again.

11. 'But those who in the forest practise asceticism
and faith,
At peace, ones who know, following the way
of alms,
Free of passion, go through the door of the sun
To where is the person of unfailing self.

12. 'Seeing the worlds built up through action, the
Brāhmaṇa
Has achieved detachment. (Not through the made is
the unmade.)[21]
To know it he should with fuel in hand
Approach a guru, learned and established in
brahman.[22]

13. 'He, knowing it, teaches to the one who has
approached him rightly,
Whose mind is peaceful, who has attained peace,
The truth by which one knows the imperishable person,
The knowledge of *brahman* in its reality.[23]

BOOK II

CHAPTER I

1. 'This is truth:

'As from a blazing fire, sparks like itself
Go forth in their thousands,
So, good man,[24] many kinds of beings come forth
From the imperishable, and go back into it too.

2. 'The person is divine, unshaped.
He is outside and inside, unborn:
Without breath, without mind, pure,
Higher than the highest imperishable.

3. 'From him breath and mind are born,
All faculties too,
Space, air, light, water,
Earth the upholder of all.

4. 'His head is fire, his eyes the moon and sun,
His ears the directions, his speech the Vedas made manifest,
His breath the air, his heart the all:
At his feet is the earth:[25] he is the inner self of all beings.

5. 'From him comes fire, whose fuel is the sun,
From the moon[26] Parjanya, on earth the plants:
A male sprinkles seed in a female.[27]
Many creatures are brought forth from the person.

6. 'From him come the *ṛc, sāman* and *yajus* verses,
initiation (*dīkṣā*),
Sacrifice, ceremonies (*kratu*), and gifts (*dakṣiṇā*),
The year, the patron of the sacrifice,
The worlds where the moon shines[28] and where the
sun does.

7. 'From him the gods are brought forth in many kinds,
Sādhyas, human beings, animals and birds,
The breath and lower breath (*prāṇāpāna*), rice and
barley, and asceticism,
Faith, truth, celibacy (*brahmacarya*) and rule.

8. 'The seven breaths[29] come forth from him,
The seven flames, fuel, the seven offerings,
The seven worlds in which there move
The breaths, seven by seven, resting in the
secret place.[30]

9. 'From him all the oceans and mountains come,
And the rivers flow in all their forms.
From him, too, all plants and their juices[31] come
By which, with the elements, the inner self is
sustained.

10. 'The person is all this,
Action, asceticism, *brahman* beyond death.[32]
Good man, the one who knows this, hidden in a
secret place,
Undoes the knot of ignorance here.

CHAPTER 2

1. 'Obvious yet hidden, called "Moving in Secret",
   Is the great place. Here is fixed
What moves, breathes and blinks.[33]
   Know that as being, as not-being, as the lovely
      glory,[34]
As beyond knowledge, the finest of creatures.

2. 'That which is blazing, and that which is subtler than
      the subtle,
   In which the worlds are fixed, and those who
      have worlds,
Is the imperishable *brahman*.
   It is breath, it is speech and mind.
It is truth, it is the immortal.
   That must be pierced, good man: pierce that.[35]

3. 'Seize as your bow the great weapon of the Upaniṣad,
   And set in it an arrow sharpened by contemplation.
Draw it with a mind that has attained the nature
      of *that*.[36]
   The target is the imperishable: pierce that.

4. 'The OṂ (*praṇava*) is the bow, the arrow the self:
   Brahman is its target, it is said.
It must be pierced by one who is not careless:
   So, like the arrow, one will become of a kind with it.

5. 'Know only that as self
   On which sky, earth and middle-air are woven,
And mind with all the breaths.
   Shun all other words.
This is the bridge to immortality.

6. 'Where the channels[37] are brought together
Like spokes in a chariot's hub
It moves within,
Becoming many.
By means of OṂ meditate on the self.
Success to you in crossing beyond darkness!

7. 'The one who is all-knowing, all-wise,
Whose greatness this is on earth,
Is the self established in the space,
In the divine city of *brahman*.[38]

8. 'It is made of mind, leader of breaths and body,
Based on food, directing the heart.
The wise see, by knowledge,
The immortal form of bliss shine out.

9. 'The knot of the heart is broken;
All doubts are cut through;
One's actions fade away
When this is seen, the higher and the lower.

10. 'In the highest golden sheath
Is *brahman*, stainless, without parts.
It is the pure, the light of lights
Which the self-knowers know.

11. 'The sun does not shine there, nor the moon and stars.
Lightning does not shine there, let alone fire.
Everything reflects its shining.
Everything is lit by its light.[39]

12. '*Brahman* is the immortal; *brahman* is in the east;
Brahman is in the west, and in south and north:
Spread out, above and below,
Brahman is all this, the greatest.

BOOK III

CHAPTER I

1. 'Two birds, companions and friends,
   Cling to the same tree.
One of them eats the sweet pippala-berry:
   The other looks on, without eating.

2. 'In the same tree a man is plunged.
   Deluded, he grieves from powerlessness:
When he sees the other, powerful one, content,
   Sees his greatness, he is freed from sorrow.[40]

3. 'When the seer sees the gold-coloured
   Maker, powerful one, person, source of *brahman*,
Knowing him, he shakes off good and evil:
   Stainless, he reaches supreme equality.[41]

4. 'He is breath which shines out through all beings:
   Knowing, one becomes a knower, who does not
      speak too much.[42]
Playing in the self, enjoying the self, performing works,
   One is the finest of the knowers of *brahman*.

5. 'The self may be won by truth, by asceticism,
   By right knowing, by constant celibacy.
Pure, it is in the body, made of light:
   That which the Yatis[43] see, their faults worn away.

6. 'It is truth that conquers,[44] not falsehood.
By truth is laid out the path to the gods
By which the Ṛṣis, their desires fulfilled,
Travel to the highest abode of truth.

7. 'Great, divine, its form inconceivable,
Subtler than the subtle, it shines out:
It is farther than the far, and yet it is at hand,
Hidden in a secret place, here, among those who see.

8. 'It is not grasped by the eye, nor yet by speech
Nor by the other gods,[45] nor by asceticism or work.
By the calming of knowledge, the meditator,
His nature purified, sees it, without parts.[46]

9. 'The subtle self may be known by consciousness
In which the breaths, fivefold, have entered.
The whole consciousness of creatures is woven with the breaths.
When that is purified, the self appears in it.

10. 'His nature purified, whatever world
He illuminates with his mind, and whatever desires he desires,
He wins that world and those desires:
So one who desires prosperity should honour the knower of the self.

CHAPTER 2

1. 'He knows the supreme place of *brahman*,
On which the all, being fixed, shines brightly.
Those wise ones, without desire, who contemplate the person
Go beyond the seed.[47]

2. 'The one who desires desires, dwelling on them,
Through desires is born here and there.
But the desires of the one who has fully attained his desire
And fulfilled himself, all pass away here.

3. 'The self cannot be won by speaking,
Nor by intelligence or much learning.
It can be won by the one whom it chooses.
To him the self reveals its own form.[48]

4. 'The self cannot be won by the weakling,
Nor through carelessness, or asceticism misapplied:[49]
But the self of the one who strives by these means
Enters the place of *brahman*.

5. 'On reaching him, the Ṛṣis, contented with knowledge,
With selves fulfilled, free from passion, at peace,
Win him who is everywhere, all around:
Wise, self-controlled, they enter the all.

6. 'Discerning well the aim of the knowledge of Vedānta,
Their nature purified through the yoga of renunciation, all the Yatis,
Having gone beyond death, at the ending time
Are liberated in the worlds of *brahman*.

7. 'The fifteen parts[50] have gone to their bases
And all the gods into their own deities:[51]
The actions and the self made of knowledge
All become one in the supreme unfailing one.

8. 'Just as flowing rivers go down into the sea
Leaving name and form behind,
The one who knows, freed from name and form,
Reaches the divine person, higher than the highest.

9. 'The one who knows the supreme *brahman* becomes *brahman*, and there is no one in his family who does not know *brahman*. He crosses over sorrow, crosses over evil: freed from the knots of the secret place, he becomes immortal.

10. 'This is taught in a *ṛc* verse:

One should teach this knowledge of *brahman* only to those
Who are skilled in ritual, learned, established in *brahman*,
Who themselves make offerings to the One Ṛṣi, having faith,
And have properly performed the "vow of the head".'[52]

11. This is the truth. The Ṛṣi Aṅgiras taught it of old. No one learns it who has not performed the vow.

Homage to the supreme Ṛṣis. Homage to the supreme Ṛṣis.

OṂ. *Gods, may we hear good fortune with our ears!*
You worthy of sacrifice, may we see good fortune with our eyes!
Having praised you with bodies strong of limb,
May we attain, lifelong, what is ordained by the gods!
May Indra, of great swiftness,
May Pūṣan, the all-knowing,
May Tārkṣya Ariṣṭanemi,
May Bṛhaspati ordain well-being for us!

OṂ. *Peace, peace, peace.*

PRAŚNA UPANIṢAD

The Teaching in Questions

OṂ. *Gods, may we hear good fortune with our ears!*
You worthy of sacrifice, may we see good fortune with our eyes!
Having praised you with bodies strong of limb,
May we attain, lifelong, what is ordained by the gods!
May Indra, of great swiftness
May Pūṣan, the all-knowing,
May Tārkṣya Ariṣṭanemi,
May Bṛhaspati ordain well-being for us!

OṂ. *Peace, peace, peace.*[1]

QUESTION I

1. OṂ. Sukeśan Bhāradvāja, Śaibya Satyakāma, Sauryāyaṇin Gārgya, Kauśalya Āśvalāyana, Bhārgava Vaidarbhi and Kabandhin Kātyāyana, intent on *brahman*, established in *brahman*, seeking the supreme *brahman*, approached the blessed Pippalāda, fuel in hand, thinking, 'He will teach us all about it.'

2. The Ṛṣi said to them, 'Live with us another year in asceticism, celibacy and faith: then ask whatever questions you wish, and if we know we will teach you all about it.'

3. Then Kabandhin Kātyāyana approached him and asked, 'Blessed one, from where are all these creatures (*prajā*) born?'

4. He told him, 'Prajāpati desired offspring (*prajā*). He raised heat.[2] Raising heat, he gave rise to a couple,[3] matter and breath, thinking, "They will produce offspring of many kinds for me."

5. 'The sun is breath; matter is the moon. Matter is all this, both the shaped and the unshaped. So shape is matter.

6. 'When the sun, rising, enters the eastern direction, it holds the living beings[4] in the east in its rays. When it illuminates the southern, the western, the northern direction, the nadir, the zenith, the intermediate directions, everything, it holds all living beings in its rays.

7. 'This same breath, Vaiśvānara, which takes all forms, rises as fire. It has been said in a verse:

8. . . . Of all forms, yellow, all-knowing,[5]
The supreme goal, the one light, giving heat.
Thousand-rayed, existing in a hundred forms,
The sun rises as the breath of creatures.[6]

9. 'The year is Prajāpati: it has two paths, the southern and the northern. Those who worship sacrifice and merit as action[7] win the moon as their world. They come back again. So Ṛṣis, desiring offspring, go to the south. This, the way to the ancestors, is matter.

10. 'But seeking the self by the northern path, by asceticism, celibacy, faith and knowledge, they win the sun. This is the support of living beings:[8] this is the immortal, the fearless; this is the supreme goal. From this they do not come back. So this is cessation. There is a verse about it:

11. They call him the five-footed father, with twelve aspects,[9]
In the upper half of the sky, possessing the land:
Others call him the shining one[10] in the lower half,
Fixed on a chariot with seven wheels and six spokes.[11]

12. 'The month is Prajāpati. Its dark half is matter, its bright half breath. So the Ṛṣis perform sacrifice in the bright half, and other folk in the other half.

13. 'Day-and-night is Prajāpati. Its day is breath, its night matter. Those who join in lovemaking by day spill their breath, but when folk join in lovemaking by night, that is chastity.[12]

14. 'Food is Prajāpati. From it comes seed, and from that all creatures are produced.

15. 'Those who practise Prajāpati's vow
Give rise to a couple.[13]
The world of Brahmā[14] belongs to them,
In whom asceticism, chastity and truth are established.

16. 'The stainless world of Brahmā belongs to them,
In whom there is no crookedness, falsehood or
artifice.'[15]

QUESTION II

1. Then Bhārgava Vaidarbhi asked him, 'Blessed one, how many gods maintain the creature? Which ones illuminate this?[16] And again, which is the finest of them?'

2. He told him, 'Space is the god: so are air, fire, water, earth, speech, mind, the eye and the ear. They illuminate it, and proclaim, "We establish and maintain this shaft."'[17]

3. 'Breath, the finest, said to them, "Do not fall into delusion. *I* establish and maintain this shaft, dividing myself into five."

4. 'They did not believe it. In its pride, it made to move upward. When it moved upward, all the others moved upward, and when it settled down, they all settled down. Just as, when the king bee moves upward, all the bees move up with him, and when it settles down, they all settle down, so do speech, mind, the eye and the ear. Satisfied, they praise the breath:

5. '"It burns as fire; it is the sun;
It is Parjanya Maghavan; it is air;
It is earth, matter, the god,
Both being and not-being, and that
which is immortal.

6. '"Like spokes in a chariot's wheel-hub,
Everything is based in breath:
Ṛc-, *yajus-* and *sāman* verses,
Sacrifice, royalty (*kṣatra*) and
priesthood (*brahman*).

7. ' "As Prajāpati, you move in the womb:[18]
It is you who are reborn;
The creatures bring tribute to you, breath,
Who rule over the breaths.

8. ' "You are the greatest bearer[19] to the gods,
The first SVADHĀ[20] to the ancestors,
The true way of the Ṛṣis,
The Atharvans and Aṅgirases.

9. ' "Breath, you are Indra with your brightness;[21]
You are Rudra, the protector;
You move in middle-air;
You are the sun, the lord of lights.

10. ' "When you rain on them,
Creatures breathe easy:
They stand with joyful looks,
Thinking, 'There will be food at our wish.'

11. ' "Breath, you are the Vrātya, the One Ṛṣi,
The eater of all, the lord of being.
We are the givers of what is fit to eat:
Mātariśvan, you are our father.

12. ' "Make that form of yours, which is established
On speech, on the ear, on the eye –
Which spreads over mind – gracious:[22]
Do not depart.

13. ' "All this that is established in the triple sky[23]
Is in the power of breath:
Protect us, as a mother does her children.
Establish splendours and wisdom[24] for us." '

QUESTION III

1. Then Kausalya[25] Āśvalāyana asked him, 'Blessed one, from where is the breath born? How does it arrive in the body? How does it divide itself up and become established? How does it support what is outside and what is concerned with oneself?'

2. He told him, 'You ask very advanced questions:[26] but since I think you are a most true Brāhmaṇa[27] I will tell you.

3. 'The breath is born from the self. It reaches up to it like the shadow to a person. It arrives in the body through the action of mind.

4. 'Just as a monarch appoints his officials, saying, "Take charge of these villages. Take charge of *these* villages", the breath sets the other breaths in their various different places.

5. 'The lower breath (*apāna*) is in the anus and the loins. The breath (*prāṇa*) itself is established in the eye and the ear, the mouth and the nostrils. The central breath (*samāna*) is in the middle: it makes equal (*sama*) all that is offered as food. From it the seven flames[28] come to be.

6. 'The self is in the heart: here are the hundred and one channels.[29] Each of them has a hundred; and every one of those has seventy-two thousand branch-channels. In them moves the diffused breath (*vyāna*).

7. 'Through one of them, the up-breath (*udāna*) rises: it leads to a pure world through pure action, to an evil one through evil, through both to the human world.

8. 'The sun rises as the external breath, for it takes care of the breath of the eye – with the deity that is in the earth supporting the lower breath, and the space between as the central breath. Air is the diffused breath.

9. 'Heat (*tejas*) is the up-breath, so when one's heat has died down one goes on to rebirth, with faculties absorbed into mind.
10. 'With whatever consciousness[30] one has, one goes to breath. The breath, joined with heat, along with the self, leads one to the kind of world that is fitting.[31]
11. 'If one, knowing this, knows the breath, one's progeny do not cease. One becomes immortal. There is a verse about it:

12. Knowing the arising, the arriving, and the place
 And the pervading in five ways
Of the breath in relation to the self,
 One attains immortality:
 Knowing, one attains immortality.'

QUESTION IV

1. Then Sauryāyaṇin Gārgya asked him, 'Blessed one, what things in the person sleep? What things in it stay awake? Which god sees dreams? Whose happiness is it? And in what are all these established?'

2. He told him, 'Gārgya, just as, when the sun sets, its rays all become one in its circle of fire, and when it rises they come out of it, time after time, so everything becomes one in the highest god, the mind. So at that time[32] a person does not hear, does not see, does not smell, does not taste, does not touch, does not speak, does not feel pleasure, does not excrete, does not move about: folk say, "He is asleep."

3. 'Only the fires of breath stay awake in this city. The lower breath is the Gārhapatya, the Anvāhāryapacana the diffused breath; since it is drawn from the Gārhapatya, the Āhavanīya is the breath (*prāṇa*), from 'drawing' (*praṇayana*).

4. 'The central breath (*samāna*) is so called because it makes the two offerings, the in breath and the out-breath,[33] equal (*sama*). The mind is the patron of the sacrifice. The fruit of the sacrifice is the up-breath (*udāna*): every day it brings the patron of the sacrifice to *brahman*.

5. 'Here, in sleep, the god experiences greatness. Whatever object of sight he has seen he sees again; whatever object of hearing he has heard he hears again; whatever he has experienced in different regions and directions he experiences again and again. What he has seen and what he has not seen; what he has heard and what he has not heard; what he has experienced and what he has not experienced; what is and what is not – he sees it all. He sees it, being all.

6. 'When he is overwhelmed by light,[34] the god sees no dreams. Now there is bliss, in this body.
7. 'Good man, just as birds flock to the tree that is their home, all of that flocks to the supreme self:
8. 'Earth and the element of earth, water and the element of water, fire and the element of fire, air and the element of air, space and the element of space, the eye and that which can be seen, the ear and that which can be heard, smell and that which can be smelled, taste and that which can be tasted, the skin and that which can be touched, the hands and that which can be held, the loins and that which can be enjoyed, the anus and that which can be excreted, the feet and the path that can be taken,[35] the mind and that which can be thought, the intelligence and that which can be understood, the ego and that with which one can identify,[36] consciousness and that of which one can be conscious, light and that which can be illuminated,[37] breath and that which can be supported.
9. 'It is the seer, the toucher, the hearer, the smeller, the taster, the thinker, the understander, the doer, the self of knowledge, the person. It flocks to the supreme imperishable self.
10. 'Good man, the one who knows the shadowless, bodiless, bloodless, pure imperishable attains the supreme imperishable. Knowing all, he becomes all. There is a verse about it:

11. Good man, the one who knows the imperishable,
In which the self of knowledge – with all gods –
Breaths and beings too, stand firm,
All-knowing, has entered into all.'

QUESTION V

1. Then Śaibya Satyakāma asked him, 'Blessed one, if someone among human beings meditates on the OṂ until he departs this life,[38] what world does he win by it?'
2. He told him, 'Satyakāma, what the OṂ is is *brahman*, both the higher and the lower: so the one who knows, by its support, reaches one or other of these.
3. If one meditates on it as having one element,[39] given knowledge by that one quickly returns to earth. The *ṛc* verses bring one to the human world. There, endowed with asceticism, celibacy and faith, one experiences greatness.
4. If one meditates on it[40] with two elements one reaches mind. One is led by the *yajus* verses to middle-air, the world of the moon. After experiencing power in the world of the moon, one comes back again.
5. 'But the one who meditates on the supreme person with three elements, as OṂ, reaches light,[41] the sun. Just as a snake is freed from its skin, he is freed from evil. He is led by the *sāman* verses to the world of *brahman*.[42] He sees the person (*puruṣa*) dwelling in the citadel (*puri-śaya*),[43] higher than the highest mass of life. There are two verses about it:

6. The three elements are death-bearing when used
 Attached to one another yet disjoined:[44]
When they are rightly used in activities
 Outside, inside and between,[45] the knower does
 not tremble.

7. By the *ṛc* verses, to this world;[46] by the *yajus* verses, to middle-air;
By the *sāman* verses, to that which the poets make known;
With the OṂ as support, the knower goes to the one
That is peaceful, unageing, immortal, fearless and supreme.'

QUESTION VI

1. Then Sukeśan Bhāradvāja asked him, 'Blessed one, Hiraṇyanābha, a king's son of Kosala, came to me and asked this question: "Bhāradvāja, do you know the person with sixteen parts?"'[47]

'I told the prince, "I do not know him. If I had known him, how could I not have told you? The one who speaks falsehood withers up, root and all, so I may not speak falsehood." He fell silent, mounted his chariot and went away. So I ask you the same: where is this person?'

2. He told him, 'Good man, the person in whom the sixteen parts arise is here, inside this body.

3. 'He[48] thought, "What needs to have departed for me to have departed? What needs to have stayed for me to stay?"

4. 'He created breath: from breath, faith, space, air, light, water, earth and the senses, mind and food: from food came strength, heat (*tapas*), the mantras, work, the worlds and, in the worlds, name.[49]

5. 'Just as the flowing rivers, heading towards the ocean, once they have reached the ocean disappear – their name and form are broken up, and it is just called "ocean" – the sixteen parts of the seer, heading towards the person, disappear – their name and form are broken up, and it is just called "person". This is without parts, immortal. There is a verse about it:

6. Know the person who is to be known –
 In whom the parts are fixed
Like spokes in a chariot's wheel-hub –
 That death may not trouble you.'

7. Pippalāda said to them, 'This is as much as I know of the supreme *brahman*. There is nothing higher than this.'
8. Praising him, they said, 'You are our father, who bring us across to the far side of ignorance.'

Praise to the supreme Ṛṣis! Praise to the supreme Ṛṣis!

OṂ. *Gods, may we hear good fortune with our ears!*
You worthy of sacrifice, may we see good fortune with our eyes!
Having praised you with bodies strong of limb,
May we attain, lifelong, what is ordained by the gods!
May Indra, of great swiftness,
May Pūṣan, the all-knowing,
May Tārkṣya Ariṣṭanemi,
May Bṛhaspati ordain well-being for us!

OṂ. *Peace, peace, peace.*

MĀṆḌŪKYA UPANIṢAD

The Māṇḍūkas' Teaching

OṂ. *Gods, may we hear good fortune with our ears!*
You worthy of sacrifice, may we see good fortune with our eyes!
Having praised you with bodies strong of limb,
May we attain, lifelong, what is ordained by the gods!
May Indra, of great swiftness,
May Pūṣan, the all-knowing,
May Tārkṣya Ariṣṭanemi,
May Bṛhaspati ordain well-being for us!

OṂ. *Peace, peace, peace.*[1]

1. The syllable (*akṣara*) OṂ is all this. To explain further: what is called past, present and future is all just OṂ. Whatever else there is, beyond the three times, that too is all just OṂ.

2. All this is *brahman*. The self is *brahman*. The self has four feet.

3. The first foot is Vaiśvānara,[2] with waking as its state, with consciousness[3] turned outwards, with seven limbs,[4] with nineteen mouths,[5] eating coarse food.

4. The second foot is Taijasa,[6] with dream as its state, with consciousness turned inwards, with seven limbs, with nineteen mouths,[7] eating choice food.

5. When, sleeping, one desires no desire and dreams no dream, that is deep sleep. The third foot is Prājña,[8] with deep sleep as its state, become one, a sheer mass of consciousness,[9] made of bliss, eating bliss, with mind as its mouth.

6. It is the lord of all: it is the knower of all: it is the inner controller:[10] it is the source (*yoni*) of all, for it is the arising and passing away of beings.

7. Not with consciousness turned inward, not with consciousness turned outward, not with consciousness turned both ways, not a mass of consciousness, not conscious, not unconscious – folk consider the fourth to be unseen,[11] inviolable,[12] unseizable, signless, unthinkable, unnameable, its essence resting in the one self, the stilling of proliferation,[13] peaceful, gracious (*śiva*), without duality (*advaita*). That is the self: so it should be understood.

8. In terms of syllables, the self is OṂ. In terms of elements,[14]

the feet are the elements and the elements are the feet: 'a', 'u', 'm'.

9. Vaiśvānara, whose state is waking, is the 'a', the first element, from āp- ('to attain'), or from its being the first of all (*ādimattva*):[15] for the one who knows this attains all desires and becomes the first (*ādi*).

10. Taijasa, whose state is dream, is the 'u', the second element, from *utkarṣa* (rising up), or from its being both (*ubhaya*): for the one who knows this raises up a lineage of knowledge and becomes equal,[16] and there comes to be no one in his family who does not know *brahman*.

11. Prājña, whose state is deep sleep, is the 'm', the third element, from *mā-* ('to measure out', 'to create'), or from *apī-* ('to merge into', 'to dissolve'):[17] for the one who knows this creates all this and becomes its dissolution.

12. The fourth, without an element,[18] is inviolable, the stilling of proliferation, gracious, without duality. So OṂ is the self. The one who knows this by self enters the self: the one who knows this.

OṂ. *Gods, may we hear good fortune with our ears!*
You worthy of sacrifice, may we see good fortune
with our eyes!
Having praised you with bodies strong of limb,
May we attain, lifelong, what is ordained by the
gods!
May Indra, of great swiftness,
May Pūṣan, the all-knowing,
May Tārkṣya Ariṣṭanemi,
May Bṛhaspati ordain well-being for us!

OṂ. *Peace, peace, peace.*

MAITRĪ UPANIṢAD

Maitri's Teaching

OṂ. *May my limbs, speech, breath, eye, ear, strength and all senses grow strong. Everything is the* brahman *of the Upaniṣads. May I not reject* brahman. *May* brahman *not reject me. May there be no rejecting. May there be no rejecting of me.*[1] *May all the* dharmas *which are in the Upaniṣads be in me, who delight in the self. May they be in me.*

OṂ. *Peace, peace, peace.*

BOOK I

1. OṂ. The fire-building of the ancients was a sacrifice of *brahman*: so, after building the fires, the patron of the sacrifice should meditate on the self.[1] Then the sacrifice becomes full and complete.[2] Who is the one that should be meditated upon? The one called 'breath'. To explain further:

2. A king called Bṛhadratha established his eldest son in the kingship: then, considering that this body is not eternal, he attained dispassion and went out to the forest. There, embarking on the highest asceticism, he stood, arms held upward, gazing at the sun. At the end of a thousand days,[3] there came into the presence of the sage the blessed Śākāyanya, a knower of the self, seeming to blaze with energy like a fire without smoke. He said to the king, 'Stand up, stand up! Choose a boon!'

Bṛhadratha paid homage to him, and said, 'Blessed one, I am not a knower of the self. We hear that you are a knower of the entity:[4] so teach us.'

'This boon was of old difficult to achieve: do not ask the question, Aikṣvāka. Choose other desires.'

Touching Śākāyanya's feet with his head, the king uttered this chant:

3. 'This body comes into being from sexual intercourse, and, devoid of understanding, comes out through the gate of urine into a hell-realm.[5] It is constructed of bones, smeared with flesh, bound up with hide,[6] filled with faeces, urine, bile, phlegm,[7] marrow, fat, marrow of the flesh[8] and many other impurities. When one exists in such a body –

'blessed one, in this body, an evil-smelling insubstantial mass of bone, skin, muscle, marrow, seed, blood, mucus,[9] tears, water of the eyes, faeces, urine, wind, bile, phlegm, what is the use of indulging in desires? In this body, afflicted with desire, anger, greed, delusion, fear, despondency, envy, being apart from what one likes and being with what one does not like,[10] hunger, thirst, old age, death, disease, grief and so on, what is the use of indulging in desires?

4. 'We see that all this is transient, like the gadflies, mosquitoes and so on, and the grass and trees that grow up and perish.[11]

'But what of these? There are others yet – great archers, some of them wheel-turning monarchs,[12] Sudyumna, Bhūridyumna, Indradyumna, Kuvalayāśva, Yauvanāśva, Vadhryaśva, Aśvapati, Śaśabindu, Hariścandra, Ambarīṣa, Nanaktu, Saryāti, Yayāti, Anāraṇya, Ukṣasena and so on. Kings Marutta, Bharata and others, though their whole tribes of relations looked on, left their great splendour and departed from this world to that world.

'But what of these? There are others yet. We see the demise of *gandharvas*, demons, *yakṣas*, ogres,[13] ghosts, imps,[14] vampires,[15] serpents, ghouls[16] and so on.

'But what of these? Among the rest, there is the drying up of great oceans, the tumbling down of mountains, the precession of the Pole Star,[17] the cutting of the ropes of wind,[18] the submergence of the earth, the departure of gods from their place. In a *saṃsāra* like this, what is the use of indulging in desires, when we see that the one who depends on them returns here again and again? You *must* lift me out of it. In *saṃsāra* I am like a frog in a sealed well. Blessed one, you are our way out.[19] You are our way out.'

BOOK II

1. The blessed Śākāyanya, very pleased, said to the king, 'Great king Bṛhadratha, banner of the house of Ikṣvāku, you will quickly achieve your purpose and become a knower of the self, renowned by the name of "Marut".[1]

'This is *your* self.'

'Which is it, blessed one?'

2. '"The one that, departing upward on the cessation of the breathing,[2] suffering yet not suffering, dispels darkness – this is the self": so said the blessed Maitri.[3] For it is said: "The blissful one that, leaving this body and entering the light beyond, appears in its own form is the self,"[4] he said. "This is the immortal, the fearless: this is *brahman*."

3. 'This is the knowledge of *brahman*, the knowledge of all the Upaniṣads, your majesty. It was taught to us by the blessed Maitri:[5] I will recount it to you.

'The Vālakhilyas,[6] as is well known, were free from evil, of intense brightness, celibate.[7] They said to Prajāpati, "Blessed one, the body is without intelligence, like a cart. Who is it that, higher than the senses, had such power as to set it up in this form, with intelligence? Who is the instigator of it? Blessed one, tell us what you know."[8]

'He told them:

4. '"The one who is famed as standing above – pure, clean, void, at peace, without breath, selfless,[9] unending, indestructible, steadfast, eternal, unborn, independent – rests in his own power. He set up the body in this form, with intelligence. He is the instigator of it."

'They said, "Blessed one, how has one like this – invisible, without wants – set it up in this form, with intelligence, and how is he the instigator of it?"

'He told them:

5. '"That subtle, ungraspable, invisible one called the person returns[10] here, without previous consciousness, with a part of himself, just like one who wakes up from deep sleep without previous consciousness. That part of him is that element of intelligence in each person, the knower of the field, with the characteristics of will, determination and conceit,[11] Prajāpati with all eyes.[12] He, as intelligence, set up the body with intelligence, and he is the instigator of it."

'They said, "Blessed one, how does such a one exist with part of himself?"

'He told them:

6. '"In the beginning there existed one, Prajāpati. Being one, he was not happy. He meditated on himself, and created many creatures. He saw them, standing like a stone, without intelligence, without breath, like a post.[13] He was not happy. He thought, 'I must enter inside them to wake them up.' He made himself into air, as it were, and entered inside them. As one, he could not,[14] so he divided himself into five and is what is called the breath, the lower breath, the diffused breath, the up-breath and the central breath.

'"Now the one that goes out upward is the breath; the one that goes together downward is the lower breath; the one that places the coarsest element of food in the lower breath and leads it (*sam-ā-nī-*) into every limb is called the central breath (*samāna*); the one that brings up or swallows down what is drunk or eaten is the up-breath; the one by which the channels are pervaded is the diffused breath.

'"The *upaṃśu* takes over from the *antaryāma*,[15] and the *antaryāma* from the *upāṃśu*. In the space between them, heat is created.[16] What heat is is the person: that person is the fire that is in all men.[17]

'"It has been said elsewhere:

> The fire which is within a person is that which is in all men, by which the food that is eaten is digested. It is its sound that one

hears when one covers one's ears like this. When one is about to depart, one does not hear this sound.[18]

'"When he had divided himself in five, 'hidden in the secret place',[19] 'made of mind, with breath as body, with light as form, of true resolve, with space as self . . .',[20] within the heart, not having achieved his object,[21] he thought, 'I must eat objects.' So he opened up holes,[22] and he goes out and eats objects through five rays (*raśmi*). The organs of perception are his reins (*raśmi*);[23] the organs of action are his horses; his chariot is the body; the mind is his driver; his whip is made of nature.[24]

'"Impelled by him the body moves around, like the wheel impelled by the potter:[25] he set up the body with intelligence, and he is the instigator of it.

'"Poets declare him to be the self.[26] As though under domination, as though overcome by the white and black fruits of actions, he wanders among bodies. But, because of his unmanifest nature, subtlety, invisibility and lack of possessiveness, he is without fixity, not an agent, though he seems an agent and fixed.

7. '"He is fixed like a watcher, pure, steadfast, unmoving, not prone to defilement, undistracted, without yearning. Remaining his own, experiencing the law (*ṛta*), he is fixed, hiding himself with a veil made of the strands (*guna*)."

BOOK III

1. 'They said, "Blessed one, if you describe in this way the greatness of this self, what is the other, different, one called *self* that, overcome by the white and black fruits of actions, goes to good and bad wombs: that wanders about to a bourn below or above, overcome by the dualities?"

2. 'Maitri said, "There *is* another, different, one, called the elemental self,[1] which, overcome by the white and black fruits of actions, goes to good and bad wombs: that wanders about to a bourn below or above, overcome by the dualities.

'"To explain further: the five subtle elements are called by the name 'element', and the five gross elements[2] are called by the name 'element'. Their coming together is called 'the body'. So the one who is said to be 'the self in the body'[3] is said to be 'the elemental self'. This self[4] is to that one as a drop of water to the blue lotus on which it rests.[5] The elemental self[6] is overcome by the strands of nature. Because it is overcome, it falls into utter delusion. Because of this utter delusion, it has not seen him resting in the self – the lord, the blessed one, the causer of action. Delighting in the mass of strands and grown dirty, unsteadfast, fickle, utterly bewildered, full of yearning, distracted, it falls into conceitedness. 'I am this: this is mine': thinking like this, it binds itself with itself[7] like a bird with a net. Overcome by the fruits that follow on from action, he wanders around."

'They said, "Which is he?"

'Maitri told them:

3. '"It has been said elsewhere:

The maker is the elemental self. The causer of action through the organs of action is the person within.[8] As a lump of iron, overcome by fire, when beaten by the smiths becomes various, so the elemental self, overcome by the inner person, when beaten by the strands becomes various. Its variousness takes this form: the mass of beings, with three strands, transformed by eighty-four hundred thousand wombs.[9] The strands are impelled by the person, as the wheel is by the thrower.[10] And as, when a lump of iron is beaten, the fire is not overcome, so that person is not overcome.[11] The elemental self is overcome on account of its close contact.[12]

4. ' "It has been said elsewhere:[13]

This body comes into being from sexual intercourse, and, devoid of understanding, comes out through the gate of urine into a hell-realm. It is constructed of bones, smeared with flesh, bound up with hide, filled with faeces, urine, bile, phlegm, marrow, fat, marrow of the flesh, and many other impurities.

5. ' "It has been said elsewhere:[14]

The elemental self is overcome by these, which are attended by darkness (*tamas*) – confusion, fear, despair, sleepiness, laziness, negligence, old age, grief, hunger, thirst, wretchedness, anger, unbelief,[15] lack of knowledge, miserliness, compassionlessness, deludedness, shamelessness, baseness, arrogance, prejudice;[16] overcome by these, which are attended by passion (*rajas*) – craving,[17] affection, lust, greed, violence, pleasure, hate, secretiveness,[18] envy, desire, unsteadfastness, fickleness, distractedness, rapacity, seeking for gain, favouritism to friends, clinging to possessions, hatred towards sense objects that are disliked and clinging to those that are liked. So it takes on various forms: it takes them on."

BOOK IV

1. 'Then those celibates, utterly amazed, came to him together and said, "Blessed one, homage to you! Teach us. You are our way: no other can be found. What method is there for the elemental self, by which one can leave it and attain union with the self?"

'He told them:

2. ' "It has been said elsewhere:

Like the waves in great rivers, what has been done in the past cannot be turned back. Like a breaker in the ocean, the coming of death is hard to ward off. Like an animal, it[1] is bound with ropes made of good and bad fruits. Like a prisoner, it is without independence. Like one in Yama's realm, it is in a state of great fear. Like one drunk with wine, it is drunk with the wine of delusion. Like one seized by evil, it is made to tremble. Like one bitten by a great snake, it is bitten by sense-objects. Like one in great darkness,[2] it is blind with passion. Like a conjuring trick, it is made of artifice.[3] Like a dream, it is a wrong seeing.[4] Like the core of a plantain tree, it is without pith. Like an actor, it changes costume in an instant. Like a wall painting, it delights the mind, but deceptively.[5]

' "And it is said:

The objects, sound, touch and the rest,
　Remain purposeless:[6]
Attached to them, the elemental self
　Cannot remember the supreme goal.

3. ' "And this is the remedy for the elemental self: study of the

knowledge of the Veda, practising one's own *dharma*, and walking according to one's own stages of life.[7] In one's own *dharma* one stores everything:[8] other things are a branch of a grass-tussock. By it one comes to share in what is higher. Established in the stages of life, one is called *ascetic*. It has been said also: 'There is no study in the knowledge of self, or purification from actions,[9] for one without asceticism.' Someone has said:[10]

By asceticism one wins truth:
  Through truth one wins mind:
By mind the self is won,
  And, having won that, one does not return.

4. '"'Brahman *is*,' said a knower of the knowledge of *brahman*.

'"'This is the gateway to *brahman*,' says one who has been freed from evil through asceticism.

'"'OṂ is the greatness of *brahman*,' says one who is well disciplined and who contemplates perpetually.

'"So *brahman* is attained by knowledge, asceticism and contemplation. The one who, knowing this, by this triad worships *brahman* goes beyond Brahmā,[11] and reaches godhead over the gods. He attains indestructible, measureless, flawless bliss. Freed from those things by which he was filled, overcome and ridden,[12] he achieves union in the self."

5. 'The Vālakhilyas said, "You speak rightly![13] You speak rightly! We have placed in mind what you have taught us, just as you said it. Now answer another question: Fire, air, the sun, time, the breath, food, Brahmā, Rudra, Viṣṇu[14] – some meditate on one of these, some on another. Tell us which is the best one."

'He told them:

6. '"These are the supreme forms of *brahman*, the immortal and bodiless. The one who is attached to any one of them here is happy in the world of that deity. Someone has said, '*Brahman* is all this. One should meditate on, praise and propitiate[15] those forms of his. Then, with them, one moves in ever higher worlds: and at the universal destruction one attains oneness with the person – with the person.'

'"There are these verses about it:[16]

Just as, without fuel, a fire
  Dies down in its own birthplace,
On the ceasing of its movements the mind
  Dies down in its own birthplace.

For the mind which, desiring truth,
  Has died down in its own birthplace
And is not deluded, the sense objects,
  In the power of desire, are false.[17]

Consciousness[18] is *saṃsāra:*
  By effort one should purify it.
As is one's consciousness, so one becomes:
  That is the eternal secret.

By the calming of consciousness
  One kills action, both pure and impure:
With self calmed, resting in the self,
  One wins unfailing bliss.

If a person's[19] consciousness
  Were as firmly attached to *brahman*
As it is to the sense-realm,
  Would not all be freed from bonds?[20]

The mind is said to be twofold,
  The pure and the impure –
Impure from contact with desire:
  Pure when apart from desire.

When, making the mind thoroughly firm,
  Free from laxity and distraction,
One reaches a state without mind,
  That is the highest state.

The mind should be kept in check
  Until it has dissolved into the heart:
This is both knowledge and liberation.
  The rest is multiplication of books.[21]

The bliss that the stainless consciousness, washed by
concentration,
May have when it has been brought into the self
Cannot be described by speech:
It is experienced directly through the inner organ.

Water in water, fire in fire,
Or space in space cannot be made out:
Just so the one whose mind has gone within
Is completely freed.

For human beings the mind is cause
Of bondage and freedom.
When attached to objects, it brings bondage:
When without object, it brings freedom, so it
is recorded.

BOOK V

1. ' "Here now is Kutsāyana's hymn of praise:

You are Brahmā, you are Viṣṇu too:
  You are Rudra, you are Prajāpati.
You are Agni, Varuṇa, Vāyu:
  You are Indra, you are the Moon.

You are Manu, you are Yama,
  You are Earth, the Unfallen[1] likewise.
For your sake and the sake of your own nature
  You rest in the sky in many forms.

Lord of all, homage to you,
  Self of all, doer of all works:
Enjoyer of all, you are the whole lifespan,
  The ruler who delights in all games.

Homage to you, peaceful self,
  Homage to you, greatest secret,
Unthinkable, immeasurable,
  Without beginning or end.

2. ' "In the beginning this was darkness (*tamas*).[2] Later, that was moved by something else, and became unbalanced. That is the form of passion (*rajas*). Passion was moved and became unbalanced. That is the form of darkness. Purity (*sattva*) was moved. From purity flowed the essence. That is the portion consisting solely of consciousness, which is the field-knower[3] in each person, Prajāpati, whose characteristics are will, determination and conceit. Brahmā, Rudra and Viṣṇu are called the

supreme forms of him. His portion of darkness is Rudra. His portion of passion is Brahmā. His portion of purity is Viṣṇu. After becoming threefold, he became eightfold, elevenfold, twelvefold, infinite-fold.[4] Because of his becoming (*udbhūtatva*), he is being (*bhūta*). The support[5] moves in the beings. He became the overlord of all beings. He is the self inside and outside – inside and outside.

BOOK VI

1. '"He carries himself (*ātman*) in two parts, the breath and the sun. These are its two paths, the inner and the outer. They both move on in a day and a night.[1] The sun is the outer self, the breath the inner self. The movement of the inner self is measured by the movement of the outer self. Someone has said, 'The one who, knowing, freed from evil, the overseer of the eye, his mind purified, based upon that, with his sight turned inwards . . .'

The going of the outer self is measured by the going of the inner self. Someone has said, 'The person made of gold within the sun,[2] who watches this earth from his golden seat, is the one who rests within, in the heart-lotus, and eats food.'

2. '"The one who rests within, in the heart-lotus, and eats food is the fire resting in the sky, the solar fire called time, the invisible one who eats all beings as food."

'"What is the lotus? What is it made of?"

'"The lotus is space. The four directions and the four intermediate directions form its petals. The breath and the sun move down its stem. One should worship them as OṂ, with the syllable, the utterances, and the Sāvitrī.[3]

3. '"There are two forms of *brahman*, the shaped and the unshaped.[4] What is shaped is the unreal. What is unshaped is the real;[5] it is *brahman*; it is light. What is light is the sun. This is OṂ. It became the self. It divided itself into three. OṂ is three elements.[6] Through them, all this is woven on it as warp and weft.[7] Someone has said, 'One should apply (*yuj-*) oneself while meditating on this: the sun is OṂ.'

4. '"Elsewhere it has been said,[8] 'What the Udgītha is, the

reverberation is: what the reverberation is, the Udgītha is. So the sun is the Udgītha: it is the reverberation.'

' "Someone has said, '. . . the Udgītha,[9] called the reverberation, the leader, with light as its form, without sleep, free from old age, free from death, with three feet,[10] with three syllables:[11] again it should be known as fivefold,[12] hidden in the secret place.'

' "Someone has said, 'The three-footed *brahman* with its roots above:[13] its branches are space, air, fire, water, earth etc. This *brahman* is called by the name of the one fig-tree. Its light is what the sun is. It belongs to the syllable OṂ, so one should worship it ceaselessly with the syllable OṂ. It alone is the awakener of this.'[14]

' "Someone has said:

> This syllable is pure.
> This syllable is supreme.
> Knowing this syllable,
> Whatever one wishes for one has.[15]

5. ' "Elsewhere it has been said, 'What OṂ is is its sound-body.'[16] Feminine, masculine and neuter are its gender-body.[17] Fire, air and the sun are its light-body. Brahmā, Rudra and Viṣṇu are its overlord-body. The Gārhapatya, Dakṣiṇāgni and Āhavanīya are its mouth-body.[18] *Ṛc, yajus* and *sāman* are its knowledge-body. BHŪḤ, BHUVAḤ and SVAḤ are its world-body. Past, present and future are its time-body. Breath, fire and the sun are its heat-body. Food, water and the moon are its growing-body. Intelligence, mind and sense of 'I' are its consciousness-body. Breath, lower breath and diffused breath are its breath-body. So by saying 'OṂ' these bodies come to be praised, worshipped and achieved. Someone has said, 'Satyakāma, what the syllable OṂ is is *brahman*, both the higher and the lower.'[19]

6. ' "Now this was unuttered.[20] Truth, Prajāpati, after raising heat, uttered 'BHŪḤ, BHUVAḤ, SVAḤ.' This is the coarsest body of Prajāpati, the world-body. SVAḤ is its head, BHUVAḤ its navel, BHŪḤ its feet, the sun its eye: for the great element of a person depends on the eye. For this element moves

by eye. Truth is the eye. Placed in the eye, the person moves among all objects. So one should worship BHŪḤ, BHUVAḤ, SVAḤ. By it Prajāpati comes to be worshipped as the self of all, the sight of all. Someone has said, 'This is the all-bearing body of Prajāpati. Everything is hidden in it, and it is hidden in all this. So one should worship.'

7. '"*Tat savitur vareṇyam.*[21] Savitṛ is the sun. He is to be chosen (*pra-vṛ-*) by one who desires the self: so say the scholars of *brahman.*

'"Now *bhargo devasya dhīmahi.* The god (*deva*) is Savitṛ. So I contemplate the one who is called its glory (*bhargas*): so say the scholars of *brahman.*

'"Now *dhiyo yo naḥ pracodayāt.* Minds (*dhiyaḥ*) are intelligences: so say the scholars of *brahman.*

'"Now *glory.* The one who is hidden in the sun, the star in the eye, is called glory. It is glory (*bhargas*) because of its going (*gati*) by light (*bhā*); or it is glory because it parches (*bhṛj-*): so say the scholars of *brahman.*

'"It is *bha* because it lights (*bhās-*) the worlds. It is *ra* because it delights (*raj-*) beings. It is *ga* because creatures go (*gam-*) into it and come (*ā-gam-*) out of it. So because it is *bha ra ga* it is *bhargas*. It is the sun (*sūrya*) because it is perpetually produced (*sū-*). It is Savitṛ because it inspires (or 'presses Soma': *su-*). It is Āditya because it carries off (*ā-dā-*). It is water (*āpaḥ*) because it causes to swell (*ā-pyā-*).

'"Someone has said, 'Where knowledge has become dual one hears, sees, smells, tastes and touches: the self knows all. Where knowledge has become non-dual, freed from object, cause and action, without speech, incomparable, indescribable, what is it? It cannot be spoken.'

8. '"The self is Īśāna, Śambhu, Bhava, Rudra,[22] Prajāpati, the All-Creator, the golden embryo,[23] truth, breath, the goose,[24] the teacher,[25] Viṣṇu, Nārāyaṇa,[26] Arka,[27] Savitṛ, Dhātṛ, Vidhātṛ,[28] the emperor, Indra, Indu.[29] He, the one who gives heat, hidden by the thousand-eyed golden egg like fire hidden by fire, is the one that one must want to know, must seek for. By granting freedom from fear to all beings,[30] going to the forest, and setting aside the objects of sense, one may win him from one's own body,[31]

. . .Of all forms, yellow, all-knowing,
The supreme goal, the one light, giving heat.
Thousand-rayed, existing in a hundred forms,
The sun rises as the breath of creatures.[32]

9. ' "So the one who knows this has both[33] as self. He meditates on the self, sacrifices to the self. This is meditation, mind resting in the practice,[34] purified mind, as praised by the wise. One should purify the mind by chanting *Touched by Leftovers*. One chants the mantra: 'Whether it be left over or touched by leftovers, or given by an evil man, or impure from a still birth, may the purifier of Vasu, may Agni and the rays of Savitṛ purify my food, and anything else that is ill-done.'

' "First one surrounds it[35] with water. One makes offering with the five: 'To the breath, SVĀHĀ! To the lower breath, SVĀHĀ! To the diffused breath, SVĀHĀ! To the central breath, SVĀHĀ! To the up-breath, SVĀHĀ!'

' "One eats the rest with speech restrained. Afterwards one surrounds it again with water. Having sipped, while sacrificing to the self, one meditates on the self with two verses, 'As breath, as fire' and 'You are all':

As breath, as fire, the supreme self
Is sought for refuge, the one with five airs:
Being pleased, may he please all,
The enjoyer of all!

You are all, you are in all men:[36]
All, being born, is upheld by you.
May all offerings enter you,
And creatures, too,[37] go where you are,
the all-immortal.

So by this method the eater does not become food again.[38]

10. ' "Something else should be known: there is a further development of the sacrifice of the self – food and the eater of food. To explain further: the person is the watcher who rests inside matter. He is the enjoyer: he enjoys the food of nature. The elemental self is its food: matter is its agent. So with its three strands it is the object of enjoyment.[39] The person rests inside.

What is seen is the proof here. Since all animals are produced from seed, the seed is the object of enjoyment.[40] By this is explained the fact that matter is the object of enjoyment. So the enjoyer is the person, nature is the object of enjoyment, and resting in it he enjoys it. The food of nature, through the development of the distinction of the three strands, is the subtle body, which begins with 'the great' and ends with 'the particularities'. In this way the fourteenfold path[41] is explained: 'This world, known as joy, sorrow and delusion, has become food.'

'"For as long as there is no bringing forth, there is no grasping of sweetness. It, too, turns into food, in three states. They are childhood, youth and old age – because of development, it becomes food. When matter has reached manifestation in this way, it can be got hold of. Then it has the sweetnesses, intelligence etc.: they are called intelligence, resolution and conceit. Now the five sweetnesses are the sense objects, likewise all the activities of the senses and the activities of the breath. So there is manifest food and unmanifest food. The enjoyer of it is free of the strands. Because he is the enjoyer, he clearly possesses consciousness. Just as, among the gods, Agni is the eater of food and Soma is food, the one who knows this enjoys food with Agni.[42] Because of the saying. 'The elemental self is called Soma and the one who has the unmanifest as his mouth is Agni', the person enjoys the three-stranded matter with the unmanifest as his mouth.

'"The one who knows this is a renouncer, a yogi and a sacrificer to the self. Just as no one touches amorous women if they have entered an empty house, the one who does not touch sense-objects is a renouncer, a yogi and a sacrificer to the self.

11. '"Food is the highest form of the self, for breath is made of food. If one does not eat, one becomes unable to think, unable to hear, unable to touch, unable to see, unable to speak, unable to smell, unable to taste, and one gives up one's breaths.

'"Someone has said, 'If one eats, one becomes filled with breath and becomes able to think, able to hear, able to touch, able to speak, able to taste, able to smell, able to see.'

'"Someone has said:

Whatever creatures depend on earth
  Are born from food.
By food they live,
  And into it go in the end.[43]

12. '"Elsewhere it has been said, 'All beings fly out day by day desiring to get food. The sun takes up food with its rays, and so gives heat. When sprinkled with food, the breaths digest.[44] By food, fire burns.'

'"Through the desire for food, all this was shaped by *brahman*.[45] So one should worship food as the self. Someone has said:

Beings are born from food:
  Born, they grow by food.
It is eaten and it eats beings,
  Hence it is called food.[46]

13. '"Elsewhere it has been said, 'Food is the form of the blessed Viṣṇu that is called the All-bearing. Breath is the essence of food; mind of breath; knowledge of mind; joy of knowledge.'

'"The one who knows this becomes endowed with food, endowed with breath, endowed with mind, endowed with knowledge, endowed with joy. The one who knows this, resting within them, eats food in whatever beings there are that eat food.

Food keeps away old age;[47]
  Food, it is said, makes folk well disposed;
Food is the breath of animals;
  Food is the eldest; food, it is said, is
    medicine.

14. '"Elsewhere it has been said, 'Food is the source (*yoni*) of all this.' Time is the source of food, the sun of time. Its form consists of the units of time, moments[48] and so on: it is the year, with its twelve parts.[49] Half of it belongs to Agni and half to Varuṇa. In the sun's course from Maghā to halfway through Śraviṣṭhā[50] it belongs to Agni, and in its upward course from

the Constellation of the Serpents to halfway through Śraviṣṭhā it belongs to Soma.[51] In it, each part of the self has nine divisions according to the corresponding progress of the sun.[52]

' "Because of the subtlety, this is the measure:[53] time is measured by it. Without a measure, there is no getting hold of the thing to be measured. Moreover, because of its separateness,[54] the thing to be measured becomes the measure for the purpose of making itself[55] known. Someone has said, 'The one who worships time as *brahman* moves on through all the divisions of time that there are, and time moves very far away from him.'

' "Someone has said:

> Because of time, beings move on;
> Because of time, they grow up;
> In time they reach their end;[56]
> Time, though unshaped, possesses shapes.

15. ' "There are two forms of *brahman*: time (*kāla*) and the timeless (*akāla*). That which was before the sun is timeless, without parts (*akala*). That which began with the sun is time, with parts (*sakala*). The form of that with parts is the year, for all creatures are born from the year; once born here, they live by the year; in the year they meet their end. So the year is Prajāpati, time, food, the nest of *brahman*, and the self. Someone has said:

> Time ripens[57] all beings
> In the great self.
> But the one who knows in what
> Time is ripened knows the Veda.[58]

16. ' "The time that has a body is the ocean of creatures. Resting in it is the one called Savitṛ, from whom the moon, stars, planets, year etc. are produced. From them comes all this here, whatever is seen in this world, fair or foul. So *brahman* has the sun as its self.[59] So one should worship the sun under the name of time: some say that the sun is *brahman*. So someone has said:

The Hotṛ, the enjoyer, the offering, the mantra,
The sacrifice, Viṣṇu, Prajāpati –
He is all these, the lord, the witness
Who shines in yonder circle.

17. '"In the beginning all this was *brahman*, one, infinite: infinite to the east, infinite to the south, infinite to the west, infinite to the north, infinite upward and downward, infinite on every side. The directions, east and so on, do not apply to it, for the supreme self is inconceivable either across, downward or upward, immeasurable, unborn, unguessable, unthinkable. He has space as his self.[60] In the universal dissolution, he is the one awake. From space he awakens this, which is pure consciousness.[61] By this it is born, and in it it meets its end. It is the radiant form of this that gives heat in the sun, and the brighter light that is in a smokeless fire, and the one who rests in the belly and digests[62] food. Someone has said, 'The one who is in fire, the one who is in the heart and the one who is in the sun are one.'

'"The one who knows this attains oneness with the one.

18. '"Then there is the method of practice called the six-limbed yoga: restraint of the breath, withdrawal,[63] meditation, maintaining,[64] thinking, concentration. When, seeing by this, one sees him, coloured like a gold piece, the maker, the powerful one,[65] the person, womb of *brahman*,[66] then knowing him one leaves behind good and evil and makes all one in the highest unfailing.[67] Someone has said:

Just as deer and birds do not resort
To a mountain on fire,
Faults never resort
To one who knows *brahman*.

19. '"Elsewhere it has been said:

When one who knows, restraining the outer mind and causing the objects of sense to enter the breath, rests without forming concepts . . .[68] Since the life which is called the breath is produced from that which is not breath,[69] it is the breath . . . One should maintain[70] the breath in what is called the fourth state.[71]

'"Someone has said:

As not-thought in the midst of thought,
  Unthinkable supreme secret,
One should meditate on thought.
  That is the subtle form[72] without dependency.

20. '"Elsewhere it has been said:

Now the supreme contemplation of this. By pressing together the palate and the tip of the tongue, by the cessation of speech, mind and breath, one sees *brahman* by investigating.[73] When, on the dissolution of the mind, by the self one sees the self, which is subtler than the subtle, shining, then, by the self seeing the self, one becomes selfless. Because one is selfless, one can be thought to be uncountable, without source – the mark of liberation.[74]

That is the highest secret. Someone has said:

By the calming of thought
  One destroys action both fair and foul:
With self calmed, resting in the self
  One wins unfailing joy.

21. '"Elsewhere it has been said:

The channel called Suṣumnā,[75] which goes upward together with the breath, cuts through the palate. When it is joined with the OṂ and the mind, the breath can go out by it. By turning back the tongue-tip against the palate and harnessing the senses, as greatness one may see greatness. Then one reaches selflessness. Because one is selfless, one no longer experiences joy and sorrow: one reaches absoluteness.[76]

'"Someone has said:

Setting up the highest before one,
  One should restrain one's breath.[77]
By the shoreless[78] one should cross to the
    other shore
  And afterwards become united (*yuj-*) in
    the head.

22. ' "Elsewhere it has been said:

There are two *brahmans* to be named: sound and the soundless. The soundless is revealed through sound. The sound is OṂ. By it one goes out upward and finds cessation in the soundless. This is the bourn, this is immortality, this is union[79] and also ultimate bliss.[80] Just as a spider goes up outwards by its thread and finds space, so one meditates on OṂ and by it goes up outwards and finds independence.

' "Others, those who profess sound, practise differently. By joining ear and thumb, they listen to the sound of the space within the heart. That is compared to seven things: rivers, a bell, a metal pot, a wheel, the croaking of frogs, rain, and the sound made in a windless place. Going beyond their separate characteristics, they meet their end in the supreme soundless unmanifest *brahman*. There they are without separate nature, indistinguishable, like different flavours combined into sweetness. Someone has said:

> There are two *brahmans* to be known,
>   The sound-*brahman* and the supreme.
> By bathing in the sound-*brahman*
>   One wins the *brahman* that is supreme.

23. ' "Elsewhere it has been said, 'What the sound is is OṂ: this is the imperishable. The peak of it is peaceful, soundless, fearless, sorrowless, joyful, content, steadfast, immovable, immortal, unfallen, constant, known as Viṣṇu: one should worship it to achieve supremacy over all. 'Someone has said:

> The god, the higher and the lower,
>   Is called by name the OṂ:
> Without sound, become void,
>   One should then concentrate on it in
>   its place in the head.

24. ' "Elsewhere it has been said:

The body is the bow; OṂ is the arrow; the mind is its point.[81] By piercing the target of darkness one comes to the darkness which is pervaded by non-darkness. Then, by piercing that which is pervaded, one has seen the supreme *brahman*, blazing like a circle of torchlight,[82] the colour of the sun, powerful, beyond the darkness. That which is in the sun shines also in the moon,[83] in fire and in lightning. By seeing it, one becomes immortal.

Someone has said:

> The meditation on the supreme entity[84] within
> Is placed on the objects of sense,[85]
> So the knowledge that is without distinction
> Becomes subject to distinction.
>
> The joy that is witnessed by the self
> When the mind is dissolved
> Is *brahman*, the immortal, the pure:[86]
> It is the bourn; it is the world.

25. '"Elsewhere it has been said:

When one's senses are hidden as if by sleep, then, unmastered, with completely pure mind one sees, as if in a dream, in a gap in the senses, the one who leads on out (*prāṇetṛ*) who is called the OṂ (*praṇava*), in the form of light, free from sleep, free from old age, free from death, and free from sorrow. Then one also becomes one who leads on out who is called OṂ, in the form of light, free from sleep, free from old age, free from death, and free from sorrow.

Someone has said:

> Since one joins or unites (*yuj-*)
> In many ways
> Breath and OṂ and all,
> It is known as yoga.
>
> Since it is the oneness of breath and mind
> And senses too,
> The renunciation of all becoming[87]
> Is named yoga.

26. '"Elsewhere it has been said:

Just as a bird-catcher draws up the waterfowl with a device made of net, and offers them in the fire that is his belly, so one draws up the breaths with the OṂ and offers them in a fire that is free from disease. Then one is like a heated pot. Just as a heated pot blazes up through contact with melted butter, grass or sticks, the one who is called 'not-breath' blazes up through contact with breath. That which blazes up is the form of Brahmā, Viṣṇu's highest step, the Rudra-ness of Rudra. Divided up into countless parts it fills the worlds.

Someone has said:

> Just like sparks from fire
> Come rays from the sun,
> And so too do breaths etc.
> Come forth in order here.

27. '"Elsewhere it has been said:

This is the brightness of *brahman*, the supreme immortal, the bodiless. The warmth of the body is its ghee. It is set, visible, in space:[88] they dispel the space within the heart with one-pointed mind[89] so that its light strikes them, as it were. Then one quickly attains the state of that,[90] just as a lump of iron placed in the earth quickly[91] attains the condition of earth. Just as fire, blacksmiths and so on have no power over a lump of iron that is in the clay-like state, thought perishes along with its support.[92]

'"Someone has said:

> The treasury[93] formed of the space in
> the heart,
> Joy, the supreme abode . . .
> It is itself,[94] and our yoga,
> And the splendour of fire and the sun.

28. '"Elsewhere it has been said:

When one has gone beyond the elements, senses and objects, then one seizes the bow whose string is the renouncer's life[95] and whose stave is steadfastness, and with an arrow made of freedom from conceit one strikes down the primal doorkeeper of *brahman*.

(That overseer of conceit, who has confusion as his crown, craving and envy as his earrings, and sloth, drunkenness and impurity as his staff of office, seizes the bow whose string is anger and whose stave is greed, and kills beings with an arrow made of wanting.) After killing him, one crosses to the farther shore of the space within the heart on the boat of the OṂ.

Then, as the space within becomes visible, slowly, as a miner in search of minerals enters a mine,[96] one should enter the hall of *brahman*. Then by the guru's instruction one should throw off the sheath of *brahman* with its four layers of net.[97] Then, pure, cleansed, void, at peace, without breath, selfless, without end, indestructible, steadfast, eternal, unborn, independent, one rests in one's own greatness. Then, seeing the one who rests in his own greatness, one looks upon the wheel of *saṃsāra* as a wheel that rolls on.

' "Someone has said:

> For the embodied one[98] who has practised for
> six months,
> Eternally freed,
> The endless supreme secret,
> The right yoga, moves on:
>
> But never for the embodied one
> Who is all ablaze,
> Pierced by passion and darkness,
> Attached to children, wife and family." '

29. After he had said this, Śākāyanya went within his heart.[99] He paid homage to him.[100] Then he said, 'O king, by this knowledge of *brahman* the sons of Prajāpati[101] mounted the path of *brahman*.

'By the practice of yoga one achieves contentment, endurance of the pairs,[102] and peacefulness. "One should not make known this supreme secret to one who is not a son, not a student, or not at peace":[103] so one should give it to one who is devoted to nothing else,[104] who is endowed with all virtues.

30. 'OṂ. One should be in a clean place, clean, resting in purity (*sattva*), studying truth, speaking truth, meditating on

truth, sacrificing to truth. Then one finds fulfilment in the true *brahman*, that delights[105] in truth. Having become other, and cut what binds one to the fruits of that,[106] one lives free from expectation towards others as to oneself, freed from fear, without desire, having attained indestructible, measureless joy. This is the ultimate digging up of the supreme treasure – freedom from desire.

'The person made of all desires, whose distinguishing mark is determination, will and conceit, is bound: the one opposite to this is freed.

'On this, some say, "Under the influence of the differentiation of nature, the strand has taken on the bondage of the self to determination."[107] When the fault of determination perishes, there is liberation. By mind one sees; by mind one hears. "Desire, imagination, doubt, trust, lack of trust, constancy, inconstancy, shame, meditation, fear – all this is mind."[108] Carried along by the floods of the strands, soiled, unsteady, fickle, greedy, yearning, unconcentrated, one goes on to conceit. Thinking, "This am I, this is mine", one binds oneself by oneself like a bird in a net.

'So the person whose distinguishing mark is determination, will and conceit is bound: the one opposite to this is freed. Therefore one should stay without determination, without will, without conceit. This is the sign of liberation; this is the path to *brahman* here; this is the opening of the door here: by it one will go to the far shore of the darkness. Here all desires are brought together. On this folk say:

> When the five knowings cease,
> Together with the mind,
> And the intelligence does not stir,
> They call that the highest bourn.[109]

After Śākāyanya had said this, he went within his heart. He paid homage to him,[110] revering him in the proper way: and, having done what was to be done, as Marut he[111] went by the northern path. One cannot get there by a lesser road. This is the road to *brahman* here. Breaking through the door of the sun, one goes up outwards.[112] On this folk say:

The one who, lamp-like, rests in the heart
Has endless rays,
White and black, brown and blue,
Tawny and faintly red.

A single one of these, set above,
Breaks through the circle of the sun,
And gains the world of *brahman*.
By it folk go to the highest bourn.

It has another hundred rays
Arrayed above
By which one wins the very own homes
Of the troops of gods.

Below them, it has rays of many forms,
Faintly glowing.
By them here the powerless one
Wanders round[113] to experience his actions.

So the blessed sun is the cause of creation, heaven and release.

31. Someone has said, 'With what as self do the senses go forth? What here goes out of them, or what controls them?'

Someone has replied, 'With the self as self. The self goes out of them, or controls them.' There are *apsarases* and *marīcis*, daughters of the sun, so-called.[114] So he eats the sense-objects with five rays.

Which one is the self? The one who is pure, cleansed, empty, said to have the primal mark of peace, is to be grasped by its own signs.[115] Some say that the sign of the one who is signless is what heat, and that which is pervaded by it, is to fire and what the most delicious[116] flavour is to water. Some say that it is speech, hearing, the eye, the ear, the breath. Others say that it is intelligence, steadfastness, memory, knowing. But those are to it what shoots are to a seed, and what smoke, flames and sparks are to fire. On this folk say:

Just like sparks from fire
Come rays from the sun,
And so too do breaths etc.
Come forth in order here.[117]

32. All breaths, all worlds, all Vedas, all gods, all beings come up from this one in the self. Its inner meaning (*upaniṣad*) is 'the truth of the truth'.[118] 'As smoke billows out in all directions from a fire that has been laid with damp fuel, just so is everything breathed out from this great being: the Ṛgveda, the Yajurveda, the Sāmaveda, the hymns of the Atharvans and Aṅgirases, history, legend, science, the Upaniṣads, verses, sūtras, explanatory passages and expositions, all beings are breathed out from it.'[119]
33. The fire which is the year has five bricks. Its bricks are spring, summer, the rains, autumn and winter. It has a head, two wings, a back and a tail. This is the man-shaped fire.[120] This is the first fire-laying of Prajāpati. With its hands it has thrown the patron of the sacrifice up to middle-air and offered him to air.

Breath is air; breath is a fire. Its bricks are the breath, the lower breath, the diffused breath, the up-breath and the central breath. It has a head, two wings, a back and a tail. This is the man-shaped fire. This is middle-air, the second fire-laying of Prajāpati. With its hands it has thrown the patron of the sacrifice up to the sky and offered him to Indra.

The sun is Indra; it is a fire. Its bricks are the Ṛgveda, the Yajurveda, the Sāmaveda, the hymns of the Atharvans and Aṅgirases, and history and legend. It has a head, two wings, a back and a tail. This is the man-shaped fire. This is sky, the third fire-laying of Prajāpati. With its hands it makes an offering of the patron of the sacrifice to the knower of the self. Then the knower of the self has thrown him up and offered him to *brahman*. There he becomes blissful, contented.
34. Earth is the Gārhapatya; middle-air is the Dakṣiṇāgni; sky is the Āhavanīya. They are the Pavamāna, Pāvaka and Śuci.[121] He makes offering in the mouth.[122] Hence the fire of digestion is the coming together of 'the Purifying', 'the Purifier' and 'the

Clean'. So fire is to be sacrificed to, thought of,[123] praised and meditated on. Taking the melted butter, the patron of the sacrifice desires to meditate on the deity:

A bird of golden hue
Is set in the heart, in the sun –
Cormorant, goose, brightness, bull –
To him we sacrifice in this fire . . .[124]

so he understands the meaning of the mantra. He should meditate on 'the lovely glory of Savitṛ' as being that of the one who rests within the intelligence. Meditating, he recollects the state of peace of mind, and places it in the self.[125]

So the recollection of the heaven of the state of *brahman* is barred to those who do not make offering to fire, think of[126] fire, or meditate on fire. So fire is to be sacrificed to, thought of, praised, meditated on.

35. 'Homage to Agni, dwelling in the earth, protector of a world! Assign a world to this patron of the sacrifice. Homage to Vāyu, dwelling in middle-air, protector of a world! Assign a world to this patron of the sacrifice. Homage to the sun, dwelling in the sky, protector of a world! Assign a world to this patron of the sacrifice. Homage to *brahman*, dwelling in everything, protector of everything! Assign everything to this patron of the sacrifice.[127]

The face of truth is concealed
By a vessel made of gold.
Reveal it, Pūṣan, to Viṣṇu,
Who has truth as his *dharma*.[128]

That person who is in the sun – I am he.'[129]

The one who has truth as his *dharma* is the sun-ness of the sun – the white form.[130] Just a portion of the energy[131] that exists within the space[132] is that which is in the middle of the sun, in the eye, and in fire. This is *brahman*; this is the immortal; this is glory;[133] this is the one who has truth as his *dharma*. Just a portion of the energy that exists within the sky is the immortal[134] which is in the middle of the sun, of which Soma and the breaths are shoots. This is *brahman*; this is the immortal; this is glory; this is the one of the nature of truth. Just a portion of the energy that exists within the sky is the *yajus* which shines in the middle of the sun. OṂ water light juice immortal *brahman* BHŪḤ BHUVAḤ SVAḤ OṂ.

> The eight-footed[135] pure goose,
> Three-threaded, subtle, unfailing,
> Blazing with the energy of double *dharmas*[136] –
> Seeing him, one sees everything.

Just a portion of the energy that exists within the sky is 'Ud',[137] in the middle of the sun. It becomes two rays. This is 'the knower of unity',[138] the one who has truth as his *dharma*. This is the *yajus*; this is asceticism; this is fire; this is air; this is breath; this is water; this is the moon; this is the pure;[139] this is the immortal; this is the realm of *brahman*; this is the ocean of light.[140] In it, patrons of the sacrifice are dissolved like salt. This is the oneness of *brahman*: in it, all desires are brought together. On this folk say:

> Like a lamp stirred by a slight breeze
> He blazes up, the one who exists among the gods[141] –
> The one who knows this is a knower of unity, a knower of duality.
> He comes to the one abode, and has that as self.

> Those who constantly move above like water-drops,
> Like lightning, the clouds' flames, in the highest heaven,[142]
> Through the power of their source, of the splendour of the flame,
> Are like crests of black-tracked fire.[143]

36. There are two forms of the light of *brahman*: the 'peaceful' is one, the 'wealthy' another. Space is the support of the peaceful one, food of the wealthy one. So one must sacrifice inside the ritual enclosure[144] with mantras, herbs, melted butter, meat, rice-cakes, the offering called *sthālīpāka*[145] and so on; and in the mouth with the food left over by the fire, thinking of the mouth

as the Āhavanīya – for wealth of brightness, for the purpose of winning meritorious[146] worlds, and for immortality. On this folk say 'One should offer the Agnihotra while seeking heaven.' By the Agniṣṭoma one wins the kingdom of Yama; by the Ukthya the kingdom of Soma; by the Ṣoḍaśin the kingdom of Sūrya; by the Atirātra one's own kingdom; by the rite that lasts to the end of a thousand years the rank of Prajāpati.

As the existence of a lamp comes
From the joining of wick, base and oil,
Both self and the pure one[147] exist
From the joining of the inner one and the egg.

37. The very own form of the sky is the supreme brightness that exists within space. The very own form of the sky that exists within space is the syllable, OṂ. It is disposed in three forms: in fire, in the sun, and in the breath. By it one perpetually wakes up, rises up, and recovers one's breath. So by OṂ one should worship the limitless brightness.

This channel takes the offering called 'abundance of food'[148] to the sun. The essence that has flowed from it rains down the Udgītha. So, because of the breaths (*prāṇa*), living beings (*prāṇa*) are creatures. On this folk say, 'The offering that is offered in the fire, it takes to the sun. The sun rains it down with its rays. So it becomes food. From that comes the uprising of beings.' Someone has said:

The offering duly cast in the fire
Attends upon the sun.
From the sun arises rain:
From rain, food; from that, creatures.[149]

38. Offering the Agnihotra, one breaks the net of greed. Then, having cut through delusion, not praising angry states, meditating on one's desire – then one breaks the sheath of *brahman* with its four layers of net. For here are the spheres of Sūrya, Soma, Agni and purity (*sattva*). Then, having broken through furthest space, one sees, resting in its own greatness, that which rests within purity, unmoving, immortal, unfallen, constant, named Viṣṇu, the foundation beneath everything, endowed with

true desire, true resolve,[150] and omniscience, independent, made of intelligence. On this folk say:

Soma rests in the midst of the sun;
Brightness rests in the midst of Soma;
Purity rests in the midst of brightness;
The unfallen rests in the midst of purity.

When one meditates on it, its body a span or a thumb in length,[151] subtler than the subtle, one attains supremacy. Here all desires are brought together. On this folk say:

The one whose body is a thumb or a span in length,
Radiant with light, double or threefold,
Brahman, greatness[152] who is praised,
As a god has entered all beings.[153]

OṂ homage: homage to *brahman*.

BOOK VII

1. Agni, the *Gāyatra*,[1] the *Trivṛt*,[2] the *Rathantara*,[3] spring, the breath, the constellations and the Vasus rise in the east: they give heat, they rain, they praise, they go back inside, they look out through an opening. He is unthinkable,[4] unshaped, profound, hidden, irreproachable, dense, deep, without strands, pure, radiant, enjoying the strands, fearsome, unceasing, lord of yogis, all-knowing, mighty, immeasurable, without beginning or end, glorious, unborn, meditative, indescribable, all-creating, self of all, all-enjoying, ruler[5] of all, within the inner part of all.

2. Indra, the *Triṣṭubh*, the *Pañcadaśa*, the *Bṛhat*, summer, the diffused breath, Soma[6] and the Rudras rise in the south: they give heat, they rain, they praise, they go back inside, they look out through an opening. He is without beginning or end, unlimited, not cut off, not to be used by another, independent, without distinguishing mark, unshaped, of endless power, Dhātṛ, the radiant.

3. The Maruts, the *Jagatī*, the *Saptadaśa*, the *Vairūpa*, the rains, the lower breath, Śukra[7] and the Ādityas rise in the west: they give heat, they rain, they praise, they go back inside, they look out through an opening. It is peaceful, soundless, fearless, sorrowless, bliss, contented, firm, immovable, immortal, unfallen, constant, known as Viṣṇu, the foundation beneath everything.

4. The Viśvedevas, the *Anuṣṭubh*, the *Ekaviṃśa*, the *Vairāja*, the autumn, the central breath, Varuṇa and the Sādhyas rise in the north: they give heat, they rain, they praise, they go back inside, they look out through an opening. He is pure within, cleansed, void, peaceful, without breath, selfless, endless.

5. Mitra-and-Varuṇa, the *Paṅkti*, the *Triṇava* and *Trayastriṃśa*, the *Śākvara* and *Raivata*, winter and the cold season, the up-breath, the Aṅgirases and the moon rise above: they give heat, they rain, they praise, they go back inside, they look out through an opening. It is called the OṂ (*praṇava*), the leader-forth (*praṇetṛ*), with light as its form, free from sleep, free from old age, free from death, free from sorrow.

6. Śani,[8] Rāhu, Ketu,[9] serpents, ogres, *yakṣas*, men, birds, *śarabhas*,[10] elephants etc. rise below: they give heat, they rain, they praise, they go back inside, they look out through an opening. He is the one who is wise, the separator,[11] within all, imperishable, pure, cleansed, illuminated, patient, peaceful.

7. He is within the heart, subtler, kindled like a fire that takes all forms. All this is food for him. All creatures are woven on him. The self is free from evil, ageless, deathless, without hunger or thirst, of true resolve, of true desire.[12] He is the supreme lord. He is the overlord of beings. He is the protector of beings. He is the separating dam.[13] He is Īśāna, Śambhu, Bhava, Rudra, Prajāpati, creator of all, golden embryo, truth, breath, the goose, teacher, unfallen, Viṣṇu, Nārāyaṇa. The one who is in fire, the one who is in the heart, and the one who is in the sun are one. Homage to you, the one who takes all forms, who are set in truth, in heaven.[14]

8. Now the diseases of knowledge:

'Your majesty, the net of delusion has its source when those who are bound for heaven[15] are defiled by those who are not bound for heaven. There are those who are always jolly, always abroad, always begging, always living by crafts; others who beg in cities, sacrificing for those for whom one should not sacrifice, students of Śūdras, Śūdras who know the sciences; others who are vagabonds, wearers of matted locks, dancers, mercenaries, who have gone forth[16] yet appear on the stage, renegades who work for kings,[17] and so on; others who pay reverence to *yakṣas*, ogres, ghosts, imps, vampires, serpents, ghouls etc., saying that they will placate them; others who falsely wear saffron robes and earrings, or carry skulls;[18] and others who by false logic, examples, jugglery and conjuring seek to find status among those who know the Vedas. One should not live with them.

They are patently thieves, and not bound for heaven.' Someone has said:

With juggleries of the non-self doctrine,[19]
With false examples and causes,
Going astray, the world does not know
The difference between knowledge and ignorance.[20]

9. Becoming Śukra, Bṛhaspati created this ignorance for the safety of Indra and the destruction of the demons.[21] By it folk teach the auspicious (*śiva*) as inauspicious and the inauspicious as auspicious: they say, 'Let there be meditation on *dharma* which is destructive of the Vedas and the rest of the sciences.' So one should not meditate on that. On the contrary, it is like a barren woman: pleasure is its only fruit, as it is of one who has fallen from the course.[22] It is not to be undertaken. Someone has said:

These two are far apart, disparate,
Ignorance and what is called wisdom.
I think Naciketas is a seeker of wisdom:
Many desires do not distract you.[23]

Whoever knows knowledge and ignorance –
Both of them, together –
By ignorance crosses over death
And by wisdom reaches immortality.[24]

Entwined in the midst of ignorance,
Wise in their own view, thinking themselves learned,
The foolish rush about,
Like blind men led by one who is blind.[25]

10. The gods and demons once approached Brahmā[26] seeking the self. They paid homage to him and said, 'Blessed one, we seek the self: teach us.'

After meditating for a long time, he thought, 'The demons seek for a different self.' So a different one was taught to them. So these foolish ones live with great attachment, destroying their raft,[27] praising falsehood: because of the conjuring, they see falsehood as truth. What is set out in the Vedas is truth. Those who know live by what is taught in the Vedas. Therefore a Brāhmaṇa should not meditate on what is not Vedic.

11. The very own form of the sky is the supreme brightness that exists within space. It is disposed in three forms: in fire, in the sun, and in the breath. The very own form of the sky that exists within space is the syllable, OṂ. So by OṂ one should worship the limitless brightness. By it one wakes up, rises up, and recovers one's breath.

There is a constant support through meditation on *brahman*. Here, in the stirring of breath,[28] it has its place in the heat which scatters light. In a stirring like that of smoke, going up into the sky along a branch it moves from limb to limb.[29] It is like the casting of salt in water, or the heat of ghee, or the range of the meditator. On this folk say, 'So why is it called "lightning-like"?' Because, even as it goes up, the whole body lights up. So by OṂ one should worship the limitless brightness.

The eye-person, who rests
  In the right eye,
Is Indra. His wife
  Rests in the left eye.

Their meeting-place
  Is in the channel that enters the heart.
The clot of blood here
  Is the energy[30] of them both.

Reaching to the eye
  And firmly set there,
That vein is a stream for the two,
  Single, while being double.

Mind strikes the fire of the body;
  That sets in motion the wind;[31]
But the wind, moving in the chest,
  Produces a soft sound.

By joining with fire from space,[32] it is harnessed in
the heart,
Subtler (*aṇu*) than an atom (*aṇu*): twice an
atom in the region of the throat;
On the tip of the tongue know it to be three
atoms' size.[33]
It comes forth as the alphabet, they say.

Seeing, one does not see death,
Nor disease, nor suffering:
Seeing, one sees everything,
Wins everything, everywhere.[34]

The one with sight, the mover in dreams,
The deeply asleep,[35] and the one who is
beyond sleep –
These are the four divisions.
The greatest of them is the fourth.

In three of them *brahman* goes on one foot;
In the last it goes on three feet.
In order to experience truth and falsehood,
The great self[36] takes on duality –
The great self takes on duality.

OṂ. *May my limbs, speech, breath, eye, ear, strength and all senses grow strong. Everything is the* brahman *of the Upaniṣads. May I not reject* brahman. *May* brahman *not reject me. May there be no rejecting. May there be no rejecting of me. May all the* dharmas *which are in the Upaniṣads be in me, who delight in the self. May they be in me.*

OṂ. *Peace, peace, peace.*

Notes

For information on names and technical terms, see the Glossary.

GĀYATRĪ MANTRA

tat savitur vareṇyam
bhargo devasya dhīmahi
dhiyo yo naḥ pracodayāt.

I include the Gāyatrī Mantra here because there are many passages in the Upaniṣads that cannot be understood without it. It is regarded as the most sacred hymn of the Ṛgveda, and in some sense as containing the essence of the Vedas. For many Hindus it forms the basis of their daily practice. (For some of the ways in which it is used in meditation and worship, see Taimni 1974.)

Properly speaking, the hymn is called Sāvitrī, the invocation of the solar deity Savitṛ, whose name means 'the one who arouses or inspires'. *Gāyatrī* is the distinctive metre in which it is composed, containing three lines of eight syllables each. (In Vedic Sanskrit, *vareṇyam* was pronounced *vareṇiam.*) The Sāvitrī is by far the best known verse in that metre.

It appears impossible to create a usable English version which divides the content between the three lines as the Sanskrit does: 'The of-Savitṛ lovely/ glory of-the-god we-meditate-on/ so that that [god] may inspire our meditations.' I felt it necessary to keep in the translation the form of three lines of eight syllables (which is important in accounts of the symbolism of the Gāyatrī, for example BU V.14) and the carrying on of meaning between the first and second lines. Within that framework I could find no way of reproducing the two uses of the root *dhī*, in the verb *dhī-*, to 'think/meditate', and the noun *dhī*, 'thought/meditation'. I hope that 'meditate' and 'mind' have a comparable effect though the two words are not derived from the same root.

ĪŚĀVĀSYA OR ĪŚĀ UPANIṢAD

The Īśāvāsya or Īśā is traditionally placed first in collections of Upaniṣads. It belongs to the Vājasaneya Saṃhitā of the White Yajurveda. Unlike the other Upaniṣads, it is included in the Saṃhitā of the Veda itself (as ch. 40), rather than being a separate section. It takes its name from its first words (n. 3 below). Some editions transpose vv. 9–11 and 12–14, and vv. 15–16 and 17–18.

The Īśāvāsya is very difficult to date. It shows clear links on the one hand with the verse passages in Bṛhadāraṇyaka IV, and on the other with the middle-period verse Upaniṣads, particularly the Śvetāśvatara. I am inclined to favour the earlier date, since the author of the latter could well have known the Īśāvāsya and been inspired by it without necessarily being close to it in time.

1. *OṂ . . . remains*: The invocation, which is used in a number of Upaniṣads, comes from BU V.1.1. The sense is that the world of ultimate reality and the world as we know it are both ultimately of the same nature and infinite.
2. *All this . . . world*: 'All this' (*sarvam idam*) is a common Upaniṣadic term for the universe: here it primarily refers to the living beings within it. The term for the world as 'moving' is *Jagatī*.
3. *Must be . . . lord*: The original, *īśāvāsyam*, is practically untranslatable. *Īśā* is the instrumental case of *īś*, 'lord', 'powerful one', from *īś-*, 'to rule, to be powerful'. Other derivatives of this verb, e.g. *īśa*, *īśanī*, are key words in SU (e.g. SU I.8 and note, III.1 and note), where they are particularly associated with Rudra. The second word is *āvāsyam*, not *vāsyam*, as is shown by the accent in the Yajurveda text. It might be derived from *vas-*, 'to dwell', *vas-*, 'to put on (clothes)', 'to wear', or *vās-*, 'to be perfumed': hence 'indwelt by', 'worn as clothing by' or 'pervaded as with perfume by' the/a lord. Probably the author of the Upaniṣad wanted us to think of all of these. The form of the verb is future passive participle, 'capable of being indwelt/worn/perfumed', 'needing to be . . .', suggesting speculation rather than outright statement. I chose 'must be pervaded' as a rather desperate compromise.
4. *Enjoy . . . abandoned*: Either in the literal sense, 'Live on food etc. that has been freely given up to you', or symbolically, 'You can freely enjoy this world without attachment so long as you understand that everything in it is pervaded by the lord.' (Thieme 1965: 89–90.)

5. *You must . . . live*: The accent in the Sanskrit shows that this is *jijīviṣa+it*, not the optative *jijīviṣet* (Thieme 1965: 92). 'One hundred years' represents the natural span of life.
6. *Sunless*: 'Sunless', reading *a-sūrya*, or 'Demonic', reading *asurya*, 'of the *asuras*'. The latter seems to me to be importing into this text later ideas about *asuras*: in the early Upaniṣads there seems no suggestion that they have a different kind of existence from the *devas*. For the verse, cf. BU IV.4.11.
7. *self-slayers*: *Ātma-han*, an enigmatic expression, since the *ātman* as the self of a being cannot be slain (CU VIII.1.5, Kaṭha II.18–19). Modern commentators have generally followed Śaṅkara (Gambhīrānanda 1957: 8–9) in taking it as equivalent to *ātma-jñāna-rahita*, 'devoid of knowledge of the self', though the strong words used would seem to suggest those who wilfully act against their own spiritual welfare and that of others, rather than the merely ignorant. Thieme (1965) takes the verse as an injunction against taking the life of any being, since each is 'pervaded by the lord'. Sharma and Young (1990) demonstrate that there was a long-lived tradition in which this verse was taken as an injunction against suicide – the more usual sense of *ātma-han*, *ātma-hatyā*.

   On this interpretation, v. 3 might well be intended as a prohibition of the practice of religious suicide by giving up food – a practice allowed under certain circumstances by, for example, the Jains. Verse 2 would then mean, 'You should live out your natural span, doing your work and taking food that has been willingly given to you. Do not fear that this will bring about bad results. Do not try to end your existence prematurely.' As Sharma and Young point out, this interpretation need not be opposed to either of the other readings. To the enlightened one who saw 'all beings in the self/ And the self in all beings' (v. 6), there would be no difference between harming another and harming oneself (or *the* self).
8. *the waters*: Or perhaps 'his works' (*apaḥ*).
9. *in the self (ātman)*: Either 'in himself' or 'in the [supreme] self' – I have tried to keep the ambiguity.
10. *Whoever . . . from it*: Cf. BU IV.4.15.
11. *the bright*: Or 'the seed' (*śukra*).
12. *They who . . . deeper*: = BU IV.4.10. This verse is clearly intended to shock the hearer into realization. The underlying sense is probably that 'ignorance' (ritual action without understanding) and 'knowledge' (understanding without action) are both

inadequate, but the latter is more dangerous because the one who relies on it is more likely to believe that it is sufficient in itself.

13. *non-becoming . . . becoming*: 'Becoming' (*sambhūti/sambhava*) and 'non-becoming'/'destruction' (*asambhūti/asambhava/vināśa*) suggest two opposed views of the nature of reality, rather like the two extremes of 'eternalism' and 'annihilationism' described in the Buddhist texts.
14. *vessel made of gold*: The sun, seen as a cover over the hole in the dome of the sky which is the way of escape from this world. Verses 15–17 are the prayer of a dying person, and are chanted at Hindu funerals. Verses 15–18 correspond to BU V.15.1–4.
15. *its dharma*: Here, its true nature or essence.
16. *Pūṣan . . . am he*: This verse is very elliptical. Perhaps the worshipper is imploring Pūṣan (identified with Ekarṣi, the One Seer; with Yama, god of death; and with Sūrya, the sun-god) to part his rays so that in dying he can pass through them to the truth, and then to close them up again behind him to protect the living. As he enters the light the worshipper becomes identified with Pūṣan.
17. *Remember the deed*: To ensure a safe passing he recalls the good actions he has done in his life.
18. *our crooked faults*: Olivelle (1996b: 251) has 'the sin that angers', taking *juhurāṇa* from the Vedic verb *hṛ-*, 'to be angry'. The verse = RV I.189.1.

BṚHADĀRAṆYAKA UPANIṢAD

The Bṛhadāraṇyaka Upaniṣad belongs to the White Yajurveda. As its name implies, it forms part of an Āraṇyaka or 'Forest Teaching', which is attached to the Śatapatha Brāhmaṇa. The books are called *adhyāyas* ('readings', or, originally, 'passages for recitation'), and the individual chapters *brāhmaṇas*, reflecting its origin.

This Upaniṣad is a vast collection of disparate material, ranging from ideas about the creation of the universe, the place of human beings within it, and their fate after death (e.g. I.2, I.4, VI.2), to spells for winning power, sex or children (VI.3–4). Best known are the sections recounting the teachings of the sage Vājasaneya Yājñavalkya: his grand debate with the scholars of the Kurus and Pañcālas (Book III), his discussions with King Janaka (IV. 3–4), and his discourse to his wife Maitreyī (II.4, IV.5). Here are formulated many of the ideas about the nature of self (*ātman*), bondage and liberation which form the basis of debate in later Indian religion.

The Bṛhadāraṇyaka Upaniṣad exists in two recensions, the Mādhyandina and the Kāṇva, which differ mainly in the numbering and arrangement of the chapters, with a few slight differences in wording (Olivelle 1996b: 309, n.2.2; 320, nn. 5.15 and 5.1; 325, n. 2.15–16). This translation follows the Kāṇva version.

BOOK I

1. *sacrificial horse*: The horse sacrifice, *aśvamedha*, was the most ambitious form of the *yajña*, or Vedic sacrifice, and the model for the other forms. It was the means by which a king established himself as a world-ruler. The consecrated horse was allowed to wander free for a year, attended by a guard of 300 warriors. Any ruler on to whose territory it wandered had to submit or fight. At the end of the year the horse was sacrificed with great ceremony, to ensure the prosperity and fertility of the kingdom. By the method of meditation described in this passage, 'one who knows this' can gain the great merit of the *aśvamedha* through internal contemplation.
2. *fire . . . men*: Agni Vaiśvānara, who embodies all the forms of fire, including the heat within living creatures. I have frequently had to choose whether to translate *agni* as 'fire' and *vāyu* as 'air' or 'wind', or to leave them as Agni and Vāyu, the names of important gods. (The scripts used to write Sanskrit do not make any distinction between capital and lower-case letters.) It should be remembered that the composers of the Upaniṣads would probably have intended us to understand *both* meanings *all* the time.
3. *middle-air*: *Antarikṣa*, the intermediate space between sky (*dyaus*) and earth (*pṛthivī*), with which it completes the three worlds: so translated to distinguish it from air (*vāyu*) and space (*ākāśa*).
4. *the directions*: The cardinal and intermediate points, vital for orientating oneself for ritual as well as everyday purposes. In reading ancient Indian texts, it should be borne in mind that in giving directions one is assumed to be facing due east, so that 'in front' can also mean 'due east', and 'on the right' also 'due south', etc.
5. *half-months*: The waxing and waning halves of the lunar month.
6. *constellations*: *Nakṣatra*, or lunar mansions: see Glossary.
7. *speech . . . voice*: Both translations of *vāc*.
8. *sacrificial vessel*: *Mahiman*, literally 'greatness', two bowls, one

of gold and one of silver, used to hold the Soma in the horse sacrifice.

9. *birthplace*: *Yoni*, literally 'womb'.
10. *Steed . . . Horse*: Different words for 'horse': *haya*, 'steed', 'racer'; *vājin*, 'warhorse', 'charger'; *arvan*, 'runner', 'courser'; *aśva*, 'horse' (the ordinary word).
11. *this*: All this, the usual Upaniṣadic terms for the universe as we know it.
12. *this . . . Death*: Death, *mṛtyu*, is here identified with Prajāpati, 'Lord of Offspring', the progenitor of the universe.
13. *Shining (arc-)*: *Arc-* means to shine or to praise.
14. *the waters*: *Āpaḥ*: see Glossary.
15. *water (ka)*: *Ka* can mean both 'water' and 'happiness'.
16. *arka*: *Arka*, 'shining', means both 'water' and – more commonly – 'the sun' and 'fire', specifically the sacred fire at the horse sacrifice.
17. *Why . . . arka*: *Tad arkasyārkatvam*, literally 'hence the waterness of water', a frequent type of usage in the Upaniṣads.
18. *brightness*: *Tejas*, light, heat, energy, the element of fire.
19. *one third . . . air*: The remaining third being fire.
20. *that one and that one*: South-east and north-east. The speaker points to them – reminding us that this was originally oral literature. Death seems already to be in a horse-like form: see below.
21. *that one and that one*: South-west and north-west.
22. *this*: Earth.
23. *Speech*: In Sanskrit grammar, *vāc*, 'speech', is feminine, and *mṛtyu*, 'death', is normally masculine, as it is here. However *aśanāyā*, 'hunger', with whom death is identified, is feminine, suggesting that he contained a female aspect even before Vāc appeared.
24. *the seed*: *Retas*, 'that which flows'. In ancient Indian physiology, both sexes were thought to produce their own kinds of seed (originating in the bone-marrow), which had to combine for conception to take place. Often in the Bṛhadāraṇyaka the word is used in a general way, to denote the power of procreation or, as here, the resulting embryo.
25. *sent it out*: *Sṛj-*, 'to emit', one of the normal Sanskrit verbs for the action of creation by a deity. The deity is seen as sending the universe out from his or her own being, or else as organizing it (*vi-dhā-*) from chaos – rarely, if ever, as making it from nothing.
26. *Bhāṇ*: Either a cry of terror or simply a baby's first cry: connected here with *bhaṇ-*, 'to speak'.

27. *the metres*: The metres of the Veda.
28. *raised heat*: Through ascetic practice (*tapas*).
29. *embodied*: *Ātmanvin*, 'possessing an *ātman*', here in the sense of 'body'. The Sanskrit has, 'that of his . . . it became a horse', the 'body' being understood.
30. *After a year . . . himself*: As the sacrificial horse is allowed to wander for a year.
31. *the animals*: The other sacrificial animals.
32. *The one who gives heat*: The sun.
33. *arka*: Here = the sacrificial fire.
34. *the worlds*: The three worlds – earth, middle-air and sky.
35. *He who . . . re-death*: 'who knows this' understood. Historically, re-death, *punarmṛtyu*, seems to appear before rebirth as the main reason for seeking freedom.
36. *sang . . . for itself*: Speech, as Udgātṛ priest, is chanting on behalf of its clients, the gods, who have commissioned the sacrifice: however, it also takes pleasure in its own activity. Perhaps it is that element of self-interest that enables the demons to corrupt it.
37. *breath (prāṇa)*: It is unclear here whether in-breath or out-breath is intended. It appears from v. 7, however, that the later rôle of *prāṇa* as the supreme breath is here taken by the breath-in-the-mouth (*āsanya prāṇa*).
38. *the eye*: As frequently in the Upaniṣads, 'the eye' represents the whole faculty of sight, not just the physical organ: and so with the other senses.
39. *himself*: Literally 'by (him)self' (*ātmanā*).
40. *adversary*: *Bhrātṛvya*, literally 'cousin' (son of one's father's brother): the hostile meaning no doubt developed because such a relative would have been a potential rival for the family inheritance – as in the Mahābhārata.
41. *good food*: *Annādya*, 'food which is fit to eat', 'suitable food': a stock expression in the early Upaniṣads. For the power of the skilled Udgātṛ to sing (*ā-gai-*) things into existence by his chanting, cf. CU I.2.13–14.
42. *he (ama)*: *Ama* seems to be an artificial word, created to provide etymologies like this. It may have been adduced from the pronoun stem *amu*, 'that', 'he' etc.
43. *attains union . . . with it*: *Aśnute sāmnaḥ sāyujyaṃ salokatāṃ*, literally 'attains co-yoked-ness, co-world-ness, of the Sāman'. *Sāyujya*, 'union', could mean either complete identification or simply close companionship.

44. *the King*: Soma.
45. *this man's*: Clearly he means himself. Oddly, however, the pronoun he uses, *tya*, normally refers to someone far away – 'yonder man'. Perhaps the Soma is playing tricks with his spatial awareness.
46. *tone (svara)*: The pitch accent necessary for proper chanting of the Vedas. In what follows, I have inserted 'good' and 'a priest' for clarity.
47. *one*: The patron of the sacrifice (*yajamāna*).
48. *it*: Probably the knowledge just imparted.
49. *he saw*: In this chapter, in which the *ātman* takes on the characteristics of a male creator-god, I have translated pronouns referring to it in the masculine gender. Where it has a more general and abstract sense, as in BU IV.3, I have treated it as neuter. In Sanskrit the word *ātman* remains masculine regardless of the sex of the person to which it refers: 'himself', 'herself', 'itself' etc.
50. *the name 'I'*: Apart from the etymologizing of *puruṣa* as 'before-burning' later in this verse, the pronoun *aham*, 'I', is apparently being connected with the verb *as-*, 'to be'.
51. *a companion*: Literally 'a second'.
52. *we two . . . portion*: *idam ardhabṛgalam iva sva[ḥ]*. Like Müller (1962) and Olivelle (1996b), I take *svaḥ* as the form of the verb 'to be', despite the syntactical oddity of a dual verb with the singular *ardhabṛgalam*: this I have assumed is because Yājñavalkya is thinking of himself and his wife individually: hence I have inserted 'each'. Others take *svaḥ* with *ātmā* understood: 'One's own [self, body] is like half a portion.' Or 'half a split pea', taking *ardha-bṛgala* as equivalent to *ardha-bidala* or *-vidala*.
53. *Then he . . . vagina (yoni)*: He blows up the flame with his (bearded) lips while rubbing with his hands. As well as the female sex-organ, *yoni* can mean the fire-hole in the Vedic fireplace.
54. *Brahmā*: We know that he is now Brahmā rather than *brahman* only because the adjective *martya*, 'mortal', later in the sentence, is in the masculine, not the neuter, gender.
55. *being mortal*: The idea that Brahmā, the Creator God, is mortal, and not even the highest of beings, may seem startling. However, in later Hinduism, Brahmā is said to be reborn at the beginning of every world cycle, from a lotus which emerges from the navel of Viṣṇu, in order to create the world. At the end, when the universe is destroyed, he vanishes back into the lotus, which is reabsorbed into Viṣṇu. The period of existence of a universe is a day of Viṣṇu; the period between universes his night, when he

sleeps on the serpent Ananta ('Endless') on the primal waters. The present passage seems to suggest that there is already a belief that the universe is cyclic, which is also perhaps a natural development of the growing belief in reincarnation.

56. *scorpion*: Uncertain. The word used is *viśvambhara*, 'all-bearer', in later usage often a name for Agni. If this is the sense here, then it means 'like fire [hidden] in the home of fire (i.e. wood)': a frequent simile. However, *viśvambhara* occurs also in the sense of 'scorpion' or some similar insect, and *kulāya* later in the sentence is normally the nest of a bird or animal.

57. *I have . . . too*: From RV IV.26.

58. *brahman*: *Brahman* is here being used specifically in its sense of 'priesthood', the essence of the Brāhmaṇa *varṇa* ('class'), alongside all its other connotations. This in turn becomes the source of the essences of the other three classes: the Kṣatriyas, warriors and rulers; the Vaiśyas (*viś*, 'the people'), farmers and merchants; and the Śūdras, artisans and labourers.

59. *He*: Although still referring to *brahman*, the pronoun has changed from neuter to masculine, perhaps through being equated with the Brāhmaṇa in the previous verse.

60. *dharma*: Here, specifically, justice.

61. *Brahman*: Or Brahmā.

62. *learns by heart*: Especially the Veda.

63. *his completeness is this*: I.e. his true completeness.

64. *fivefold*: The sacrificial animal, like the human being, is fivefold presumably because it has a head and four limbs, five breaths, five senses, and five organs of action. Humankind may perhaps also be fivefold because it consists of the four *varṇas* and the outcast group that falls outside them.

65. *mixed*: Pure and impure.

66. *huta . . . prahuta*: Two forms of offering to the gods, the first specifically the pouring of an offering into the fire, the latter a more general term for sacrifice.

67. *one . . . lesser sacrifice*: 'One should not be an *iṣṭi*-sacrificer (-*yājuka*).' *Iṣṭi* has two meanings, depending on whether it is derived from *yaj*-, 'to sacrifice', or *iṣ*-, 'to wish'. In the Vedic period the first meaning was uppermost, and *iṣṭi* meant an offering of fruit, butter etc. that did not include Soma or animal sacrifice. So *iṣṭi-yājuka* would imply 'one who offers a lesser sacrifice' (presumably less nourishing to the gods). Here, however, it may mean (instead or as well) 'one who sacrifices for a wish' (that is, for his own needs, rather than to support the gods).

68. *first . . . offering*: 'First' added for clarity.
69. *imagination*: *Saṃkalpa*.
70. *It may . . . may not*: Perhaps meaning that *vāc* ('speech', 'voice') includes both words, which describe objects, and other sounds – natural noises, instrumental music etc. – which do not.
71. *They two*: Which two? Hume (1995) and Radhakrishnan (1994) both say, 'fire and the sun'. These two entities, however, are both masculine: not an insuperable problem for Upaniṣadic mythology, but we would have expected an explanation. The answer, I think, is 'sky and the sun'. In the Veda, *div*, *dyaus*, 'sky', is generally a male deity, Dyauspitṛ, Father Sky, a recognizable Indo-European parallel to Zeus, Jupiter (*Dius-pater) and Tyr/Tiw. In classical Sanskrit, however, *dyaus* is feminine when it means 'sky', masculine only when it means 'day'. Even in the Ṛgveda, Dyāvā-Pṛthivī, 'sky and earth', can be two sisters, as well as husband and wife. This solution is satisfying because it means that in each instance the 'body' component is feminine (earth, sky, the waters), and the 'form of light' masculine (fire, sun, moon). It is supported by BU VI.4.22.
72. *the moon goes*: At this period in India, the moon was thought to be farther away than the sun. Both, of course, were believed to orbit the earth.
73. *of sixteen portions*: *Kalā*. The fifteen portions are those by which the moon appears to grow or decrease night by night on the way from new to full and back. The invisible sixteenth portion is incarnated in all living beings.
74. *new-moon night*: *Amāvāsya*, the night on which the moon is invisible – literally 'when it stays at home'.
75. *He has . . . wheel-rim*: Literally 'He has got away with the rim.' Olivelle (1996b: 20) takes this exclamation of relief as referring to a thief: 'He got away with just the wheel-plate.'
76. *through a son*: I.e. through begetting and handing on to a son, as described.
77. *a Brāhmaṇa*: I assume from context that a Brāhmaṇa is meant.
78. *called putra*: The author seems to be linking *putra*, 'son', with *pū-*, 'to purify', and *trai-*, 'to protect'.
79. *vows*: *Vrata*, voluntary observance undertaken for a specific end (*vṛ-*, 'to choose').
80. *middle breath*: *Madhyama prāṇa*, another variation on the theory of *prāṇa*.
81. *called 'breaths' after it*: The senses and other organs are often called *prāṇas* in the Bṛhadāraṇyaka.

82. *breathe out and breathe in*: This is clearly the meaning of *prāṇ-* and *apān-* here. Some form of meditation based on awareness of the breathing is clearly intended.
83. *with him*: With Vāyu, the wind-god, or with it, the breath. (In any case, they are being closely identified.) For the phrasing, cf. BU I.3.22 and note.

BOOK II

1. *I must . . . brahman*: Olivelle gives this as 'Let me tell you a formulation of truth (*brahman*).'
2. *a thousand cows*: 'Cows' are understood.
3. *A . . . Janaka*: Ajātaśatru is perhaps secretly thinking of the occasion in SBr XI.6.2 when Janaka defeats Yājñavalkya in debate. (David Melling, in conversation.)
4. *Soma*: 'Soma' is understood.
5. *unvanquished army*: Or 'unvanquished weapon'. *Vaikuṇṭha* (perhaps 'not blunted', 'undefeated'), here a title of Indra, later became a title of Viṣṇu, and then the name of Viṣṇu's heaven.
6. *the courageous*: *Viṣāsahi*, from the frequentative form of *vi-sah-*, 'to conquer' or 'to endure': 'much-conquering', or 'much-enduring'.
7. *What is like him*: I.e. sons.
8. *a companion*: *Dvitīya*, literally 'a second'.
9. *embodied*: *Ātmanvin*. The parallel passage at KauU IV.16 includes 'the person who is in the body (*śarīra*)'.
10. *as your student*: This phrase is understood.
11. *against the natural order*: *Pratiloma*, literally 'against the [body-] hair', i.e. stroking in the wrong direction, the usual term for actions that are felt to be in the opposite order to the natural one: often used, for example, of marriages in which the woman is of a higher class or caste than the man. Here a Brāhmaṇa, supposedly the very embodiment of *brahman*, is asking for teaching about it from a Kṣatriya. Actions done in the right order are *anuloma*, 'with the hair'.
12. *hitā*: 'causeway, dike', but with the double meaning of 'wholesome, good'. The existence of these channels was perhaps suggested by those observed in the lungs.
13. *citadel of the heart*: Speculative translation of *purītat*, some organ of the body in or near the heart. The word is obscure, but seems to suggest *pur* or *purī*, 'citadel'. Previous translators have 'pericardium' (the bag of fibrous tissues surrounding the heart),

but it seems more likely that some smaller, more subtle, organ than the heart is intended – perhaps the same one as the *hṛdayasya agra*, 'summit of the heart', mentioned in BU IV.4.2. The aorta would look like such a summit.

14. *this*: The body.
15. *this*: The head.
16. *The baby . . . rope*: Olivelle (1996b: 26) takes the baby (*śiśu*) as a young animal ('youngling') such as a foal, though the riddle would seem also to apply to a baby in the mother's womb, with the mother's breath as the post, the chorion and amnion as covering (see CU III, n. 37), and the umbilical cord as the rope.
17. *brahman*: Or Brahmā. Here the Seven Ṛṣis, named in v. 4, are related to the senses or 'breaths' within the head: see Mitchiner 1982: 283–7. The Seven Ṛṣis are also present in the sky, as the seven brightest stars of the Great Bear, which can also be seen as a vessel (cf. its American name, the Big Dipper), and perhaps also as an animal (the group of four stars) with a tethering rope (the three stars of the tail or handle). The verse is based on AV XIX.49.8.
18. *These two*: The ears.
19. *These two*: The eyes.
20. *These two*: The nostrils.
21. *Speech*: I.e. the mouth.
22. *the present and the beyond*: *sac ca tyac ca*, 'both that which is [*sat* = 'being'] and that yonder [*tyat*, demonstrative pronoun denoting an object at a distance]'.
23. *the one who gives heat*: The physical sun.
24. *the circle*: Of the sun.
25. *rain-mite*: *Indragopa*, a tiny mite (an arachnid, of the genus *Trombiidae*, not an insect or a beetle). It is noted for its brilliant velvety red colour, and for appearing in vast numbers at the start of the rains: see Lienhard 1978.
26. *White lotus*: *Puṇḍarīka*, the normal word for a lotus in the Upaniṣads. It generally refers to the white species – however, see CU I.6.7 and its n. 18.
27. *symbolic statement*: *Ādeśa*: cf. CU III, n. 6.
28. *This state*: The household stage of life. Yājñavalkya has two wives: Maitreyī and Kātyāyanī; see also BU IV.5.
29. *priesthood . . . over*: Olivelle (1996b: 29) takes this as a curse: 'May the priestly power forsake . . .' (taking the verb as an injunctive aorist). I take it as meaning that, if the person thinks of these

good things as other than the self, not only will he lose them, but he has never really had them.

30. *lute*: *Vīṇā*.
31. *consciousness*: *Saṃjñā*, here perhaps as the faculty which labels and distinguishes between objects.
32. *honey*: *Madhu*. This image suggests mutual dependence and nourishment, as between bees and honey.
33. *radiant, immortal person*: Literally the person made of brightness (*tejomaya*), made of immortality (*amṛtamaya*).
34. *in respect of oneself*: *Adhyātman*, 'on the level of the body, senses etc.', as distinct from, for example, the level of gods and celestial powers.
35. *Twin heroes . . . honey*: = RV I.116.12.
36. *Aśvins . . . secret*: = RV I.117.22.
37. *magical powers*: *Māyā*, the power of making and shaping, especially of what others see, and hence of magical illusion (*mā-*, 'to measure', 'to shape'). The verse is RV VI.47.18.
38. *of the teaching . . . received it*: I have added 'of the teaching' and 'received it' for the sake of clarity.
39. *Pautimāṣya*: I.e. a different member of the Pautimāṣya family.
40. *Mṛtyu Prādhvaṃsana*: 'Death son of Destroyer'.
41. *Pradhvaṃsana*: 'Destroyer'.
42. *Ekarṣi*: 'The One Ṛsi'.
43. *Vipracitti*: 'Poet's Mind', 'Inspired Mind'. Generally the name of a demon (*asura*).
44. *Vyaṣṭi*: 'Individuality', as distinct from 'Samaṣṭi', 'Totality'.
45. *Sanāru . . . Sanātana . . . Sanaga*: 'Ancient', 'Eternal', and 'Goer of Old'.
46. *Parameṣṭhin*: 'Stander at the Highest'.

BOOK III

1. *for the priests*: *Dakṣiṇā*. The patron (*yajamāna*), who commissions the sacrifice, can be a 'twice-born' (initiated) man of any of the upper three classes – here the Kṣatriya king, Janaka.
2. *the truest Brāhmana*: *brahmiṣṭha*, literally '*brahman*-est'.
3. *called*: We know that Yājñavalkya is calling, perhaps from a distance, because instead of the expected form *sāmaśrava iti* we have *sāmaśravā3 iti*: i.e. instead of the final short vowel of the vocative we have one of triple length, longer than a long syllable.
4. *Hotṛ*: See *priests* in the Glossary.

5. *bright . . . fortnights*: The waxing and waning halves of the lunar month.
6. *graspers . . . over-graspers*: According to Olivelle (1996b: 309, n. 2.1), there is a pun here. In the ritual, the *graha*, grasper, is a cup used to draw out Soma and the *atigraha*, or over-grasper, is an offering of extra cupfuls of Soma. In the body, the *graha* is a sense-organ and the *atigraha* the sense-object.
7. *He who knows this*: 'who knows this' understood.
8. *the god's*: The sun-god's.
9. *between*: Between ocean and sky.
10. *woven, as warp and weft*: *Otaṃ protaṃ ca*. Olivelle (1996b: 40) suggests, 'woven back and forth': i.e. the waters, for example, are woven by the shuttle going back and forth, forming the weft, and the air is the warp thread on which they are woven. In the traditional interpretation, which I have followed, the waters would be the warp and weft threads, and the air the loom itself.
11. *moments, hours*: *Nimeṣa* is properly [the duration of] the blink of an eye, *muhūrta* a period of forty-eight minutes.
12. *All this . . . Vasus*: Relating 'Vasus' to *vas*-, 'to dwell'?
13. *He who purifies*: Vāyu – wind, air.
14. *have the Brāhmaṇas . . . for them*: Literally 'have the Brāhmaṇas made you their remover of burning embers?' (*aṅgārāvakṣayaṇa*, perhaps = 'fire-tongs'). Yājñavalkya is trying to warn Śākalya not to overreach himself. Śākalya's name, Vidagdha, means both 'clever' and 'burnt-up'. A lengthened vowel at the end of the question suggests that Yājñavalkya has raised his voice, perhaps in exasperation.
15. *when . . . heart*: 'Baby' and 'father' added for clarity.
16. *the centre*: *Dhruvā diś*, literally 'the fixed direction'.
17. *the person . . . teaching*: *Aupaniṣada puruṣa*, 'the person of the Upaniṣad', who provides the hidden connection between the *puruṣas* described in vv. 10–17.
18. *Is reborn . . . died*: Taking it as *añjasā* + *apretyasaṃbhavaḥ*. This seems to fit the context better than *añjasā pretyasaṃbhavaḥ*, 'is reborn directly, when it has died'.

BOOK IV

1. *to give audience*: Added for clarity.
2. *to teach him*: Added for clarity, following Śaṅkara's interpretation of *yathā mātṛvān pitṛvān ācāryavān*, mother, father and teacher being in succession the main influences on a boy's life

(Mādhavānanda 1934: 399–400). Others take this passage as 'It is as [obvious as] if someone were to say that he had a mother . . .', which, however, seems a little forced.

3. *one-footed brahman*: *Brahman* understood, in the sense either of the reality to be understood or of a formulation of teaching.
4. *I give . . . elephant*: *Hasty-ṛṣabhaṃ sahasraṃ dadāmi* – 'I give a thousand [cows] possessing an elephant-bull.' Olivelle (1996b: 53) has 'with bulls and elephants', which I think is forcing the grammar somewhat, as well as raising the question of what Yājñavalkya, a priest, not a warrior or a courtier, was expected to do with the elephants.
5. *of being killed*: *Vadha*, 'killing' (specifically execution), in legal texts also covering other forms of corporal punishment. (From *vadh-*, 'to strike', 'to kill'.)
6. *Indha*: 'The Kindler'.
7. *Virāj*: 'The Queen'.
8. *the Videhas . . . at your service*: Countries such as Videha are at this date seen primarily in terms of their people: the Videhas; 'at your service' added for clarity.
9. *But once . . . boon*: 'Once' added for clarity. The reference is to an occasion mentioned in SBr XI.6.2.10, when, after the king had taught him about the symbolism of the Agnihotra, Yājñavalkya granted him this boon.
10. *dreaming sleep*: 'Dreaming' added for clarity.
11. *creates*: Emits them from himself (*sṛj-*), as a god does.
12. *the sleeping*: This is plural, probably referring to the *prāṇas* – senses and other bodily functions.
13. *the goose who flies alone*: *Eka-haṃsa*, 'the one goose', a sacred bird, whose symbolism comes from both its beauty and its long migratory flights. In ancient Indian literature *haṃsa* always means 'goose', never 'swan' or 'flamingo', as it is often translated. Specifically, *haṃsa* or *rājahaṃsa* is a mainly white form of the Indian goose (*Anser indicus*), while *kalahaṃsa* is the greylag goose (*Anser anser*): see Vogel 1962. In Celtic Christianity the wild goose is a symbol of the Holy Spirit (Revd Dr Tony Ellis, in conversation: for a contemporary example of its use in worship, see Bell and Maule 1989: 1).
14. *it*: I.e. the *puruṣa*.
15. *but they are wrong*: Added for clarity.
16. *for my liberation*: Olivelle (1996b: 60) takes this as 'for *your* liberation (i.e. from the boon – cf. Kaṭha n. 8)': hence 'you'll have to tell me more than that to get yourself released'.

17. *deep sleep*: *Suṣupta*, 'dreamless sleep', as distinct from *svapna*, 'dreaming sleep'.
18. *When*: In dream.
19. *a murderer*: *Bhrūṇaha*, said to be the killer either of an embryo or of a learned Brāhmaṇa – both being regarded as particularly heinous crimes.
20. *because it is imperishable*: Or 'because he is imperishable': literally 'because of imperishability' (*avināśitvāt*).
21. *of Brahmā*: Or 'of *brahman*'.
22. *pipal-berry*: The pipal or pippala tree is the sacred fig, *Ficus religiosa*.
23. *They say*: Of the dying man.
24. *former experience*: *Pūrvaprajñā*. Here *prajñā* seems to refer to that which the person has experienced through his senses, etc. during life: it is distinguished from his pure consciousness at the point of death (*vijñāna*) and from his knowledge or learning (*vidyā*) which is linked with his actions (particularly ritual ones), *karman*.
25. *a weaver*: As Olivelle points out (1996b: 318, n. 4.4), *peśaskārī* is a female weaver (masc. *peśaskāra*), not a goldsmith, as often previously translated. Pāli has *pesakāra*, 'weaver'.
26. *of Brahmā*: Or of *brahman*.
27. *so is what he gets back*: Or 'so is what he comes to resemble'.
28. *brahman*: Or 'Brahmā' (here and in the next line).
29. *They who . . . deeper*: = IU 9.
30. *Those worlds . . . departing*: Cf. IU 3.
31. *this . . . place*: The body, or the universe.
32. *the five . . . peoples*: Or perhaps 'Every one of the five peoples'.
33. *separating . . . together*: Or 'holding these worlds so that they do not split apart'.
34. *the hymn*: Apparently not from the Ṛgveda, though the word *ṛc* is used.
35. *a Brāhmaṇa*: Socially speaking, Janaka is a Kṣatriya, but in the spiritual sense he is a Brāhmaṇa, as one who knows *brahman*.
36. *Brahmā*: Or *brahman*.
37. *Kātyāyanī . . . in it*: Meaning not, I think, that Kātyāyanī knows only 'what all women know', but that she knows what every priest's wife knows: what food and robes her husband will need for each ritual, etc. Cf. BU II.4.
38. *consciousness*: *Saṃjñā*.
39. *this*: Masc., probably referring to the self.
40. *Now . . . Pautismāṣya*: Cf. BU II.6 and notes.

BOOK V

1. *Teach us, father*: In the Upaniṣads, young people address their parents as *bhavat* and *bhavatī*, which previous translators have rendered as 'sir' and 'madam'. In modern English this is far too chilly – though in the eighteenth century it would not have been. *Bhavat* and *bhavatī* are formal but friendly modes of address. Lacking a real English equivalent, I have simply translated them in this context as 'father' and 'mother', which seem to carry a similar degree of formality.
2. *You understood*: As Śaṅkara notes (Mādhavānanda 1934: 565–7), each class of beings hears the sound as the teaching that it most needs. The gods, who are inclined to be self-indulgent, hear it as self-control; human beings, who are inclined to be possessive, hear it as generosity; and the demons, who are inclined to be cruel, hear it as compassion. T. S. Eliot alludes to this passage in *The Waste Land*, Part V, 'What the Thunder Said'.
3. *hṛ-da-yam*: *Hṛdayam*, the nominative singular of *hṛdaya*, 'heart'.
4. *goes (i-)*: Several parts of the verb *i-*, 'to go', contain the sound *ya*, e.g. *yanti*, 'they go'.
5. *That is that*: I.e. our present reality, in this verse called *satya*, 'truth', is the same as the ultimate reality, *brahman*.
6. *wonder*: *Yakṣa*, a word later specialized to mean one of a class of nature-spirits, but in the Upaniṣads a more general term for a mysterious entity.
7. *sa-ti-yam*: *Satiam* in Vedic pronunciation.
8. *falsehood in the middle*: *Anṛta*, 'falsehood', 'wrong', is the opposite of *ṛta*, 'right order', 'the law', the Vedic equivalent of *dharma*. The reasoning here seems to be that 't' is the only sound common to *satya* and *anṛta*.
9. *depart*: I.e. die.
10. *BHŪḤ*: BHŪḤ, BHUVAḤ and SVAḤ are *vyāhṛti*, 'utterances', sacred words representing the different levels of the cosmos. BHŪḤ signifies earth, BHUVAḤ middle air (*antarikṣa*), and SVAḤ sky.
11. *supports (pratiṣṭhā)*: I.e. feet. From our point of view, the *puruṣa* is upside down. (From his, no doubt we are.) Cf. the upside-down tree in Kaṭha VI.1 and MaiU VI.4. For the importance of a firm basis or support, see Glossary under '*Prati-sthā-*'.
12. *SVĀHĀ . . . SVADHĀ*: *SVĀHĀ* and *VAṢAṬ* (roughly 'Hail!') are cries uttered at the moments of offering during sacrifices to

the gods. *HANTA* ('Come!' 'Look!' 'Hey!') prefaces remarks to fellow human beings. *SVADHĀ* ('Blessing!') is uttered during offerings to the ancestors.

13. *that which is in all men*: Agni Vaiśvānara.
14. *digested*: Literally 'cooked'.
15. *tabor*: *Lambara*, said to be a musical instrument, type unspecified. But if the word is onomatopoeic it must surely refer to some kind of drum.
16. *When one suffers . . . asceticism (tapas)*: This chapter suggests that the most unwelcome experiences can be used for spiritual training.
17. *Vi . . . knows this*: *Vi-ram-* means 'to cease', 'to abandon'. Perhaps Prātṛda's father means that by understanding *vi* and *ram* one attains the cessation of suffering.
18. *a hero*: A heroic son.
19. *eight syllables*: Pronouncing *dyauḥ* in the Vedic way as *di-auḥ*. For the Gāyatrī, see GM and notes. Most Sanskrit metres have four lines (or half-lines, as they are most commonly written) which are accordingly known as *pādas* or *padas*, 'feet' or 'quarters'.
20. *vyāna*: Pronounced as *viāna*.
21. *turīya*: Literally 'fourth', but a less usual term than *caturtha*, the ordinary word. Its meaning is specialized to denote the transcendent fourth outside any set of three – e.g. the state of mind that is other than waking, dream and dreamless sleep. Here it is the fourth 'foot' to complete the three 'feet' of the Gāyatrī that can be chanted and heard.
22. *the one who gives heat (tap-)*: The sun.
23. *darkness*: *Rajas*, a wide term that may mean 'cloud', 'dust', 'darkness', 'impurity', 'passion'.
24. *gayas*: *Gaya* in this sense seems to be a word invented to account for the etymology of *Gāyatrī*.
25. *Some . . . as an Anuṣṭubh*: There are several alternative Sāvitrīs (invocations of Savitṛ), including some in other metres. Anon. (1968: 436) considers the present passage to be a warning against teaching the student the version in *Anuṣṭubh* ('*śloka*') verse. The *Anuṣṭubh* that he quotes is RV V.82.1: for a translation, see CU V.2.7.
26. *One may pray*: Added for clarity. This verse contrasts strangely with the advice given in V.2.1–3, though it is of a piece with the somewhat competitive attitude to life found elsewhere in the Bṛhadāraṇyaka, and even more in the Vedas. It seems curious

that the desire to frustrate an enemy is put ahead even of the desire to do well oneself.

27. *an elephant, carrying*: Perhaps meaning that Buḍila Āśvatarāśvi is carrying knowledge as an elephant might carry goods – unable to use it himself; or that he is carrying an unnecessary burden of past wrong-doing.

28. *even if . . . much evil*: This seems to have been put in to explain the morally doubtful advice in the previous verse. The repeated *iva*, 'as it were', suggests that the author does not want us to take it too literally.

29. *The face . . . gold*: See IU 15–18 and notes.

BOOK VI

1. *finest*: *Vasiṣṭhā*, 'best', 'richest', in feminine gender, agreeing with *vāc* (speech).

2. *the eye . . . rough ground*: The eye rests equally comfortably on a smooth or a rough object.

3. *The one . . . attained in it*: Literally 'To the one who knows prosperity (*sampad*) comes (*sam-pad-*) whatever desire he desires. The ear is prosperity, for all the Vedas are attained (*abhi-sam-pad-*) in it.' The verb *sam-pad-*, 'to come to', 'to befall to', is used always of agreeable things. The noun *sampad*, 'prosperity', is derived from it.

4. *increases . . . animals*: Literally 'procreates by means of offspring and by means of [domestic] animals'.

5. *flying things*: *Pataṅga*, here of flying insects rather than birds, since the list is of creatures considered impure for human beings to eat. In the Bṛhadāraṇyaka, vegetarianism is not yet taken as the norm – see BU VI.4.18.

6. *being . . . entourage*: Literally 'having himself waited on'.

7. *called, 'Young man!'*: Here and in what follows in the Sanskrit the final syllables of each line of dialogue have been marked extra long, suggesting that the prince and the young man are calling to one another, in a kind of challenge, rather than speaking conversationally. I have here and there attempted to suggest this with the words 'he called'.

8. *father . . . mother*: Sky and earth.

9. *princeling*: *Rājanya-bandhu*, 'relative of royals', a pejorative term for a Kṣatriya. There is perhaps an unintended compliment here, since the Kṣatriya turns out to know more about *brahman* than the Brāhmaṇa youth.

10. *by announcing*: As he is of a higher class than his teacher he does not have to touch his feet.
11. *That world*: Sky.
12. *From that offering a person arises*: Which answers the question about the number of offerings that have to be made before the waters (which appears as rain in v. 10) take on a human voice, rise up, and speak.
13. *worship faith as truth*: Or 'truly worship faith'. Śraddhā may be regarded as a goddess: she is sometimes said to be the mother of Bṛhaspati (Mitchiner 1982: 244).
14. *the six months . . . northward*: Approximately 21 December to 21 June.
15. *of Brahmā*: Or 'of *brahman*'.
16. *the six months . . . southward*: Approximately 21 June to 21 December.
17. *King Soma*: Identified with the moon.
18. *sweeps . . . smears around*: Cleanses the site by sweeping it and smearing with cow-dung.
19. *stirred mixture*: *Mantha*, prepared as described in BU VI.3.13.
20. *you who cross our desires*: A goddess who is both Vidharaṇī, 'the Separator', and, when favourable, Saṃrādhanī, 'the Reconciler'.
21. *the finest*: Feminine, referring on to 'speech' in the following verse. The terminology is explained in BU VI.1.1–6.
22. *hiṅ*: The sound uttered at the beginning of the sacrifice by the Prastotṛ.
23. *recited*: By the Adhvaryu priest.
24. *recited back*: By the Agnīdhra priest.
25. *what burns . . . wet*: Lightning in the cloud?
26. *Āmaṃsy . . . mahi*: Obscure: possibly 'You think: think on your power.' The equivalent passage in CU has, '*Amo nāmāsy amā hi te sarvam idam*' – see CU V.2.6 and note.
27. *We . . . lovely*: This and what follows are three lines of the Gāyatrī, with the 'sweetness verses' and the ritual utterances between. Because of the differences in word-order between the languages, the English translation of the first two lines here does not exactly reproduce their content in the Sanskrit: see GM notes.
28. *Sweetly*: Sweet/sweetly, sweet-filled: *madhu*, *madhumat*, whose basic meaning is 'honey', 'honey-bearing' (as in BU II.5). The verses are found at RV I.90.6–8 and Vājasaneyī Saṃhitā 13.27–9.
29. *lord of the wood*: *Vanaspati*, 'forest tree'.
30. *the lineage*: Of the teaching, as in e.g. BU VI.5.

31. *Four things*: I.e. used in this sacrifice.
32. *rice . . . vetch*: This list is rather obscure, and almost certainly includes varieties that are no longer cultivated. *Aṇu* and *priyaṅgu* are both members of the millet (*Panicum*) family, hence 'millet' and 'panic seed' in the translation. *Māsura* and *khalva* are thought to be pulses, the former a variety of lentil, the latter an unknown species. Following Olivelle (1996b: 87), I have used 'peas' for the latter. *Khalakula* seems to be a member of the vetch family, leguminous plants that in ancient times were grown for food in various parts of the world.
33. *pressing-stone*: *Grāvan*: (a) the stone used to press the Soma; (b) the male sex-organ.
34. *poured*: Or emitted (*abhi-sṛj-*), used (a) of the Soma-offering; (b) of the sexual act; (c) of the cosmic act of creation. The creative act of Prajāpati is recounted here to provide a precedent for the rituals described in the rest of the chapter, which are concerned mainly with sex and childbirth.
35. *Vājapeya sacrifice*: 'Drink of strength', considered one of the most powerful forms of Soma sacrifice, offered only by Kṣatriyas aspiring to kingship or Brāhmaṇas seeking the highest status.
36. *merit*: *Sukṛta*, good action. This chapter seems to reflect the anxiety of men undertaking spiritual practice about losing their hoarded energy through sexual intercourse (which, for those living the household life, was also part of their duty to the ancestors). Later, followers of Tantra attempted to solve the problem through yogic techniques. The Bṛhadāraṇyaka, typically, attempts to solve it through knowledge.
37. *descendants of Brāhmaṇas*: Literally 'grandsons of Brāhmaṇas': men who are born into the Brāhmaṇa class, but do not have the knowledge that should go with it.
38. *If it . . . recite over it*: I have expanded this passage slightly, following Śaṅkara's commentary on these verses. Another interpretation is simply, 'If he should see himself in water, he should recite over it . . .' However, this seems an abrupt change of subject here. (Mādhavānanda (1934: 649) omits most of this passage from his translation.)
39. *when . . . dirty clothes*: At the end of the seclusion during menstruation – see v. 13. Śaṅkara takes this sentence as being part of what the man should say: 'She [my wife] is the beauty among women . . .' In what follows, I have inserted the words 'a man', 'a woman', 'the couple' where necessary for clarity. (Mādhavānanda (1934: 649) omits much of this.)

40. *strike*: Or touch (*upa-han-*, elsewhere used of ordinary or ritual physical contact, e.g. v. 13). It is not clear whether actual or symbolic violence is intended. Neither would seem to the modern mind to fit very easily with the reverence for the woman advocated e.g. in v. 2.
41. *You*: Addressed to Kāma, the god of love and desire.
42. *breathe out . . . in*: *Abhi-prāṇ-*, *apān-*, breathe out into her and then breathe back in?
43. *opposite . . . to normal*: *Pratiloma* – see BU II, n. 11.
44. *learned daughter*: Śaṅkara (Mādhavānanda 1934: 653) considers that the daughter's learning will be confined to the domestic area, disregarding the examples of Maitreyī and Gārgī Vācaknavī in this same Upaniṣad.
45. *meat from . . . a bull*: Modern editors, such as Panoli (1994–6, Vol. 4), are troubled by this recommendation to eat beef (as they seem not to be by the apparent encouragement of domestic violence in v. 7). Śaṅkara accepts and interprets the passage as it stands (Mādhavānanda 1934: 654). It is not clear whether beef-eating was regarded as generally acceptable at this time: the present passage is describing not an ordinary meal, but a piece of sympathetic magic to bring about the conception of a son who will be a 'bull among men'.
46. *sthālīpāka*: 'Cooking in a dish'. *Sthālī* is familiar in its Hindi form as the *thālī* tray of Indian cuisine.
47. *touch-offering*: *Upaghāta*, again from *upa-han-* (n. 41). The food is symbolically offered to the gods by touching the dish before the couple eat.
48. *Get up . . . husband*: Part of RV X.25.22, a verse of the wedding-hymn.
49. *I am . . . she*: *Ama*, *sā*, cf. I.3.22 and note, CU I.6 and notes.
50. *in the direction of the hair*: *Anuloma*: either in a literal sense or, perhaps, 'in the natural way'.
51. *mixed*: Mixed with yoghurt. In this and what follows, I have inserted words such as 'the son' where necessary for clarity.
52. *That breast . . . to suck*: Variation of RV I.164.49; 'my baby' added for clarity.
53. *Heroine*: Taking *vīre* as vocative feminine. It could be locative masculine: hence 'To a hero you have borne a hero.'
54. *heroes*: I.e. her husband and many sons.
55. *The son of Pautimāṣī*: This list differs widely from those in BU II.6 and IV.6. The names from 'son of Pautimāṣī (*pautimāṣī-putra*)' to 'the son of Prāśnī' (*prāśnī-putra*, near the end of v. 2) are

all metronymics. But Pautimāṣī's son and the Pautimāṣya of the other lists could well be the same person. The family name is unusual in itself; and in the Upaniṣads name-formation has not yet settled into the classical Sanskrit pattern of suffixing *-ya* for patronymics and *-eya* for metronymics (cf. *Āditya*, 'son of [goddess] Aditi', and *Āruṇeya*, 'son of [man] Āruṇi').

56. *who lived ... house*: As a student.
57. *as far as 'the son of Sāñjīvī'*: Whereas vv. 1–3 take the lineage back to Āditya, the sun-god, v. 4 takes it back to *brahman*, as in the other lineage chapters.
58. *us two*: Teacher and student.
59. *a hero's work*: *vīrya*, the heroism of studying to realize *brahman*. The invocation is found in TA 8.1.1 and 9.1.1.

CHĀNDOGYA UPANIṢAD

The Chāndogya Upaniṣad belongs to the Sāmaveda, and contains much technical information for the use of the Udgātṛ priests who are responsible for the Udgītha, or loud chanting of that Veda, at the sacrifice. *Chāndogya* means 'of the Chandogas' or chanters of the Vedic metres, from *chandas*, 'metre', + *gai-*, 'to sing'. Like the Bṛhadāraṇyaka, the Chāndogya is a great compilation of material of different kinds. It conveys much of its teaching through stories featuring such vivid characters as Satyakāma, Jabālā and Raikva. Book VI, in which Uddālaka Āruṇi teaches his son Svetaketu Āruṇeya about the nature of self, has been particularly influential in the development of Hindu thought.

BOOK [INVOCATION]

1. *of me*: And/or 'by me'. The invocation is found also at PG III.16.1.

BOOK I

1. *contemplate ... Udgītha*: *Upās-*, 'contemplate' or 'worship' something as a symbol of something else, as in BU II.1. There is a hint of a pun here, since *akṣara*, as well as 'syllable', can also mean 'imperishable' – cf. BU III.8.8–11.
2. *final essence*: *Rasatama*, literally 'essence-est'. 'Quintessence'

would have been appropriate but for its connotations of 'fifth', whereas this is the eighth in the sequence.

3. *threefold knowledge*: Ṛgveda, Yajurveda and Sāmaveda.
4. *one sounds . . . OṂ*: The ways of chanting that are appropriate to the three Vedas.
5. *When . . . overcome them*: An abbreviated retelling of BU I.3.
6. *What . . . not be seen*: Or the beautiful and the ugly. This version of the story seems not to differentiate between the two pairs (a) good and evil and (b) pleasant and unpleasant. Presumably, because consciousness is flawed, one can (a) do wrong and (b) experience what is unpleasant, (b) being the result of (a).
7. *With it*: With the breath in the mouth.
8. *the one who gives heat*: The sun.
9. *This one and that one*: The Udgītha and the sun.
10. *'svara' . . . 'pratyāsvara'*: *Svara* (1) from *svṛ-*, 'to sound' (or, in some senses, 'to shine'); *svara* (2) apparently a variant of *svar*, 'sky', sun' (as in the *vyāhṛti* SVAḤ); *pratyāsvara* from *prati-ā-svṛ-*, 'to shine (or sound) back towards'.
11. *between-breath . . . breathing in*: These must surely be the meanings of *prāṇa*, *apāna*, *vyāna* and their related verbs here.
12. *neither breathing out . . . in*: Each part of the *sāman* is sung in one breath.
13. *hymn-sequence*: *Stoma* (from *stu-*, 'praise'), a sequence of verses sung by the Udgātṛ and his assistants.
14. *whatever . . . while chanting*: As often in the Chāndogya, the end of a topic is marked by the repetition of the last few words.
15. *have many*: I.e. sons.
16. *This*: The earth.
17. *sā . . . ama*: For *sā* and *ama*, see BU I.3.22 and its n. 42. The comparisons here depend on the fact that a *sāman*, or verse of the Sāmaveda, is usually adapted from a *ṛc*, or verse of the Ṛgveda.
18. *monkey-face lotus*: *Kapyāsa puṇḍarīka*, a lotus resembling a monkey's face (*kapi+āsan*), or, according to Śaṅkara (who derives *āsa* from *ās-*, 'to sit': Gambhīrānanda 1983: 54), a monkey's behind. The resemblance is said to be one of colour, making this a reddish tawny lotus instead of a white one – the normal meaning if *puṇḍarīka*. Perhaps this is a folk name of some specific plant.
19. *Ud*: According to van Buitenen (1962: 57), the use of Ud as the name of a divine being in the sun is 'not just derived from the first syllable of *udgītha*, but also from a mystical interpretation of RV 1.50.10. "*úd vayáṃ támasas pári jyótis páśyanta uttarám/deváṃ devatrā sūryam aganma jyótir uttamám.*" "Looking high up

beyond darkness at the higher light we have gone to the sun, god among gods, the higher light."' The composer of the present passage takes Ud as a name, rather than as 'high up'. Van Buitenen quotes AA III.2.4, where the Ṛgvedic verse is interpreted in the same way.

20. *minstrels*: *Geṣṇa* would seem to mean 'one who desires to sing', a desiderative form of *gai-*, 'to sing', which fits the context here. Śaṅkara interprets it as 'finger-joints' (Gambhīrānanda 1983: 55).
21. *He rules . . . gods*: In the Sanskrit, *iti* at the end of this sentence suggests that it is a quotation.
22. *This one's . . . form*: 'This one', the person in the eye; 'that one', the person in the sun.
23. *What . . . back to*: Literally what is its *gati*, 'going', or ultimate destination (and hence its source, too).
24. *When . . . hailstones*: Literally when the Kurus were struck by hailstones (or possibly locusts – *maṭacī*). There was a famine, but no shortage of water – see v. 4.
25. *elephant-keeper's village*: *Ibhyagrāma*, said to be a village belonging to man who is rich enough to keep an elephant (*ibha*), though it is equally possible that Ibhya is the headman's name. In the following passage I have repeated the names of the speakers where the pronouns seemed ambiguous.
26. *If . . . up to me*: To save his life Uṣasti accepts the beans, despite the ritual impurity of eating *ucchiṣṭa*, leftovers (an instance of *āpad-dharma*); but since water is available elsewhere he does not feel able to accept that.
27. *praising-place*: The *āstāva*, where the Udgātṛ and his assistants, the Prastotṛ and Pratihartṛ, sit to chant the *sāman*.
28. *Prastotṛ . . . split apart*: The singing of the *sāman* is typically divided up as follows: the Prastāva, 'prelude', sung by the Prastotṛ; the Udgītha, sung by the Udgātṛ; the Pratihāra, 'response', sung by the Pratihartṛ; and the Nidhana, 'finale', sung by all three. The whole is preceded by the Hiṅkāra, 'humming'. The whole *sāman* corresponds to one or more stanzas of a hymn, adapted for chanting by the insertion of syllables called *stobhas*, and the sections sung by different priests often overlap, the Udgātṛ, for example, beginning the Udgītha before the Prastotṛ has finished the Prastāva. For details of *sāman*-chanting, with musical examples, see Staal 1983, especially W. Howard, 'The Music of Nambudiri Unexpressed Chant (Aniruktagāna)', in Vol. 2: 311–42.

29. *The patron of the sacrifice*: I.e. the king.
30. *all the priestly offices*: It seems that just the priestly offices of the Udgātṛ group are intended.
31. *the Udgītha of the dogs*: There seems no reason to assume that satire is intended, though perhaps some shock value is intended in placing the *sāman* in the mouths of animals regarded as unclean. Perhaps the implication is that the chanter should desire the higher benefits of the sacrifice as earnestly as the dogs desire food and drink.
32. *Just as . . . one another*: As the priests move around in a circle, each holding on to the robe of the one in front, each dog holds the tail of the one in front. The Bahiṣpavamāna ('externally purifying') is the ritual by which the priests purify the outside of the sacrificial area.
33. *OṂ . . . OṂ*: Many of the syllables are marked as extended to three beats to imitate the style of chanting.
34. *hāu . . . ī*: These are *stobhas*, ritual cries inserted into verses in *sāman*-chanting.

BOOK II

1. *sāman . . . (sāmnā)*: There is a play here on three different words *sāman*, which may or may not be related: (1) verse of the Sāma-veda; (2) prosperity; (3) kindness, diplomacy.
2. *The seasons . . . rich in seasons*: The seasons are made suitable (*kḷp-*, cf. CU VII, n. 17) for him, and he becomes *ṛtumat*, 'a possessor of seasons', rich in the good things that the seasons bring.
3. *sevenfold sāman in speech*: The sevenfold *sāman* separates the Hiṅkāra and the Ādi, 'beginning', and inserts the Upadrava, 'accessory part', sung by the Udgātṛ.
4. *huṃ . . . Nidhana*: *Huṃ* here may represent nasal sounds, or *stobhas* in general. The names of the other parts of the chant are associated with the prepositions of Sanskrit: *pra*, 'towards'; *ā*, 'all the way to/from'; *ud*, 'up'; *prati*, 'against' or 'across'; *upa*, 'up to'; *ni*, 'down'. Between them they seem to suggest most possible forms of action.
5. *Everyone thinks*: Added for clarity.
6. *Its form*: Added for clarity, here and in the rest of the chapter.
7. *The domestic animals . . . go 'hiṃ'*: The ritual sound *hiṃ*, pronounced *huṃ*, is said to resemble the lowing of a cow for her calf.
8. *before evening falls*: Literally 'before the latter part of the day

(*aparāhṇa*)', a period of time that in this context seems not to correspond precisely to either 'afternoon' or 'evening', but to include part of each.

9. *victory over the sun*: Or perhaps: 'the victory of the sun'.
10. *the sticks*: Added for clarity.
11. *invites a woman*: 'A woman' etc. added for clarity.
12. *Hair*: *Loman*, usually the hair of the body.
13. *shares . . . with the deities*: Cf. BU I.3.22 and its n. 43, BU I.5.23.
14. *vowels . . . Death*: The linguistic terms used are *svara*, vowels; *ūṣman*, the consonants ś, ṣ, s, ḥ (and ṃ), translated here as sibilants; and *sparśa*, normally the contact-consonants, k, kh, g . . . m, but here perhaps including also the semi-vowels.
15. *There are three . . . immortality*: On this passage, see Olivelle 1996b: 334–5, and his article (1966a). He considers that the one who rests in *brahman* is specifically 'the one who practises OṂ', which fits the context here, though in general I think he tries to narrow the meaning of *brahman* too much. 'Believes in' added for clarity, though it is warranted by the quotation-word *iti*.
16. *sounds*: Literally 'syllables' (*akṣara*).
17. *morning pressing*: The three Soma-pressings carried out in the course of the day are the *prātaḥsavana*, the morning pressing; the *mādhyandina savana*, the midday pressing; and the *tṛtīya savana*, the third (evening) pressing.
18. *morning recitation*: *Prātaranuvāka*, the recital of verses of invitation to the sacrifice at the beginning of the *prātaḥsavana*. In this chapter, terms such as 'the patron of the sacrifice' have been inserted for clarity.
19. *Open . . . ā*: These verses were chanted in the ornate *sāman* style, indicated in the Sanskrit by the marking of lengthened syllables (some as long as eighteen beats) and *stobhas* inserted between syllables, e.g. of 'kingship' here.
20. *element*: *Mātrā*, 'element' or 'most basic part', for example the smallest component of speech.

BOOK III

1. *horizontal cane*: The bamboo cane from which the honeycomb hangs.
2. *larvae*: *Putrāḥ*, literally 'sons', 'offspring'.
3. *honey-veins*: *Madhunāḍī*, often translated as 'honey-cells'. However, the passage evidently visualizes the honey not in static

containers, but in streams flowing outwards from a centre, just as light radiates from the sun.

4. *the nectar . . . nectar*: Literally 'those immortal [waters] are [its] waters'. Curiously, in English 'nectar' can mean either the drink of the gods (*amṛta*) or the juice of flowers (here called waters – *āpaḥ*). I hope that the resulting word-play, not in the original, may help to give a flavour of the many Sanskrit puns that have had to be left untranslated.
5. *good food*: *Annādya*: see BU I, n. 41. The bees are pictured as distilling the essence from the nectar by a process similar to either cooking or brooding.
6. *now*: Added for clarity.
7. *secret symbolic statements*: *Guhyāḥ . . . ādeśāḥ*. *Ādeśa* means a symbolic statement conveying an aspect of truth for meditation. Examples are *tajjalān* (see n. 18), and 'not this, not this' (*neti neti*) in BU II.3.6. See Ranade and Belvalkar 1927: 388–90.
8. *nectars*: Here 'nectar' translates *amṛta* – see n. 4. Chapters 6–10 refer back to chs. 1–5, so that the Vasus are feeding on the nectar distilled from the Ṛgveda, the Rudras on that from the Yajurveda, and so on.
9. *this form*: I.e. the red form of the sun.
10. *above . . . below*: I.e. in the zenith and in the nadir respectively.
11. *inner . . . brahman*: *Brahmopaniṣad.*
12. *to his offspring*: Or 'to creatures'.
13. *this whole earth*: 'Earth' implied by 'this' (f.).
14. *this is greater than that*: I.e. this knowledge is greater than any wealth. The expression each time ends with *iti*, suggesting that this is what is (or should be) in the teacher's mind when he makes this choice.
15. *all this . . . come to be*: *Idaṃ sarvaṃ bhūtaṃ yad idaṃ kiṃca*, literally 'all this [that has come into] being, whatever it is'. The universe seems to be pictured here as one great living thing (*bhūta*).
16. *so far . . . sky*: Based on RV X.90.3. For the feet of the Gāyatrī, see BU V.14.
17. *divine channels*: *Devasuṣi*, suggesting both 'channels of the gods' and 'channels which are gods'.
18. *Tajjalān*: *Tad+ja+la+an*, traditionally said to mean 'born from (*ja*), absorbed back into (*la*), and breathing (*an*) that (*tad*)'.
19. *intention*: *Kratu*, the will or intelligence that leads to action.
20. *of true resolve*: *Satyasaṃkalpa*, 'having a will (*saṃkalpa* – see CU VII.4.1 and note) which [invariably] comes true'.

21. *be changed into*: Or 'attain'.
22. *<name>*: The name of the son to be protected. The speaker prays that the four goddesses named in v. 2 will dote on and protect his child as they would their own.
23. *the morning pressing*: For the symbolism in this chapter see CU II.24 and notes.
24. *cause . . . to stay*: Or 'cause all this to shine'. Cf. BU III9.2–5 and note.
25. *Why do you*: Addressing the disease.
26. *When . . . initiation*: On the day of initiation (*dīkṣā*), the patron and his wife keep a strict fast.
27. *When . . . upasads*: On the days of the *upasads* (preparatory days – see Glossary), a small amount of fluid is allowed, but no food.
28. *hymns and recitations*: *Stutaśastras. Stuta* is the same as the *stoma*, sung by the Udgātṛ and his assistants. *Śastra*, 'praise', is recited by the Hotṛ and his assistants.
29. *gifts to the priests*: *Dakṣiṇā*.
30. *She will . . . sacrifice*: Or, 'He will beget!' 'He has begotten!', but also 'He will press [Soma]! He has pressed [Soma]!' ('Of the sacrifice' added for clarity.)
31. *bath at the end*: *Avabṛtha*, the bath taken by the patron and his wife to end the *yajña*.
32. *Kṛṣṇa son of Devakī*: This is perhaps the earliest mention of Kṛṣṇa in literature.
33. *the subtlest . . . breath*: *Prāṇasaṃśita*, from *sam-śo-*, 'to sharpen', so presumably the subtlest part of the breath. Each of these descriptions is in the neuter gender: 'You are [that which is] unperishing . . .'
34. *Yes . . . sky*: Some texts include only part of this verse (SV.I.1.10, a variant of RV VIII.6.30), 'Yes . . . Of the primal seed', and run it together with the following one: 'Yes, seeing above darkness the highest light/Of the primal seed/Seeing, each for himself, the highest . . .'
35. *Seeing . . . light*: VS XX.21, based on RV I.50.10.
36. *That was being*: Or perhaps, 'It became being', though the verb used is *āsīt*, not *abhavat*.
37. *chorion . . . amnion*: The chorion (*jarāyu*) and the amnion (*ulba*) are the outer and inner sacs surrounding an embryo. The authors primarily seem to have in mind a mammalian birth, though comparable organs are found in a bird's egg.
38. *amniotic fluid*: Literally 'the water of the bladder' (*udaka vāsteya*). The blood-vessels (*dhamani*) are presumably those which

pass through the chorion and placenta and nourish the embryo. This interpretation would fit the symbolism, since we would then have the rivers running from the mountains to the sea. These organs would have been known even in ancient times, since traces of them are found in the afterbirth.

BOOK IV

1. *great-grandson*: *Pautrāyaṇa*, son's son's son (of Janaśruta).
2. *geese*: *Haṃsa*: see BU IV, n. 13.
3. *Yoke-man*: *Sayugvat*, 'possessing a *sayuj* (or yoked pair of animals)' – often translated as 'the man with the cart'. Olivelle (1996b: 340, n. 1.3) translates this title as 'the gatherer', suggesting that it is 'probably a technical term of the dice game referring to the method of gathering up the winnings'. He seeks to link it with the doctrine of drawing together (*saṃvarga*, CU IV.3 and notes). The rules of the ancient Indian dice game are very obscure, but there seems no evidence that *sayugvat* was a dicing term, and we know, from v. 8, that Raikva owned (or at least lived under) a cart (*śakaṭa*).
4. *What . . . Yoke-man*: Or 'That man – how is he Raikva, the gatherer' – Olivelle 1996b: 128.
5. *Just . . . kṛta throw*: 'Throw' and 'of the dice' added for clarity, here and below. The *kṛta* throw seems to have scored ten, the sum of the scores of all the other throws. In any case, it was an unassailable throw: a player throwing *kṛta* won immediately, without further plays (Handelman and Shulman, 1997: 64).
6. *chamberlain*: *Kṣattṛ*. One of his functions is to sing the king's praises. He has paid Janaśruti some compliment, to which Janaśruti replies by quoting the words of the geese, in the hope that his chamberlain will be able to clear up the mystery.
7. *Brāhmaṇa*: Olivelle (1996b: 128) emends to *abrāhmaṇa*, 'non-Brāhmaṇa'. However, I feel that this loses the impact of the next sentence. The text (rather pointedly, perhaps) does not tell us how long it took for the chamberlain to find Raikva.
8. *He called . . . 'So what?'*: In the Sanskrit, *Are*, with its final syllable marked extra long to show that Raikva is shouting, seems to suggest indifference or contempt. Raikva is evidently a man of few social graces: cf. CU IV.2.3, 5, where he addresses the well-meaning king as 'Śūdra'.
9. *worship*: *Upās-*.
10. *at the king's behest*: I have taken *asmai*, 'for him', as meaning

'for the king', though some take it as 'for Raikva': 'where the king lived with Raikva [as his student]'. The place-name probably means 'Raikva's Parṇa (= *palāśa*, i.e. Butea Frondosa) Trees'.

11. *drawer-together*: *Saṃvarga*, 'that which consumes or absorbs (*sam-vṛj-*) all things': cf. KauU II.7 and notes.
12. *Ka*: Ka, 'Who?', as the name of a god has its origins in RV X.121, which has the refrain 'Who is the god whom we should worship with the oblation?' The answer given in that hymn is Prajāpati, who is identified with Hiraṇyagarbha, the golden embryo. As a result, Ka becomes a synonym for Prajāpati: see W. D. O'Flaherty 1981: 26–9.
13. *There are five . . . Virāj*: Referring to the groups of deities and of bodily functions mentioned in vv. 2–3. The *kṛta* throw is worth ten, and the metre Virāj ('Queen') has ten syllables per *pāda*.
14. *lineage*: *Gotra*. Satyakāma addresses his mother as *bhavatī*: cf. BU V, n. 1.
15. *You can say . . . Jābāla*: Jabālā wants the boy to give the impression that he is the son of a man called Jabāla, by forming a patronymic rather than a metronymic from her name. 'Satyakāma' means 'loving truth'.
16. *as my teacher*: Added for clarity.
17. *The bull called*: In this and the parallel passages, the last syllable of 'Satyakāma' is marked extra long to show that the speaker is calling to him. According to Śaṅkara (Gambhīrānanda 1983: 269–77), the four symbolic beings who teach Satyakāma represent four gods: apart from Agni himself, they are Vāyu (the bull), Sūrya (the goose) and Prāṇa (the cormorant).
18. *fraction*: *Kalā*, specifically a sixteenth: cf. BU I.5.14–15 and its n. 73.
19. *Shining*: Or Visible (*prakāśavat*).
20. *Madgu*: Previous translators of this passage have called it 'water-bird' and 'diver-bird', but references to it elsewhere all seem consistent with its being a cormorant (*Phalacrocorax carbo*), a familiar bird on the great rivers of India. For example in Mbh, the *madgu* is a water-bird listed with the duck, the goose and the crane (III.155.50); it follows the heron in a list of creatures not to be eaten by a Brāhmaṇa (XII.37.18); and it has a distinctive neck, since a being of demonic appearance is described as *madgugrīva*, '*madgu*-necked' (IX.44.70). According to a commentator on Manu quoted by the St Petersburg Dictionary, the *madgu* is so called because it dives (*ni-majj-*) and eats fish!
21. *Abiding*: *Āyatanavat*, 'possessing an abode'.

22. *has the best results*: *Sādhiṣṭhaṃ prāpati*: 'attains the best', assuming that *prāpati* is equivalent to *prāpnoti*, or 'causes [one] to attain the best' if it is an irregular form of *prāpayati*.
23. *return home*: I.e. at the end of their studies.
24. *Kha*: *Kha* is equivalent to *ākāśa*, 'space': cf. BU V.1. For Ka see n. 12. Here *ka*, like *kha*, is in the neuter gender: 'What?' rather than 'Who?'
25. *Earth . . . I am he*: In keeping with the usual way of working from coarser to more subtle aspects in teaching, 'Earth, fire, food, the sun' should probably be regarded as outer forms of the person seen in the sun, who is identified with the *ātman*: and similarly with the deities mentioned in chs. 12 and 13.
26. *where they go back to*: Their *gati*: see CU I, n. 23.
27. *but then . . . different*: 'Then' added for clarity.
28. *it goes . . . eyelids*: I.e. the ghee or water does not stick to the eye itself, let alone the person who is seen in it.
29. *they*: *Sic.* The subject of this chapter suddenly changes to the plural number.
30. *a person . . . not human*: *Puruṣo 'mānavaḥ*, 'a person who is not a descendant of Manu'.
31. *in the whirlpool of Manu*: *Mānavam āvartam*. It is interesting to compare this passage with BU VI.2.15–16: there are both similarities and differences.
32. *The one who purifies*: Air.
33. *morning recitation*: *Prātaranuvāka*, cf. CU II, n. 18.
34. *closing verse*: *Paridhānīyā* [*ṛc*].
35. *he extracted*: *Pra-vṛh-*: cf. Kaṭha II.13 and its n. 22.
36. *salt*: Said to mean borax. The idea seems to be that one uses a subtler form of any substance in order to mend it.
37. *to the north*: I.e. in an auspicious direction.
38. *the mare . . . Kurus*: It does not seem necessary, as Hume does (1995: 226), to emend *aśvā* ('mare') to *śvā* ('dog'), since the composer could well have been thinking of a mare protecting her foal. The Brahmā priest has to go wherever the sacrifice 'turns back' through error, and put it right.

BOOK V

1. *eldest and best*: For CU V.1.1–5 cf. BU VI.1–5. The Chāndogya version of the story is shortened and simplified, and the faculty of procreation is omitted from the group of *prāṇas*.
2. *finest*: Here, oddly, 'finest' (*vasiṣṭha*) is masculine, even though

referring to *vāc* (speech): similarly in CU V.1.13 and V.2.4, in both of which it is feminine in the corresponding BU passage.

3. *The one . . . divine and human*: 'To the one who knows prosperity (*sampad*) come (*sam-pad-*) his desires, both divine and human.' Cf. BU VI, n. 3.
4. *Now . . . the best*: Cf. BU VI.1.7–14.
5. *If one . . . sprout*: Cf. BU VI.3.7–12.
6. *Amo . . . idam*: Obscure: perhaps 'You are called he (*ama* – see BU I, n. 42): for all this is your she (taking *amā* as the feminine of *ama*)', or '. . . for all this is at home (*amā*) in you'. Cf. BU VI.3.5 and note.
7. *most sustaining for all*: *Sarvadhātama*, 'most all-refreshing', *sarva+dhe-* in the sense of 'suckle, nourish'. For the composer of the Upaniṣad, it may also have been associated with *dhā-*, hence, 'most all-upholding'. The English 'sustaining' seems to contain both ideas. The verse is RV V.82.1.
8. *might*: Added for clarity.
9. *sees a woman*: I.e. in a dream.
10. *Śvetaketu Āruṇeya . . . you*: Cf. BU VI.2.
11. *he cried*: In this question and the next two the last vowel is lengthened to three beats.
12. *a single one of them . . .* : Here Śvetaketu repeats the questions to his father.
13. *you . . . that*: Added for clarity.
14. *amnion*: *Ulba*, cf. CU III.19.2 and its n. 37.
15. *faith, asceticism*: *Śraddhā tapa iti*: ambiguous. 'What is called "faith" [or] "asceticism"' or 'What are called "faith" [and] "asceticism"'? The equivalent BU passage (VI.2.15–16) places asceticism with the *second* path.
16. *stored-up merit*: *Iṣṭāpūrta*, the merit accumulated (*pūrta*) through sacrifice (*iṣṭā*) and other virtuous acts, or perhaps 'sacrifice and accumulated [merit]'.
17. *They live . . . beans*: The grammar changes in CU V.10.5 from the plural, referring to the beings in the world of the ancestors, to the singular, referring to the natural phenomena into which they have turned, and back again in CU V.10.6, when the beings have again taken individual form.
18. *enters . . . bed*: With the guru's wife.
19. *the self of all men*: *Ātman vaiśvānara*, 'the *ātman* within all beings', a concept developed from that of *agni vaiśvānara*, 'the fire (of life) within all beings' (BU I.1.1 and its n. 2). Later, the term is specialized to refer to just one form of the *ātman* (e.g.

ManU 3) but here it seems to be used of the self in the widest sense.

20. *worship*: *Upās-*.
21. *Soma . . . again*: 'Soma' added for clarity.
22. *as identified with himself*: *Prādeśamātra abhivimāna*, with the individual parts (*prādeśa*) as the measure (*mātrā*), referring them individually back to himself (*abhi-vi-man-*). Olivelle (1996b: 146) takes *abhivimāna* as equivalent to *ativimāna*, 'When someone venerates this self . . . as measuring the size of a span and as beyond all measure'.
23. *the earth . . . feet*: Oddly, the pattern in which the identification is reiterated is changed here: we would have expected, 'His feet are "Support".'
24. *Wait around*: *Pari-upās-*: similarly all beings attend upon (*upās-*) the Agnihotra.

BOOK VI

1. *There once . . . Āruṇeya*: 'A boy' added for clarity.
2. *difference of shape . . . reality*: *Vikāra*, 'apparent difference or change of shape', is less real than the underlying reality (*satya*).
3. *In the beginning . . . produced*: Cf. CU III.10 and its n. 36; BU I.2.1.
4. *It created heat*: Throughout Books VI and VII, I have translated *tejas*, referring here to the fire element, as 'heat', rather than 'brightness', as elsewhere. I have kept the English word 'fire' for *agni*. The verb used of the act of creation is *sṛj-*, 'to emit' or 'to let go'.
5. *created differences . . . form*: *nāmarūpe vyākarot*: *vi-ā-kṛ-* encompasses both 'to make different' and 'to make manifest', since difference is characteristic of the realm of *saṃsāra*.
6. *each . . . threefold*: The repetition stresses that each individual one is in three parts. The red, white and black forms (CU VI.4.1) seem to foreshadow the three *guṇas* (*rajas*, *sattva* and *tamas*) of Sāṅkhya philosophy.
7. *consumed*: Literally 'eaten'.
8. *fractions*: *Kalā*, cf. CU IV, n. 18.
9. *'the leader of food' (aśanāyā = hunger)*: *Aśanāyā*, 'desire for food, hunger', is a derivative of *aśana*, 'food', from *aś-*, 'to eat'. The present passage links the second element with *nī-*, 'to lead'.
10. *'leader of water' (udanyā = thirst)*: Linking *udanyā*, 'desire for water, thirst', with *uda[ka]*, 'water', + *nī-*, 'to lead'.

11. *This subtle . . . self*: *Etadātmyaṃ idaṃ sarvaṃ*, 'all this [universe] is *etadātmya*, having this (*etad*, the subtle essence) as its *ātman*'.
12. *You are that*: *Tat tvam asi*, perhaps the most famous saying in the Upaniṣads. Olivelle (1996b: 349), following Brereton (1986), rejects this traditional interpretation, on the grounds that in Vedic grammar, 'the neuter pronoun *tat* ("that") cannot stand in apposition to a masculine pronoun (here *tvam*, "you") . . . Thus if the author had wanted to assert the identity between "that" and "you", he would have used the masculine of "that"; the phrase would then read *sa tvam asi*.' He therefore takes *tat* in an adverbial sense, referring back to what has gone before: 'And that's how you are, Śvetaketu.' I confess I am not convinced. The examples that Brereton gives are not entirely parallel. In any case, there are numerous places in the Upaniṣads where the authors have departed from the strict rules of grammatical gender to make a teaching point: there are several in the Chāndogya itself. In III.17.6, for example, we have a series of neuter adjectives agreeing with a *tvam* which appears to stand for the masculine *ātman*. The most obvious meaning of the words *sa tvam asi* would have been '*You* are', leaving the hearer to wonder '*What* am I?'
13. *reach my goal*: *Sam-pad-*, 'prosper, be successful'.
14. *makes himself false*: Because he is denying the truth. This passage embodies the belief in the 'act of truth', a formal statement of truth which has miraculous powers, on which the innocent suspect can draw.
15. *As he would not then be burnt . . .* : So the wise one is not injured by *karman*? By speaking truth he identifies himself with truth, which cannot be injured. Here mention of the subtle part (*aṇiman*) is omitted, but it is clearly being identified with the inner truth.

BOOK VII

1. *the fourth*: Here the Atharvaveda seems closer to being regarded as the official fourth Veda than it is in the BU (II.4.10, IV.5.11).
2. *the Veda of Vedas*: Grammar, without which the Vedas themselves cannot be understood.
3. *ancestral rites*: *Pitrya*, 'rites for the ancestors (*pitṛs*)'.
4. *arithmetic*: *Rāśi*, here probably in the sense of 'amounts', 'calculations'.
5. *portents*: *Daiva*, literally 'that which is of the gods', but generally in the sense of 'fate' or 'fortune'.
6. *treasure-finding*: *Nidhi*, 'that which is put away', 'treasure'.

7. *disputation*: *Vākovākya*, 'dialogue', apparently contracted from *vākopavākya*, 'speech and reply', no doubt implying skill in debates like this one.
8. *the single way*: *Ekāyana*, 'the one way [to live]', ethics.
9. *the knowledge of the gods*: *Devavidyā*, said to mean etymology, also essential for the understanding of the Vedas.
10. *the knowledge of priesthood*: *Brahmavidyā*: here in the sense of 'knowledge proper to Brāhmaṇas' rather than 'knowledge of the supreme reality'.
11. *the knowledge of ghosts*: Or perhaps 'knowledge of the elements', or 'knowledge of beings' (*bhūtavidyā*). However, exorcism seems an appropriate skill, not covered elsewhere in the list.
12. *the knowledge of royalty*: *Kṣatravidyā*, said to be a synonym for 'archery', though no doubt it could cover other forms of knowledge appropriate to Kṣatriyas. Perhaps placed here in the list (rather than where one would expect it, after *brahmavidyā*) because it rhymes with the following item.
13. *the knowledge of the constellations*: *Nakṣatravidyā*, 'the science of the lunar mansions', an early form of astrology.
14. *the knowledge . . . serpents*: *Sarpadevajanavidyā*. Or 'serpents and (other) divine people'. Gonda (1981: 13) notes that in Vedic literature *devajana* seems to be euphemistic – 'not infrequently found in passages that refer to serpents or serpent demons'. The *vidyā* is presumably power over such beings, and access to the knowledge that they possess.
15. *Worship*: *Upās-*.
16. *heat*: *Tejas*, see CU VI, n. 4.
17. *Will (saṃkalpa)*: The key words in this chapter are derived from the verb *kḷp-*, 'to shape [something] in accordance with . . .', 'to make suitable'. Will (*saṃkalpa*) is the faculty that shapes the intentions and fits them for action.
18. *Intelligence (citta)*: The key words here are derived from the verb *cit-*, 'to think of', 'to perceive'. *Citta* here is a more purposeful kind of mental activity than the *manas* referred to in CU VII.3.
19. *He is nobody*: *Nāyam asti*, 'He is not', or perhaps (with *vidvān* understood) 'He does not know.'
20. *Meditation*: *Dhyāna*, from *dhyai-*, 'to think', 'to contemplate', here as a spiritual practice bringing great karmic rewards.
21. *Understanding*: *Vijñāna*, 'knowledge' or 'understanding'.
22. *pay attention*: *Upa-sad-* generally means 'to serve', 'to attend upon', but here seems to be used in a wider sense.
23. *ten nights*: Fewer than the fifteen days suggested in CU VI.7.

24. *living things*: *Prāṇāḥ*, 'breaths', instead of the more usual *prāṇinaḥ*, '[beings] possessing breath': cf. the usage of *pāṇa* in the Pāli formula *pāṇātipātā veramaṇī*, 'to refrain from assault upon life (= living beings)'.
25. *greater*: *Bhūyas*, neuter, rather than the expected *bhūyān*, agreeing with *smaraḥ* (memory, masculine).
26. *You are killing . . . Brāhmaṇa*: Literally 'You are a patricide! You are a matricide! . . . You are a Brahmanicide!'
27. *speaks boldly*: Is *ativādin*, 'one who speaks beyond (*ati-vad-*) the normal limits' – a doubtful quality in one without knowledge, but proper in one with knowledge beyond the normal limits.
28. *action*: *Kṛti*, suggesting the process of acting, rather than *karman*.
29. *The seer*: *Paśya*, 'one who sees (*paś-*) things rightly'.
30. *The one . . . wiped away*: Both Nārada, to whom the teaching of Book VII is given, and future students of this Upaniṣad.
31. *Skanda*: Skanda, 'Leaper', here suggests one who leaps over to the 'farther shore of darkness'. He is later known as Kārttikeya, the general of the army of the gods.

BOOK VIII

1. *lotus-house*: *puṇḍarīka veśman*, 'a dwelling [which is] a [white] lotus', visualized as within the heart.
2. *If folk . . . would say*: A more obvious interpretation would be, 'If [folk] were to ask one . . . one should say.' However, the expression 'he said' (*uvāca*) in CU VIII.3.4 suggests that chs. 1–3 represent the teaching of some specific person, perhaps Sanatkumāra (as in Book VII), or Prajāpati (anticipating chs. 7–12 below).
3. *of true desire*: *Satyakāma*, here primarily meaning 'having desires which [invariably] come true', rather than 'desiring the truth', though of course it is the fact that it desires only truth that enables this to happen.
4. *of true resolve*: *Satyasaṃkalpa*, cf. CU III, n. 20.
5. *Just as here people . . . perish*: Ambiguous. Probably, 'Just as here people follow [a king] at [his] command, and so [as a reward] live in whatever place . . . they wish for, [there, people who have performed acts of merit in the hope of reward receive worlds as their reward. But,] just as here worlds won by action perish [e.g. when the king's favour is lost], there worlds won by merit perish [when the merit is used up].'
6. *If one . . . fathers*: 'When one knows the self and the true desires'

is to be understood. *Pitṛloka* seems not to have its usual meaning of 'world of the ancestors', since separate worlds of mothers, brothers etc. are mentioned below. Śaṅkara considers that fathers, mothers etc. from previous births appear to him as objects of enjoyment, a metaphorical understanding of *loka* (Gambhīrānanda 1983: 584–7).

7. *women*: Or 'wives'.
8. *there*: *Atra*, literally 'here', but referring to the self.
9. *go to it every day*: I.e. in deep sleep.
10. *The blissful one*: *Samprasāda*, 'complete peace', the self during deep sleep.
11. *sa-tī-yam*: Cf. BU V.5.1.
12. *a dam . . . not run together*: Cf. BU IV4.22 and note.
13. *studentship*: Or specifically 'celibacy' (*brahmacarya*).
14. *seeking (iṣṭvā)*: The participle *iṣṭvā* has the double meaning of 'having sacrificed', from *yaj-*, and 'having wished', from *iṣ-*.
15. *'a sequence of sacrifices' (sattrāyaṇa)*: 'A course (*ayana*) of long sacrifices' (*sattra*, a particularly long and elaborate form of Soma sacrifice).
16. *'silent practice' (mauna)*: The practice of the *muni* or silent sage: cf. BU III.5.
17. *'a period of fasting . . . (na naśyati)*: Pun on *an-āśaka* ('not eating') and *a-nāśaka* ('not destroying').
18. *the sky . . . here*: I.e. the world after earth and middle-air: or perhaps 'in the third sky (i.e. heaven) from here', visualizing a hierarchy of heavens. The names of the oceans Ara and Ṇya seem to have been invented for this passage, to give an esoteric etymology for *araṇya*, 'forest'. There is a hint of a further pun on *ārṇava*, 'ocean'.
19. *Airaṃmadīya*: 'Of refreshment and intoxication/bliss'.
20. *Somasavana*: 'Soma-pressing'.
21. *Aparājitā*: 'Unconquered'.
22. *Prabhu*: 'Lord'.
23. *channels of the heart . . . red*: Cf. BU IV.3.20 and IV.4.9.
24. *When . . . obstruction*: Cf. IU 15–16 and BU V.5, V.10.
25. *A hundred and one . . . departing*: Cf. Kaṭha VI.16.
26. *smart*: Literally 'well-adorned'. Presumably Indra and Virocana are to change from the simple robes of the *brahmacārin* to their normal kingly garb.
27. *have this . . . teaching*: *Etadupaniṣad*, 'having this as [their] Upaniṣad'.

28. *The self . . . here*: Virocana misunderstands the teaching, identifying the self with the body.
29. *alms*: Gifts got by begging.
30. *seems to be stripped*: Reading *vicchādayantīva*, 'they strip it as it were': var. *vicchāyayantīva*, 'they wound it as it were'.
31. *It merges and dissolves*: *Vināśam apīto bhavati*, 'it has merged into dissolution'. During dreamless sleep, though the self is not destroyed, the consciousness of it vanishes.
32. *the highest person*: *Uttama puruṣa*, above the *puruṣas* mentioned in the next verse: cf. BU III.9.26.
33. *the person of the eye*: *Cākṣuṣa puruṣa*.
34. *The nose*: *Ghrāṇa*, literally 'the [sense of] smell', here refers to the physical base of the sense.
35. *From . . . the dark*: This (deliberately) enigmatic saying perhaps means, 'From this world (dark because clouded by ignorance), I go to the many-coloured world of the gods: from there I go to the (dark because mysterious) world of *brahman*.'
36. *Rāhu's mouth*: Rāhu is an eclipse demon: cf. MaiU VII.6 and its n. 9.
37. *That which contains them*: *Te yadantarā*, 'that which they are inside of'.
38. *the Brāhmaṇas . . . people*: I.e. the three 'twice-born' classes, 'the people' (*viś*) representing the Vaiśyas.
39. *To the white . . . slimy*: *Śyetam adatkam adatkaṃ śyetaṃ lindu*. To old age, death, or rebirth in a new womb? The ambiguity is compounded by the fact that the repeated word *adatka*, normally taken as *a-dat-ka*, 'without teeth', may also have been understood as *adat-ka*, 'devouring', from *ad-*, 'to eat'.
40. *virtuous children*: *Dhārmika*. 'Children' added for clarity.
41. *at the due times*: E.g. at the sacrifice.

TAITTIRĪYA UPANIṢAD

The Taittirīya Upaniṣad belongs to the Black Yajurveda. Its three books are called Valli, or 'creeper': Śikṣāvalli (see n. 3), Brahmavalli – and Bhṛguvalli. They form books 7–9 of the Taittirīya Āraṇyaka, which is attached to the Taittirīya Brāhmaṇa of that Veda.

Some editions, such as that of Shastri (1970), include summaries of the contents at the end of each section. As these consist mainly of the first word or two of each verse in the Sanskrit, they are untranslatable, and I have omitted them.

1. *kind*: *Śam*, 'bringing health and well-being', cf. RV III.5 and note. The original begins each phrase with the word: *śaṃ no mitraḥ śaṃ varuṇaḥ* etc. The invocation is found at RV I.90.9, AV XIX9.6, 7.
2. *brahman*: Or possibly Brahmā. However '*brahman* manifest' below is certainly the neuter form. The first phrase occurs at AB VIII.9.5, but 'homage to you, Vāyu . . . *brahman* manifest' seems to be found only in the TA and TU.
3. *I will speak . . . truth*: Or 'I will speak of you as law: I will speak of you as truth.' Found at SG VI4.7 and MG I.4.4 as well as in TA and TU.
4. *May that . . . speaker*: Found at MG I.4.4 as well as in TA and TU.
5. *Pronunciation*: *Śikṣā*, the *vedāṅga* concerned with the pronunciation of the Vedas.
6. *Letter . . . sequence*: The aspects of pronunciation are *varṇa*, 'letter'; *svara*, 'tone', the pitch accent of Vedic Sanskrit; *mātrā*, 'length'; *bala*, 'strength', 'stress'; *sāman*, 'song', 'intonation'; *santāna*, 'continuity'.
7. *us two*: Teacher and student.
8. *Regarding . . . connector*: A distinctive feature of the style of the Taittirīya Upaniṣad is the frequency with which it breaks sentences between verses, perhaps reflecting the way in which it was meant to be chanted.
9. *She*: Śrī, as goddess of prosperity.
10. *soon*: Reading *'ciram* for *[a]ciram*. Reading *ciram* would mean 'for a long time'.
11. *prosperity, wool-clad*: *Śrī lomaśā*, 'prosperity in the form of wool [-bearing animals]'.
12. *come in peace*: *Śam* (see n. 1) *āyantu*, which rhymes with *pra māyantu* and *damāyantu* in the two preceding lines.
13. *Just as the months (while days grow old)*: Just as months [flow on], so that days (*ahar*) grow old (*jṛ-*) – *aharjaram*.
14. *Take refuge in me*: *Pra-pad-*, more often used of a worshipper or subject going to a deity or ruler than the other way round.
15. *utterances*: *Vyāhṛti* – see Glossary.
16. *MAHAḤ*: 'Greatness.'
17. *the two halves of the palate*: Literally 'the two palates' (*tāluke*).
18. *birthplace*: *Yoni*, the opening through which Indra (here = *ātman*) is born from this body into the next world.
19. *He exists . . . head*: Literally 'He exists where the end of the hair is, parting the two skulls of the head' – a reference to the fontanelle

or *brahmarandhra* – cf. AU III.12, 14, where again the self is identified with Indra.

20. *cuticle*: *Carman*, literally 'hide', the skin as the outer covering of the body as distinct from *tvac*, the skin as organ of touch.
21. *the words*: Spoken by the Adhvaryu.
22. *recitations*: *Śastra*, cf. CU III.17.3 and note. ŚOṂ is a *stobha*, or ritual sound inserted into chanting.
23. *response*: *Pratigara*, to the Hotṛ.
24. *sets it going*: *Prasauti*: var. *prastauti*, 'sings the Prastāva', which, however, is the job of the Prastotṛ, not the Brahmā.
25. *one*: The *yajamāna*.
26. *Satyavacas*: 'Of true speech'.
27. *Taponitya*: 'Constant in asceticism'.
28. *the racehorse*: *Vājin*, i.e. the sun.
29. *beneficial*: *Kuśala*, an almost untranslatable word covering 'good', 'healthy', 'wholesome' and 'skilful'.
30. *with largesse*: With *śrī*.
31. *restrained*: *Yukta*, from *yuj-*, 'to yoke'.
32. *dedicated*: *Āyukta*, perhaps 'appointed [to that office]'.
33. *us two*: Teacher and student. This is the same invocation as at the end of BU.
34. *in the secret ... heaven*: I.e. both within the heart and in the highest heavenly realm (*parame vyoman*, a Vedic form of the locative).
35. *the wise one*: *Vipaścit*: cf. Kaṭha II.18.
36. *self*: Here said to = body. But clearly the teacher is pointing to different parts of his body as he gives this teaching: I think that on the word *ātman* he points to his heart. The comparison is to a brick fire-altar, which is symbolically both a man and a bird. Cf. MaiU VI.33–4.
37. *the panacea*: *Sarvauṣadha*, 'the (herbal) medicine of all'.
38. *This ... that one*: *Tasya puruṣavidhatām anv ayaṃ puruṣavidhaḥ*: 'This person-shaped one is according to the person-shapedness of that one.' The being is conceived as a series of sheaths, each more subtle than the one outside it, but corresponding to it in form.
39. *It is ... previous one*: Each successive sheath is to the one before as the *ātman* is to the body.
40. *knowledge*: *Vijñāna*.
41. *Folk ... as being*: Presumably one becomes 'somebody' rather than 'nobody' in society.

42. *If . . . win it*: Each question ends with an extended vowel, suggesting that it is chanted.
43. *the present and the beyond*: *Sac ca tyac ca*, cf. BU II.3.1 and note.
44. *From not-being . . . born*: Cf. CU III.19.1 and, apparently disagreeing with it, CU VI.2.1–2.
45. *Well done*: Cf. AU II.3.
46. *breathe . . . draw breath*: The two verbs are *an-* and *prāṇ-*.
47. *of one . . . knower*: Reading *viduṣo manyamānasya*. Śaṅkara reads *viduṣo 'manyamānasya*, 'of one who knows but does not think' (Gambhīrānanda 1957: 346). The state of completeness and fullness must be that described in BU IV3.23–31. When a sense of duality arises, fear can creep in.
48. *From this . . . run on*: Similar to Kaṭha VI.3.
49. *That is one human joy*: Cf. BU IV.3.33.
50. *The one . . . nothing*: A variation on the verse in TU II.4.
51. *HARI OṂ*: It is unclear why, uniquely in the Principal Upaniṣads, HARI OṂ is used here in preference to OṂ. Later, Hari becomes a well-known name for Viṣṇu, and Kṛṣṇa as his incarnation: here it seems to be simply a *stobha* (cf. n. 22).
52. *stands . . . heaven*: *Parame vyoman*, cf. n. 33.
53. *The one who . . . fame*: For phraseology, cf. CU II.8–12.
54. *get food . . . possible*: To give to any guest (or beggar) who may need it.
55. *This food . . . first*: 'For another' added for clarity. The sense seems to be that in as much as anyone has food prepared for the other person, he himself will receive food.
56. *'getting and enjoying'*: *Yogakṣema*: see also Kaṭha II.2 and note.
57. *dying-around*: *Parimara*, cf. KauU II.12.
58. *adversaries*: *Bhrātṛvya*, cf. BU I.3.7 and its n. 40.
59. *Oh, bliss . . . bliss . . .* : *Hāvu, hāvu, hāvu*, said to be an exclamation of joy. The *hā*, like many other syllables in the passage, is marked extra long, to show that it is chanted like a *sāman*.
60. *universe*: Or 'world' (*bhuvana*).
61. *sun*: Or 'sky'. (*Suvar* as in the *vyāhṛti*.)

AITAREYA UPANIṢAD

The Aitareya Upaniṣad belongs to the Ṛgveda. It forms part of the Aitareya Āraṇyaka, named after the teacher Mahidāsa Aitareya.

1. *Be . . . for the Veda*: I.e. to prevent my knowledge of it from being lost. 'My speech . . . for the Veda' = MG IV.4.8.

2. *I hold . . . together*: *Saṃvasāmi* here seems to be used in a causative sense: 'I cause to stay together.'
3. *I will speak . . . truth*: Cf. the invocation to TU.
4. *In the beginning . . . blinking*: Cf. BU I.2. This primal *ātman* appears to be identified with Prajāpati.
5. *heavenly water*: *Ambhas*, the water above the sky.
6. *a man*: *Puruṣa*. This translation seemed more appropriate in this context, as here the person is visualized in specifically masculine form.
7. *He heated him up*: Cf. CU II.23.2. The process is like that of a bird brooding its egg.
8. *like an egg*: *Yathāṇḍam*. We would perhaps have expected *yathāṇḍasya*, 'as on an egg', since the *puruṣa* apparently corresponds to the egg, the sense-organs to cracks appearing in the shell, and the senses themselves to the chicks.
9. *sight*: Here *cakṣus*, 'eye', is used for the sense of sight as distinct from *akṣan*, the physical eye: similarly with *śrotra* and *karṇa* for the sense of hearing and the physical ear.
10. *flew down . . . ocean*: Or perhaps 'plunged down into'. The verb *pra-pat-* can refer either to flying or to falling. However, the passage seems to be carrying on the bird simile implicit in Book I. The deities – the natural phenomena that are the external correspondences of the senses – have hatched out and flown to the great ocean (*saṃsāra?*), looking for land to settle on. Until that has been found (in v. 3), they have to float on the water.
11. *The self . . . thirst*: 'Self' and 'the man' added for clarity. It appears that it is the introduction of hunger and thirst (desire in its most elemental form) into the *puruṣa* that makes it into a potential dwelling-place for the deities.
12. *well done*: *Sukṛtam* (neuter).
13. *tried to escape behind him*: *Aty-ajighāṃsat*, an otherwise unknown form, thought to be an irregular desiderative from *ati-hā-*, 'to escape'.
14. *now*: *Atra*, here and now in this world.
15. *lower breath*: *Apāna*, as the force of digestion, which also carries away the body's waste products: presumably why it was the only one with which the *puruṣa* could seize the primal food while it was behind him.
16. *If . . . by speech*: *Yadi vācābhivyāhṛtam*, literally 'if it has been uttered by speech', etc.
17. *down-breathing*: *Abhyapānitam*, 'it has been breathed down over', perhaps implying the process of digestion.

18. *the parting*: Of the skull.
19. *three kinds of sleep*: Literally 'three sleeps'.
20. *this state . . . this state*: Waking, dreaming sleep and dreamless sleep? Or the latter two plus the 'fourth state'?
21. *What . . . another*: *Kim ihānyaṃ vāvadiṣad iti. Vāvadiṣat* is another of the Aitareya's peculiar verb forms: it seems to be a combined intensive and desiderative of *vad-*, 'to speak'. Hume (1995: 297–8, n. 5) offers a number of suggestions, favouring, 'Of what here would one desire to speak as another?' He seems to have overlooked the fact that *vad-* can take the accusative of the person addressed, as well as of the subject discussed, and that whatever type of secondary verb it is is in the imperfect tense: 'he/she/it has wished [with consequences that still exist] to speak repeatedly to . . .' I believe that this passage is a counterpart to that in BU I.2.4–5 and I.4.2–3, in which the lonely *ātman/puruṣa*, desiring a companion, creates another self. Here the other, finding itself created, wonders, 'What was it that wanted someone else to talk to, and so created me?' He gets his answer when he sees the *brahman*, a neuter entity, so answering Hume's objection to a neuter subject and a masculine object.
22. *He cried*: The final vowel is lengthened, suggesting that the *puruṣa* is crying out, in pleasure or surprise.
23. *Though . . . the mysterious*: Cf. BU IV.2.2.
24. *He . . . departs*: The son takes the ageing father's place in sacrifices etc., and the father dies.
25. *While . . . with speed*: = RV IV.27.1.
26. *consciousness . . . knowledge*: It is not clear how far the author is being systematic about the different kinds of mental activity listed. The first four are all forms of the verb *jñā-*, 'to know', modified by different prefixes: *saṃjñāna*, translated as 'consciousness', is 'knowing-together', often used of the naming faculty of mind; *ājñāna*, 'perception', is 'knowing-up-to', often used of the recognizing faculty; *vijñāna*, 'discrimination', is 'knowing-in-different-directions', knowing things apart; *prajñāna*, 'knowledge', is 'knowing-towards', often used of wisdom or knowledge in general.
27. *intelligence*: *Medhas* (var. *medhā*), whose underlying meaning seems to be one of 'strength', hence mental power.
28. *vision . . . thought*: These three are all abstract nouns expressing the action of verbs: *dṛṣṭi*, from *dṛś-*, 'to see'; *dhṛti*, from *dhṛ-*, 'to bear'; and *mati*, from *man-*, 'to think'.
29. *consideration*: *Manīṣā*, also from *man-*.

30. *swiftness*: *Jūti*, from *jū-*, 'to hurry'.
31. *memory*: *Smṛti*, from *smṛ-*, 'to remember'.
32. *resolve . . . will*: The list concludes mainly with aspects of will: *saṃkalpa*, 'resolve', CU VII.4.1 and note; *kratu*, 'intention', often that which desires to perform sacrifice; *kāma*, 'desire'; and *vaśa*, 'mastery, control over others'. 'Life', the odd one out in this list, is *asu*, cf. BU II.1.10.
33. *elements*: *Mahābhūta*, perhaps the gross elements of Sāṅkhya.
34. *finely mixed*: *Kṣudramiśra*, 'mixed with the small': perhaps = the *tanmātra* or subtle elements.
35. *the sweat-born*: Insects.
36. *is led by knowledge*: Or perhaps 'having knowledge as eye' (*prajñānetra*). In this passage, *prajñā* and *prajñāna* seem to be used interchangeably.
37. *wise*: *Prajña*.
38. *he*: Vāmadeva.

KAUṢĪTAKĪ UPANIṢAD

The Kauṣītakī Upaniṣad belongs to the Ṛgveda, and forms Books III–VI of the Kauṣītaki or Śāṅkhāyana Āraṇyaka of the Kauṣītaki (Śāṅkhāyana) Brāhmaṇa. It has two main recensions: A, originally published in the Ānandāśrama Sanskrit Series, and B, published in the Bibliotheca Indica series. Except where otherwise stated, I have followed B in the main translation, and have given the A readings in the notes. I have not noted small differences which do not affect the meaning. Where verse numberings differ, as in Book II.4 – end, I have followed B.

BOOK [INVOCATION]

1. *My speech . . . speech*: MG 4.4.8: cf. invocation for AU. The invocation for the Kauṣītakī Upaniṣad has been put together from a number of sources, some of them apparently garbled. I am very grateful to Dr John D. Smith for helping me to unravel it.
2. *May you . . . youth*: *Āvir āvir maryo 'bhūr*, 'May you become (or, you have become) visible, visible as a (young) mortal man': cf. SV I.435 (= I.1.5.9), *āvir maryā ā vājaṃ vājine agmaṃ savituḥ savaṃ*, thought to mean 'Openly mortals bringing booty have come to Savitṛ's pressing.'
3. *By knowledge . . . place*: Reminiscent of MG IV.4.8.

4. *With this . . . together*: Cf. AU invocation.
5. *Homage to Agni . . . from your sight*: This comes from AG VIII.14.18, *bhūmim upaspṛśed agna iḍā nama iḍā . . . mā te vyoma saṃdṛśi*. In *agna iḷā/iḍā* there is probably a reference to RV III.24.2, *agna iḷā sam idhyase vītihotro amartyaḥ; juṣasva sū no adhvaram*, 'O Agni, you are kindled with the libation, immortal Vītihotra; be well pleased with our sacrifice!' For 'Gracious lady (*śivā*), be most healing to us, compassionate Sarasvatī' I have followed AG: it has vocatives, which make better grammatical sense than the nominatives of the Kauṣītakī text. 'Let us not be separated from your sight' takes *vyoma* (pronounced in Vedic as *vioma*) as a form of *vi-yu-*, 'to separate'.
6. *Unerring mind . . . harm*: SG VI4.1.

BOOK I

1. *Gāṅgyāyani*: Var. Gārgyāyani. 'As priest' added for clarity at the end of the sentence.
2. *When . . . arrived*: A has, 'As he sat there'.
3. *Son . . . is there*: A. B has, 'You are the son of Gautama. Is there . . .'
4. *is there . . . in a world*: This passage is deliberately riddling and obscure. The closed place (*saṃvṛta*) is ambiguous: is it a barrier which will prevent the patron of the sacrifice from going further, so that he has to come back, or one which will prevent him from having to come back? In either case, the reference is to the two paths to the other world – cf. BU VI.2 and CU V.3.
5. *as a student*: Phrase added for clarity.
6. *with its latter . . . again*: Reading *aparapakṣeṇa prajanayati*. Var. *aparapakṣe na prajanayati*, 'in the latter half it does not give birth to them'.
7. *a worm . . . a person*: A has the creatures in a different order, and omits the boar.
8. *From the shining . . . realm*: The shining (or 'wise' – *vicakṣaṇa*) and fifteenfold is the moon, where the ancestors live. (For its fifteen parts, see BU I.5.14–15 and its n. 73.)
9. *being reborn*: *Upajāyamāna*, used in this sense in Mbh and BhG (Hume 1995: 303) – or perhaps just an emphatic way of repeating the idea 'born'.
10. *as the twelfth . . . father*: The speaker is identifying himself with the year, which contains twelve or thirteen lunar months. His father is presumably the sun.

11. *I know that . . . that*: *Tad vide prati tad vide*, perhaps 'I know the way that leads to the gods: I know the other way, too.' Alternatively, *prati tad vide* may simply mean 'I know it very well' (cf. the English colloquialism 'I know it backwards').
12. *Seasons . . . immortality*: Taking it as the imperfect tense. It could be imperative: 'Seasons, bring me to immortality!'
13. *to Vāyu's world*: A follows this with 'to Āditya's [the Sun's] world'.
14. *to Brahmā's world*: Or to '*brahman*'s world'. Almost all the references in Book I could bear either translation: the only instances where the form of the word is quite unambiguous are *brahmaivābhipraiti*, 'approaches *brahman*' (I.4. twice), and *tam brahmā pṛcchati*, 'Brahmā asks him' (I.5).
15. *the lake, Āra*: Cf. CU VIII.5.3, where the ocean is called Ara.
16. *watchmen, the Muhūrtas*: Following Olivelle (1996b: 203), who is presumably emending the word *yeṣṭiha*, which is otherwise unknown, to **yaṣṭiha*, 'one who strikes with a stick', hence 'watchman'. The traditional interpretation of this obscure passage is that the world of Brahmā has moments (*muhūrta*) called Yeṣṭiha, speculatively translated as 'swift-moving' (cf. Vedic *yeṣṭha*). This item would then be in reverse order from the rest of the list, where the feature of the Brahmā-world comes *after* its name. *Muhūrta* is either a moment or a period of forty-eight minutes (cf. BU III, n. 11).
17. *Vijarā*: 'Free from old age'.
18. *Ilya*: 'Of refreshment' (*ilā*).
19. *Sālajya*: Obscure: perhaps a variant of some compound of *śālajya*, 'having a sāl tree as bowstring'.
20. *Aparājita*: 'Unconquered'.
21. *Vibhu*: 'Extensive', 'pervading'. In CU VIII.5.3 it is called Prabhu.
22. *Vicakṣaṇā*: 'Shining': cf. n. 14.
23. *Amitaujas*: 'Of unlimited power'.
24. *Mānasī . . . worlds*: The names of these two nymphs mean 'of mind' and 'of the eye'. I take *jagatī* ('the two [moving] worlds', i.e. heaven and earth) with them, since mind and eye can fairly be said to weave the world as we experience it. Olivelle (1996b: 204) takes Jagatī with what follows, as the title of Ambā and Ambālī (for *ambayāvī*).
25. *Ambās . . . Ambāyavīs*: 'Mothers and (?) nurses': *ambāyavī* is clearly a derivative of *ambā*, 'mother' (often as a general term of affection and respect).

26. *Ambayā*: 'Ladies (?)': another derivative of *ambā*.
27. *Brahmā*: See n. 14.
28. *they run away from him*: As time no longer affects him. See Kau UI, n. 16.
29. *by awareness one discerns*: In this Upaniṣad *prajñā* is used in a broader sense than the usual 'wisdom' or 'knowledge', so I have translated it as 'awareness' and the verb *pra-jñā-* as 'to be aware'. It is the quality by which one *vipaśyati*, 'discerns', 'has insight'.
30. *Soma-stems*: Or 'moon-beams' (*somāṃśu*).
31. *sets . . . on it*: Literally 'mounts it with just one foot'. He has to pass a further test before he can sit down on it.
32. *seed for a wife*: *Bhāryāyai retas*. A has *bhāyā[ḥ] etad*: 'this [which is] of light'.
33. *made of brahman*: See Kau U I, n. 14.
34. *By what my neuter names*: A changes the order of the feminine and neuter names.
35. *By the breath*: *Prāṇa* appears here the second time as the physical organ of smell.
36. *Brahmā . . . The waters*: Brahmā added for clarity. Hume (1995: 307, n. 2) plausibly suggests that there is a play here on *āpaḥ*, 'the waters', and *āp-*, 'to attain'.

BOOK II

1. *Mind . . . its maid*: A has the servants in a different order.
2. *a messenger*: Or 'messengers'. This paragraph not in A.
3. *dharma . . . not ask*: *Dharma* presumably in the sense of what naturally happens to such a person, as well as of the right way for him to behave. A has, 'of the one who asks'.
4. *at . . . junctures*: This phrase not in A.
5. *strews, and sprinkles*: Grass and water respectively. A adds, 'and purifies'.
6. *with the spoon*: A adds, 'or with a bowl or with a metal cup'.
7. *longing . . . gods*: *Daiva smara* – desire (*smara* = *kāma*) as connected with the *devas* of the bodily functions.
8. *makes offerings . . . butter*: A has, 'builds a fire and makes offerings . . .'
9. *constantly*: A adds, 'unceasingly'.
10. *The Uktha is brahman*: Cf. BU I.6.
11. *recitations*: *Śastra*, cf. CU III.17.3 and note.
12. *of the sacrifice*: *Aiṣṭika*, 'connected with the offering (*iṣṭi*)'. (A has *aiṣṭaka*: 'of the [sacrificial] bricks [*iṣṭakā*]'.)

13. *This . . . Indra*: A has, 'This is the self of a person. The one who knows this becomes self.'
14. *The all-conquering Kauṣītaki*: A just has, 'He'.
15. *the sacred thread*: One of the earliest references to the *yajñopavīta*, at this date put on for specific rituals, not worn all the time.
16. *fetched water*: A has, 'having sipped water'.
17. *the drawer*: In this verse Kauṣītaki uses three related epithets for the sun, *varga*, *udvarga* and *saṃvarga*, all derivatives of the verbal root *vṛj-*, 'to absorb (and so remove from somewhere else)'. Cf. *saṃvarga*, CU IV.3.1 and note.
18. *So it draws . . . by night*: Not in A.
19. *In the same way . . . method*: This clause omitted in A.
20. *when . . . round*: A has simply, 'on the new moon night'.
21. *cast . . . at it*: A has, 'speech casts . . .'
22. *Since . . . a son*: A has, 'Since your well-formed heart/ Rests in the moon in the sky,/ Mistress of Immortality,/ May I not mourn for harm to a son.' (Cf. the verse in v. 10.) The version in B is addressed to the moon: that in A to the wife. They are being identified in terms of their power to give offspring. 'Well-formed' (*susīma*) is literally 'having a good border or parting (*sīman*)', of a woman with beautifully parted hair.
23. *Wax! . . . to you*: = RV I.91.16a and IX.31.4a.
24. *May juices . . . to you*: = RV I.91.18a.
25. *Stem . . . to wax*: Or 'Ray that the Ādityas cause to wax!' (= AV VII.81.6a, with *ādityā* replacing the original *devā*).
26. *the turn of Indra*: A has, 'the turn of the gods', as in the following verse.
27. *the shining*: *Vicakṣaṇa*, cf. KaU I, n. 8.
28. *the people*: *Viś*, referring to the Vaiśya class (as the 'kings' are the Kṣatriyas).
29. *Then . . . before her*: A has, 'Then his offspring do not pass away before him.' For the verse, cf. n. 22.
30. *sniff . . . head*: For the 'sniff-kiss', see Hopkins 1907. Hopkins regards this ancient mode of greeting (breathing in over someone's head while making a humming sound, compared to the lowing of cattle) as a 'savage' method, pre-dating and later superseded by the mouth-kiss. One can only suggest that the ancient Indian sages were more observant of human behaviour than E. W. Hopkins. Presumably the process of inhaling the person's smell after a long absence originated as a way of satisfying oneself as to their identity and health. (Mouth-kissing is mentioned in BU VI.4.9ff., but in a sexual context.)

31. *<name>*: Only A has *asau*, denoting that the appropriate name is to be spoken, here and below.
32. *then embraces him*: This phrase not in A.
33. *<name>*: A adds, 'He utters his name'.
34. *who . . . the remnant*: *Ṛjīṣin*, 'possessing the *ṛjīṣa* (or remnant of the third pressing of Soma)' – here a title of Indra. Verse adapted from RV III.36.10a (with 'to him' replacing 'to us').
35. *Bestow . . . goods*: = RV II.21.6a.
36. *goes to the air*: A. B has, 'goes to the directions', which does not fit with the parallel passage in v. 13.
37. *the southern . . . northern*: The Himalaya and Vindhya ranges.
38. *Now . . . supremacy*: What follows is a variation on the story in BU VI.1.1–14 and CU V.1.
39. *It lay . . . a log*: A omits, 'not breathing, dry'.
40. *all of them together*: Literally 'together with all these': the author is probably thinking principally of the breath leaving with the other faculties.
41. *Entering the air*: Not in A.
42. *the one who knows this*: This phrase omitted in A.
43. *handing-on*: For a different handing-on ceremony, see BU I.5.17–20.
44. *lies there*: A has, 'himself lies there'. In practice presumably the father would get someone else to do the tasks mentioned.
45. *lies down over him*: Literally 'approaches him from above' (*upariṣṭād abhipadyate*).
46. *With the son . . . him*: A has, 'he [the father] sits facing him'.
47. *The father . . . mind in me*: This item not in A.
48. *The father . . . awareness in me*: A has, 'thoughts, that which is to be known, and desires' instead of 'awareness'.
49. *goes out*: A adds, 'eastward'.
50. *of brahman*: A inserts, 'may good food,'.
51. *go forth*: As a wandering ascetic.
52. *they should provide . . . be provided*: A has, 'As he [the father] provides him, so he should be provided.' 'Funeral rites' added for clarity.

BOOK III

1. *manly deeds*: *Pauruṣa*, 'manliness', from *puruṣa* here in the sense of the male.
2. *I slew . . . Tvaṣṭṛ*: Indra's victory over Viśvarūpa, the three-headed

son of Tvaṣṭṛ, is first mentioned in the Ṛgveda, X.8.8.9 and X.99.6.

3. *Arunmukha sorcerers ... wolves*: These sorcerers (*yati*) are thought to be the same as the Arurmaghas, miserly beings mentioned in AB VII.28.
4. *Prahlādīyas*: Attendants of the demon Prahlāda.
5. *Paulomas*: The sons of the *asura* Puloman. (Indra carried off and married Puloman's daughter, Śacī, often called Paulomī.)
6. *Kālakañjas*: Black-haired ones? – a group of *asuras* said to have been turned into stars.
7. *murder*: *Bhrūṇahatyā*: cf. BU IV.3.22 and note.
8. *Though ... his face*: I.e. he does not blanch. Radhakrishnan's version, 'If he wishes to commit a sin ...' (1994: 774), is misleading: *cakṛṣaḥ* is the genitive of the perfect, not the desiderative participle. The sense is that the person who attains knowledge does not suffer evil karmic consequences from past wrongdoing: not that he can cheerfully carry on doing wrong!
9. *worship ... life*: B has, 'worship me as the self of awareness'.
10. *in this world*: B has, 'in that world'.
11. *true resolve*: *Satya saṃkalpa*: cf. CU III, n. 20.
12. *would be able ... aware of*: Literally 'would be able to make aware of' (*śaknuyāt ... prajñāpayitum*), but a passive sense seems to be required here.
13. *This ... the breath*: Not in B.
14. *each to its proper place*: I.e. the sense of sight to the eyes, that of hearing to the ears, etc.
15. *But ... breath is*: This paragraph not in A.
16. *consciousness*: *Citta*, cf. CU VII, n. 18.
17. *with all thoughts*: A adds, 'When he wakes up ... the worlds from the gods' – as in v. 3 above, but out of place here.
18. *What ... the breath is*: This sentence not in A.
19. *Speech ... to it*: I.e. speech is one part of awareness, and name is the object in the outer world which corresponds to speech. The senses arise from the self, via the breath, in order to experience their objects.
20. *The mind ... desires*: A has *prajñā* ('awareness') instead of *manas*, 'mind', and 'thoughts, what is to be understood, and desires' as its external element.
21. *Rising ... names*: Once one has gained the use of the faculties through awareness, one has access to all the objects of them.
22. *Rising to the mind ... thoughts*: A has, 'Rising to thought (*dhī*)

through awareness, by thought one wins all thoughts, that which is to be known, and desires.'

23. *My mind . . . action*: A has, 'Our (dual) mind was elsewhere: we were not conscious of this action', and similarly with the sentence on movement and the feet. This would mean that here the words are being spoken by the faculties under discussion, instead of by the person, as in B.
24. *one should know the seer*: A has, 'one should know the knower of form'.
25. *the ruler of the world*: *Lokeśa.* A has *sarveśa*, 'lord of all'.

BOOK IV

1. *Gārgya Bālāki . . . brahman*: I have annotated this version of the encounter only where it differs from that in BU II.1.
2. *In the sun . . . truth*: This summary of the contents of the chapter is missing in some manuscripts.
3. *King Soma*: This appears only in A.
4. *the self of truth*: A has, 'the self of brightness' (*tejas*).
5. *Bālāki . . . in the air*: A reverses the order of vv. 7 and 8.
6. *with offspring, with animals*: A has, 'filled with offspring and animals, and he and his offspring do not move on before their time'.
7. *among others*: *Vā anyeṣu.* A has *evānv eṣa*, so that the sentence now means, 'becomes courageous accordingly'.
8. *the self of brightness*: Var. *nāmnasyātmā*, 'the self of name'.
9. *the shadow*: A has, 'the echo'.
10. *gets offspring . . . companion*: I.e. has a wife who gives him children.
11. *the echo*: A has, 'the sound that follows one as one moves'.
12. *life*: *Asu*, the breath of life, as in BU II.1.10. A has *āyu*, the lifespan.
13. *the person who is in sound*: A has, 'the person of shadow'.
14. *before his time*: A adds, 'neither he nor his offspring'.
15. *the person . . . dream*: A has, 'the self of awareness by which a person, asleep . . . dream'.
16. *offspring . . . lifespan*: A has only, 'offspring, animals'.
17. *of speech*: A has, 'of name'.
18. *as your student*: Added for clarity.
19. *contrary . . . form*: A form (*rūpa*) which is *pratiloma*, cf. BU II, n. 11. A has, 'it would be' in place of 'I think it' at the start of the sentence.

20. *the channels of a person*: A has, 'the channels of the heart'.
21. *The breath . . . nails*: This sentence not in A.
22. *scorpion's nest*: *Viśvambhara*, cf. BU I, n. 56.

KENA UPANIṢAD

The Kena Upaniṣad, called after its first word, belongs to the Sāmaveda. It forms part of the Talavakāra or Jaiminīya branch of that Veda, and is sometimes called the Talavakāra Upaniṣad. The numbering and division of the verses within it vary in different recensions. The metre in the verse portions is very irregular, and not all the mss. divide it into books.

1. *of me*: And/or 'by me'. Invocation as for CU.
2. *Urged on . . . ear*: The questions (in italics) are spoken by the student, the rest by the teacher.
3. *Knowing this*: Added for clarity. Another possibility is to take these as two separate statements: '. . . The wise renounce these [presumably the eye etc., not the "eye of the eye" etc.] and become immortal.
4. *It is different . . . to us*: Cf. IU vv. 10, 13.
5. *eyes*: Perhaps = sights. It is plural, not dual, so perhaps refers to the sense of sight in general (in all beings).
6. *breathe . . . breath*: *Prāṇ-*, *prāṇa*, perhaps referring to the sense of smell.
7. *which is you*: Or 'which you [know]'.
8. *unknown*: Reading *'veditam*, 'unknown', for *veditam*, 'known', following Olivelle (1996b: 228). The following verses then represent the method of contemplation that the teacher is recommending to the student.
9. *If here . . . destruction*: Cf. BU IV.4.14.
10. *wonder*: *Yakṣa*, denoting a mysterious entity rather than, as in later usage, a member of a particular class of nature spirits. It is here in the neuter gender, stressing its impersonal character. *Yakṣa* is used in a similar sense in BU V.4, where it could be either masculine or neuter in gender.
11. *Umā Haimavatī*: Perhaps the earliest mention of this goddess, here appearing as a personification of the knowledge of *brahman*.
12. *touched it closest*: Manuscripts add, 'they were the first to know it as *brahman*'. As Olivelle (1996b: 343–4) points out, this was

almost certainly copied from the following verse, as the syntax does not fit here.

13. *imagination*: *Saṃkalpa*. The moment of realization in the mind is compared to the flash of lightning.
14. *the beloved*: *Tadvana*, a rare word said to mean 'greatly loved': perhaps from *tad* + *vana*, either 'that beloved' or 'beloved of that', depending on whether we take it as a *karmadhāraya* or a *tatpuruṣa* compound. *Vana* is thought to come from the Vedic root *van-*, 'love', 'desire', 'win' – cf. Latin *Venus*, *venerare*, and English 'win'.
15. *secret teaching of brahman*: *Brāhmī upaniṣad*.
16. *in the end*: Reading *ante*. Reading *anante* gives, 'in an endless . . . heavenly world'.
17. *highest*: Reading *jyeye*, 'senior', 'superior' (?). Reading *'jyeye* gives, 'in an unconquerable heavenly world'.

KAṬHA UPANIṢAD

The Kaṭha Upaniṣad is traditionally assigned to the Black Yajurveda, or sometimes to the Atharvaveda. Its chapters are called Vallī, literally, 'creeper, climbing plant'. Some editions divide the work into two books, with our Books I–III forming the chapters of Book One and IV–VI the chapters of Book Two. In translating and commenting on this Upaniṣad I have been greatly indebted to D. H. Killingley's unpublished 'Notes on the Kaṭha Upaniṣad'. The frame-story of the boy Naciketas and Yama, the god of death, is one of the best-loved in the Upaniṣads.

The Kaṭha Upaniṣad shows theistic and devotional tendencies, the supreme reality being visualized with the attributes of several of the Vedic gods and goddesses, especially with those of Agni.

1. *OṂ . . . peace*: Invocation as at the end of BU.
2. *a sacrifice . . . possessions*: A *sarvavedas* sacrifice involved the giving in gifts (*dakṣiṇā*) of all the patron's possessions, particularly cattle, but not his land, which belonged to the community. The frame-story of this Upaniṣad is based on TB III.11.8, which gives it as the story of the origin of the Nāciketa-fire.
3. *Of cattle*: Added for clarity.
4. *Daddy*: Uniquely in the Upaniṣads, Naciketas calls his father by the familiar term *tata*. He is clearly much younger than the other sons we encounter, and has yet to go and live in the house of a teacher (at about twelve years old, cf. CU VI.1.2). His simple and

straightforward approach to life seems to suggest a child of eight to ten years old.

5. *I go*: Obedient to his father's word, which cannot be revoked since it was made at the sacrifice, Naciketas sets off for the house of Yama, the god of death. As D. H. Killingley points out (1981, 1983: 4), Uśan Vājaśravasa does not have to kill his son, who 'has offered himself as a dakṣiṇā, not as a victim'. Presumably Naciketas chants vv. 5–6 as he walks to Yama's house.

6. *As fire . . . everything*: Yama is absent when Naciketas arrives. (It is not Naciketas's time to die, so Yama is not expecting him.) When he returns home, a voice warns him that a Brāhmaṇa has waited in his house without food or drink to quench his anger.

7. *Brahmā*: Here as a respectful title for a Brāhmaṇa.

8. *Auddālaka Āvuṇi*: Son or descendant of Uddālaka Āruṇi. I think it refers to the father. Some take it to refer to the son, reading *mat-prasṛṣṭam* instead of *mat-prasṛṣṭah*, so that 'released by me' refers to the son. However, the father, too, has to be released by Yama – from the consequences of his rash words.

9. *How to . . . there*: Literally 'the attainment of an endless world, and a firm basis [in it]'.

10. *the beginning of the world*: *Lokādi*, 'the beginning of the world', or perhaps 'the world, etc.' that can be won through the sacrifice.

11. *chain*: *Sṛṅkā*, a word apparently not known outside this Upaniṣad and other passages based on it, but possibly cognate with *śṛṅkhalā*, 'chain', 'elephant fetter'. Here it seems to refer to something desirable, like a gold necklace. In Kaṭha II.3 it is something that brings bondage. Killingley (1981, 1983: 11) suggests that Yama offers it 'in the hope that Naciketas will inadvertently waste his third boon by accepting it'. But it may simply be a symbolic way of referring to the gift of the knowledge of the Nāciketa-fire.

12. *Who does the three works*: *Triṇāciketa*, one who has built three Nāciketa-fires. The other triads mentioned in this verse may refer to the same actions, or to other groups of three, such as (1) earth, middle-air and sky, or father, mother and teacher; and (2) sacrifice, study and gifts, or sacrifice, gifts and asceticism. See Killingley 1981, 1983: 12.

13. *building the fires*: *Nicāyya*, 'having built' [the fires], or 'having revered' [the god].

14. *this threesome*: See n. 12.

15. *fair ladies . . . instruments*: The list of temptations may seem at

first glance slightly incongruous, but in fact Yama may be trying to suit his audience. Fair ladies (*rāmā*) could hardly be omitted from any list of worldly temptations, but Naciketas is probably still at an age at which chariots are more interesting than girls.

16. *matter . . . away*: *Sāṃparāya*, 'that which is connected with passing away (*saṃparāya*, from *sam-parā-i-*, "to pass on", "to die")'.
17. *for the sake . . . enjoying*: *Yogakṣemāt*, 'from [the desire for] the getting and enjoying [of goods]'.
18. *chain*: *Sṛṅkā*, as in n. 11.
19. *The childish . . . away*: 'The matter of his passing away (*sāṃparāya*) does not appear to the fool (*bāla*, literally 'child', but often used of the spiritually unaware).'
20. *I know . . . permanent*: Some consider this verse part of Yama's teaching, on the grounds that Naciketas has not yet performed the ritual to which he gave his name. But the timescale of this Upaniṣad is that of the divine, not the human, world. Naciketas could well have carried out the ritual, under Yama's instructions, around I.15. Or it could be a prayer on the part of the composer of the Upaniṣad (see Killingley 1981, 1983: 34).
21. *the study . . . self*: *Adhyātmayogādhigama*, the study of yoga *adhyātmam*, 'concerned with [one]self', rather than *adhidaivatam*, 'concerned with deities', or *adhibhūtam*, 'concerned with beings'. The use of *adhyātma* in the sense of 'supreme self' is a post-Upaniṣadic development.
22. *Drawing out . . . dharma*: Zaehner (1966: 174) translates *pravṛhya dharmyam* as 'Let him uproot all things of law'. However, it is clear from its use in Kaṭha VI.17 that *pra-vṛh-* means to take something out *to keep it* (and discard the rest), not to throw it away.
23. *I consider . . . this*: *Vivṛtaṃ sadma naciketasaṃ manye*, literally 'I consider Naciketas an open dwelling [for this knowledge].' Here I agree with Hume (1995: 348), against, it seems, all the other translators! Olivelle (1996b: 237) has, 'To him I consider my house to be open, Naciketas', presumably reading *vivṛtam sadma naciketaḥ saṃmanye*. Others seem to take *naciketasaṃ* as an adjective: 'I consider the house open of/for Naciketas', though *nāciketasaṃ* would have been expected – e.g. Radhakrishnan (1994: 614): 'I know that such a house is wide open unto Naciketas.' (Perhaps he means us to understand it as an accusative of extent, 'open with respect to/in the case of Naciketas', though I know of no comparable usage in the Upaniṣads.)

24. *the wise one*: *Vipaścit*, literally 'of inspired mind', here seems to refer to the wise inner self rather than to the wise person. Cf. BhG II.20, which instead of *vipaścit* refers to *śarīrin*, the embodied (self) mentioned in BhG II.18.
25. *If the slayer . . . slain*: This famous verse is very close to BhG II.19. It has been suggested, therefore, that it must be a late addition to the Kaṭha Upaniṣad, borrowed from the Bhagavad-gīta, on the grounds that it is more appropriate there, as part of the dialogue on the battlefield. However, it seems equally apposite here, placed in the mouth of Death himself. From many examples in the Upaniṣads and elsewhere, it seems clear that verses containing memorable summaries of teaching had wide currency, and were available to be adapted as needed by the composers of spiritual works.
26. *will*: *Kratu*, the desire by which one accomplishes Vedic rituals. Here the yogi has gone beyond that stage.
27. *the creator's favour*: *Dhātuḥ prasādāt*, 'the favour of Dhātṛ'. The alternative reading, *dhātuprasādāt*, would mean 'through the calming of the elements'.
28. *(madāmada)*: Intensive of *mad-*, 'to be happy'? Or *mada* + *amada*, 'both delighted and not-delighted'?
29. *those with the five fires*: Householders.
30. *undisciplined*: *Ayukta*, literally 'unyoked'. So in the next verse 'disciplined' is *yukta*.
31. *The unmanifest . . . unmanifest*: The terminology here is similar to that of the Sāṅkhya *darśana*. Here, however, *puruṣa* is regarded as higher than *avyakta* (= *prakṛti*), and by implication as the source of it and all the other levels of existence; whereas in classical Sāṅkhya *puruṣa* and *prakṛti* are both autonomous and externally existent.
32. *Stand up . . . pay attention*: It seems curious that these injunctions are all in the plural, unless they are proverbial.
33. *seen*: Or 'worshipped' (*nicāyya*).
34. *go into . . . wait*: *Mṛtyor yanti vitatasya pāśam*, literally 'go into the noose of spread-out Death'. *Vitata*, 'spread out', more naturally applying to *pāsa*, 'noose', the lasso-like weapon with which Death catches living beings, is here transferred to its owner (who is of course also speaking the words).
35. *sexual contacts*: Or 'mutual contacts'.
36. *honey-eater*: The self as experiencer within the individual, identified in the verse with the cosmic self, 'lord of past and future'.
37. *He who . . . that*: The syntax of this verse and the next are rather

unorthodox in terms of classical Sanskrit. However, it is clear that *brahman* is being successively identified with different aspects of deity, first in the form of the primeval male, and then in the form of Aditi, the mother of the gods.

38. *the eleven-gated city*: The body – the gates being either the two eyes, two ears, two nostrils, mouth, sex-organ, anus, navel and *brahmarandhra* or fontanelle, or the faculties (five sense-organs, five organs of action, and mind).
39. *As the goose . . . law*: A verse found several times in the Yajurveda, e.g. VS X.24, where (according to SBr VI.7.3.11) it refers to Agni in his various forms. 'Sky' added for clarity.
40. *the gods*: Or 'the Viśvedevas'. In any case, they are regarded as deities present in every being, in the form of the senses and other faculties.
41. *So that . . . body*: Literally 'For the embodiment of the possessor of the body' (*śarīratvāya dehinaḥ*), or, if *dehinaḥ* is taken as nominative plural, 'Some possessors-of-bodies go into a womb for embodiment . . .'
42. *Others . . . motionless*: *Sthānum anye'nusaṃyanti*. Zaehner (1966: 180) translates this as 'Others pass into a lifeless stone.' But the idea of rebirth in, for example, a stone or even a tree-stump seems improbable. Could 'the motionless' actually be a *higher* state: 'Others go into a changeless [world]'?
43. *by another's light*: Added for clarity.
44. *its branches below*: The upside-down tree with its roots above and branches below is a perennial Indian symbol: see Killingley 1981, 1983: 54. There is possibly an even earlier example of its occurrence than RV I.24.7, on the Indus Valley seal showing a tree with unicorn heads (Allchin and Allchin 1982: 211, pl. 8.16). Dr Karel Werner has suggested in conversation that the tree here should be upside down if the script is to be in the same place as on most other Indus Valley seals. Here, too, the tree is a pipal or pippala (*aśvattha* or sacred fig, *Ficus religiosa*).
45. *that moves*: *Jagat*, 'the world', viewed as constantly moving (*gam-*): cf. IU 1.
46. *in the worlds of creation*: Reading *sargeṣu lokeṣu*, 'in the worlds (which are) creations' (from *sṛj-*). An alternative reading is *svargeṣu lokeṣu*, 'in the heavenly worlds'.
47. *In oneself . . . shadow*: It appears in successively clearer form in higher and higher worlds. (As Killingley points out (1981, 1983: 57), 'the ancient Indian mirror was a polished slab of stone or metal', and so not particularly clear.)

48. *Knowing . . . grieve*: Literally 'Knowing the separate state of the senses, and that which is the rising and setting of those that arise separately . . .' The wise one realizes that experiences, pleasant or unpleasant, which impinge upon his senses are external, and do not affect the *ātman*.
49. *The unmanifest . . . great*: For the Sāṅkhya terminology, cf. Kaṭha III.11 and note.
50. *without mark*: *Aliṅga*, 'without defining characteristics'.
51. *five knowings*: Through the senses.
52. *of both*: The 'both' are perhaps the two forms of self, cf. Kaṭha IV.5 and note.
53. *When all . . . here*: = verse in BU IV.4.7.
54. *A hundred and one . . . directions*: = verse in CU VIII.6.6.
55. *by wisdom*: Or 'steadfastly' (*dhairyeṇa*).

ŚVETĀŚVATARA UPANIṢAD

The Śvetāśvatara Upaniṣad, like the Kaṭha, to which it is clearly related, is an Upaniṣad of the Black Yajurveda. It is called after the teacher mentioned in VI.21, whose name means 'possessing white mules' – symbolically, perhaps, 'having pure faculties': cf. the chariot simile in II.9 and in Kaṭha III.3–6, 9. Apart from the introductory line it is all in verse, though the metre is somewhat irregular. In contrast to the Kaṭha, it has no ritual content: it comes from a community of ascetics who have left the household life and its rituals behind (VI.21). Nor is there a frame-story: the format, in which the teaching is the answer to a question asked at the start, is reminiscent of the Kena.

Its philosophy is a form of Sāṅkhya, in which creation emanates from the dual principles of *puruṣa* and *prakṛti*, 'spirit' and 'matter', or (since *prakṛti* is an active principle, including mind and senses as well as the body) 'man' and 'nature'. However, it reconciles the two principles with its theistic world-view by subordinating them both to 'the god' (*deva*, unusually used almost in the sense of 'God' with a capital G). This *deva* has characteristics of the Vedic Agni and Savitṛ, but above all of Rudra, who has already taken on titles and characteristics of Śiva. *Puruṣa, prakṛti* and *deva* are regarded as distinct entities, each present in every being. *Ātman* is used as a synonym for *puruṣa*: it is implied, though not stated, that there are multitudes of separate *puruṣas*. *Brahman* is sometimes identified with *deva*, and sometimes seen as containing all three entities. Complete liberation is thought to require knowledge of, and devotion to, the god. This Upaniṣad contains probably the earliest explicit reference to bhakti (VI.23) and early references to Sāṅkhya, Yoga and Vedānta (VI.13, 22).

Recently, Thomas Oberlies (1998, 1995) has questioned the accepted date for this Upaniṣad and its early place within the sequence of Indian texts. He points to the large number of verses shared between the Upaniṣad and the Bhagavadgītā. Since, for example, the syntax of III.17 (see SU III, n. 17) fits much more easily at the place where it is found in the Bhagavadgītā, he considers that the verse must originally have belonged there, and that the Śvetāśvatara must therefore be more recent. He places it as late as the second or third century CE, though this surely depends on the date of the Bhagavadgītā, which is itself arguable: most scholars today place it around the second century BCE.

An attractive feature of Oberlies's theory is that it provides a believable setting for the unusual philosophy of this Upaniṣad. This then no longer represents an early, undeveloped, version of Sāṅkhya, but a later one, which seeks to reconcile Sāṅkhya with a developing theism.

I have found D. H. Killingley's unpublished 'Notes on the Śvetāśvatara Upaniṣad' indispensable in understanding this text.

BOOK [INVOCATION]

1. *OṂ . . . peace*: Invocation as at start of IU and BU.

BOOK I

1. *What . . . brahman*: *Kiṃ kāraṇaṃ brahma*. Other possible interpretations include, 'What is the cause? [Is it] *brahman*?' and (taking it as *kiṃkāraṇaṃ brahma*) 'What does *brahman* have as its cause?' Elsewhere in the text, however, *brahman* is synonymous with the original cause, so I have taken it as 'What is the cause, i.e. *brahman*?', equivalent to the perennial question of the Upaniṣads, 'What do you worship as *brahman*?'
2. *Should we . . . person*: Presumably all theories current when the Upaniṣad was composed. The first five suggest atheistic theories of origin. A womb (*yoni*) perhaps suggests a mother-goddess; for creation from a person or man (*puruṣa*), see RV X.90 and BU I.4. The Upaniṣad regards each of these theories individually as too simplistic.
3. *A conjunction . . . sorrow*: It also rejects any combination of these theories, considering that they do not account for the existence

of the *ātman* (which it considers axiomatic). Yet it considers that there must be something higher than the *ātman*, since that is incapable of controlling its own conditions of existence.

4. *the method of meditation*: *Dhyānayoga*; cf. SU II.8–15.
5. *the god's ... strands*: The god's own power (*devātmaśakti*) is hidden by the strands (*guṇa*) that he himself generates in the world. It is also possible to take it as 'the god, the self and the power (= *prakṛti*), hidden by [their] own strands'. The term *guṇa* may or may not be used in its technical Sāṅkhya sense of the strands of *sattva* (brightness), *rajas* (passion) and *tamas* (darkness) as constituents of everything in the world.
6. *one rim*: The unity of the cosmos: 'wheel' added earlier for clarity. The riddle is deliberately obscure, and the following identifications, derived mainly from Killingley 1983 and Johnson 1930, are conjectural.
7. *three tyres*: The three *guṇas*.
8. *sixteen ends*: Five sense-faculties, five action-faculties, mind, and the five elements.
9. *Half a hundred spokes*: Obscure.
10. *twenty counter-spokes*: Perhaps the ten faculties without mind, plus the gross and subtle elements (*mahābhūta* and *tanmātra*). It is not clear what the 'counter-spokes' (*pratyarā*) of a wheel might be.
11. *Six eights*: Johnson (1930: 858–9) suggests that some of these sets of eight may be among those intended (based on the classic Sāṅkhya text, the *Sāṅkhya-kārikā* of Īśvarakṛṣṇa, which can be found with English translation in Larson 1979: 255–77):
    - (i) Eight forms of *prakṛti*: five elements plus *buddhi*, *manas* and *ahaṃkāra*.
    - (ii) Eight forms of psychic power (*siddhi*, 'accomplishment', or *aiśvarya*, 'mastery') achieved by yogis: minuteness, lightness, ability to reach anywhere, irresistible will, greatness, control, lordship over the body, locomotion at will.
    - (iii) Eight first results of yoga, as in SU II.13.
    - (iv) Eight forms of *tamas* ('darkness' or 'ignorance'): false identification of the *puruṣa* with any of the forms of *prakṛti* in (i) (*Sāṅkhya-kārikā* 48).
    - (v) Eight follies (*moha*): identification of the powers in (ii) with *mokṣa*, 'liberation' (*Sāṅkhya-kārikā* 48).
    - (vi) Eight accomplishments (*siddhi*): reasoning, instruction by a teacher, study, suppression of suffering in relation to (a) the

self, (b) beings and (c) deities, knowledge learned from a friend, and gifts (*Sāṅkhya-kārikā* 51).

(vii) Eight gods or classes of gods: Brahmā, Prajāpati, Indra, ancestors, *gandharvas*, *yakṣas*, *rākṣasas* (powerful demons such as Rāvaṇa), *piśācas* (malevolent beings said to be fond of raw flesh).

12. *one rope . . . shape*: Desire.
13. *Three . . . roads*: Bad rebirth, good rebirth and liberation from rebirth.
14. *one illusion . . . causes*: *Puruṣa* and *prakṛti*, or possibly merit and demerit, as causes of rebirth.
15. *five streams*: Five sense faculties.
16. *wild . . . sources*: *Pañcayonyugravakrām*. Johnson (1930: 863–4) emends the last element to *-nakrām*, so that instead of 'wild . . . sources' we would have, 'with fierce crocodiles which are the five sources (*yoni*)', which he identifies with the five elements, earth, water, fire, air and space.
17. *five perceptions*: Five sense-perceptions.
18. *five whirlpools*: Five sense-objects.
19. *five sufferings*: The five sufferings (*duḥkha*) are presumably the five afflictions (*kleśa*): *avidyā*, 'ignorance'; *asmitā*, 'belief in personal existence'; *rāga*, 'desire'; *dveṣa*, 'hatred'; *abhiniveśa*, 'clinging to worldly existence'.
20. *Fifty divisions . . . each*: Obscure.
21. *rest to all*: As ambiguous in Sanskrit as it is in English. *Sarvasaṃstha*, 'that in which everything rests/come to rest', could mean either that in which all that has been created is maintained or that into which it all perishes again. For the second meaning there is the pairing with *sarvājīva*: for the first there is the usage in SU VI.17, in which *īśasaṃstha* clearly means 'resting/remaining as the lord'.
22. *goose*: *Haṃsa* (cf. BU IV.3.11–12 and its n. 13), here representing the self.
23. Hume (1995: 395) splits the verse differently: '. . . the soul . . . flutters about./ Thinking that itself (*ātmānam*) and the Actuator are different./ When favored by Him, it attains immortality.' However, the whole tendency of this Upaniṣad is to distinguish between the god and the individual self. As in the Kaṭha, not only knowledge but the favour of the deity are held to be necessary for liberation.
24. *In it . . . imperishable*: This can be taken as either 'In it are the triad, [i.e.] the good support (*su-pratiṣṭhā* = *prakṛti*) and the

imperishable (*akṣara* = *ātman*) [plus a third, unstated member = *deva*]' or 'In it are the triad: [it is] the good support and the imperishable.'

25. *The powerful one*: *Īśa*, from *īś-*, 'to rule', 'to be powerful', of the god, contrasted here with the self which is *anīśa*, 'powerless', because it is attached to the world and imagines itself to be autonomous.
26. *There are . . . enjoyment*: In the riddling language typical of this Upaniṣad, *aja* and *ajā* mean 'unborn (male)' and 'unborn (female)', as well as 'billy-goat' and 'nanny-goat'. The female is *prakṛti*, the two males the unbound *deva* and the bound *puruṣa*: see also SU IV.5 and note. All three (the triad) are contained within the infinite self, which here is equated with *brahman*.
27. *not an actor*: *Akartṛ*. This self only appears to perform actions.
28. *the taker*: *Hara*, here probably referring to the self as 'taker' or 'receiver' of the results of *karman*, not to a name of Śiva.
29. *immortal imperishable*: *Amṛta* ('immortal') + *akṣara* (cf. n. 25).
30. *entity (tattva) and more*: There appears to be no English translation of *tattva* which covers all its meanings in the Śvetāśvatara. It literally means 'thatness': its normal meaning is 'truth' or 'reality' (as in the Vedic verse, SU II.1), but in Sāṅkhya it has the technical sense of one of the entities regarded as the basic principles of creation. (In the nominative case it is *tattvam*, and in later Vedānta it was used to refer to the teaching *tat tvam asi*, 'you are that' – see CU VI.8.7 and its n. 12.) Olivelle (1996b: 254) takes *tattvabhāvāt bhūyaś ca* as 'further, . . . by becoming the same reality as him', which seems to run counter to the distinction between *deva* and *ātman* stressed in this Upaniṣad.
31. *artifice (māyā)*: Following Killingley (1983: 15–16), I have translated *māyā* in this Upaniṣad as 'artifice' rather than 'illusion', and *māyin* as 'artificer'. For Sāṅkhya, the universe is not pure illusion, but a reality whose nature is misunderstood by beings caught up in it. 'Artifice' also conveys the idea that *māyā* is something cleverly made (*mā-*) by the god.
32. *absolute*: *Kevala*, 'alone'. For Sāṅkhya, liberation was a state not of complete union, but of the *puruṣa*'s realizing its separation from *prakṛti*. I have taken *kevala* as representing *kevalaḥ*, the nominative case. It is equally possible, as Olivelle does (1996b: 254), to take it as representing *kevale*, the locative: 'in the absolute'.
33. *the mark*: *Liṅga*, its essential characteristics. Fire is believed to be latent in fuel.

34. *river-beds*: *Srotas* normally means a river or stream (from *sru-*, 'to flow'), but here the author clearly has in mind a river-bed in the dry season, from which water may be got by digging.
35. *inner . . . brahman*: *Brahmopaniṣad*.

BOOK II

1. *from earth*: Or 'for earth' (depending on whether *pṛthivyā* is taken as the sandhi form of *pṛthivyāḥ* or of *pṛthivyai*). Verses 1–5 are found also in the Black Yajurveda, TS IV.1.1.1–5, and, with variations, in VS XI.1–5. They originally accompanied offerings to the god Savitṛ (SBr VI.3.1.12–17), but here are applied to the symbolic offering of meditation. Savitṛ, the solar deity who raises the mind to a higher level, is being identified with *deva*. Each of the five verses begins with a form of the verb *yuj-*, 'to yoke', referring to harnessing of the mind.
2. *inspiration*: *Sava*, '[soma-] pressing', 'impelling' or 'inspiration' (the functions of Savitṛ). Originally the verse meant that the speakers were physically present at a ritual in honour of Savitṛ: in the present context they are subject to his inspiration.
3. *for the heavenly world*: *Suvargeya*, adjective from *suvarga*, the Vedic form of *svarga*, heaven: *suvargeyāya*, 'for [the attainment of] that which is of heaven'. 'Strive' or 'make offering' is to be understood.
4. *the hero's path*: I.e. the sun's path. 'Your', in the previous line, is dual: in its original context (RV X.13.1), the verse is addressed to the two *havirdhānas*, carts in which the offerings are brought to the sacrifice.
5. *Where . . . Mind appears*: 'Mind' (*manas*) here refers to the special state of mind associated with the ritual. The 'wind' that arises is the breath of the priest who kindles the fire.
6. *With Savitṛ . . . perished*: One should make the Vedic lore (*brahman*) one's source (*yoni*) and hence one's destination, knowing that one is supported by one's previous good deeds (*pūrta*).
7. *its three parts*: I.e. head, neck and torso.
8. *With soundless . . . and so on*: *Śabdajalāśrayādibhiḥ*, 'with sound, water, a dwelling etc.', would seem to mean 'with sounding water, a dwelling etc.'. However, as Johnson points out (1930: 877–8), though water is necessary for the yogi, sound, even that of water, is to be avoided. The simplest emendation is to read *'śabda-*, as the sandhi form of *aśabda-*, 'soundless'. Alternatively, Johnson

suggests emending *śabda-* to *śāda-* or *śaṣpa-*, both meaning 'grass' (necessary for the yogi's bed and seat).

9. *harbingers . . . brahman*: Forms of light or sound that arise in the meditator's vision or hearing as concentration grows stronger.
10. *When earth . . . yoga*: As the subtle forms of the five elements arise in his consciousness, the elements within the yogi's own body are purified, producing the changes described in vv. 12 and 13.
11. *being bright*: I.e. by nature.
12. *But when . . . bonds*: Whereas v. 14 has described a level of attainment reachable by one's own efforts, the attainment of v. 15 requires knowledge of the deity.
13. *The god . . . way*: = VS XXXII.4.
14. *to the god . . . praise*: Variant of TS V.5.9.3 = AV VII.87, where the god is called Rudra, not *deva*.

BOOK III

1. *powers*: *Īśanī*, a feminine derivative of *īs-*, 'to rule', a power appropriate to Rudra-Śiva (*īśa* or *īśvara*): cf. *śakti*.
2. *Protector . . . in again*: I.e. he is preserver and destroyer as well as creator (v. 4).
3. *Eyes . . . earth*: = RV X.81.3, where it refers to Viśvakarman, 'All-maker' (= Tvaṣṭṛ, the craftsman of the gods, noted for his powers of *māyā*).
4. *the golden embryo*: This (*hiraṇyagarbha*) first appears in RV X.121 as the source of creation. The present passage places the god before even the golden embryo.
5. *most healing*: *Śantama*, 'most health-giving'. As Killingley points out (1983: 9), 'the word śam "well, happily; welfare, health" belongs especially to Rudra, being used in his names Śaṃkara and Śambhū, both meaning "causing welfare, making well"'. The verse is TS IV.5.1c = VS XVI.2.
6. *Mountain-dweller . . . thing*: = TS IV.5.1d/VS XVI.3.
7. *Higher than that*: *Tataḥ param*. Higher than what? To make it 'higher than Rudra' would contradict the rest of the Upaniṣad. If, as Hume believes (1995: 400, n. 5), it is 'higher than the universe', we would expect *ataḥ param*, 'higher than this'. If we take *tataḥ* in the sense of 'therefore', the connection is still unclear. Zaehner (1966: 208, n. 5) takes it as referring back to the golden embryo (v. 4), which seems strained. He also takes the next word,

brahmaparam, as 'than Brahman higher', though there seems little reason not to take it as a synonym of *paraṃ brahma*, in SU I.7. (*Brahmaparam* recurs at SU V.1.) Perhaps, as Killingley suggests (1983: 10), the verse has been taken from another context, where the connection was clearer.

8. *No one*: Here *kiṃcid* (neuter) is replaced by *kaścid* (masculine), though the adjectives agreeing with it remain neuter. The tree in the sky is probably the upside-down tree of Kaṭha VI.1.
9. *than that*: The same problem as in n. 7
10. *gracious one (śiva)*: In the Śvetāśvatara, 'Śiva' seems to be in the process of changing from one of the god's many titles to his principal name.
11. *being . . . onward*: *Sattva* here probably refers to all being, rather than just to the *guṇa* of that name.
12. *Ruling . . . attainment*: The god is thought of as having the power to choose who will reach the highest level of spiritual attainment.
13. *Is shaped . . . mind*: Reading *hṛdā manvīśā manasā'bhikḷpto*, as in SU IV.17. In the present verse there is a variant, *manvīśo*, so that this line would read, 'The wise one, is shaped by the heart, the mind.' In any case, the sense is that the *puruṣa*, though originally without the strands (*guṇa*), is moulded by the characteristics of the being in which it is born.
14. *The person . . . length*: = RV X.90.1.
15. *The person . . . food*: = RV X.90.2.
16. *With hands . . . world*: = BhG XIII.13.
17. *Seeming . . . of all*: Syntactically, this verse is set apart from what surrounds it by the fact that *īśāna*, 'ruler', and all the terms describing it, are the accusative case. This may be because it is borrowed from elsewhere (lines a and b = BhG XIII.13: d = IX.18b). In context, it can be taken as an exclamation of wonder at the qualities of the deity.
18. *Embodied . . . outside*: Here the 'goose' is *deva* rather than *puruṣa*. It is both within the individual being and outside it. The 'nine gates' are the two eyes, two ears, two nostrils, mouth, sex-organ and anus: cf. the 'eleven-gated city' in Kaṭha V.1 and note.
19. *Subtler . . . at an end*: Variant of Kaṭha II.20.
20. *Self of all*: *Sarvātman*: alternatively, 'having all selves', cf. SU V, n. 6.

BOOK IV

1. *through . . . ways*: *Bahudhā śaktiyogāt*: alternatively, 'through union with his power (*śakti* = *prakṛti*) in many forms'.
2. *That is fire . . . Prajāpati*: = VS XXXII.1.
3. *You are woman . . . side*: = AV X.8.27.
4. *moth . . . red eyes*: 'Moth' translates *pataṅga*, 'flying thing', generally not used of birds. (Śaṅkara interprets it as 'bee', presumably because it is glossy black (Gambhīrānanda 1986: 143).) The green being with red eyes could be a butterfly or a parrot. As Killingley remarks (1983: 13), 'The exact meaning is not important, as 4ab is merely a selection of phenomena all of which are manifestations of God; the colours contrast with the statement that God is colourless (1a).'
5. *The one . . . lightning*: I.e. the rain-cloud.
6. *With the nanny-goat . . . enjoyment*: For the three goats/unborn ones see SU I, n. 26. The female, *prakṛti*, produces creatures which, like herself, are of three basic colours (cf. CU VI.4). Later, the three colours were associated with the three *guṇas* – red with *rajas*, white with *sattva*, and black with *tamas* – and that may already be implied here. The male who 'lies' with her (in a somewhat un-goatlike manner) is *puruṣa* in a state of bondage. The one who abandons her is *deva*. Hume (1995: 403) and others translate *bhuktabhogām* as though it were *bhuktabhogaḥ*, but, as Zaehner notices (1966: 210), it is *prakṛti* who has 'had her pleasure': i.e. it is the female principle that initiates the process of creation.
7. *Two birds . . . eating*: = RV I.164.20. We do not know precisely what the verse meant for the Vedic Ṛṣi, but for the author of the Śvetāśvatara the tree was *prakṛti* and the two birds *puruṣa* and *deva*. The verse is found again at MuU III.1.1.
8. *from powerlessness (anīśayā)*: Instrumental of *anīśa*, which I take as 'non-power', 'lack of power'. Olivelle (1996b: 259) takes it as meaning 'non-lord' (f.): 'one person grieves, deluded by her who is not the Lord'.
9. *In the same . . . sorrow*: = MuU III.1.2.
10. *To one . . . here*: = RV I.164.39, TB III.10.9, 14, TA II.11.1, AV IX.10.18.
11. *The great lord*: *Maheśvara*, later a usual title of Śiva, though in Mbh also used of Indra.
12. *worshipful*: *Īḍya*, a Vedic epithet particularly associated with Agni, found also in SU VI.5, 7.

13. *Overlord ... offering*: Based on RV X.121. Lines cd = RV X.121.3cd; line a = AV XIX.46.4b; line c = VS XX.20.32b.
14. *than ... butter*: Or 'from clarified butter'. The god is compared to an imaginary, even subtler, product (*maṇḍa*, which usually refers to the scum on boiled rice or to a distilled liquor) which bears the same relation to ghee as ghee does to curds or curds to milk.
15. *all-maker*: *Viśvakarman*, cf. SV III, n. 3.
16. *magnanimous*: *Mahātman*, often used in the epics as an epithet of heroes. It is a *bahuvrīhi* (possessive) compound, literally 'having a great self', not a synonym of *mahat ātman*, 'the great self'.
17. *the lovely ... Savitṛ*: *Tat savitur vareṇyam*, the first line of the Gāyatrī Mantra ('glory' added for clarity). There is a reminiscence of this mantra in the use of the unusual word *vareṇya*, 'lovely', literally 'worth choosing', in SU V.4.
18. *propitious*: *Dakṣiṇa*, literally 'right-hand' (and 'southern', because directions are always given as if one is facing east): hence 'skilful' and 'auspicious'. The phraseology is reminiscent of TS V.5.7.3a and RV V.3.3.
19. *Do not ... offerings*: = RV I.114.8, TS IV.5.10.3 and VS XVI.16.

BOOK V

1. *Kapila*: Kapila here seems to be identified with the golden embryo. Followers of the Sāṅkhya system identify this Kapila with their founder of the same name. The use of the present tense emphasizes the timelessness of the god.
2. *The god ... field*: The spreading out and drawing together of the nets represent the alternate creation and reabsorption of universes.
3. *When ... of all*: *Bhūyaḥ sṛṣṭvā yatayas tateśaḥ sarvādhipatyaṃ kurute mahātmā*. This passage is syntactically confusing and possibly corrupt. Both *yatayaḥ* and *mahātmā* are in the nominative case, and the indeclinable participle *sṛṣṭvā* could agree with either: 'Having created again, the Yatis, and likewise the lord, the magnanimous one does/makes the overlordship of all.' The Yatis ('wizards') are demiurges who take a part in the process of creation. Some texts have *patayaḥ*, 'the lords', for *yatayah*.
4. *the draught-ox*: I.e. the sun.
5. *those who ... womb*: I.e. all beings that are born from wombs.
6. *womb of all*: *Viśvayoni*. Alternatively, 'possessing all wombs' –

cf. 'possessing all faces . . .' in SU III.11. However, there *sarva-* rather than *viśva-* is used, and in line c here the universe is called *sarvam etad viśvam*, 'all this whole'.

7. *the womb of brahman*: *Brahmayoni*, probably meaning 'the source of the Vedas': alternatively, 'the source of Brahmā'.
8. *The overlord . . . actions*: The *ātman*, wandering through *saṃsāra* in accordance with its *karman*.
9. *With a form . . . awl*: The *tattvas* are seen as constituting a series of sheaths which make up what we think of as the being. The sheath that contains intention (*saṃkalpa*) and *ahaṃkāra* is thumb-sized, and inside that is a finer sheath with just *buddhi* and *ātman*.
10. *The life . . . infinity*: The *jīva* (or *ātman*) by itself is finer still, yet is also capable of attaining infinity (*ānantyāya kalpate*). This core does not possess any of the external characteristics of a being, such as sex (see v. 10).
11. *By intention . . . born*: This verse seeks to explain how this subtle core undergoes conception, growth and birth into a conscious being.
12. *Because . . . another*: Beings suppose that their bodies, circumstances etc. are the result of some external agency, rather than of their own past actions.
13. *'nestless' by name*: Taking *anīḍākhya* as *a-nīḍa* ('without a nest [*nīḍā*] or permanent abode', 'bodiless') + *ākhya*. Olivelle (1996b: 262) takes it as *anīḍ-ākhya* ('Without-a-Lord'), from *an-īś*.
14. *of the creation of parts*: Perhaps 'of creation with all its parts', or 'of the creation which consists of parts' (as distinct from the original unity).

BOOK VI

1. *By one . . . self*: Killingley (1983: 23) suggests, 'The one may be prakṛti, or the individual self; the two may be the unmanifest and the manifest prakṛti, or the self and prakṛti; the three are the three guṇas; the eight are the five elements, plus three elements of personality – buddhi, ahaṃkāra and mind.'
2. *being . . . entity*: Or 'in reality other' (*tattvato'nyaḥ*).
3. *efficient cause*: *Nimittahetu*, in Indian philosophy the agent which works on the material cause (*upādāna*), as the potter works on clay to make the pot.
4. *proliferation*: *Prapañca* – the process by which multiplicity evolves from the original unity. Killingley (1983: 24) suggests

that it is derived from *pañca*, 'five', reflecting the belief that creation evolves in fives (elements, senses, etc.). (Perhaps there is also the idea of a hand opening up, revealing its five fingers.)

5. *supreme power*: *Parā śakti*. Although the god's power is not here specifically identified as his consort, there is already potential for the development of this idea.
6. *mark*: *Liṅga*, perhaps specifically of the signs of sex, cf. SU IV.3 and V.10.
7. *spider-like . . . brahman*: For the image of the spider (*tantunābha*, 'thread-navelled one'), cf. BU II.1.20, MuU I.1.7 and MaiU VI.22. There is the implication that the universe is both part of the god's substance and something in which he conceals himself. The spider's web is also a net – cf. SU III.1 and V.3.
8. *Sāṅkhya and Yoga*: Apparently the earliest mention of the Sāṅkhya *darśana*, already paired with Yoga.
9. *Permanent . . . impermanent*: Or 'Permanent among the permanent', reading *nityo nityānāṃ*, for *nityo 'nityānāṃ*. Verses VI.12–13 are very close to Kaṭha V.12–13.
10. *The sun . . . light*: = Kaṭha V.15. Here, however, I have translated the pronoun as 'he' rather than 'it', to reflect the more personal view of deity in the present context.
11. *fire . . . water*: Like the fire in the depths of the ocean, believed to be ready to destroy the world at the end of the aeon.
12. *Lord of . . . mind*: *Pradhānakṣetrajñapati*: *pradhāna* = *prakṛti*; *kṣetrajña*, 'field-knower', = the conscious individual.
13. *stability*: *Sthiti*, the continued existence of the universe, or perhaps stillness as opposed to bondage.
14. *shines . . . intelligence*: Or 'shines with self as his intelligence' (*ātmabuddhiprakāśa*).
15. *purifier*: *Pavitra*, a purifying implement, such as the sieve of wool used to purify the Soma.
16. *The supreme . . . student*: Cf. BU VI.3.12 and CU III.11.5–6.
17. *the great-hearted one*: *Mahātman*, cf. SU IV, n. 16.
18. *highest devotion*: *Parā bhakti*: probably the earliest mention of the importance of devotion to the god (and to the guru).
19. *OṂ . . . peace*: Invocation as at end of BU.

MUṆḌAKA UPANIṢAD

The Muṇḍaka Upaniṣad belongs to the Atharvaveda. It does not belong to any Atharvaveda Brāhmaṇa, though it attributes its teaching to Aṅgiras, one of the sages of that Veda. Its title seems to be derived from *muṇḍa*, 'bald', referring to ascetics who have shaved their heads as a symbol of renunciation. The individual books are themselves called *muṇḍaka*, and the chapters *khaṇḍa*, 'sections'.

1. *good fortune*: *Bhadram*, either as neuter adjective, '[that which is] fortunate', or as adverb, 'fortunately', 'auspiciously'. The invocation occurs in several places in Vedic literature, the earliest being RV I.89.8.
2. *the all-knowing*: *Viśvavedas*, 'all-knowing' or 'all-possessing'. I have departed from the literal wording of the original verse in an attempt to convey something of its rhythm. Literally, 'Well-being for us [may] Indra, of great swiftness,/ Well-being for us [may] Pūṣan, the all-knowing,/ Well-being for us [may] Tārkṣya Ariṣṭanemi,/ Well-being for us may Bṛhaspati ordain!'
3. *Phonetics*: *Śikṣā*, the study of the correct pronunciation of the texts. The six forms of knowledge mentioned in the verse are the Vedāṇgas, or limbs of the Veda.
4. *ritual*: *Kalpa*, the Vedāṅga concerned with ritual practice.
5. *astronomy*: *Jyotiṣa*, 'the science of the lights', covering what we now think of as astronomy, astrology and mathematics. As a Vedāṅga, it was used to determine the times at which sacrifices should be held.
6. *invisible*: *Adreśya*, not found elsewhere, but thought to be a variant of *adṛśya*.
7. *without colour*: *Avarṇa*, also 'without (social) class', paralleling *agotra*, 'without lineage'.
8. *emits . . . on to it*: *Sṛjate gṛhṇate ca*, often translated as 'emits and draws in [its thread]'. However, *gṛhṇate*, an irregular form of *grah-*, is not an obvious verb to use of reabsorption, and the other examples given in this passage are all concerned with the process of outward proliferation.
9. *From food . . . immortality*: We are to assume that (sacrificial) works arise from the combination of breath, mind, truth and the worlds.
10. *the triple knowledge*: The Veda. (The feminine noun *vidyā*, 'knowledge', is understood.)

11. *the world . . . deed*: Cf. Kaṭha III.1. Verses 1–6 seem to make a case for ritual activity, which is countered in 7–13.
12. *the seventh*: The seventh rebirth.
13. *Kālī . . . called*: The names of the tongues of flame (all feminine) are 'Black', 'Terrible', 'Swift as mind', 'Very red', 'Of very smoky colour', 'Possessing sparks' and 'Taking all forms'. The title 'goddess' (*devī*), specifically attached to the last, is clearly intended to apply to all of them.
14. *they are blazing*: 'They' is masculine: presumably we are to understand 'the fires' rather than 'the tongues'.
15. *dweller above*: Perhaps Indra.
16. *well-won*: *Sukṛta*, '[won by] good action.'
17. *the eighteen forms of sacrifice*: According to Hume (1995: 368, n. 3), 'the four Vedas, each including Saṁhitā, Brāhmaṇa and Sūtra, and in addition the six Vedāṅgas which are enumerated at Muṇḍ. I.I.5'. According to Śaṅkara, 'the sixteen priests, the [patron's] wife and the patron' (Gambhīrānanda 1958: 103). In any case, the message is that one should not place reliance in external forms.
18. *Living . . . blind*: Almost identical to Kaṭha 2.5 and a verse in Maitri 7.9.
19. *the doers of works*: *Karmin*, literally 'possessing action': relying on ritual actions for a place in a higher world.
20. *stored-up merit*: *Iṣṭāpūrta*, cf. CU V.10.3 and note.
21. *Not . . . unmade*: The thought of the Brāhmaṇa, who realizes that the unmade *brahman* cannot be realized through made things, such as rituals.
22. *a guru . . . brahman*: Along with SU VI.23, one of the earliest references to the guru.
23. *reality*: *Tattvataḥ*: cf. SU I, n. 30.
24. *good man*: I.e. Śaunaka.
25. *At . . . the earth*: Or 'from his feet [comes] the earth'. Unlike the other *devas*, the earth is not actually identified with a part of him.
26. *From the moon*: Literally 'from Soma'.
27. *a female*: Literally 'a young woman' (*yoṣit*), apparently in a deliberate echo of the discourse given in BU VI.2.9–16 and CU V.4–10.
28. *shines*: Literally 'purifies' (or 'blows', like the wind). The worlds are those of the gods and of the ancestors.
29. *The seven breaths*: According to Śaṅkara, the two eyes, two ears, two nostrils and mouth, compared here to the seven flames of the

external sacrifice (cf. MuU I.2.4). Each has its fuel (the sense-objects) and its world (its sphere of activity) (Gambhīrānanda 1958: 124).

30. *in the secret place*: Within the heart.
31. *juices*: *Rasa*, 'juice' or 'essence', the basic nourishment of creatures.
32. *beyond death*: Or perhaps, 'supreme immortal': *parā+mṛta* or *para+amṛta*.
33. *Obvious . . . blinks*: These three lines = AV X.8.6.
34. *the lovely glory*: *Vareṇya* (*bhargas*, 'glory', understood, from the Gāyatrī Mantra).
35. *pierce that*: *Viddhi*, imperative of both 'pierce' (*vyadh-*) and 'know' (*vid-*).
36. *that has . . . of that*: *Tadbhāvagatena*: var. *tadbhāgavatena*, 'having that as lord'.
37. *the channels*: Of the heart.
38. *divine city of brahman*: Cf. CU VIII.1.
39. *The sun . . . light*: = Kaṭha V.15.
40. *Two birds . . . sorrow*: Verses 1–2 = SU IV.6–7.
41. *equality*: *sāmya*, 'sameness': it is not clear whether this means identity with *brahman* or simply equanimity of mind.
42. *who does not speak too much*: Or perhaps 'There is none who out-speaks him', depending on whether *ativādin* is being used in a good or a bad sense (cf. CU VII.15.4 and note).
43. *Yatis*: Here as ascetics, 'strivers'.
44. *It is . . . conquers*: *Satyam eva jayate*, the motto of the modern Republic of India.
45. *the other gods*: Here = the sense organs.
46. *without parts*: It cannot be seen merely as a sum of parts: cf. SU VI.5 and VI.19.
47. *the seed*: The seed of rebirth?
48. *The self . . . form*: = Kaṭha II.23.
49. *asceticism misapplied*: *Tapasaḥ . . . aliṅgāt*, 'through the non-mark of asceticism'.
50. *The fifteen parts*: Perhaps the five breaths, the five sense organs, and the five organs of action.
51. *all the gods . . . deities*: The sense-organs have become united with the corresponding deities – sight with fire, hearing with the directions, etc.
52. *vow of the head*: *Śirovrata*, said by Śaṅkara to mean the observance of carrying fire on the head (Gambhīrānanda 1958: 171). It

seems more likely, however, that the composer of this Upaniṣad was thinking of the practice of shaving the head – hence the title of the Upaniṣad.

PRAŚNA UPANIṢAD

The Praśna Upaniṣad is assigned to the Atharvaveda. As with the Muṇḍaka, it does not form part of an Atharvaveda Brāhmaṇa, but it attributes its teachings to one of the sages of that Veda – in this case Pippalāda. The individual books are themselves called *praśna*, 'questions'.

1. *OṂ . . . peace*: For the invocation, see MuU nn. 1–2.
2. *He raised heat*: *Tapo 'tapyata*: cf. BU I.2.6 and note.
3. *a couple*: *Rāyi*, 'matter', is feminine, *prāṇa*, masculine. Prajāpati both turns into and produces from himself a fruitful couple (*mithuna*) – cf. BU I.4.3.
4. *living beings*: Literally 'breaths' (*prāṇa*).
5. *all-knowing*: *Jātavedas*.
6. *Of all . . . creatures*: = verse in MaiU VI.8. Though called a *ṛc*, this is apparently not from the Ṛgveda.
7. *merit as action*: *Iṣṭāpūrte*, cf. CU V.10.3 and note. 'Action' represents *kṛta*, perhaps as the winning throw of the dice (CU IV.1.4 and note) or perhaps as being 'enough' ('it is done') – Olivelle 1996b: 401.
8. *of living beings*: Or 'of the breaths' (*prāṇa*).
9. *five-footed . . . aspects*: With five seasons and twelve months. The verse = RV I.164.12.
10. *the shining one*: *Vicakṣaṇa*, cf. KauU I.2 (verse) and note.
11. *seven wheels . . . spokes*: Said by the commentators to mean the seven horses of the Sun-god and *six* seasons of the Indian year (spring, summer, rainy season, autumn, winter, and cold season). ('Chariot' earlier added for clarity.) The sense of the verse is perhaps 'Whereas some identify him with the year, others identify him with the sun in his chariot.' The hymn from which the verse is taken is deliberately obscure: see the translation and comments by Wendy O'Flaherty (1981: 75–83).
12. *chastity*: Literally 'celibacy' (*brahmacarya*).
13. *a couple*: *Mithuna*, like Prajāpati himself in n. 3.
14. *of Brahmā*: Or 'of *brahman*'.
15. *artifice*: *Māyā*, cf. SU I.10 and its n. 31.

16. *this*: *Etat*, neuter, so not 'the creature' (*prajā*, fem.). Probably the body (see next note), but possibly 'all this' (= the universe).
17. *shaft*: *Bāṇa*, 'arrow', here referring to the body.
18. *womb*: Or 'embryo' (*garbha*).
19. *the greatest bearer*: Of offerings (*vahnitama*), 'bearer-est', superlative of Vahni (= Agni).
20. *SVADHĀ*: The cry uttered when making offerings to the ancestors: cf. BU V.8 and note.
21. *brightness*: *Tejas*.
22. *gracious*: *Śivā*: cf. SU III.3–5 and notes.
23. *the triple sky*: I.e. the three worlds – sky, middle-air and earth.
24. *splendours and wisdom*: *Śrīś ca prajñāṃ ca*, suggesting benefits both material and spiritual.
25. *Kausalya*: The spelling of Kauśalya/Kausalya varies in the text.
26. *You ask . . . questions*: *Ati-praśnān pṛcchasi*: cf. CU VII.15.4 and note.
27. *a most true Brāhmana*: *Brahmiṣṭha*, cf. BU III.1.2 and its n. 2.
28. *seven flames*: Cf. MuU II.8.
29. *hundred and one channels*: Cf. BU II.1.19.
30. *consciousness*: *Citta*.
31. *the kind . . . fitting*: *Yathāsaṃkalpitaṃ lokam*, 'a world such as has been shaped by one's will to fit one': cf. CU VII.4.
32. *at that time*: In dreaming sleep.
33. *the in-breath and the out-breath*: *Ucchvāsa-niḥśvāsa*, both components of *prāṇa*, the 'upper breath', which is *not* the 'out-breath' or 'in-breath' taken separately.
34. *When . . . light*: In dreamless sleep.
35. *the path . . . taken*: Literally 'that which can be gone'.
36. *the ego . . . identify*: *Ahaṅkāraś cāhaṅkartavyaṃ ca*, 'the I-maker and that which can be made I'.
37. *light . . . illuminated*: *Tejaś ca vidyotayitavyaṃ ca*. Here *tejas* is visible light: the same word is used earlier in the list for the fire element.
38. *until . . . life*: *Prāyaṇāntaṃ*, 'to the end of departing'.
39. *element*: *Mātrā*, literally 'measure', is the smallest element of speech. In Sanskrit grammar the 'o', though pronounced as a pure vowel, is regarded as originating in a diphthong, 'a' + 'u'. The nasalisation 'ṃ' represents, and interchanges with, the consonant 'm'. So 'OṂ' can be understood as three sounds in one. (A *mātrā* is not precisely the same as the 'phoneme' of modern linguistics,

which I think would apply to the 'o' of actual speech rather than to the 'a' + 'u' of which it is made up.)

40. *one meditates on it*: Added for clarity.
41. *light*: *Tejas*.
42. *brahman*: Or Brahmā.
43. *person . . . (puri-śaya)*: Cf. BU II.5.18.
44. *The three elements . . . disjoined*: The three *mātrās*, 'a', 'u' and 'm', individually lead only to finite worlds, and so still belong to the realm of death. When joined together as OṂ, they transcend it. There is multiple punning here on derivatives of *yuj-* in the senses of 'to use' and 'to join'.
45. *Outside, inside and between*: The *mātrās* are perhaps being equated with the three states of waking, dreaming and dreamless sleep, as in ManU 9–11.
46. *world*: Added for clarity.
47. *sixteen parts*: Cf. BU I.5.14.
48. *He*: The person. The implied answer to the questions that follow is that the person departs as soon as breath has departed, and stands firm (*prati-sthā-*) when breath stands firm.
49. *He created . . . name*: Cf. the sequences name . . . breath and speech . . . abundance in CU VII.1–15 and 16–23.

MĀṆḌŪKYA UPANIṢAD

The Māṇḍūkya Upaniṣad is assigned to the Atharvaveda. It is a primary source of Advaita (non-dualist) Vedānta, through its commentary, the Māṇḍūkya Kārikā of Gauḍapāda (*c.* eighth century), Śaṅkara's teacher's teacher.

1. *OṂ . . . peace*: For the invocation, see MuU nn. 1–2.
2. *Vaiśvānara*: 'Of all men': often a name for Agni – see BU I, n. 2.
3. *consciousness*: *Prajñā*, which here means knowledge in a much broader sense than that of knowing specific objects.
4. *seven limbs*: Head, eyes, mouth, ears, lungs, stomach and feet.
5. *nineteen mouths*: The five sense organs; the five organs of action (speech, handling, locomotion, reproduction and excretion); the five breaths; mind (*manas*); intellect (*buddhi*); thought (*citta*); and sense of individuality (*ahaṃkāra*). (See Guénon 1981: 91–4.)
6. *Taijasa*: 'Of light (*tejas*)', 'radiant'.
7. *seven . . . mouths*: The body as one experiences it in dream seems to have the same organs and senses as the physical one, though

the objects with which it comes into contact – its 'food' – are subtler.

8. *Prājña*: 'Of knowledge', 'of consciousness' (from *prajñā*).
9. *consciousness*: *Prajñāna*, 'knowing', another derivative of *pra-jñā-*, 'to know'.
10. *inner controller*: For the inner controller (*antaryāmin*), see BU III.7.
11. *unseen*: Reading *adṛṣṭam*. Var. *adṛśyam*, 'invisible'.
12. *inviolable*: *Avyavahārya*, 'not able to be dealt with'. The verb *vy-ava-hṛ-* means 'to have dealings with' in any of a large number of ways – business, legal, social etc.
13. *proliferation*: *Prapañca* (cf. SU VI.6 and note). Here it is shown on the level of the microcosm, in the tendency of the mind to depart from its still centre and become caught up in outer things. When *prapañca* is stilled, the mind (or the universe) returns to its original unity.
14. *elements*: *Mātrā*: cf. PU VI.3–6 and notes.
15. *ādimattva*: Equivalent to *ādima-tva*, a common doubling of 't' before 'v': literally 'first-of-all-ness', an abstract noun from *ādima*, the superlative of *ādi*, 'first'. The short 'a' is the commonest sound in Sanskrit and the first letter in the scripts in which it is written, as well as in *aum*. Curiously, the words used to illustrate its qualities here all begin with the long 'ā'.
16. *equal*: With it (the lineage of knowers of *brahman*)? With anyone with whom he has dealings? *Samāna* has a wide range of meanings, including 'the same', 'equal' and 'whole, unified'. Since here it is used to explain *ubhayatva*, 'both-ness', the sense of this verse is perhaps that not only will 'the one who knows this' raise up a lineage of knowers of *brahman*, but *both* he and they will be equal and united in this knowledge. But it could also mean that he becomes equal-minded amid *both* joy and sorrow. Śaṅkara (Gambhīrānanda 1958: 222) thinks that 'the one who knows this' is treated equally by all: 'he does not become an object of envy to his enemies, as he is not to his friends'.
17. *from apī- (to merge into, to dissolve)*: Although *apī-* does not begin with 'm', it contains the related labial sound, 'p'. In what follows, 'The one who knows this', like a god, creates and reabsorbs his own world.
18. *without an element*: Or 'measureless' (*a-mātra*).

MAITRĪ UPANIṢAD

This Upaniṣad, variously called the Maitrāyaṇī, Maitrāyaṇa, Maitri or Maitrī, belongs to the Maitrāyaṇa tradition of the Black Yajurveda. It is named after one of the teachers in it, Maitreya or Maitri. In the present translation I have mainly followed the 'Text of the Vulgate' in van Buitenen's edition (1962); but, unlike van Buitenen, I have preferred to keep the simpler and better-known title for the Upaniṣad.

The position of the Maitrī is ambiguous, and it is even harder to date than the rest of the Upaniṣads. As van Buitenen says (1962:5):

> It is neither a 'principal' or 'classical', nor yet entirely a 'minor' upaniṣad, but falls somewhere between these uncertain and arbitrary categories . . . Macdonell concludes that its late date is undoubted: 'It is in fact a summing up of the old upaniṣadic doctrines with an admixture of ideas derived from the Sāṃkhya doctrine and Buddhism.'

Van Buitenen has attempted to reconstruct the original Upaniṣad, a teaching on the symbolism of fire-building closely related to that in TU Book II, though most of the existing Upaniṣad is clearly much later.

He disputes (pp. 6–7) the extent of Buddhist influence on the text as we have it, though the vocabulary includes many words more frequently found in Buddhist sources (Ranade and Belvalkar, 1927: 124–30).

[INVOCATION]

1. *of me*: And/or 'by me'. Invocation as for CU.

BOOK I

1. *should meditate on the self*: Thereby identifying the domestic rite of lighting the fire (*agnidhyāna*) with the Vedic sacrifice.
2. *OṂ. The fire-building . . . complete*: Van Buitenen (1962: 14, 29–36) considers that this material belongs to the original Upaniṣad, which resumes at VI.33. According to this theory, everything between is *upākhyāna* or additional explanation.
3. *a thousand days*: Reading *sahasrāhasya*. Var. *sahasrasya*, 'a thousand [years?]'.
4. *the entity*: *Tattvavid*, cf. SU I.10 and its n. 30.
5. *a hell-realm*: *Niraya*, 'down-going', generally a Buddhist word

for a hell (*naraka* being the usual Hindu term), though it is found also in ManU and Mbh.

6. *hide*: *Carman*, skin as the physical covering of the body as distinct from *tvac*, the skin as organ of touch: cf. TU I.7, where it is translated as 'cuticle'.
7. *bile, phlegm*: Bile (*pitta*) and phlegm (*kapha*), together with air (*vāta*), form the three humours of ancient Indian physiology.
8. *marrow of the flesh*: *Vasā*, thought of as a kind of marrow within flesh, as distinct from *majjā*, the marrow within bones.
9. *mucus*: *Śleṣman*, elsewhere often a synonym of *kapha* (see n. 7).
10. *being apart . . . not like*: *-iṣṭaviyoga-aniṣṭasaṃprayoga-*, a clear reminiscence of part of the Buddhist definition of suffering, *appiyehi sampayogo dukkho piyehi vippayogo dukkho* – 'Being with what is not dear is suffering; being apart from what is dear is suffering.' (From the Pāli version of the Dhammacakkapavattana Sutta, *Saṃyutta Nikāya* LVI.11.)
11. *trees . . . perish*: A double sandhi, *-vanaspataya udbhūta-* (from *-vanaspatayaḥ udbhūta-*), has been combined again to form *-vanaspatayodbhūta-*. Such irregular sandhis are a feature of this Upaniṣad.
12. *wheel-turning monarchs*: *Cakravartin*, 'wheel-turner', monarch ruling the entire world.
13. *ogres*: *Rākṣasa*, powerful demons such as Rāvaṇa.
14. *imps*: *Gaṇa*, 'troops' of demigods, especially those attendant on Śiva.
15. *vampires*: *Piśāca*, malevolent beings said to be fond of raw flesh.
16. *ghouls*: *Graha*, 'seizers', following Zaehner 1966: 220. *Graha* can also be the word for a planet.
17. *the precession of the Pole Star*: Because of the phenomenon of the precession of the equinoxes, the earth's celestial poles have a small yearly movement, turning full circle in about 28,000 years. As a result, Polaris, though it is called *dhruva*, 'the fixed', will not always remain the closest star to the north pole.
18. *the ropes of wind*: Believed to hold the planets in their orbits. The astronomical ideas here are characteristic of the second century on: see Pingree 1981: 12–13.
19. *our way out*: *Gati* here = the way we can go.

BOOK II

1. *Marut*: Wind-god, identifying the king with *prāṇa* = air.
2. *the breathing*: Called *ucchvāsa*, perhaps to distinguish the process of breathing from the *prāṇas*.
3. *the blessed Maitri*: Vulgate edition. The Southern edition has just, 'the blessed one'.
4. *The blissful one . . . self*: CU VIII.3.4.
5. *the blessed Maitri*: Vulgate edition. The Southern edition has, 'the blessed Maitreya'.
6. *the Vālakhilyas*: Said to be a group of 60,000 thumb-sized Ṛṣis who surround the chariot of the sun: hence, presumably, their intense bright energy (*tejas*).
7. *celibate*: *Ūrdhvaretas*, 'with seed kept above' in order to conserve their ascetic energy (*tapas*).
8. *tell us . . . know*: V. SM has, 'tell us this'.
9. *selfless*: Reading *anātmā* (V). SM has *anīśātmā*, 'whose self has no ruler'.
10. *returns*: Or 'exists' – *āvartate*.
11. *will, determination and conceit*: This triad recurs in this Upaniṣad, representing the qualities that distinguish the embodied self from the pure self. Will (*saṃkalpa*) is that which imagines or shapes; determination (*adhyavasāya*) seems to be that which becomes fixed on some object or idea; conceit (*abhimāna*) is that which causes us to think of ourselves as better (or, for that matter, worse) than our fellow beings.
12. *with all eyes*: *Viśvākṣas* (SM). V. has *viśvākhyas*, 'called all'. In either case, what is referred to is the embodied self within (or looking out from) every being.
13. *like a post*: The syntax here is odd: we should have expected the accusative, *sthāṇum iva*.
14. *he could not*: V. SM has, 'did not enter'.
15. *upāṃśu . . . antaryāma*: Vessels (*graha*, cf. BU III, n. 6) used in pressing the Soma. The process of digestion is being compared to the pressing.
16. *heat is created*: Literally 'one has created heat': var. 'the god has created heat'.
17. *the fire . . . all men*: Agni Vaiśvānara, cf. BU I.1 and its n. 2.
18. *The fire . . . sound*: BU V.9.
19. *hidden . . . place*: TU II.1.
20. *made of . . . self*: CU III.14.2.

21. *object*: *Akṛtārtha*. There seems to be a pun on two senses of *artha*, 'purpose' and 'sense-object'.
22. *holes*: For the senses: cf. Kaṭha IV.1.
23. *The organs . . . (raśmi)*: Van Buitenen (1962: 101) emends *buddhīndriyāni yāni* to *buddhīndriyāni khānīmāni*: 'The organs of perception are these holes: they are his reins.'
24. *made of nature*: *Prakṛtimaya*: cf. the introduction to the SU notes.
25. *wheel . . . potter*: Wheel-thrown pottery was known in the Indian subcontinent from around the fourth millennium BCE, and the potter working at the wheel would have been a familiar sight throughout the Upaniṣadic period.
26. *Poets . . . self*: SM omits *kavayaḥ*, just giving the indefinite, 'They declare it . . .'

BOOK III

1. *elemental self*: *Bhūtātman*, a lower level of 'self', related to the elements (*bhūta*) of the universe.
2. *five subtle . . . five gross elements*: *Tanmātra* (var. *tanmātrā*) and *mahābhūta*, in Sāṅkhya the subtle and gross levels of the five traditional elements.
3. *the self in the body*: V ('the self' understood). SM has just 'is said to be "the body"'.
4. *This self*: SM version, in which 'this self' seems to refer to the *bhūtātman*. V. has, 'this immortal self', suggesting the higher self.
5. *on which it rests*: Phrase added for clarity.
6. *elemental self*: Added for clarity.
7. *itself with itself*: *Ātmanā+ātmānam*.
8. *The maker . . . within*: Based on MDh XII.12.
9. *eighty-four hundred thousand wombs*: SM. V has, 'transformed in eighty-four forms'.
10. *thrower*: SM. I have taken *cakrin*, 'possessing/using a wheel', as a pottery term – cf. MaiU II.6. V has, 'by the potter'.
11. *is not overcome*: Taking *abhibhūyati* as a passive with active endings.
12. *close contact*: With the elements or strands.
13. *elsewhere*: Above, MaiU I.3.
14. *elsewhere*: Apparently not traced. (Henceforth I mark the quotations only when their sources have been traced.)

15. *unbelief*: *Nāstikya*, the state of being a *nāstika*, one who says *nāstika*, 'There is not.'
16. *prejudice*: *Asamatva*, 'unevenness', apparently not found in this sense elsewhere, but clearly suggesting not treating people (or life's vicissitudes) equally.
17. *craving*: *Tṛṣṇā*, literally 'thirst', but here clearly distinguished from the physical need to drink, *pipāsā*, included in the list of *tamas* qualities. *Tṛṣṇā* as a *rajas* quality must mean the basic tendency to desire: cf. the Buddhist usage of *tṛṣṇā* (Pāli *taṇhā*) as the basic form of desire that sets in motion the round of suffering.
18. *secretiveness*: *Vyāvṛtatva*. (So Hume (1995: 419): the state of being covered or hidden?)

BOOK IV

1. *it*: The elemental self.
2. *like one in great darkness*: SM. V has, 'like a great darkness'.
3. *made of artifice*: *Māyāmaya*: cf. BU II.5.19 and note, PU I.16 and SU I.10 and its n. 31.
4. *wrong seeing*: *Mithyādarśana*: cf. the Buddhist expression *mithyādṛṣṭi* (Pāli *micchādiṭṭhi*), 'wrong view'.
5. *delights . . . deceptively*: *Mithyāmanorāma*. 'Falsely [as in previous note] delighting the mind' – perhaps with a *trompe l'œil* effect.
6. *purposeless*: *Artha* here as goal or point, not sense-object.
7. *stages of life*: *Āśrama*, a stage of life, with its appropriate behaviour.
8. *In one's . . . everything*: SM. V has, 'This is the vow of own *dharma*.'
9. *purification from actions*: SM. V has, 'success in actions' (*karmasiddhi* for *karmaśuddhi*).
10. *someone has said*: *Evaṃ hy āha*, an indefinite expression repeatedly used in this Upaniṣad, '[some person or text] has said'. Zaehner (1966) takes it each time as 'he [i.e. Maitri] said'.
11. *Brahmā*: Probably not *brahman*.
12. *ridden*: *Rathita*, probably meaning 'used as a chariot'.
13. *speak rightly*: *Abhivādin*, 'speaking properly' – the opposite of *ativādin*, 'speaking beyond limits'. Some emend *abhivādy asi* to *ativādy asi*, *ativādin* in a good sense – cf. CU VII.15.4 and note.
14. *Brahmā, Rudra, Viṣṇu*: An early reference to these gods as a triad.
15. *and propitiate*: *Nihnuyāc ca*. With an alternative interpretation

of the verb *ni-hnu-*, Hume (1995: 422) interprets this as 'meditate upon, and praise, but then deny'. However, the text clearly speaks of moving up *with* them [the forms] – *tābhiḥ [= tanūbhiḥ] saha*, not beyond them.

16. *these verses about it*: In V these verses occur at VI.34.
17. *And is . . . false*: Reading *indriyārthāvimūḍhasya*. Literally 'And is not deluded by the sense objects, [those sense objects], in the power of desire, are false.' An alternative reading (followed by Hume 1995: 447) is *indriyārthavimūḍhasya*. To make sense of this, the verse must be divided in two, so that the first half follows on the sense of the previous verse: 'For the mind which, desiring truth, has died down in its own birthplace. But for the one deluded by the sense objects, [those sense objects], in the power of desire, are false.' This still leaves the genitive cases in the first half of the verse unexplained.
18. *consciousness*: *Citta*.
19. *a person's*: *Jantu*, elsewhere in the Upaniṣads referring to any being (Kaṭha II.20, SU III.20): here apparently referring to a human being.
20. *Would not . . . bonds*: Literally 'Who would not be freed . . . ?'
21. *of books*: Or 'of knots'.

BOOK V

1. *the Unfallen*: *Acyuta*, often a name of Viṣṇu and Kṛṣṇa.
2. *darkness*: Here *tamas* is one of three strands (*guṇa*).
3. *field-knower*: The conscious mind, cf. SU VI.16.
4. *threefold . . . infinite-fold*: The threefold is clearly Brahmā, Viṣṇu and Siva with their three *guṇas*. Van Buitenen (1962: 134) suggests that the eightfold is the eight *prakṛtis* (*avyakta*, *buddhi* and *ahaṃkāra* + five elements); that the elevenfold is the ten *indriyas* (sense-organs and organs of action) + *manas*; and (following the commentator Rāmatīrtha) that the twelvefold is the ten *indriyas* + *manas* + *buddhi*.
5. *the support*: *Pratiṣṭhā*, perhaps equated with *prakṛti*, as in SU I.7 and note.

BOOK VI

1. *They both . . . night*: Both human life and the sun move in cycles of a day and a night.
2. *The person . . . sun*: Cf. CU I.6.6.

3. *with the syllable . . . Sāvitrī*: I.e. with the syllable OṂ itself, the utterances (*vyāhṛti*) BHŪḤ, BHUVAḤ and SVAḤ, and the Gāyatrī Mantra.
4. *There are . . . unshaped*: Cf. BU II.3.1.
5. *real*: Or 'true' (*satya*).
6. *OṂ is three elements*: Cf. PU V.1–5, ManU *passim*, and notes.
7. *as warp and weft*: A reminiscence of BU III.6 and III.8.
8. *Elsewhere . . . said*: CU I.5.1.
9. *. . . the Udgītha*: Presumably one should understand, 'Contemplate the self as the Udgītha . . .'.
10. *three feet*: The states of waking, sleep and dreaming?
11. *three syllables*: 'a' + 'u' + 'm'?
12. *fivefold*: From the five *prāṇas*.
13. *The three-footed . . . roots above*: Based on RV X.90.3–4: cf. Kaṭha VI.1.
14. *this*: The universe, or being.
15. *This syllable . . . has*: A variation of Kaṭha II.16, with *puṇyam*, 'pure', for *brahman*.
16. *sound-body*: *Svanavatī tanū*, 'body possessing sound'.
17. *gender-body*: *Liṅgavatī* ('possessing sex or gender'), with *tanū* understood – and likewise with the following list of bodies.
18. *its mouth-body*: As the fires which receive the offering.
19. *Satyakāma . . . lower*: Slightly adapted from PU V.2.
20. *this was unuttered*: I.e. the universe, 'in the beginning'.
21. *Tat savitur vareṇyam*: See the notes to GM.
22. *Īśāna . . . Rudra*: Names which become associated with Śiva.
23. *the golden embryo*: Cf. SU III.4 and note.
24. *the goose*: *Haṃsa*: cf. *ekahaṃsa*, BU IV.3.11 and its n. 13.
25. *the teacher*: Or 'ruler' (*śāstṛ*).
26. *Nārāyaṇa*: Descendant of man (*nara*): in MDh I.10 identified with Brahmā, but in later texts generally with Viṣṇu.
27. *Arka*: 'The Shining', here as a name for the sun: cf. BU I.2.1 and its n. 13.
28. *Dhātṛ, Vidhātṛ*: Dhātṛ, the Disposer, and Vidhātṛ, the Ordainer, later often identified with Brahmā.
29. *Indu*: The moon.
30. *By granting . . . beings*: By abstaining from harming them.
31. *and setting . . . body*: Or 'and placing the objects of sense outside one's own body, one may win him'.
32. *Of all . . . creatures*: PU I.8.
33. *both*: Breath and the sun.
34. *resting in the practice*: Taking *prayogasthaṃ* with *manas*, gives

'resting in the practice (*prayoga*)'. Taking it with *dhyānaṃ*, 'medication', gives, 'as found in the texts' (another sense of *prayoga*).

35. *it*: The breath, cf. BU VI.1.14 and CU V.2.2.
36. *in all men*: *Vaiśvānara*.
37. *all offerings . . . creatures, too*: Assuming that *āhutayaś ca sarvāḥ prajās* . . . is an elliptical way of saying *āhutayaś ca sarvāś ca prajās* . . .
38. *does not . . . again*: Because he will not be reborn.
39. *the object of enjoyment*: *Bhojya*, 'that which is to be enjoyed'.
40. *the seed . . . enjoyment*: Because (domestic) animals (*paśu*) are enjoyed by human beings as food and by gods in the sacrifice.
41. *fourteenfold path*: The fourteenfold *tattvas* of the subtle body (*liṅga*), from the great (*mahat*) to the *viśeṣas*, particularities or separate elements. The whole passage, with its references to matter (*pradhāna*) and nature (*prakṛti*), has a strongly Sāṅkhya flavour.
42. *enjoys food with Agni*: Hume (1995: 431) suggests that, 'like Agni, [he] is not defiled by the impurities of the food eaten'.
43. *Whatever . . . end*: TU II.2.1.
44. *digest*: Literally 'cook'.
45. *by brahman*: Or 'by Brahmā'.
46. *Beings . . . food*: TU II.2.1.
47. *Food . . . old age*: *Annam eva vijarannam*. Van Buitenen (1962: 140) suggests that this 'strange form' may be 'a resanskritisation of a [Prakrit] *vejaraṇṇam vaijaraṇyam*: "something that fends off senility"'.
48. *moments*: *Nimeṣa*, cf. BU III.8.9 and note.
49. *with its twelve parts*: *Dvādaśātmaka*, 'having a twelvefold self or body'. The twelve are the months: there may also be an implied reference to the signs of the zodiac – see below, n. 50.
50. *Maghā . . . Śraviṣṭhā*: The lunar mansion of Maghā, which includes the fixed star Regulus in Leo, occupies 0° Leo to 13° 20' Leo of the sidereal zodiac. Śraviṣṭhā (= Dhaniṣṭhā, consisting of the stars of the constellation Delphinus) occupies 23° 20' Capricorn to 6° 40' Aquarius sidereal. As the two solstices must be opposite one another, we are presumably meant to take 'halfway through Śraviṣṭhā' as meaning 0° Aquarius sidereal rather than as the literal midpoint, 13° 20' Capricorn sidereal. To find a date when the solstices really occurred at these points, we would need to go back to around 1800 BCE. This passage clearly cannot be as ancient as this. It is possible that it contains memories of an

earlier time, though, as Indian astronomer/astrologer/mathematicians (*jyotiṣins*) early understood the phenomenon of the precession of the equinoxes, they could just as well have extrapolated it from their observations. (Roebuck 1992: 94–102, 18–21.)

51. *upward course . . . Soma*: The sun actually moves *from* 'halfway through Śraviṣṭhā' *to* 'the Constellation of the Serpents' (Āśleṣā, 16° 40' Cancer to 0° Leo sidereal).
52. *nine divisions . . . sun*: Each month is *navāṃśaka* – 'has nine divisions', each of which is also a quarter of a lunar mansion. The precision implied here suggests that the months are being equated with the signs of the zodiac. In later Indian astronomy/astrology, the 108 *navāṃśas* are particularly significant, reconciling the solar and lunar reckonings of planetary movement.
53. *Because . . . the measure*: Because of the subtlety of time (or of the *navāṃśas*), the year (or the month) is the measure.
54. *because . . . separateness*: Or 'because of its being made of parts (*pṛthaktva*)'.
55. *itself*: Time? The year?
56. *they reach their end*: *Astaṃ niyacchanti*, 'they go down in the west', like the heavenly bodies.
57. *ripens*: *Pac-*, 'to cook, 'to ripen' or 'to digest'.
58. *the one . . . Veda*: Taking *mahātmani* with the first half of the *śloka*. Van Buitenen (1962: 141) takes it with the second half: 'he who knows the great ātman in which time itself is cooked'. *Mahātman* here is evidently a *karmadhāraya* compound, 'the great self', not a *bahuvrīhi*, 'possessing great self', as in the earlier Upaniṣads (Kaṭha I.16, SU IV.17 and SU VI.23). (Cf. *śāntātman* in MaiU V.1, stanza 4, which I have taken simply as 'peaceful self'.
59. *has the sun as its self*: Or 'is the self of the sun'.
60. *has space as his self*: Or 'is the self of space'.
61. *pure consciousness*: *Cetāmātra*, apparently not known to Monier-Williams's Sanskrit dictionary, but clearly related to *citta*.
62. *digests*: Literally 'cooks'.
63. *withdrawal*: Of the senses from their objects.
64. *maintaining*: *Dhāraṇā*, 'holding [an object] in mind'.
65. *the powerful one*: *Īśa*, cf. SU I.8 and note.
66. *womb of brahman*: *Brahmayoni*, cf. SU V.6 and note.
67. *unfailing*: *Avyaya*, cf. *akṣara*.
68. *without forming concepts*: *Niḥsaṃkalpa*. There seems to be a break in the text here.
69. *not breath*: Or 'without breath' (*aprāṇa*).

70. *maintain*: *Dhārayet*: cf. *dhāraṇā* (n. 64).
71. *the fourth state*: *Turyākhya*, i.e. neither waking, dreaming nor dreamless sleep.
72. *subtle form*: *Liṅga*.
73. *investigating*: *Tarka*.
74. *Because . . . liberation*: The grammar here is a little odd. 'On account of selflessness, one [or he] is to be thought of as uncountable, without source (*ayoni*) [both masc.], the mark of liberation.'
75. *Suṣumṇā*: Perhaps the earliest mention by name of the channel Suṣumṇā, through which, according to Tantric teaching, energy rises up through the body via the *cakras*. When it reaches the topmost *cakra*, just above the fontanelle, enlightenment is attained.
76. *absoluteness*: *Kevalatva*: cf. SU I.11 and note.
77. *breath*: Literally 'air' (*anila*).
78. *By the shoreless*: Or 'By what is not the shore'.
79. *union*: *Sāyujya*, cf. BU I.3.22 and its n. 43, CU II.20.2 and note.
80. *ultimate bliss*: *Nirvṛtatva*.
81. *The body . . . point*: Cf. MuU II.2.3–4.
82. *a circle of torchlight*: *Ālātacakra*, the illusory circle of light formed by whirling a source of light.
83. *the moon*: Soma, here a synonym for the moon.
84. *entity*: *Tattva*, cf. SU I.10 and its n. 30.
85. *the objects of sense*: *Lakṣya*, the 'targets' of the senses.
86. *the pure*: Or 'the seed' (*śukra*).
87. *becoming*: Or 'being' (*bhāva*).
88. *in space*: *Nabhas*, i.e. within the heart.
89. *mind*: Added for clarity.
90. *that*: The light.
91. *quickly*: Reading *yathācireṇa* as *yathā* + *acireṇa*: or 'eventually', reading it as *yathā cireṇa*.
92. *along with its support*: Hume (1995: 440) adds, '– and is not overcome'.
93. *the treasury*: *Kośa*, used of various kinds of receptacle or container.
94. *itself*: Or 'ourself/ourselves'.
95. *the renouncer's life*: *Pravrajyā*, 'going forth' (to become a religious wanderer) or the state of such a wanderer.
96. *as a miner . . . mine*: Mining was known in India from the Mauryan period. Extensive remains of deep mines, with wooden pit-props, have reliable radiocarbon dates of third–second

century BCE. The metals which were mined included copper, lead, silver and zinc (Craddock et al., 1989).

97. *sheath . . . four layers of net*: For the four layers of the sheath (*kośa*), see MaiU VI.38.
98. *the embodied one*: *Dehin*, cf. Kaṭha V.7 and note.
99. *went within his heart*: Or 'became the one within Bṛhadratha's heart'?
100. *He . . . to him*: The syntax suggests that Śākāyanya paid homage to Bṛhadratha, as now being liberated. Another possible interpretation is that Bṛhadratha paid homage to Śākāyanya, as his guru. See n. 110, below.
101. *the sons of Prajāpati*: The Vālakhilyas.
102. *the pairs*: Of opposites: pleasure and pain, praise and blame, etc. This passage is perhaps to be taken as a further piece of Śākāyanya's teaching.
103. *One should not . . . peace*: Cf. BU VI.3.12 and SU VI.22.
104. *devoted to nothing else*: Or 'devoted to no other [teacher]' (*anany-abhakta*).
105. *that delights*: *Abhilāṣiṇi*, agreeing with *brahmaṇi*, seems improbable: we should have expected this description to refer to the meditator.
106. *Having . . . of that*: Another tricky passage. *anyas tatphalacchinnapāśo*: van Buitenen (1962: 146) thinks there has been a lacuna in the text, and takes it as 'The other, whose ropes that tie him to the results of his actions have been cut'. So he translates the whole sentence as 'The other, whose ropes that tie him to the results of his acts have been cut, who has no worldly hopes, who, as an ātman, has no fear for others, attains permanently to indestructible, unmeasurable bliss.'
107. *to determination*: Plus will and conceit.
108. *Desire . . . is mind*: = BU I.5.3.
109. *When . . . bourn*: Kaṭha VI.10.
110. *He . . . to him*: Here it seems clear that Bṛhadratha is paying homage to Śākāyanya (cf. n. 100).
111. *he*: Bṛhadratha: cf. MaiU II.1 and note.
112. *Breaking through . . . outward*: Cf. BU V.10.1.
113. *Wanders round*: In *saṃsāra* (*saṃ-sṛ-*).
114. *apsarases . . . so-called*: Or *apsarases*, *marīcis* and *bhānavīs*, though the position of *ca* suggests the interpretation that I have followed. The rays of the sun (*marīci*) are being regarded as divine females, *apsarases* or heavenly nymphs and *bhānavī*, 'connected with, or daughters of, Bhānu, the sun'.

115. *signs*: *Liṅga*.
116. *most delicious*: Or most subtle (*śivatama*). Flavour is the essence of water, as heat is of fire.
117. *Just like . . . here*: As in MaiU VI.26.
118. *Its inner . . . truth*: Cf. BU II.1.20.
119. *As smoke . . . from it*: Cf. BU IV.5.11.
120. *man-shaped fire*: Van Buitenen (1962: 88–9) considers this teaching on the symbolism of the fire, which carries on the theme of MaiU I.1, to be the core of the original Upaniṣad, and most of what comes in between to have been added as *upākhyāna*, or additional explanation. Cf. the symbolism of the altar, which is both a man and a bird, in TU II.1–5.
121. *Pavamāna, Pāvaka and Śuci*: 'Purifying', 'Purifier' and 'Clean', three offerings made into the fires at the sacrifice – 'so by transference, applied, as epithets, to the fire itself' (Hume 1995: 446).
122. *He makes . . . mouth*: Southern text, *haviṣkṛtam etenāsye 'nnam*, 'food is offered by him in the mouth' – 'he' being the patron of the sacrifice, and so symbolically any eater of food who knows this. V has *āviṣkṛtam etenāsya yajñam*, 'by this the sacrifice becomes manifest'.
123. *thought of*: Punningly, also 'built up' (*cetavya*).
124. *A bird . . . fire*: For the four symbolic beings, cf. CU IV.5–8 and notes. Here brightness (*tejas*) replaces the *agni* of the earlier text.
125. *in the self*: V adds here, ' "There are these verses about it: Just as, without fuel, a fire . . . brings freedom, so it is recorded" ', which are in IV.6 in the Southern tradition.
126. *think of*: Or 'build up'.
127. *Homage to Agni . . . sacrifice*: For the ritual, cf. CU II.24.5 ff.
128. *The face . . . dharma*: Cf. IU 15 and BU V.15.1, but with *viṣṇave* for *dṛṣṭaye*.
129. *That person . . . he*: Variation of IU 16.
130. *The one . . . white form*: Cf. CU I.6.5–6, I.7.4–5 and III.2.3.
131. *energy*: *Tejas*.
132. *within the space*: *Nabhas*, i.e. within the heart.
133. *glory*: *Bhargas*, a reference to the Gāyatrī.
134. *the immortal*: Or 'the nectar' (*amṛta*).
135. *eight-footed*: Referring to the cardinal and intermediate points (Zaehner, 166: 241)?
136. *double dharmas*: Reading *dvidharmāṇāṃ* (perhaps referring to higher and lower truth?). V has *dvidharmo 'ndhaṃ*, 'blind to the twofold *dharmas*, blazing with energy' (perhaps referring to the pairs of opposites).

137. *Ud*: Cf. CU I.6.7.
138. *the knower of unity*: *Savit*, perhaps from *sa*, 'together', + *vid*, 'knowing': not found elsewhere, but in the verse contrasted with *dvaitavit* ('knower of duality').
139. *the pure*: Or 'the seed' (*śukra*).
140. *the ocean of light*: *Bhānu arṇava*, 'the ocean which is light (or the sun)'.
141. *exists among the gods*: 'Or 'goes among the gods' (*antargaḥ surāṇāṃ*, literally '[is] a goer-among of the gods'). I have assumed that *antarga* here is being used in the same sense as *antargata* earlier in this paragraph, where, as often in Sanskrit, 'going' or 'having gone' somewhere simply means being there.
142. *in the highest heaven*: *Parame vyoman*, cf. TU II.1 and its n. 34.
143. *fire*: Added for clarity.
144. *ritual enclosure*: *Vedi*, here probably of the entire ritual area rather than just the fire-altar.
145. *sthālīpāka*: Cf. BU VI.4.19.
146. *meritorious*: *Puṇya*.
147. *the pure one*: Probably the sun.
148. *abundance of food*: Van Buitenen (1962: 54–60) suggests emending *annabahu* to *anābhū*, which in MDh I.6.1.41b is said to be a channel which takes offerings to the sun.
149. *The offering . . . creatures*: = MDh III.76.
150. *true desire, true resolve*: Cf. CU VIII.1.5 etc.
151. *a thumb in length*: Cf. Kaṭha IV.12–13 and VI.17; SU V.8. The span (*prādeśa*) is a measure of twelve thumbs (*aṅguṣṭha*).
152. *greatness*: *Mahas*, cf. TU I.5 and note.
153. *beings*: Or worlds (*bhuvanāni*).

BOOK VII

1. *the Gāyatra*: The *Gāyatra* (here = *Gāyatrī*) and the others named second in the lists (VII.1–5) are all metres used in Vedic hymns.
2. *the Trivṛt*: 'Threefold'. The *Trivṛt*, *Pañcadaśa* ('fifteen'), *Saptadaśa* ('seventeen'), *Ekaviṃśa* ('twenty-one'), *Paṅkti* ('pentad'), *Triṇava* ('three times nine') and *Trayastriṃśa* ('thirty-three') are all *stomas*, or hymn-sequences chanted by the Udgātṛ and his assistants (cf. CU I.3.10 and note).
3. *the Rathantara*: The *Rathantara*, *Bṛhat*, *Vairūpa*, *Vairāja*, *Śākvara* and *Raivata* are *sāmans*: cf. CU II *passim*, especially chs. 12, 14 and 16, and KauU I.5.
4. *He is unthinkable*: In this and the following verses, some of these

sets of descriptions are in the masculine gender, others in the neuter. I have marked this by translating the former with 'he is' and the latter with 'it is'.

5. *ruler*: *Īśāna*.
6. *Soma*: Here apparently distinct from the moon, who as *candramas* is mentioned in MaiU VII.5. (Though Varuṇa occurs in two different forms.)
7. *Śukra*: 'Bright/pure one' or 'Seed', the guru of the *asuras*, from about the second century CE identified with the planet Venus.
8. *Śani*: 'Slow one': the planet Saturn.
9. *Rāhu, Ketu*: Eclipse demons, representing the lunar nodes, points where the apparent paths of the sun and moon cross, and eclipses can occur. As a planetary deity, Rāhu ('Seizer') is the more ancient, originally personifying both lunar modes (cf. CU VIII.13). Ketu ('Comet') originally seems to have represented such phenomena as comets and meteors: the date at which he became a fully fledged planetary deity is controversial. The present passage seems to treat him as such: if the reference is original, it seems to be earlier than any of those in Markel 1990.
10. *śarabhas*: Mythical beasts with eight legs, said to be stronger than an elephant.
11. *the separator*: *Vidhāraṇa*, cf. the separating dam (*setu vidhāraṇa*) in v. 7.
12. *of true resolve . . . desire*: A slight variation on CU VIII.1.5.
13. *the separating dam*: Cf. BU IV.4.22 and (var.) CU VIII.4.1.
14. *in heaven*: *Nabhas*. Van Buitenen (1962: 88–9) regards verses VII.1–7 as part of the original Upaniṣad, and the passages after 'rest . . . in heaven' as editorial additions. However, the references to astrological deities, especially Rāhu and Ketu, seem to me to suggest a later date.
15. *bound for heaven*: *Svargya*, 'destined for a heavenly world'.
16. *who have gone forth*: *Pravrajita*. Some take this as a separate item in the list: Hume (1995: 455), for example, has, 'religious mendicants, actors . . .', presumably taking it to refer to those who have gone forth outside the Vedic tradition. The verb *pra-vraj-*, 'to go forth', is often used of the ordination of Buddhist and Jain monks and nuns, but it is also what Yājñavalkya is about to do in BU IV.5.2. Moreover, *pravrajyā* is praised within the Maitrī itself (VI.28 and its n. 95).
17. *renegades . . . kings*: 'Those who have fallen into working for kings', as spies etc. Since Hume's translation of this phrase could hardly be bettered, I have adapted it, with thanks.

18. *others who ... carry skulls*: Those who bear the emblems of different traditions of holy men, without keeping the vows appropriate to their way of life.
19. *juggleries ... doctrine*: *Nairātmyavāda-kuhaka*, clearly a hit at Buddhism. The author appears to be trying to distance himself from the apparent sympathy for Buddhist ideas that he shows elsewhere, e.g. at MaiU VI.20, where to be *nirātman*, 'selfless', is a desirable state.
20. *The difference ... ignorance*: Reading *vedāvidyāntaraṃ*: var. *vedavidyāntaraṃ*, 'what is within the knowledge of the Veda'.
21. *Becoming Śukra ... demons*: Bṛhaspati, the guru of the gods, is said to have taken on the form of Śukra, the guru of the demons, to teach them false doctrine – often said to be that of the Cārvākas or materialists. Later, in the Purāṇas, Viṣṇu takes on the same role, when he is described as becoming incarnate as the Buddha and Mahāvīra to confuse the demons.
22. *the course*: I.e. of right conduct.
23. *These two ... you*: Variation of Kaṭha II.4.
24. *Whoever ... immortality*: = IU 11.
25. *Entwined ... blind*: Variation of Kaṭha II.5 and MuU I.2.8.
26. *Brahmā*: Or *brahman*.
27. *their raft*: With which they should cross to the other shore of *saṃsāra*.
28. *of breath*: Added for clarity.
29. *from limb to limb*: Of the tree.
30. *energy*: *Tejas*. This passage is almost a verse paraphrase of BU IV.2.2–4.
31. *the wind*: *Māruta*, here equated with breath.
32. *from space*: *Khaja*, 'born of the space [within the heart]'; punningly also invoking fire 'of friction' (*khaja*, churning or stirring).
33. *Subtler ... size*: Or perhaps, 'Subtler (*aṇu*) than subtle (*aṇu*): twice as subtle in the region of the throat; on the tip of the tongue know it to be three times as subtle.' This verse seems to suggest a theory of the *cakras*.
34. *Seeing ... everywhere*: Variation on the verse in CU VII.26.2.
35. *deeply asleep*: *Supta* ('asleep') is here equivalent to *suṣupta*, referring to dreamless sleep.
36. *the great self*: *Mahātman*, cf. VI.15 and its n. 58.

Glossary

I have not usually included the names of people who are mentioned only once and about whom nothing else appears to be known. Words in bold italics denote cross-references.

Abhipratārin Kākṣaseni See ***Śaunaka Kāpeya***.
Adhvaryu See ***priests***.
Ādi See CU II, n. 3.
Aditi 'Boundless', goddess of space, mother of the ***Ādityas***.
Āditya 'Son of ***Aditi***', name of a group of gods of solar character, usually twelve in number, and often identified with the sun in the twelve months of the year. In BU, Āditya is the regular word for 'sun', and has generally been translated as such.
Agni Fire and its god, believed to carry the sacrificial offerings to the heavenly world: in the Upaniṣads, often as ***Vaiśvānara***. For the fire ***element***, the word ***tejas*** is generally preferred.
Agnīdhra 'Fire-kindler', assistant of the ***Brahmā priest***, responsible for maintaining the sacrificial ***fires***.
Agnīdhrīya fire A fire lit for certain ***sacrifices*** in addition to the three main ***fires*** (***Āhavanīya***, ***Dakṣiṇāgni*** and ***Gārhapatya***); associated with the ***Agnīdhra*** priest.
Agnihotra The daily fire ***sacrifice***.
Agniṣṭoma 'Praise of Agni', a five-day ***sacrifice***, carried out on behalf of a ***Brāhmaṇa*** seeking to win heaven.
Ahaṃkāra (or *ahaṅkāra*) Literally 'the I-maker': the sense of 'I' or ego – distinct from the self, or ***ātman***. In ***Sāṅkhya*** philosophy, within the psyche and the universe, the stage at which an apparent self-awareness emerges within nature (***prakṛti***).
Āhavanīya fire 'Offering-fire', lit in the east of the sacrificial area.
Aikṣvāka 'Descendant of Ikṣvāku', ***Bṛhadratha***.
Ajātaśatru A king of Kāśī, probably not the same as the Ajātasattu of Magadha of the Buddhist tradition – see Introduction.
Ājīvikas, the A religious movement founded around the fifth century

BCE by Makkhali Gosāla, said to have been a contemporary and sometime follower of Mahāvīra, the founder of ***Jainism***. The Ājīvikas believed that, in order to achieve liberation, the individual had to live out (*ā-jīv-*) his or her own destiny – a view criticized by members of other religions on the grounds that it denied responsibility for one's actions. The Ājīvika religion survived in southern India until ät least the fourteenth century CE, but has now disappeared.

Ākāśa 'Space', 'ether', often regarded as a fifth ***element***, along with earth, water, fire and air.

Akṣara (1) 'Imperishable, unfailing'; (2) 'syllable'. As (1), with overtones of (2), often a synonym for ***OṂ***.

Ambhiṇī 'Powerful', with ***Vāc***, one of only two female teachers mentioned in the lineage lists of the Bṛhadāraṇyaka (BU VI.5.3).

Ancestors Translation of *pitṛ*, 'fathers', 'parents' – deified ancestors worshipped in the ***Śrāddha*** ceremony, which enabled them to maintain a place in their special realm.

Aṅgiras Name of a Vedic sage and of his family, priests associated with the ***Atharvans***. (In MuU I.1 also appearing as *Aṅgir*, apparently for the sake of the metre.) With *Atharvan*, it is also a name for the verses of the ***Atharvaveda***.

Āṅgirasa Descendant of ***Aṅgiras***.

Antarikṣa 'Middle-air', the intermediate space between sky (***dyaus***) and earth (***pṛthivī***), with which it completes the three worlds: so translated to distinguish it from air or wind (***vāyu***) and space (***ākāśa***).

Anumati 'Favour', personified as goddess of the day before full moon. (Cf. ***Sinīvalī***.)

Anuṣṭubh A metre of thirty-two syllables in four ***pādas*** – the *śloka*, the most common metre in Sanskrit verse from the epics on.

Anvāhāryapacana = ***Dakṣiṇāgni fire***.

Āpad-dharma 'Misfortune-***dharma***': alternative standards of behaviour permissible in times of natural disaster or war, when it may not be possible to keep to the rules of conduct, food or livelihood appropriate to one's *dharma* in normal times.

Āpaḥ 'The waters' – always plural, and in the Upaniṣads generally retaining the numinous quality that it has in the ***Vedas***, where these beings are regarded as goddesses. (More ordinary words for water are singular: where possible I have kept this distinction in the translation.) Also used for the ***element*** of water.

Apāna A ***prāṇa***: see Introduction, under 'Key Concepts'.

Apsaras Heavenly nymph, female counterpart of *gandharva*.

Āraṇyaka 'Forest Teaching', the third part of each of the four ***Vedas***, consisting of exploration of the inner meaning of the ritual.

Aryaman 'Companion', an *Āditya* protecting hospitality.
Āruṇi See *Uddālaka Āruṇi*.
Āśramas Four stages of life, designed to integrate both household life and renunciation into the social structure: the stages are those of the *brahmacārin*, student of the *Vedas*; *gṛhastha*, or householder; *vanaprastha*, forest-dweller; and *sannyāsin*, wandering renouncer.
Asuras, 'Powerful Ones', demons, rivals to the gods or *devas*. (In the myths, *asuras* by no means always behave badly, or *devas* well.)
Aśvamedha The horse-*sacrifice*: see BU I.1 and notes.
Aśvapati Kaikeya A king of the Kekayas, and a teacher in CU V.11–24 and SBr X.6.1.2.
Aśvin 'Horseman', title of the twin heavenly physicians Dasra and Nāsatya, students of the sage *Dadhyac Ātharvaṇa*, BU II.5.16–19.
Atharvan Name of a Vedic sage and of his family, priests associated with the *Aṅgirases*. (In MuU I.1 also appearing as *Atharva*, apparently for the sake of the metre.) With *Aṅgiras*, it is also a name for the verses of the *Atharvaveda*.
Ātharvaṇa Descendant of *Atharvan*.
Atharvans and Aṅgirases, hymns of the Upaniṣadic term for the *Atharvaveda*.
Atharvaveda The *Veda* consisting of hymns for the rituals of the *Atharvan* and *Aṅgiras* priests. In the early Upaniṣads, it is still seen as somewhat apart from the *Ṛgveda, Yajurveda* and *Sāmaveda*.
Atirātra 'Overnight', a form of *Soma sacrifice*.
Ātman 'Self': see Introduction under 'Key Concepts'.
Ayāsya Āṅgirasa One of the seers of the *Ṛgveda*.
Baka Dālbhya A sage mentioned in CU I.2.13 and I.12, and in JB I.9.2.
Bālāki the Proud (*Dṛpta-Bālāki*) See *Gārgya Bālāki*.
Bārku Vārṣṇa A teacher mentioned in BU IV.1.4, and also in SBr I.1.1.10.
Bhadra 'Auspicious', a *sāman*.
Bhaga '(Good) Fortune', an *Āditya*.
Bhakti Loving devotion, especially as a way of spiritual practice.
Bhṛgu Vāruṇi *Varuṇa*'s son and student in TU III.
BHŪḤ A *vyāhṛti* representing the world of earth.
BHUVAḤ A *vyāhṛti* representing the world of middle-air (*antarikṣa*).
Brahmā (1) An important god, embodying the priestly power; (2) a priest, expert in all three *Vedas*, responsible for silently overseeing the whole process of the *sacrifice* and correcting any mistakes; (3) in Kaṭha I.9, a polite mode of address to a *Brāhmaṇa*. In classical Hinduism, sense (1) comes to predominate: Brahmā is regarded as

the first member of the main triad of gods, as the Creator, along with *Viṣṇu* the Preserver and *Śiva* the Destroyer.

Brahmacārin A celibate student living in a teacher's house and studying the *Vedas*.

Brahmacarya The practice of the *brahmacārin*: religious studentship, celibacy.

Brahmadatta Caikitāneya A teacher mentioned in BU I.3.24, and in JU I.37 and I.59.

Brahman See Introduction, under 'Key Concepts'.

Brāhmaṇa (1) The second part of each of the four *Vedas*, containing material on the conduct and meaning of ritual; (2) a 'Brahmin', a member of the priestly class.

Brahmanaspati 'Lord of *brahman*', a deity identified with *Bṛhaspati*.

Bṛhadratha A royal sage, student of *Śākāyanya* in MaiU.

Bṛhaspati 'Lord of Sacred Speech', the priest of the gods, later identified with the planet Jupiter.

Bṛhat 'Great', a *sāman* addressed to *Indra* in *Bṛhatī/Śatobṛhatī* metre.

Bṛhatī, 'Great' (f.), a metre of thirty-six syllables in four *pādas*, often alternated in Vedic poetry with the *Śatobṛhatī* (forty syllables).

Buddhi Intellect or intelligence: in everyday usage, the intellect or seat of thought; in a *Sāṅkhya*-influenced technical sense, the mirror of consciousness or primary evolute of nature. In Sāṅkhya, this is the first stage of evolution of both the world and the psyche: when the original unmanifest state of nature (*prakṛti*) becomes disturbed, the *sattvaguṇa* predominates, producing the *tattva* of *buddhi* in the psyche, and *mahat*, its equivalent, in the cosmic realm. Since Sāṇkhya regards *prakṛti* as unconscious, and only *puruṣa* as genuinely conscious, *buddhi* is regarded as a mirror formed of *prakṛti* but reflecting *puruṣa*.

Buḍila Āśvatarāśvi Also called *Vaiyāghrapadya*, a *Brāhmaṇa* mentioned at BU V.14.8 and at CU V.11–16.

Cakra Literally 'wheel', one of the centres of energy in the body according to *Tantra* and *Yoga*. The main *cakras* are said to be those of earth, at the base of the spine; water, in the sexual area; fire, at the navel; air, in the heart; space, in the throat; and mind, in the forehead, between the brows. Each *cakra* has its own name, colour, sacred syllables and meditation symbols, and is visualized as a lotus of a different number of petals. The unmanifest is represented by the *sahasrāra* ('thousand-spoked') *cakra*, seen as a thousand-petalled lotus just above the fontanelle on top of the head: liberation is believed to occur when the energy known as Kuṇḍalinī, in most beings dormant in the lowest *cakra*, is awakened and arises to the *sahasrāra cakra* through the channel known as ***Suṣumnā***. (The spelling is frequently Anglicized to 'chakra' – see the Sanskrit Pronunciation guide.)

Caṇḍāla A member of a caste formerly regarded as untouchable.

Chandas Poetic metre, especially of the ***Vedas***: (in pl.) sometimes a synonym for the Vedas themselves. The metres are themselves viewed as sacred, and sometimes personified as goddesses.

Constellations See ***Nakṣatra***.

Dadhyac Ātharvaṇa A sage whose curious name ('Yoghurt-Sprinkler') suggests a connection with nourishment and sustenance. He had received the honey-teaching from ***Indra***, but could not pass it on under penalty of having his head cut off. The ***Aśvin*** twins wanted the teaching, and Dadhyac promised to give it to them. Before he did, the Aśvins replaced his head with that of a horse, so that when Indra cut off the horse-head they were able to put back Dadhyac's original head. The exchange of heads seems to suggest a shamanistic experience.

Dakṣiṇā The gift to the priests at the end of a ***sacrifice***.

Dakṣiṇāgni fire The 'southern fire', also called *Anvāhāryapacana*, lit in the south of the sacrificial area.

Darśana 'Seeing', 'view', hence religious or philosophical system. There were many *darśanas* current in the late centuries BCE and early centuries CE, many of them – such as those of the ***Jains*** and Buddhists – being regarded by Hindus as heterodox. So a system of Six Darśanas was developed as part of the process of defining Hindu orthodoxy. The Six are (1) Nyāya, 'rule', logic, the study of reasoning and debate; (2) Vaiśeṣika, 'atomism', the study of the nature of things; (3) ***Sāṅkhya***, 'enumerationism', the study of the evolution from first causes of the world as we perceive it; (4) ***Yoga***, 'yoke', 'application', spiritual practice, the physical, mental and moral disciplines designed to lead to liberation; (5) Mīmāṃsā, 'inquiry', the science of scriptural exegesis, concerned especially with understanding and correct practice of Vedic ***sacrifice***, and based on the ***Brāhmaṇas***; (6) ***Vedānta***, 'The end of the Veda', the study of the inner meaning of the ***Vedas***, based on the Upaniṣads. (The better-known use of *darśana*, as the auspicious sight of a divine person or image, does not seem to occur in the Upaniṣads.)

Death See ***Mṛtyu***, ***Yama***.

Demons See *asuras*.

Devas 'Bright Ones', the gods: often used of the powers in the microcosm (sight, breath etc.) as well as those in the macrocosm (sun, air etc.).

Dharma Cosmic law, the right order of things, one's proper role in life. I have generally left it untranslated.

Dhātṛ 'Disposer', 'Arranger', a creator-god, in the *Vedas* associated with *Savitṛ* and the *Ādityas*: later identified with *Prajāpati* and *Brahmā*.

Dīkṣā The initiation of the *yajamāna* and his wife at the beginning of the *sacrifice*.

Direction (*diś*) The directions, or cardinal points (sometimes including the intermediate points, and/or zenith and nadir), are important in Vedic ritual and may be personified as goddesses (CU III.15.2). 'The directions' is often a way of saying 'the space around us'. In the lists of correspondences between macrocosm and microcosm, they are linked with the sense of hearing, presumably because space as experienced by hearing extends in all directions, whereas that experienced by the other senses is limited in different ways: e.g. the field of vision extends only in front.

Dyaus Sky and its god (occasionally goddess – see BU note I.71).

Ekarṣi (Eka-Ṛṣi) The One Seer, a prototype of the *Ṛṣi*: see Mitchiner 1982: 306–7.

Elements (*bhūta*, 'being', 'having come to be') Most schools of thought in ancient India believed that matter was made up of either four elements – earth (*pṛthivī*), water (*āpaḥ*, *udaka*), fire (*tejas*), and air (*vāyu*) – or five: the above plus space/ether (*ākāśa*). The proportion of the earth element present was thought to determine size, weight, and hardness or softness; of the water element, cohesiveness; of the fire element, heat or cold; and of the air element, motion. *Sāṅkhya* theory analyses the elements into two different levels. The gross elements (*mahābhūta*, 'great elements') make up physical matter, while the subtle elements (*tanmātra*, 'having the measure of that', i.e. 'only that') are seen as the constituents of a pure kind of matter directly experienced by the sense organs. Subtle earth is experienced as sound, touch, colour, taste and smell; water as sound, touch, colour and taste; fire as sound, touch and colour; air as sound and touch; and space as sound.

Fire, sacrificial Of central importance in Vedic ritual, in which *Agni*, as fire-god, was belived to carry offerings to the gods. See *Agnīdhrīya, Āhavanīya, Dakṣiṇāgni* and *Gārhapatya*.

Gandhāra The north-western region of the Indian subcontinent, including a large part of modern Pakistan.

Gandharva In later literature *gandharvas* are generally known as heavenly musicians, male counterparts of the *apsarases*; in the Upaniṣads they appear as demigods with their own world, and (in

BU III.3.1 and III.7.1) as beings that may possess human women who then act as oracles.

Gārgī Vācaknavī A woman disputant in the great debate of BU III (see BU III.6 and III.8).

Gārgya (fem. *Gārgī*) The family name of several people mentioned in the Upaniṣads.

Gārgya Bālāki A teacher who overreaches himself in BU II.1 and Kau IV.

Gārhapatya fire The householder's fire, into which the *yajamāna* and his wife make their offerings. It is lit from the domestic fire, which the householder maintains throughout his household life, and the other sacrificial *fires* are lit from it. Alternatively, the householder may maintain all three sacrificial fires permanently.

Gautama 'Descendant of Gotama': *gotra* name of several important figures in the Upaniṣads, including *Uddālaka Āruṇi, Śvetaketu Āruṇeya, Hāridrumata Gautama* and *Naciketas*. (Gotama was one of the Seven *Ṛṣis* – see BU II.2.3–4 and notes.) Curiously, the name Gautama (often in its *Pāli* form, 'Gotama') is best known as the family name of the Buddha, who was a *Kṣatriya*. He came from a community of north-east India and Nepal called the Sakyas (Sanskrit 'Śakyas'), one of a number of tribes or clans who lived in a semi-democratic system in which each head of a family was called a 'king' (*rājan*) and was entitled to attend the tribal assembly. It appears that many of these Kṣatriya tribes used *Brāhmaṇa gotra* names, though no one entirely knows why. (They certainly did not keep to the rule forbidding marriage within the *gotra*.)

Gāyatra A *sāman* in *Gāyatrī* metre: in CU II.11 and Mai U VIII.1 equivalent to *Gāyatrī*.

Gāyatrī 'She who sings', a metre of twenty-four syllables in three *pādas*; specifically, the most famous verse in that metre (see GM notes).

Ghee (Sanskrit *ghṛta*) Clarified butter, poured into the fire as an offering in the Vedic *sacrifice*.

Glāva Maitreya A sage who in CU I.12 is mentioned either as synonymous with *Baka Dālbhya* or as an alternative source of his teaching.

Gods See *devas*.

Gośruti Vaiyāghrapadya A student of *Satyakāma Jābāla* in CU V.2.3 and also in SA IX.7.

Gotra Exogamous lineage within the *Brāhmaṇa* class, derived in the paternal line from one of the ancient sages: see e.g. *Gautama*.

Guṇas The three 'strands' or qualities from which existence as we know it is composed: *sattva* (goodness, brightness, purity), *rajas* (passion) and *tamas* (darkness). This doctrine seems to be foreshadowed in CU VI.4.1, is referred to throughout SU (see e.g. I.3. IV.5 and notes), and appears in developed form in MaiU III.3–5 and V.2.

Hāridrumata Gautama Teacher of ***Satyakāma Jābāla*** in CU IV.4 and IV.9.

Hiṅkāra A humming resonation at the start of a ***sāman***, said to resemble the lowing of cattle. Despite the name, the sound made is *huṃ*, not *hiṃ*: see also CU I, n.28.

Hotṛ See ***priests***.

Ilā (or *Iḍā*, *Iḷā*, *Irā*) 'Refreshment', a goddess personifying the offerings of milk and ***ghee***. She is called *Maitrāvaruṇī*, daughter of ***Mitra*** and ***Varuṇa***, because she was born through the favour of those two gods.

Indra 'Lord', an ***Āditya***, king of the ***devas***, a god of sky and weather, wielder of the thunderbolt and destroyer of demons and monsters. In the ***Vedas*** he appears as a ***Soma***-drinking, womanizing roisterer, conquering his enemies sometimes by treacherous means. KauU III.1 has Indra acknowledging his turbulent past, while portraying him as a being who has now become free of it through knowledge of the truth. We find a similar reformed Indra in Buddhist and ***Jain*** texts, in which he is portrayed as having become a devotee of the Buddha and Mahāvīra respectively. (See also Kena III.11–12 and IV.2–3.)

Indradyumna Bhāllaveya Known from episodes in CU V.11–14 and SBr X.6.1.1, in which he is taught by ***Aśvapati Kaikeya***.

Īśāna 'Lord', an early name for ***Śiva***.

Jabālā Mother of ***Satyakāma Jābāla*** (CU IV.4).

Jagatī 'Moving' – a metre with forty-eight syllables in four ***pādas***.

Jains, Jainism The Jain religion in its present form was founded by Mahāvīra, 'Great Hero', around the fifth century BCE: the term 'Jain' (Sanskrit *Jaina*) means a follower of the Jina, 'Conqueror', another of Mahāvīra's titles. Jainism still has a following in western and southern India, and among Indian diaspora communities. It lays great stress upon non-violence (*ahiṃsā*).

Jaivali Pravāhaṇa (also Pravāhaṇa Jaivali) A ruler of Pañcāla mentioned in BU VI.2, CU I.8.1 and CU V.3–10.

Jana Śārkarākṣya One of a group of five ***Brāhmaṇa*** householders taught by Aśvapati Kaikeya in CU V.11–24.

Janaka of Videha A wise and generous king who debates with ***Brāhmaṇas*** in several episodes of BU and SBr. In the latter (XI.6.2) he overcomes ***Yājñavalkya, Śvetaketu Āruṇeya*** and another Brāhmaṇa in debate, and then teaches Yājñavalkya about the symbolism of the fire-*sacrifice*: hence the boon mentioned in BU IV.3.1.

Jānaśruti Pautrāyaṇa 'Jānaśruti the Great-Grandson [of Janaśruta]', a king apparently known only from CU IV.1.

Jāratkārava Ārtabhāga A disputant in BU III.2, also mentioned in SA.

Jātavedas 'Knower/Possessor of What is Born (?)', a title of ***Agni***.

Juhū Goddess of the eastern direction in CU III.15.2. 'Juhū' is usually a name for the sacrificial ladle – 'she who repeatedly makes offerings'.

Ka 'Who?': as name of ***Prajāpati***, see CU IV, n. 12.

Kabandha Ātharvaṇa A *gandharva* mentioned in BU III.7. While '*Ātharvaṇa*' is a priestly title, 'Kabandha' is a name associated later with demonic beings. Cf. ***Sudhanvan Āṅgirasa***.

Kahola Kauṣītakeya A disputant in BU III.5, who appears also in SBr II.4.3.1.

Karman (or *karma*) 'Work', 'action'. Often in the early Upaniṣads, *karman* has its Vedic meaning of 'work', specifically ritual activity. The earliest uses of the word in its current sense, of any willed activity viewed as bringing appropriate results in this or a future life, appear to be in BU III.2.13 (where the idea is presented as a new one) and in BU IV.4.5–6. I have preferred the form *karman*, derived from the Sanskrit stem (the more usual academic practice), to *karma*, from the nominative case, because in colloquial English usage the latter seems to have taken on meanings that are almost opposite to the Sanskrit ones, including 'fate' or 'destiny'.

Kāśi Present-day Varanasi (Benares).

Kātyāyanī A wife of ***Yājñavalkya***.

Kauravyāyaṇī A granddaughter (son's daughter) of Kuru. The identity of her son (BU V.1.1) appears not to be known.

Kauṣītaki An important teacher, after whom the Kauṣītaki Brāhmaṇa and Upaniṣad are named, and mentioned also in SA II.17 and XV.1 and elsewhere. It is not known whether the Kauṣītaki of CU 1.5.2 is the same man.

Kṛṣṇa Devakīputra Mentioned in CU III.17.6 as a pupil of one Ghora Āṅgirasa. If he is not the same as the Kṛṣṇa (also son of Devakī) of the epics, it is surely a remarkable coincidence. However, it is impossible to tell from this passage whether he is already regarded as a divine incarnation, or simply as a human teacher. (The spelling is often Anglicized to 'Krishna' – see the Sanskrit Pronunciation guide.)

Kṣatriya A member of the second class (***varṇa***): the warriors and rulers. In theory, kings were supposed to be Kṣatriyas, though this has not always been the case. (It seems likely that, in the early period, men who succeeded in becoming king were regarded de facto as Kṣatriyas.)

Kuru The land and and people of present-day eastern Punjab and Haryana; also the name of a family, and apparently of an individual (BU V.1.1).

Madhuka Paiṅgya A student of ***Yājñavalkya*** (BU VI.3.8) mentioned as a teacher in SBr XI.7.2.8.

Madra Land and people of the north-west of the Indian subcontinent, around the area of present-day Punjab.

Maghavan 'Possessing Might', a title of ***Indra***, and sometimes (e.g. in PU II.5) of ***Parjanya***.

MAHAḤ A ***vyāhṛti*** introduced in TU 1.5.1.

Mahat 'The great': in the ***Sāṅkhya*** philosophy, the correspondence on the cosmic scale to ***buddhi*** within the individual.

Mahāvṛṣa A land and people in present-day Punjab.

Mahidāsa Aitareya The teacher of AB, AA and AU, mentioned in CU III.16.7 and JB IV.2.11.

Maitreyī A wife of ***Yājñavalkya***.

Maitri (or Maitreya) The teacher after whom MaiU is named.

Manas In everyday use, 'mind'; as a philosophical term, the mind organ, the organizing principle of sense experiences and seat of the emotions: see ***Sāṇkhya, tattva***.

Mantra A sequence of sacred sounds used as an object of meditation: in the Vedic literature the term often refers to the Vedic hymns themselves.

Manu Ancestor and lawgiver of the human race: traditionally the author of texts on law (*Mānava Dharmaśāstra* or Laws of Manu) and ritual (*Mānava Gṛhyasūtra*).

Marut A member of a group of storm-gods, 7, 49 or 180 in number, similar to the ***Rudras***, but attendant upon ***Indra***. In MaiU, a name for ***Bṛhadratha***, perhaps identifying him with the breath.

Mātariśvan In the earlier ***Vedas*** a form of ***Agni***, or a closely related deity; in the Upaniṣads, identified with ***Vāyu***, the wind-god. Later he becomes a separate deity, as ***Indra***'s charioteer.

Matsya A land and people in present-day Rajasthan.

Māyā The magical, creative and illusory powers of a god.

Middle-air See ***antarikṣa***.

Mitra, 'Friend', an ***Āditya***. In the ***Vedas*** often paired with ***Varuṇa*** as Mitrāvaruṇau ('Mitra-and-Varuṇa'), apparently as gods of the day and night skies. Although Mitra is not very prominent in the Vedas, he has been an influential deity elsewhere: Mithra, his Iranian equivalent, remained a significant figure in ancient Persian religion, and as Mithras became the subject of a popular cult among the Roman legions.

Mokṣa Liberation from ***saṃsāra***.

Mṛtyu Death and its god. In the Kaṭha Upaniṣad and elsewhere, generally synonymous with ***Yama***. In BU I.2.1 death is a primal force of creation, equivalent to ***Prajāpati***. In BU I.4.11 Mṛtyu appears as a deity, distinct from Yama. In BU II.6.3 and IV.6.3 he appears as a teacher, son of Pradhvaṃsana, 'Destroyer'.

Naciketas The young hero of the Kaṭha Upaniṣad.

Naimiṣa A sacred forest whose location is unknown.

Nāka Maudgalya A teacher mentioned in BU VI.4.4 and TU I.9.1.

Nakṣatra Constellation: specifically lunar mansion – one of the twenty-seven or twenty-eight constellations through which the moon passes in the course of the sidereal month. The *nakṣatras* formed a lunar zodiac, which preceded the introduction into India of the solar zodiac and was afterwards combined with it.

Nārada An important sage, first encountered in AV, who seeks for teaching from ***Sanatkumāra*** in CU VII.

Nārāyaṇa 'Descendant of Man', a primeval sage, in MaiU VII.7 apparently already identified with ***Viṣṇu***.

Naudhasa A ***sāman*** attributed to a sage called Nodhas.

Nidhana The final part of a ***sāman***: see CU I, n. 28.

OṂ The most important sacred sound, in PU and ManU analysed into three *mātrā* or elements, 'a' + 'u' + 'm'. This syllable takes on vital importance in later Hinduism, the three *mātrās* being taken as symbols of the divine triad, ***Brahmā, Viṣṇu*** and ***Śiva***. Today, the character 'OṂ' in the Devanāgarī script – ॐ – is frequently used as a symbol of Hinduism.

Pādas (or *padas*) Literally 'feet' or 'quarters', the divisions of a stanza of ***Sanskrit*** verse. Most metres have four such divisions – hence the name. The ***Gāyatrī*** has three.

Pāli One of the ***Prakrit*** languages, in which the canonical texts of the Theravāda (Southern Buddhist) tradition are preserved.

Pañcāla A people and land in western Uttar Pradesh: with ***Kuru***, the heartland of Vedic civilization.

Paṅkti A metre of forty syllables in four ***pādas***.

Pārikṣita A descendant of Parikṣit, a king of the ***Kuru*** line.

Parjanya The rain-god.

Paśu (Domestic) animals, especially those fitted for ***sacrifice***.

Paulkasa A member of a caste formerly regarded as untouchable.

Pipal (Sanskrit *pippala* or *aśvattha*) The sacred fig, *Ficus religiosa*. This tree has been sacred in the Indian subcontinent from a very early period: its distinctive heart-shaped leaves are depicted on Indus Valley seals of the second millennium BCE – see Allchin and Allchin 1982: 211, pl. 8.16. It is the same species of tree under which the Buddha sat to become enlightened.

Pippala See ***pipal***.

Pippalāda A teacher in PU: important also in AV.

Pitṛ See ***ancestors***.

Prācīnaśāla Aupamanyava One of a group of five ***Brāhmaṇa*** householders taught by Aśvapati Kaikeya in CU V.11–24.

Prācīnayogya Son of Prācīnayoga ('Ancient Yoga'): title of ***Satyayajña Paulusi***, of a teacher mentioned at BU II.6.2, and of the student in TU I.6.2.

Pradhāna 'Matter', in ***Sāṅkhya*** philosophy a synonym for ***prakṛti***.

Prajāpati 'Lord of Offspring', the progenitor of the universe.

Prakrit A member of a group of Middle Indian languages (including ***Pāli***), part-way between the Old Indian languages of Vedic and classical ***Sanskrit*** and most of the modern languages of northern India. The Buddha, Mahāvīra (see ***Jainism***) and Makkhali Gosāla (see ***Ājīvikas***) all taught in Prakrit languages, in order to reach beyond the educated classes who knew Sanskrit.

Prakṛti 'Nature', in ***Sāṅkhya*** philosophy covering matter, body, mind and senses – everything, in fact, that is not ***puruṣa***. See the introduction to the SU notes.

Prāṇa 'Breath': used of the five breaths (see Introduction, under 'Key Concepts'); of the first of the five, the process of respiration; of the senses; of bodily functions in general; of life; and of living beings.

Praṇava 'Reverberation', in CU 1.5.1 identified with ***OṂ***, and in the later Upaniṣads used as a synonym for it.

Prastāva See CU I, n. 28.

Prastotṛ 'Praiser', a ***priest***, assistant to the ***Udgātṛ***.

Pratardana Daivodāsi A king mentioned in KauU II.5 and III.1.

Pratihāra See CU I, n. 28.

Pratihartṛ 'Responder', a ***priest***, assistant to the ***Udgātṛ***.

Prati-sthā- (verb) 'To stand firm, be established, be supported'. This and its derivatives, such as ***pratiṣṭhā*** (noun, f.), 'firm basis, support', are key words in the Upaniṣads, representing a recurrent theme in Vedic religion. It is not enough to achieve prosperity, high status or a heavenly realm: one also has to be secure from falling away from it.

Prātṛda Mentioned as a student in BU V.12.2, and also as a teacher named Bhalla in JB III.31.4.

Pravāhaṇa Jaivali See *Jaivali Pravāhaṇa*.

Priests (*ṛtvij*, 'sacrificing in season') Four priests, each with three assistants, were required for a full-scale ***sacrifice*** (*yajña*). The Hotṛ or invoker, a specialist in the ***Ṛgveda***, was responsible for invoking the gods; the Adhvaryu or officiant, a specialist in the ***Yajurveda***, for the physical activities – preparing the altar and implements, lighting the fire, and immolating the sacrificial animal; the Udgātṛ or chanter for chanting the ***Sāmaveda***; and the Brahmā, who had to know all three ***Vedas***, for overseeing the whole process and correcting any mistakes.

Pṛthivī The earth and its goddess; the earth ***element***.

Puruṣa 'Man', 'person' – see Introduction, under 'Key Concepts', and (for ***Sāṅkhya*** usage) the introductory part of the SU notes.

Pūṣan 'Nourisher', a solar deity regarded as protecting domestic animals and making roads safe.

Raikva Sayugvat See CU IV.1–3 and its n. 3.

Raivata (or *Revatī*) A ***sāman*** based on the ***Revatī*** verse.

Rājana 'Shining', a ***sāman***.

Rajas 'Dust', 'passion', the ***guṇa*** of passion and anger, associated with the colour red.

Rājñī 'Queen', goddess of the western direction in CU III.15.2.

Rathantara 'Crossing by Chariot (?)', a ***sāman*** addressed to ***Indra*** in *Bṛhatī/Śatobṛhatī* metre.

Ṛc A verse of the ***Ṛgveda***, recited at the ***sacrifice*** by the ***Hotṛ*** and his assistants. In the plural it often means 'the Ṛgveda', and has been translated as such.

Revatī 'Wealthy': the name of the verse RV 1.30.13, which begins with the word *revatī*; (also *Raivata*), a ***sāman*** based on this verse.

Ṛgveda The first of the ***Vedas*** containing hymns, dialogues, philosophical speculations, and both public and personal prayers.

Ṛṣi 'Seer', specifically one of the poets of the ***Vedas***.

Ṛṣis, Seven The Seven Ṛṣis are seven great sages identified with the principal stars of the Great Bear/Big Dipper. Their usual names are Gotama, Bharadvāja, Viśvāmitra, Jamadagni, Vasiṣṭha, Kaśyapa and Atri (BU II.2.4), though other groups are known. All are regarded as the ancestors of important ***Brāhmaṇa*** lineages (***gotra***): see ***Gautama***. (For a detailed study, see Mitchiner 1982.)

Ṛta 'Right order', the Vedic equivalent of ***dharma***. I have usually translated it as 'law'.

Rudra 'Howler', 'He Who Weeps': in BU a storm-god. In SU, Rudra is identified with the supreme deity, and already has many titles and attributes of ***Śiva***. In MaiU he has all the characteristics of Śiva, including his place in the supreme triad (IV.5), though that name is not used. The *Rudras* are eleven storm-gods, sons of Rudra. In CU III.7.1 they seem to be identified with the ***Maruts***.

Sacrifice (*yajña*) The ritual at the heart of Vedic religion: see Introduction, under 'Background'. The most elaborate kinds of sacrifice took many days to perform, and could require as many as sixteen ***priests***. The other main participants were the ***yajamāna***, or 'patron of the sacrifice', and his senior, lawfully married wife (*dharma-sahacāriṇī*, 'co-performer of ***dharma***'). The sacrificial ***fires*** played a central part in the ritual, as the means by which the offerings were carried to the realm of the gods; so too did the ***Soma*** plant, from which the sacred drink was pressed. Probably the definitive account of the sacrifice is that of Frits Staal (1983), who witnessed a modern performance of the ritual and chronicled every aspect of it, publishing his account in two large illustrated volumes, with audio-cassettes and a video recording. For a brief but useful account of the sacrifice, see Gambhīrānanda 1983: 675–9.

Sādhya Perhaps 'to be propitiated', powerful beings living in middle-air (***antarikṣa***). According to the Agni Purāṇa, they are twelve: Manas (Mind), Mantṛ (Thinker), ***Prāṇa***, Nara (Man), Apāna (Lower Breath), Vīryavat (Courageous), Vibhu (Pervading), Haya (Horse), Naya (Conduct, Policy), Haṃsa (Goose), ***Nārāyaṇa***, Prabhu (Lord). See Daniélou 1964: 303, 470.

Sahamānā 'Conquering' or 'Enduring', goddess of the southern direction in CU III.15.2.

Śākāyanya The teacher in the frame-story of MaiU.

Śakti 'Power': in classical Hinduism, the active power of a god, often personified as a goddess, his consort – especially important in the religious traditions associated with ***Śiva*** and his consort, Pārvatī or Umā (see ***Umā Haimavatī***).

Śākvara A ***sāman*** in ***Śakvarī*** metre.

Śakvarī 'Powerful', a Vedic metre of fifty-six syllables arranged in seven ***pādas***, rather than the more usual four: also used of the ***Śākvara sāman***.

Sāman A verse from the ***Sāmaveda***, chanted at the ***sacrifice*** by the ***Udgātṛ*** and his assistants (see CU I, n. 28). In the plural it often means 'the Sāmaveda', and has been translated as such.

Samāna A ***prāṇa***: see Introduction, under 'Key Concepts'.

Sāmaśravas A student of ***Yājñavalkya*** in BU III.1.2.

Sāmaveda The third of the ***Vedas***. Many of its verses are shared with the ***Ṛgveda***, but here they are designed to be chanted aloud by the ***Udgātṛ*** and his assistants: see CU I, n. 28.

Saṃhitā The earliest part of each of the four ***Vedas***, collections of hymns, prayers etc.: 'the Vedas' as distinct from the ***Brāhmaṇas, Āraṇyakas*** and Upaniṣads.

Saṃsāra The realm of death and rebirth.

Sanatkumāra 'Eternal Youth/Bachelor', a son of ***Brahmā***.

Sandhi ('join') A prominent feature of the ***Sanskrit*** language (but found to a lesser extent in others, such as Welsh), in which, within the sentence, the end of one word and the beginning of the next affect one another and sometimes coalesce.

Śāṇḍilya A teacher of CU III.14, prominent also in SBr.

Śaṅkara (or Śaṃkara) (*c.* 788–820) A great Hindu philosopher also known as Śaṅkarācārya ('Śaṅkara the teacher') and Ādiśaṅkara ('the first Śaṅkara'). Śaṅkara expressed his ideas both through original works and through commentaries on existing texts, including the Bhagavadgītā and eleven of the Upaniṣads. His commentaries, which are published alongside the texts in many Indian editions of the Upaniṣads, are indispensable for understanding the way in which the Upaniṣads are seen in the Hindu tradition. Śaṅkara interpreted the texts in terms of Advaita or non-dualist ***Vedānta***, in which any distinction between the world and the supreme reality is viewed as the result of illusion (***māyā***). (Śaṅkara is also one of the names of ***Rudra/Śiva*** (see SU II, n. 5); the philosopher is thought by many to be an incarnation of Śiva. The title 'Śaṅkarācārya' is also borne by the heads of the monasteries that he is believed to have founded, influential figures within Hinduism.)

Sāṅkhya (or Sāṃkhya) One of the Six ***Darśanas*** or orthodox schools of Hindu philosophy. It is a strongly dualist and realist system, regarding the original principles of ***puruṣa*** and ***prakṛti*** as eternally distinct. The *puruṣa* is the self, both on the cosmic scale and in each being: it corresponds to the ***ātman***, though every *puruṣa* is regarded as distinct, whereas in non-dualist schools all *ātmans*, and indeed ***brahman*** as the supreme *ātman*, are seen as being ultimately one. The *puruṣa* is unaffected by the process of creation, which is initiated by *prakṛti* in response to the presence of *puruṣa*. *Puruṣa* and *prakṛti* are sometimes translated as 'mind' and 'matter', but, since *prakṛti* also includes almost everything that we regard as mind, they are better translated as 'consciousness', or even 'spirit', and 'nature'. All creation is thought to be made up of three ***guṇas***, which were originally evenly mixed and in balance: their disturbance, separation and recombination caused the stages of creation (see ***tattva***). Both Kaṭha and SU use Sāṇkhya-like terminology, while differing in some aspects of their thought from classical Sāṅkhya.

Sanskrit An ancient Indian language of the Indo-Iranian sub-group of the Indo-European family – one of the classical languages of religion and culture in India. The Sanskrit of the Upaniṣads varies from text to text, and seems to cover a wide range of periods and styles. The early Upaniṣads, especially BU and AU, quite frequently break the rules of the grammarians, and give the impression of being rather close to the spoken language of their time. (Some usages are similar to those of the ***Prakrit*** languages.) The middle and later ones, on the whole, keep closer to the classical form of the language, apart from MaiU, which has some quirky forms (especially of ***sandhi***) apparently characteristic of the Maitrāyaṇa lineage of texts. Most of the Upaniṣads also contain quotations from the hymns of the ***Vedas***, which are in an earlier form of Sanskrit ('Vedic'), containing words and grammatical forms that were lost in classical Sanskrit.

Sarasvatī In the ***Vedas***, goddess of a sacred river; in later Hinduism, identified with ***Vāc*** as goddess of wisdom.

Sattva Literally 'goodness': the ***guṇa*** of brightness or purity, associated with the colour white.

Satya 'Truth', often in reference to higher levels of reality, in contrast with our normal view of existence.

Satyakāma Jābāla Mentioned in BU IV.1.6 and VI.3.11–12, and most famously in CU IV.4–9.

Satyayajña Pauluṣi Also called *Prācīnayogya*: one of a group of five ***Brāhmaṇa*** householders taught by Aśvapati Kaikeya: CU V.11 and V.13.

Śaunaka Kāpeya A teacher said in JB to be the household priest of Abhipratārin Kākṣaseni, with whom he is mentioned in CU IV.3.5. A possibly different Śaunaka is mentioned in MuU 1.3.

Savitṛ 'He Who Inspires/Presses ***Soma***', the solar god sought for poetic and spiritual inspiration.

Sāvitrī 'Of ***Savitṛ***', the proper name of the verse usually known as the ***Gāyatrī***.

Sindhu The river Indus and the area surrounding it.

Sinīvalī Goddess of the day when the new moon first becomes visible each month. She is *pṛthuṣṭhukā*, 'wearing her hair in a broad curly fringe like a bull's poll [*stukā*]', presumably like the fringe of the moon's crescent. She is paired with Rākā, goddess of the full-moon day: both are invoked for help in childbirth.

Śiva 'Gracious', in the ***Vedas*** a title associated with ***Rudra***: perhaps euphemistically, as he is a god with a dangerous side. In SU it is not quite clear whether 'Śiva' is still just a title, or whether it is now the name of the god, who already bears many of the other titles and attributes of Śiva. In later Hinduism, Śiva is the third of the divine triad (see ***Brahmā***, ***Viṣṇu***): the Destroyer (or, more accurately, Reabsorber) of the universe.

Ṣoḍaśin 'In Sixteen Parts', a form of ***Soma sacrifice***.

Soma The sacred plant (probably a species of *Ephedra*: see Brough, 1971) and the drink pressed from it, which seems to have had hallucinogenic properties. Soma played an important part in the Vedic ***sacrifice***, and was itself worshipped as a god. Later, it was frequently identified with the moon and its god, since the moon was visualized as a receptacle of Soma to be drunk by the gods and ancestors.

Speech, voice See ***Vāc***.

Śraddhā 'Faith', the state of mind proper to one performing a ***sacrifice***, sometimes personified as a goddess.

Śrāddha 'Of Faith', an offering to the ancestors.

Śramaṇa A wandering spiritual seeker, practising outside the conventional stages of life: see 'The Background' and n. 21 in the Introduction.

Śrī Prosperity or glory, often as a goddess, and later identified with Lakṣmī, goddess of beauty and good fortune.

Śruti 'That which is heard', literature regarded by Hindus as 'revealed', as distinct from *smṛti*, 'that which is remembered'.

Stobha Ritual exclamation used in chanting and mantras – e.g. 'HUṂ', 'SOṂ'.

Subhūtā 'Well-Being', goddess of the northern direction in CU III.15.2.

Sudhanvan Āṅgirasa A ***gandharva*** mentioned in BU III.3. 'Sudhanvan' means 'having a fine bow', i.e. an archer, whereas '***Āṅgirasa***' is a priestly title: cf. ***Kabandha Ātharvaṇa***.

Śūdra A member of the fourth class (***varṇa***): the artisans and labourers.

Śukra 'Bright', 'seed'; sometimes as the priest of the ***asuras***, later identified with the planet Venus.

Sūrya The sun and its god.

Suṣumnā (or Suṣumṇā) The central channel believed to link the ***cakras*** in the body.

Sūtra Literally 'thread', a saying or collection of sayings on a specific topic, e.g. *Dharmasūtra* or *Vedānta-sūtra*. Some *sūtras*, such as those on grammar, deliberately cultivate a very terse, almost coded, style, while others, such as the *Kāma-sūtra* (on love and sex), are written in plain prose. The word (often in the ***Pāli*** form *sutta*) is also used of the discourses of the Buddha. It is not known precisely what the author of BU IV.1.2 and IV.5.11 meant by *sūtra* – or indeed by 'history' (*itihāsa*), 'legend' (*purāṇa*), 'science' (*vidyā*) or even

'Upaniṣad' – since the texts that currently bear these names seem to have been compiled later than BU itself. Perhaps he had in mind the sayings of famous teachers, many of which were incorporated into the Upaniṣads.

Svadhā A ritual shout during offerings to the ancestors: see BU V.8 and note.

SVAḤ A ***vyāhṛti*** representing the world of sky or heaven.

Svāhā A ritual shout during offerings to the gods: see BU V.8 and note.

Śvetaketu Āruṇeya Son of ***Uddālaka Āruṇi*** and member of the ***Gautama gotra***, he appears as a young man somewhat too full of his recent education in BU VI.2, CU V.3–10 and KauU I.1–2.

Śvetāśvatara The teacher of SU, apparently not known elsewhere.

Śyaita A ***sāman***, presumably from *śyeta*, 'white'.

Tamas 'Darkness', the ***guṇa*** of ignorance, associated with the colour black.

Tantra (1) 'Loom', 'framework', 'treatise', the name of certain texts, both Hindu and Buddhist; (2) the teachings embodied in these texts – a way of spiritual practice that seeks to use the body and its drives as a means to liberation by transforming, rather than rejecting, them. Tantra is viewed as a rapid but dangerous path, characterized by transgressive rituals, which are practised either in reality (in 'left-handed' forms of Tantra) or symbolically (in 'right-handed' forms). Hindu Tantra is generally associated with the worship of ***Śiva*** and ***Śakti***. See ***cakra***.

Tapas The root *tap*-means 'to be hot', hence 'to suffer'. *Tapas* is ascetic practice – suffering voluntarily undergone – and the spiritual energy (another kind of heat) raised through it. The creation stories of the early Upaniṣads (e.g. CU II.23, AU I) regard *tapas* as part of the process of creation, analogous to the heat necessary to brood an egg.

Tārkṣya Ariṣṭanemi 'Tārkṣya Whose Wheel-Rim is Undamaged', in Vedic literature a divine horse. By the epic period he comes to be regarded as a divine bird, either Garuḍa, the king of birds, himself or one of his brothers.

Tattva One of the twenty-five basic entities of ***Sāṅkhya*** philosophy: (1) ***prakṛti***, from which emanates (2) *buddhi/mahat*, intelligence/the great; (3) *ahaṃkāra*, sense of 'I', ego; (4–8) five *tanmātra*, subtle ***elements*** (space, air, fire, water, earth); (9–13) five *mahābhūta*, gross elements (ditto); (14–18) five senses (ear, skin, eye, tongue, nose); (19–23) five organs of action (speech, hand, foot, excretory organs, sex organs); and (24) *manas*, mind. (25) is ***puruṣa***, equivalent to *ātman*.

Tejas Light, heat, energy, the element of fire.

Triśaṅku A king who, though he had offended several of the Seven *Ṛṣis*, found favour with another of them, Viśvāmitra, and with his help was set in the sky in the constellation of Orion (Mitchiner 1982: 180–81, 253).

Triṣṭubh A metre of forty-four syllables in four *pādas*.

Tvaṣṭṛ 'Carpenter', the heavenly craftsman, possessed of the power of *māyā*.

Udāna A *prāṇa*: see Introduction, under 'Key Concepts'.

Udaṅka Śaulbāyana Mentioned in BU IV.1.3, and also in TS VII.5.4.2.

Uddālaka Āruṇi An important teacher, BU III.7, BU VI.4.4, CU III.11.4, CU V.11ff.; teacher to *Yājñavalkya*, BU VI.3.7, BU VI.5.3; father and teacher to *Śvetaketu Āruṇeya*, CU VI *passim*, KauU I.1, and in BU VI.2 under his family name of *Gautama*. See also Kaṭha n. 8.

Udgātṛ See *priests*.

Udgītha The loud chanting of the *Sāmaveda* at the *sacrifice*: for details, see CU I, n. 28.

Uktha A group of verses from the *Ṛgveda* chanted at the *sacrifice*.

Ukthya 'Accompanied by *Ukthas*', a form of *Soma sacrifice*.

Umā Haimavatī (daughter of Himavat = Himalaya) The goddess later known as Pārvatī, 'daughter of the mountain', consort of Śiva: one of the most important deities in later Hinduism. In Kena III.12–IV.1 she appears as a personification of the knowledge of *brahman*.

Upadrava See CU nn. 29 and 38.

Upasads Days of preparatory offerings between the initiation (*dīkṣā*) and the *Soma sacrifice* itself – e.g. the twelve days prescribed to prepare for the ritual in BU VI.3.1.

Uśan Vājaśravasa Father of *Naciketas*, son (or descendant) of *Uddālaka Āruṇi* (so possibly a brother of *Śvetaketu Āruṇeya*); a member of the **Gautama** family who curses his son: Kaṭha I.1, I.11 and n. 8.

Uṣasta/Uṣasti Cākrāyaṇa A disputant in BU III.4; an expert in the *Sāmaveda*, CU I.10–11.

Uśīnara An unknown place and people.

Vāc Speech and its goddess: with *Ambhiṇī*, one of only two female teachers mentioned in the lineage lists of the Bṛhadāraṇyaka (BU VI.5.3).

Vairāja A *sāman* in *Virāj* metre.

Vairūpa A *sāman* of the Vairūpas (descendants of Virūpa), a group of *Aṅgiras* priests.

Vaiśvānara 'Of All Men/People': in the earliest Upaniṣads, usually a title of *Agni*, in the form of the heat within all beings; later of *ātman* or *prāṇa* as present within all beings.

Vaiśya A member of the third class (*varṇa*): the farmers and merchants.

Vaiyāghrapadya Son of Vyāghrapada ('tiger-foot'), the patronymic of several teachers.

Vājasaneya See *Yājñavalkya*.

Vālakhilya According to the Bhāgavata Purāṇa, a group of sixty thousand thumb-sized *Ṛṣis* who surround the chariot of the sun: see Daniélou 1964: 323.

Vāmadeva A Vedic *Ṛṣi* mentioned in BU I.4.10 and AU IV.5.

Vāmadevya A *sāman* of the Ṛṣi *Vāmadeva*.

Varṇa 'Colour', each of the four divisions of society: *Brāhmaṇas*, *Kṣatriyas*, *Vaiśyas* and *Śūdras*.

Varuṇa An *Āditya*, god of the sky (in the *Vedas*); of the ocean (in later Hinduism).

Vasu The eight 'good' or 'wealthy' gods, mainly deities of elements and celestial phenomena: in Kaṭha V.2 the Vasu = the sun?

Vāyu Air, wind and its god; the air *element*.

Vedāṅga Subsidiary studies to the *Vedas*: see MuU I.1.5 and notes.

Vedānta 'The end of the Veda', a term originally applied to the Upaniṣads themselves: the *darśana* or philosophical school concerned with the inner meaning of the Vedic literature, especially the Upaniṣads. Vedānta itself developed into a number of different schools, typified by the Advaita (non-dualist) philosophy of *Śaṅkara*, the Viśiṣṭādvaita (modified non-dualism) of Rāmānuja (*c.* 1017–1137) and the Dvaita (dualism) of Madhva (*c.* 1197–1276). All found justification for their ideas in the *Vedas* and the Upaniṣads. Differences among these schools, as well as between them and the Buddhists, *Jains* and *Ājīvikas*, at times became as acrimonious, though rarely as bloody, as the theological disputes of Europe.

Vedas The most ancient part of Hindu scripture: see Introduction, under 'Background'.

Vidagdha Śākalya A disputant in BU III.9; mentioned in BU IV.1.7 and in SBr XI.6.3.3.

Videha A land and people in northern Bihar.

Virāj 'Ruler', usually f., 'Queen': as wife of *Indra* (BU IV.2.3); as a metre (three *pādas* of ten syllables), CU IV.3.8 (Olivelle 1996b: 341, n. 3.8). In the *Ṛgveda* too, Virāj appears as both the female principle of creation (precursor of *prakṛti*) and as the metre (O'Flaherty 1981: 30–31, 33–4).

Virocana King of the *asuras*.

Viṣṇu 'Pervader', an ***Āditya***, noted in the early Upaniṣads, as in the ***Vedas***, chiefly for crossing the universe in three strides (Kaṭha II.9): in MaiU he has his later role as one of the supreme triad of gods, the Preserver, alongside ***Brahmā*** the Creator and ***Rudra*** (***Śiva***) the Destroyer.

Viśvāvasu 'All-Wealthy', 'All-Good', a ***gandharva*** who tries to claim *droit de seigneur* over brides.

Viśvedeva In the ***Vedas***, 'All the Gods', the gods as a group; by the period of the Upaniṣads 'the All-Gods', a particular group of divine brothers.

Vivasvat 'Radiant One', Sūrya, the sun-god: father of ***Yama*** and ***Manu***.

Vrātya A wandering ascetic outside the normal stages of life (***āśramas***). In later times the term became one of contempt, but in AV XV the *vrātya* is the subject of a hymn of praise. The *vrātya* of the ***Atharvaveda*** is perhaps a precursor of the ***śramaṇa***: see 'The Background' and n. 20 in the Introduction.

Vyāhṛti An 'utterance', one of a number of sacred words representing the different levels of the cosmos. BU and CU have ***BHŪḤ, BHUVAḤ*** and ***SVAḤ***. TU introduces ***MAHAḤ***. Later texts know of others, as different levels of existence are distinguished.

Vyāna A ***prāṇa***: see Introduction, under 'Key Concepts'.

Waters See ***āpaḥ***.

Worlds (*loka*) There are numerous references in the Upaniṣads to multiple worlds, and it is not always possible to determine exactly which ones are intended. 'The two worlds' are generally this world and the afterlife; 'the three worlds' often earth, sky and ***antarikṣa***, seen as the abodes of human beings, gods and ancestors. We also find various longer lists of worlds inhabited by different groups of divine beings (e.g. in BU III.6.1, BU IV.3.33 and TU II.8). From an early period, Indian thinkers seem to have been at ease with the concept of multiple worlds and enormous reaches of space and time.

Yajamāna The one who commissions the ***sacrifice***. He must be a 'twice-born' (initiated) man of any of the upper three classes, accompanied by his lawful wife. Following Olivelle 1996b and Gonda 1981, I have preferred to translate him as 'patron of the sacrifice', rather than as the more literal but misleading 'sacrificer'.

Yajña See ***sacrifice***.

Yājñavalkya The great sage to whom the principal teachings of SBr and BU are attributed. The Vājasaneya recension of the ***Yajurveda*** bears his family name.

Yajñāyajñīya A ***sāman*** of the ***Agniṣṭoma***.

Yajurveda The second of the ***Vedas***. It shares much of its material with the *Ṛgveda*, but adapted to the needs of the *Adhvaryu* and his assistants. There are two main recensions: the 'Black Yajurveda', in which the verses are mixed with explanatory *Brāhmaṇa* material, and the 'White', in which they are unmixed.

Yajus A prayer or formula from the *Yajurveda*, uttered at the *sacrifice* to accompany the actions of the *Adhvaryu*. In the plural, it often means the Yajurveda, and has been translated as such.

Yakṣa Usually, a nature spirit, connected with trees etc.; in BU V.4.1, Kena III.2, a wonder, mystery or mysterious entity.

Yama The son of *Vivasvat* (Sūrya), god of *dharma* and ruler of the dead. Often synonymous with *Mṛtyu* (Death).

Yati 'Striver', variously as demiurge (SU V.3 and note), as malevolent wizard (KauU III.1 and note) and as enlightened ascetic (MU III.1.5 and III.2.6).

Yoga Literally 'application', 'yoke', 'union' – from *yuj-*, 'to join, yoke, apply oneself'. A multi-layered term in Asian religions: (1) any way of spiritual practice, such as *bhakti-yoga*, the way of devotion, or *jñāna-yoga*, the way of knowledge; (2) a specific way of spiritual practice, involving meditation and (often) physical posture, found in all South Asian religious traditions; (3) the Hindu form of (2), systematized as one of the Six *Darśanas*, often paired with *Sāṅkhya*, to which it is very close in its theoretical aspect; (4) apparently a later development, but found in MaiU, union (e.g. with supreme reality) as the goal of spiritual practice.

Yoni Literally 'womb' or 'female sex-organ'; metaphorically the source, origin or birthplace of anything.

Index

PENGUIN CLASSICS

The Classics Publisher

'Penguin Classics, one of the world's greatest series' JOHN KEEGAN

'I have never been disappointed with the Penguin Classics. All I have read is a model of academic seriousness and provides the essential information to fully enjoy the master works that appear in its catalogue' MARIO VARGAS LLOSA

'Penguin and Classics are words that go together like horse and carriage or Mercedes and Benz. When I was a university teacher I always prescribed Penguin editions of classic novels for my courses: they have the best introductions, the most reliable notes, and the most carefully edited texts' DAVID LODGE

'Growing up in Bombay, expensive hardback books were beyond my means, but I could indulge my passion for reading at the roadside bookstalls that were well stocked with all the Penguin paperbacks . . . Sometimes I would choose a book just because I was attracted by the cover, but so reliable was the Penguin imprimatur that I was never once disappointed by the contents.

Such access certainly broadened the scope of my reading, and perhaps it's no coincidence that so many Merchant Ivory films have been adapted from great novels, or that those novels are published by Penguin' ISMAIL MERCHANT

'You can't write, read, or live fully in the present without knowing the literature of the past. Penguin Classics opens the door to a treasure house of pure pleasure, books that have never been bettered, which are read again and again with increased delight' JOHN MORTIMER

BAMBA SUSO
AND BANNA KANUTE

Sunjata

Famous across West Africa from Guinea to the Gambia, through Mali and into Burkina Faso, the heroic exploits of Sunjata – based on events in the early thirteenth century – are still constantly being reinterpreted in many different media.

Sunjata started life as a gluttonous and slow-witted child, but went on to become a celebrated warrior, who defeated the Susu overlords and founded the great Mali empire, which lasted two centuries. Equally crucial was the role of his sister Nene Faamaga, who seduced his arch-enemy Sumanguru into revealing the secret magical powers which made him invulnerable.

These stories remain central to the culture of the Mande-speaking peoples. This book brings together translations of live performances by two leading Gambian *Jalis* (or bards). Where Banna Kanute's exciting version is all about violent action, supernatural forces and the struggle for mastery, Bamba Suso uses far more dialogue to reveal his insight into human relationships. A map, notes and lists of characters (many of whom have several names) help non-specialists gain access to one of the major epic traditions of Africa.

Translated and annotated by GORDON INNES
Edited with an introduction and additional notes by
LUCY DURÁN *and* GRAHAM FURNISS

Early Greek Philosophy

The Pre-Socratics, the first heroes of Western philosophy and science, paved the way for Plato, Aristotle and all their successors.

Democritus' atomic theory of matter, Zeno's dazzling 'proofs' that motion is impossible, Pythagorean insights into mathematics, Heraclitus' haunting and enigmatic epigrams – all form part of a revolution in human thought which relied on reasoning to justify its conclusions and forged the first scientific vocabulary.

Although none of their original writings have come down to us complete, patient detective work enables us to reconstruct the crucial questions they asked and their absorbing answers. Here Jonathan Barnes brings together the surviving Pre-Socratic fragments in their original contexts, allowing modern readers to get to grips with these pioneering thinkers, whose ideas remain at the centre of philosophical debate. The revised edition of the collection has been updated to take account of further research and a major new papyrus of Empedocles.

Revised edition
Translated and edited by JONATHAN BARNES

Sagas of Warrior-Poets

A famous poet and fighter spends an illicit night with a woman he failed to marry long ago. Her husband has no choice but to seek redress . . .

All the Icelandic sagas portray a world well aware of the power of words: to praise, to blame, to curse and to taunt. Yet these five stories are unusual in putting a skald, or poet, centre stage and building the plot around his travels to seek fame, his doomed love for a married woman and his hostilities against her menfolk.

Although the mainly thirteenth-century authors drew on semi-historical traditions about people and events over two centuries before, they portrayed vivid and enduring scenes of everyday life in the farmsteads of windswept Iceland – making hay, hunting seals, rounding up sheep and struggling through blizzards. Most of the poet-heroes are notably difficult characters, whose restless energy threatens the peace of their communities, and whose own faults, as much as fate, bar them from happiness. Full of fights, invective and voyaging, these sagas also deploy their terse prose and intricate verse to explore human motive and behaviour in non-aristocratic society, and as such they are almost unique in the medieval literature of Europe.

Edited with an introduction by DIANA WHALEY

HOMER

The Iliad

'Look at me. I am the son of a great man. A goddess was my mother. Yet death and inexorable destiny are waiting for me'

One of the foremost achievements in Western literature, Homer's *Iliad* tells the story of the darkest episode in the Trojan War. At its centre is Achilles, the greatest warrior-champion of the Greeks, and his refusal to fight after being humiliated by his leader Agamemnon. But when the Trojan Hector kills Achilles' close friend Patroclus, he storms back into battle to take revenge – although he knows this will ensure his own early death. Interwoven with this tragic sequence of events are powerfully moving descriptions of the ebb and flow of battle, of the domestic world inside Troy's besieged city of Ilium and of the conflicts between the gods on Olympus as they argue over the fate of mortals.

E. V. Rieu's acclaimed translation of *The Iliad* was one of the first titles published in Penguin Classics, and now has classic status itself. For this edition, Rieu's text has been revised, and a new introduction and notes by Peter Jones complement the original introduction.

Translated by E. V. RIEU
Revised and updated by PETER JONES *with* D. C. H. RIEU
Edited with an introduction and notes by PETER JONES

HOMER

The Odyssey

'I long to reach my home and see the day of my return. It is my never-failing wish'

The epic tale of Odysseus and his ten-year journey home after the Trojan War forms one of the earliest and greatest works of Western literature. Confronted by natural and supernatural threats – shipwrecks, battles, monsters and the implacable enmity of the sea-god Poseidon – Odysseus must test his bravery and native cunning to the full if he is to reach his homeland safely and overcome the obstacles that, even there, await him.

E. V. Rieu's translation of *The Odyssey* was the very first Penguin Classic to be published, and has itself achieved classic status. For this edition, Rieu's text has been sensitively revised and a new introduction added to complement his original introduction.

'One of the world's most vital tales ... *The Odyssey* remains central to literature' MALCOLM BRADBURY

Translated by E. V. RIEU
Revised translation by D. C. H. RIEU
With an introduction by PETER JONES

Beowulf
A Verse Translation

'With bare hands shall I grapple with the fiend, fight to the death here, hater and hated! He who is chosen shall deliver himself to the Lord's judgement'

Beowulf is the greatest surviving work of literature in Old English, unparalleled in its epic grandeur and scope. It tells the story of the heroic Beowulf and of his battles, first with the monster Grendel, who has laid waste to the great hall of the Danish king Hrothgar, then with Grendel's avenging mother and finally with a dragon that threatens to devastate his homeland. Through its blend of myth and history, *Beowulf* vividly evokes a twilight world in which men and supernatural forces live side by side, and celebrates the endurance of the human spirit in a transient world.

Michael Alexander's landmark modern English verse translation has been revised to take account of new readings and interpretations. His introduction discusses central themes of *Beowulf* and its place among epic poems, the history of its publication and reception, and issues of translation.

'A foundation stone of poetry in English' ANDREW MOTION

Revised edition
Translated with an introduction and notes by
MICHAEL ALEXANDER